A HISTORY OF WOMEN'S POLITICAL THOUGHT IN EUROPE, 1400–1700

This ground-breaking book surveys the history of women's political thought in Europe, from the late medieval period to the early modern era. The authors examine women's ideas about topics such as the basis of political authority, the best form of political organisation, justifications of obedience and resistance, and concepts of liberty, toleration, sociability, equality, and self-preservation. Women's ideas concerning relations between the sexes are discussed in tandem with their broader political outlooks; the authors demonstrate that the development of a distinctively sexual politics is reflected in women's critiques of marriage, the double standard, and women's exclusion from government. Women writers are also shown to be indebted to the ancient idea of political virtue, and to be acutely aware of being part of a long tradition of female political commentary. This work will be of tremendous interest to political philosophers, historians of ideas, and feminist scholars alike.

JACQUELINE BROAD is an Honorary Research Associate in the School of Philosophy and Bioethics at Monash University. She is author of *Women Philosophers of the Seventeenth Century* (2002) and co-editor with Karen Green of *Virtue, Liberty, and Toleration: Political Ideas of European Women, 1400–1800* (2007).

KAREN GREEN is Associate Professor in the School of Philosophy and Bioethics at Monash University. She is author of *Dummett: Philosophy of Language* (2001) and *The Woman of Reason* (1995).

A HISTORY OF WOMEN'S POLITICAL THOUGHT IN EUROPE, 1400–1700

JACQUELINE BROAD
AND
KAREN GREEN
Monash University

CAMBRIDGE
UNIVERSITY PRESS

CAMBRIDGE UNIVERSITY PRESS
Cambridge, New York, Melbourne, Madrid, Cape Town, Singapore, São Paulo, Delhi

Cambridge University Press
The Edinburgh Building, Cambridge CB2 8RU, UK

Published in the United States of America by Cambridge University Press, New York

www.cambridge.org
Information on this title: www.cambridge.org/9780521888172

First published 2009

Printed in the United Kingdom at the University Press, Cambridge

A catalogue record for this publication is available from the British Library

Library of Congress Cataloguing in Publication data
Broad, Jacqueline.
A history of women's political thought in Europe, 1400–1700 / Jacqueline Broad,
Karen Green.
p.   cm.
Includes bibliographical references and index.
ISBN 978-0-521-88817-2 (hardback)
1. Political science–Europe–History.   2. Women in politics–Europe–History.
3. Women–Europe–Attitudes–History.   4. Europe–Politics and government.
I. Green, Karen, 1951–   II. Title.   III. Title: Women's political thought
in Europe, 1400–1700.
JA84.E9B76 2008
320.082'094–dc22
2008038190

ISBN 978-0-521-88817-2 hardback

For
Jeremy, Annalena, and Bethany
and
Tamsin, Michael, and Alexandra

Contents

Preface

It is a common view that in the history of political thought there are no female figures on a par with men such as John Locke and Thomas Hobbes. Our background and training in philosophy gave us little reason to doubt this received wisdom. But our first defence – to quote Judith Drake (*fl.* 1696–1723) – is that a man ought no more to boast of 'being Wiser than a Woman, if he owe his Advantage to a better Education, and greater means of Information, then he ought to boast of his Courage, for beating a Man, when his Hands were bound'.[1] When it comes to the history of ideas in Europe from 1400 to 1700, women had their hands bound in many respects: through their lack of formal education in political rhetoric, their official exclusion from citizenship and government, the perception that women ought not to be involved in political affairs, and the view that it was immodest for a woman to write at all. But there is a remarkable number who escaped their bonds: some were educated to a high degree, some were self-educated, some attained the highest levels of government and political authority, others were counsellors and companions to queens; many wrote political commentaries in the guise of religious or prophetical works, and many of them defended their writings with appeal to biblical and secular precedent. Taken collectively, their works laid the foundations for subsequent generations of European women whose demands for equality in education, employment, and political representation are still not entirely met.

We began this project with the modest aim of showing simply that there is a history of women's political thought in Europe from 1400 to 1700. The result is an amalgam of our joint areas of expertise: Karen

---

[1] [Judith Drake], *An Essay In Defence of the Female Sex. In which are inserted the Characters Of A Pedant, A Squire, A Beau, A Vertuoso, A Poetaster, A City-Critick, &c. In a Letter to a Lady. Written by a Lady* (London: Printed for A. Roper, E. Wilkinson, and R. Clavel, 1696), p. 20.

Green on women thinkers from the late medieval to the early modern period in Italy and France, and Jacqueline Broad on women of the early modern period in England. As historians of philosophy, we take a common philosophical approach to these women's writings: we focus primarily on concepts, ideas, and arguments rather than historical events and political actions (though we do discuss such subjects when they are relevant). We cannot claim to have written a definitive or comprehensive history: the terrain is simply too vast, and many of the political issues are too complex to be adequately addressed in a historical-intellectual overview. As a result, this book offers only one of many possible histories that could have been written. We do not discuss women from Germany, Spain, or the Netherlands. We do not comprehensively cover the implicit political themes in women's poetry, plays, and fictional works (though we do discuss some). We do not, moreover, offer a detailed account of how women have a different way of thinking politically compared to men, or a history of political thought 'in a different voice'. Had we attempted to discuss male thinkers by way of comparison, the end-product would have been gargantuan or else excessively simplistic.

There are at least three themes that emerge out of our research. First, we find that many women entered into the political discourse of their time aware that they were marked by men as political outsiders and inferiors. At risk of being anachronistic, we suggest that almost all the women we discuss were conscious of their *gender*. In many cases, this awareness influenced their political thinking such that they recognised the implications of their theories for women as a social group. Whether it be the idea that women are capable of political virtue, or that women's participation is vital to a flourishing political community, or justifications of women's subordination and arguments in favour of passive obedience to men, most female political thinkers made women politically visible. In this respect, we intend our work to be a consciousness-raising exercise: we hope to promote the idea that the female subject did exist, despite being a forgotten or repressed feature in the history of European political thought. Secondly, the study of these women demonstrates that the thought of early modern women has as much continuity with what came before as with what came after. For many scholars, the seventeenth century represents a crucial period in which modern ideals – such as feminism, liberalism, democracy, and secular political thought in general – first emerged on the political landscape. But we find that the early modern women have a great deal in common with their female predecessors in the late medieval era and the Renaissance, especially when it comes to the topics of political virtue, the religious foundations of political authority and marriage, and the comparative virtues of men and women. Thirdly, we found that many women writers were aware of their female predecessors and contemporaries, and that several fashioned themselves as part of a female intellectual tradition. Some continental women made a conscious effort to represent themselves as part of a female 'republic of letters'; some cited past queens and other female political figures as inspiration for their reflections; and others saw themselves as part of a long tradition of women (especially biblical women and sibyls or prophetesses) who spoke with authority on political subjects.

This book would not have been possible without the generous financial assistance of the Australian Research Council. The council awarded us a large Discovery Project grant in 2004 for the purposes of carrying out research into the history of women's political thought, and we are extremely grateful to them and to the anonymous ARC reviewers who saw the merit in our original proposal. We also thank the participants in our 2005 conference, 'Toward a History of Women's Political Thought, 1400–1800', many of whom contributed to our early thinking about who and what should be included in such a history. We are especially grateful to our keynote speakers at the conference – Hilda L. Smith, Sarah Hutton, Patricia Springborg, and Catherine Müller – for sharing their incomparable expertise in the area; to Earl Jeffrey Richards, for his participation and his ongoing support; and to Lisa Curtis-Wendlandt, for her help in organising the event. We are also grateful to the French Embassy for their sponsorship of Catherine Müller's participation, and to Edouard Mornaud of the Alliance Française de Melbourne, for organising this assistance and for providing the conference venue. We thank Springer Press for their permission to reproduce (in Chapter 6) sections of Jacqueline Broad's essay 'Liberty and the Right of Resistance: Women's Political Writings of the Civil War Era in England', published in our edited collection, *Virtue, Liberty, and Toleration: Political Ideas of European Women, 1400–1800*, edited by Jacqueline Broad and Karen Green (Dordrecht: Springer, 2007). We are also grateful to the church of Santa Trinità in Florence, Italy, for granting their kind permission to use Domenico Ghirlandaio's image *Sibilla* (from the Sassetti Chapel) on our dust-jacket. We would like to thank Hilary Gaskin and the anonymous CUP reviewers, for their many helpful and sensible suggestions on our draft manuscript; our colleagues in the Philosophy Department at Monash University, Melbourne, including Dirk Baltzly, John Bigelow, Sandra

Bolton, Fiona Leigh, Justin Oakley, and Rob Sparrow; and our families (especially Sandra Broad), for their terrific support and encouragement. Finally, our work would have been poorer without the contribution of our research assistant, Nicole Kouros, who brought to the project both skills in Italian and a deep knowledge of Dante, as well as offering invaluable assistance in the preparation of the final manuscript.

Introduction

In *Some Reflections Upon Marriage* (1700), Mary Astell (1666–1731) wryly observes that it is 'Men who dispute for Truth as well as Men who argue against it; Histories are writ by them, they recount each others great Exploits, and have always done so.'[1] It might have pleased Astell to learn that, more than three hundred years later, many women would also be historians, and that women's exploits now rate a mention in the standard history books. More recently, women's intellectual history has also begun to receive scholarly attention. In the case of the history of political thought, there have been several articles about women's political ideas, and a few monographs devoted to individual figures,[2] as well as collections of essays on female political thinkers in particular historical periods and locations.[3] Recent developments in this area are partly due to the fact that women's political texts are now more publicly available than ever before.[4] But Astell's observation still holds true in one respect: even

[1] Mary Astell, *Reflections Upon Marriage*, in *Astell: Political Writings*, ed. Patricia Springborg, Cambridge Texts in the History of Political Thought (Cambridge University Press, 1996), p. 77.
[2] See Kate Langdon Forhan, *The Political Theory of Christine de Pizan* (Aldershot: Ashgate, 2002); Barbara Stephenson, *The Power and Patronage of Marguerite de Navarre* (Aldershot: Ashgate, 2004); Anna Battigelli, *Margaret Cavendish and the Exiles of the Mind* (Lexington: University Press of Kentucky, 1998); Patricia Springborg, *Mary Astell: Theorist of Freedom from Domination* (Cambridge University Press, 2005); and Virginia Sapiro, *Vindication of Political Virtue: The Political Theory of Mary Wollstonecraft* (Chicago and London: The University of Chicago Press, 1992).
[3] Consider, for example, Hilda L. Smith (ed.), *Women Writers and the Early Modern British Political Tradition* (Cambridge University Press, 1998); Tjiske Akkerman and Siep Stuurman (eds.), *Perspectives on Feminist Political Thought in European History from the Middle Ages to the Present* (London: Routledge, 1998); and Jacqueline Broad and Karen Green (eds.), *Virtue, Liberty, and Toleration: Political Ideas of European Women, 1400–1800* (Dordrecht: Springer, 2007).
[4] The accessibility of English women's texts has been vastly improved by online collections such as *Early English Books Online* (*EEBO*) and *Eighteenth-Century Collections Online* (*ECCO*). There are also now a few anthologies of women's political writings: Lynn McDonald (ed.), *Women Theorists on Society and Politics* (Waterloo, Ontario: Wilfrid Laurier University Press, 1998); Hilda L. Smith and Berenice A. Carroll (eds.), *Women's Political and Social Thought: An Anthology* (Bloomington: Indiana University Press, 2000); Kirstin Waters (ed.), *Women and Men Political Theorists: Enlightened Conversations* (Malden, MA, and Oxford: Blackwell Publishers, 2000); and Hilda L. Smith, Mihoko

though the best-known histories of political thought are no longer written solely by men, they still tend to be *about* men – especially well-known men, such as Plato, Aristotle, Dante, Machiavelli, Hobbes, Locke, and Rousseau. In this book, we aim to redress the imbalance by providing a history of women's political thought in Europe from the late medieval to the early modern period. The names of the women we discuss may not all be as familiar as those of the men: our subjects include Christine de Pizan, Isotta Nogarola, Cassandra Fedele, Laura Cereta, Marguerite de Navarre, Queen Elizabeth I of England, Jeanne d'Albret, Arcangela Tarabotti, Moderata Fonte, Lucrezia Marinella, Marie le Jars de Gournay, Katherine Chidley, Elizabeth Poole, Priscilla Cotton, Margaret Fell Fox, Queen Christina of Sweden, Madeleine de Scudéry, Margaret Cavendish, Elisabeth of Bohemia, Elinor James, Joan Whitrowe, Anne Docwra, Damaris Masham, Mary Astell, and Gabrielle Suchon – among others. Though some of these women are no longer famous, many of them were known by, and compared to, famous male theorists of their time and discussed similar political issues in their works.

Some scholars might doubt the need to devote a book to female political thinkers alone. They might argue that it is easier to assess the significance and coherence of women's political ideas when they are placed alongside those of the other sex; and they might point out that, apart from their gender, these women have very little in common socially, geographically, chronologically, or ideologically speaking. But these are observations that might be made about the majority of histories of political thought – histories that are seriously incomplete because they ignore women thinkers. In any case, we do not completely disregard male thought. Many of the women we discuss developed their work in response to male authors, and so we do consider the political ideas of men such as Aristotle, John of Salisbury, Dante, John Knox, Thomas Hobbes, and John Locke.

But we also think that women's consciousness of gender in their political thought is enough to warrant giving them a volume of their own. It has been a common criticism of male political theorists that they tend to forget about women, or that women are rendered invisible in their

Suzuki, and Susan Wiseman (eds.), *Women's Political Writings, 1610–1725*, 4 vols. (London: Pickering and Chatto, 2007). The Cambridge University Press series 'Texts in the History of Political Thought' includes *Astell: Political Writings*; Margaret Cavendish, *Political Writings*, ed. Susan James (2003); Christine de Pizan, *The Book of the Body Politic*, ed. and trans. Kate Langdon Forhan (1994); and Mary Wollstonecraft, *A Vindication of the Rights of Men and a Vindication of the Rights of Woman*, ed. Sylvana Tomaselli (1995).

political discussions of family and citizenship. In her highly influential work *The Sexual Contract* (1988), Carole Pateman observes that, in the standard histories of social contract theory, there is a great, repressive silence about women: their subordination to men is assumed but never explicitly acknowledged.[5] She argues that prior to the original contract (a pragmatic justification of political authority and obedience), there must be another agreement made between men for the purpose of dominating and controlling women – the sexual contract. More recently, Hilda L. Smith has argued that the early modern concept of citizenship implicitly excludes women.[6] Though 'the citizen' is intended to be a universal concept, applicable to both men and women, on closer inspection it turns out to be reflective of male experience alone. In this book, we do not deny that men have thought of themselves as paradigm citizens.[7] But we do offer a somewhat revised history of political thought: we show that not all political writing in the pre-Enlightenment era renders women invisible, or fails explicitly to mention the female sex and their political subordination or exclusion.[8] We examine what happens when the 'subjects' start to speak (to borrow a post-modern phrase) or when women of the past developed their own political theories and opinions. For some modern feminists, the results may be surprising, and, perhaps, sometimes disappointing.[9] Against their misogynist critics, these women defend their capacity for political virtue, they argue for women's prudence, they defend female monarchs, and they call for female liberty of conscience against the tyranny of men. Yet many are intolerant and conservative, critical of those who bring about social disorder for the sake of religious freedom and they are committed to individual virtue and passive obedience to authority. In some cases, there is also acceptance, and even justification, of women's subordination to men.

---

[5] Carole Pateman, *The Sexual Contract* (Stanford University Press, 1988).

[6] Hilda L. Smith, *All Men and Both Sexes: Gender, Politics, and the False Universal in England, 1640–1832* (University Park, PA: Pennsylvania State University Press, 2002).

[7] In addition, we do not deny that when male theorists such as Hobbes, Locke, and Rousseau do mention women, they typically offer justifications of women's subordination to men. On this topic, see Susan Moller Okin, *Women in Western Political Thought* (Princeton University Press, 1979).

[8] To be fair, in a more recent article, Pateman observes that a history of political thought without women's ideas is but a 'truncated and partial' story; see Carole Pateman, 'Women's Writing, Women's Standing: Theory and Politics in the Early Modern Period', in Smith (ed.), *Women Writers and the Early Modern British Political Tradition*, pp. 365–82 (esp. 367).

[9] See Margaret King, *Women of the Renaissance* (Chicago: University of Chicago Press, 1991), p. 237, and Joan W. Scott, *Only Paradoxes to Offer: French Feminists and the Rights of Man* (Cambridge, MA: Harvard University Press, 1996). Both King and Scott express disappointment at the conservatism of the historical women they study.

Often, as Mary Astell observed in 1700, these women 'Love their Chains' and think 'as humbly of themselves as their Masters can wish'.[10] Instead of calling for equal liberty, many women emphasise the duty of all human beings to accept subordination to a higher authority. Such women insist that even a prince is subordinate to God, and that love of God and humility are virtues that men (as well as women) ought to acquire. But whatever the viewpoint, these female political thinkers do not forget about women: they consider the implications of their general political theories for women as well as men. In this respect, regardless of a lack of radicalism in some areas, a history of women's political thought can offer a different political perspective to that of the standard, exclusively male, histories.

A major methodological question raised by this research is: what constitutes political thought and what counts as a political text? In modern political theory, politics is often regarded as a separate sphere from ethics. Theorists concentrate on questions concerning power, the foundations and limits of political authority, the nature of political obligation, and the tensions between liberty and distributive justice. On this reading, the key concepts – to put it rather simply – are *rights* and *obligations*, whether they are the rights (or entitlements) and obligations of sovereigns, or the rights and obligations of subjects, and so on. Political texts are those that discuss sovereign power (such as democratic, oligarchic, or monarchic power) and the relations between sovereigns and subjects. Among the texts we consider, some conform to this paradigm and others do not. In the later chapters of this work, we examine women's ideas about the basis of political authority, their theories about the best forms of political organisation, their justifications of political obedience or political resistance, and their various concepts of liberty in both the family and the state. We also discuss the extent to which these ideas about authority, obedience, and liberty are applied to the situation of women. But we maintain that this modern paradigm of political thought is open to question: it is the result both of the occlusion or forgetting of an earlier political tradition, and of the exclusion of women and their concerns from standard political theory. Our research thus expands the domain of the political in two respects. First, it returns to the ancient Aristotelian paradigm in which politics and ethics are united rather than opposed. Secondly, it includes sexual politics, and so we cover texts such as Marguerite de Navarre's *Heptameron* and Madeleine de Scudéry's *Clélie* which are not usually thought of as political.

---

[10] Astell, *Reflections*, p. 29.

For Aristotle and the Stoic writers Seneca and Cicero (who accepted the Aristotelian framework), the key political concepts are not rights and obligations but *virtue* and *the good*.[11] Aristotle's political thought begins with the premise that an individual's participation in the political community is necessary in order for that individual to attain the good life (*eudaimonia*). In Aristotle's *Politics*, the city-state or *polis* is not regarded as external to, or pitted against, the individual, but rather as the natural means by which the individual is able to achieve the good. When Aristotle discusses the best form of political organisation, he discusses it with regard to the form that will best promote the good life, and he sees the virtues as habits that are conducive to this end. In this tradition ethics, the nature of virtue, and politics are inextricably connected. Developing Aristotle's thought, the Stoics identify the good life with a life of virtue, while the Epicureans make virtue a means to pleasure in a broad sense (identified with *eudaimonia*). The Aristotelian approach to political thought focuses on the appropriate character and virtues of members of the *polis*, on issues such as civic friendship, and the best organisation for promoting the best kind of life – topics that have not been central to modern political thought. In the late medieval and Renaissance periods, the Aristotelian political outlook was adapted by Giles of Rome, John of Salisbury, and St Thomas Aquinas. During this period, the writings of Aristotle and his Roman descendants, particularly Seneca and Cicero, shaped and informed the subject matter of political philosophy, for both male and female authors alike.

Women writers of the fifteenth century adapt and critique this tradition. The Aristotelian subject matter arises most strongly in their defence of women's capacity for virtue. Their approach can be summed up by the idea, expressed by Christine de Pizan, that the good of the city is the good of all its inhabitants, male as well as female. They insist that women are capable of exercising all the virtues, and should be encouraged to develop them. In his *Politics*, Aristotle implies that women do not have the prime political virtue of prudence (*phronesis*), or the capacity to discern good from evil in their practical deliberations. By denying women this capacity, he appears to justify the exclusion of women from political authority, their subordination to men, and their lack of qualification for full citizenship. Women such as Christine de Pizan, Elizabeth I, and Lucrezia Marinella explicitly challenge Aristotle's denial of prudence to the female

---

[11] For a nice summary of this topic, see C. C. W. Taylor, 'Politics', in *The Cambridge Companion to Aristotle*, ed. Jonathan Barnes (Cambridge University Press, 1995), pp. 233–58 (esp. 233–5).

sex and his exclusion of women from participation in the *polis*. Other women, such as Laura Cereta, Marguerite de Navarre, and Madeleine de Scudéry, question his assumptions concerning the nature of virtue. Humility is not a virtue recognised by Aristotle, but these women exploit the tradition of Christian virtue and promote humility in opposition to arrogant pagan morality. Opposing Aristotelian and medieval representations of women as morally inferior, women defend their moral worth, question men's virtue, and propose new paradigms of the relations between men and women. Based on a reading of Christianity according to which grace is offered to the powerless, Marguerite hints that women may be spiritually and morally superior to men. Marinella goes further and adapts Platonist doctrine to establish women's moral superiority and the injustice of their subjection to men. We thus demonstrate the existence of a well-established tradition of women's thought grounded in a Christian synthesis of classical Aristotelian and Stoic political ideas, which elevates women's political contribution by equating the good life with the exercise of virtue.

In pre-Enlightenment Europe, political thought was intertwined not only with ethics and virtue, but also with religion and salvation. The synthesis of political and religious thought continued well into the seventeenth century: a strong religio-political outlook can be found in the works of Marie le Jars de Gournay, Elizabeth Poole, Mary Pope, Elinor James, Gabrielle Suchon, and Mary Astell, among others. These women uphold a divine conception of kingship and a view of monarchs as God's instruments on earth; they have a pastoral conception of the monarch as a protector of souls as well as bodies; and they offer Scripture-based arguments in favour of obedience to both just rulers and irreligious tyrants. Some women also offer biblical arguments in favour of women's political subordination to men. But in other women's writings of the time, religion is not the entirely conservative or limiting force that we might expect it to be.[12] The writings of English women petitioners during the Civil War, and Quaker women such as Priscilla Cotton, Mary Cole, Margaret Fell Fox, and Anne Docwra, reveal that the Bible can be interpreted in a politically progressive fashion. These women argue in favour of egalitarianism, liberty of conscience, social justice for the poor, and the toleration of religious diversity. They do not argue in favour of full citizenship for women, or their freedom from political subordination to men but they do highlight

---

[12] On this topic more generally, see Patricia Crawford, *Women and Religion in England 1500–1720* (London and New York: Routledge, 1993).

women's equal interest in liberty of conscience (or freedom of worship), they argue in favour of women's spiritual equality with men, and they defend the authority of women to speak in church. The long-lived popularity of Aristotelian and Stoic ideas concerning good government and virtue is apparent in other women's writings. In the late seventeenth century, in the works of Damaris Masham, Gabrielle Suchon, and Mary Astell, we start to see arguments in favour of women's intellectual cultivation both for the sake of the country, and for the sake of women's own virtue and salvation.

Our expansion of the domain of political thought results in a broadening of the texts that we read as political. Modern political theorists tend to concentrate their studies on prose treatises that deal exclusively with issues of power and the legitimacy of the state. Niccolò Machiavelli's *The Prince* (1532), Thomas Hobbes's *Leviathan* (1651), and John Locke's *Two Treatises of Government* (1689) form the backbone of contemporary academic discussion on historical political theory. Some of the works that we examine conform to this standard. Christine de Pizan's *Book of the Body Politic* (1407) and *Book of Peace* (1412–14), and Marie le Jars de Gournay's 'Farewell of the Soul of the King' (1610) are political treatises that concentrate on the practice of good government and the relative rights and responsibilities of monarchs and subjects. The politics of relations between the sexes is also discussed in polemical writings that are not too different from the standard political treatises: Christine de Pizan's *Book of the City of Ladies* (1405), Moderata Fonte's *The Worth of Women* (1600), Arcangela Tarabotti's *Paternal Tyranny* (1643), Marie le Jars de Gournay's *The Equality of Men and Women* (1624), and perhaps Mary Astell's *Some Reflections Upon Marriage* (1700) are cases in point. But many women's works fall outside the standard models. Often women writers express their ideas about the ideal state, relations between the sexes, and other political issues through fiction, poems, pamphlets, petitions, and plays. In doing so, they were typically following the fashion of the era in which they wrote. In the early modern period and before, men sometimes expressed their political views through the medium of poetry, as in John Milton's *Paradise Lost* (1667), and in fictional pieces, such as Thomas More's *Utopia* (1516), and Jonathan Swift's *Gulliver's Travels* (1726). In the following chapters, we include a discussion of some of the most influential works in these genres, though it has been impossible to comment on every politically significant literary production by a woman.

This leads us to a final methodological question: what are the criteria for inclusion in our history? Why do we include some writers and not others? Needless to say, the first criterion is gender: because we propose to address the forgotten or neglected history of women's political thought, the political texts in our study must be written by women. In the case of multi-authored and anonymous or pseudonymous works, this is not a straightforward matter. We know that Elizabeth I played a significant role in the writing of her speeches and prayers, but there is evidence that these were also the products of collaboration with male counsellors. Similarly, though many women's petitions of the English Civil War era were written from a female point of view, and were presented to parliament by women, there is some question about women's authorial role in the petitions. We include discussion of both Elizabeth and the Civil War women, however, because there is plausible evidence on the side of female authorship: Elizabeth was a highly educated, authoritative woman who played a hands-on role in the fashioning of her public persona; and there is historical and textual evidence that Katherine Chidley may have played a leading part in the writing of the Leveller women's petitions. Second, we include only those women writers who articulate a coherent political viewpoint, according to the definition of political thought discussed above. In some cases, such as those of the English queens Mary I and Mary II, there is simply not enough extant material to discern any particular viewpoint. The same problem arises with regard to Princess Elisabeth of Bohemia and Queen Christina of Sweden, though we do briefly discuss their extant opinions in relation to wider political themes.

Many historiographical conclusions might be drawn from our account of women's political ideas. According to the standard, all-male accounts, the history of political thought is a history in which natural justifications of political authority (such as patriarchalism and divine right theory) are overthrown by conventional or contractual theories;[13] biblical and authority-based arguments are replaced by appeal to reason and rational principles, and the religious world view gives way to the secular, liberal philosophy of the Enlightenment – a philosophy in which liberty, equality, and toleration play a central role. But these accounts may be the result of historians concentrating on works that ground future trends, rather than those that express widely accepted platitudes of the period in question. Recent revisionist historians have challenged the idea of a smooth and uncomplicated progress toward Enlightenment political ideals. The study of women's political writings may also lead to a shift in

---

[13] See Gordon J. Schochet, *The Authoritarian Family and Political Attitudes in 17th Century England: Patriarchalism in Political Thought* (New Brunswick and London: Transaction Books, 1988).

our thinking about such progress. These texts come with little scholarly baggage, and so the reader must evaluate them on their own terms: we must pay attention to what the women actually said rather than what current scholars say about them. Taken collectively, women's political writings offer a different – and, in many cases, a woman-centred – perspective on central problems and classic works within the history of political thought. Their texts can be an affront to our modern ways of thinking. Seemingly familiar political concepts – such as prudence, liberty, toleration, equality, and self-preservation – have quite different connotations when discussed in their original religio-political contexts. In addition, our study shows that feminist political thought has had a longer pre-history than many theorists have recognised. The gender concerns of pre-Enlightenment women may not always be secular or liberal in content, but they are nevertheless recognisably feminist or proto-feminist in spirit.

Finally, it must be noted that many of these women acknowledge the existence of their female predecessors. Some continental women, such as Madeleine de Scudéry, make a conscious effort to represent themselves as part of a female 'republic of letters'. Many women cite past queens and other female political figures, such as Joan of Arc and the Amazons, as inspiration for their political writings. Others legitimate their political activism in print by appealing to a long tradition of women, especially biblical exempla and sibyls or prophetesses, who were authoritative political advisers. There is also a plausible case to be made for the continuing influence of Christine de Pizan: many women who exercised political authority in the Renaissance period – including, in France, Anne de Beaujeu, Margaret of Austria, Louise of Savoy, and Marguerite de Navarre – were familiar with Christine's works; and in England, it seems likely that Elizabeth I and Margaret Cavendish also had access to Christine's writings. Many would agree that, in order to move forward politically, women need to develop a consciousness of themselves as political actors and theorists who belong to a tradition of female thought. In writing this history, we hope to have contributed to women's growing historical self-consciousness, and to have demonstrated that women made a far more profound contribution to the development of European political ideas than has been generally acknowledged.

CHAPTER I

Christine de Pizan

Christine de Pizan (1364–1430) lived in France from the reign of Charles V, through the madness of Charles VI, until the year in which the appearance of Joan of Arc secured the succession of Charles VII. Christine thus suffered the effects of the conflict between the Armagnacs and Burgundians, which had one of its murderous climaxes in the Cabochien uprising of 1413. During this period, she wrote a number of works promoting princely virtue, often intended for Louis of Guyenne, the eldest son of Charles VI, and Isabeau de Bavière, who, she hoped, might ultimately take over the government and secure the peace. She also wrote during a period that famously consolidated the authority of vernacular literature. Against the background of the dissemination of translations of classical thought to a courtly and lay audience, promoted by Charles V, Christine was able to establish herself as an authoritative female writer. In 1403, Philip the Bold, Duke of Burgundy, invited her to write a history of Charles V. In response Christine painted an idealised portrait of this king, whose prudence, justice, and capacity to maintain the peace and prosperity of France constituted for her the ideal princely government. Christine also wrote works defending women, for which she is now best known. In this chapter, we examine the way in which her meditation on the nature of good government interconnects with her defence of women's authority.

As a child, Christine travelled from Venice, where she was born, to Paris, where she lived most of her life, and wrote the vast majority of her works. She undertook this journey because of the fame of her father, Tomasso Pizzano, a contemporary of Francesco Petrarch (1304–74). Some years earlier, he had been invited to the court of the French king, Charles V, and had been persuaded to remain in Paris. His daughter and wife followed him, taking the long and arduous journey across the Alps a few years later. Thus in her person Christine could be said to have embodied the humanist project of *translatio studii*, the dissemination of classical knowledge from the heartland of classical thought to the more distant corners of Europe.[1] In *Christine's Vision* (1405), she attributes her voyage to the call of Fama, fame and fortune, thus staking a claim to cultural immortality anticipating the attitude of later Renaissance authors. Yet she also often invokes a Stoic distrust of Fortune, and warns of the precariousness of reputation.[2] As a widow, she would discover her intellectual vocation: the task of developing and promoting a classical vision of good government, grounded in the thought of Aristotle, Cicero, Seneca, Augustine, Boethius, and their medieval descendants, Thomas Aquinas and Dante. She articulated this vision in many works, both in poetry and prose, and quite uniquely, she attempted to make the political wisdom and concept of the good life to be found in these authors available to a female as well as a male audience.

Christine de Pizan was widowed some time during 1389–90 and turned to writing verses in the last years of the fourteenth century. Initially these were laments, regretting the loss of her young husband, the trials of widowhood, and the loneliness of her condition. Gradually her verses became more political. In 1399, she composed a poem in the form of a letter by the God of Love in which she complains about the disloyal way in which men represent and treat women.[3] In 1400, this poem was followed by one of her most widely disseminated works, the *Letter of Othea*. Here Christine identifies the goddess 'Othea' with prudence and wisdom. Through the character of Othea, Christine tells 100 stories drawn from the history of Troy, intended to advise an adolescent prince or knight about virtue and vice.[4] There followed a period of extraordinary productivity

[1] For developments of this idea, see Lori Walters, 'Christine de Pizan as Translator and Voice of the Body Politic', in *Christine de Pizan: A Casebook*, ed. Barbara K. Altmann and Deborah McGrady (New York: Routledge, 2003), pp. 25–42; and Lori Walters, 'The Royal Vernacular: Poet and Patron in Christine de Pizan's *Charles V* and the *Sept Psaulmes Allégorisés*', in *The Vernacular Spirit. Essays on Medieval Religious Literature*, ed. Renate Blumenfeld-Kosinski, Duncan Robertson, and Nancy Bradley Warren (New York: Palgrave, 2002), pp. 145–82. For Christine's careful inscription of herself into the cultural memory, see Margarete Zimmerman, 'Christine de Pizan: Memory's Architect', in Altmann and McGrady, *Christine de Pizan: A Casebook*, pp. 57–77.

[2] Christine de Pizan, *Le Livre de l'advision Cristine*, ed. Christine M. Reno and Liliane Dulac (Paris: Champion, 2001), pp. 6 and 15; Christine de Pizan, *Christine's Vision*, trans. Glenda K. McLeod (New York: Garland, 1993), pp. 5 and 13. Later in the work Opinion promises Christine that her fame will live in the future and her works will be appreciated by a wise prince: see *L'advision*, ii.22, pp. 89–90; *Christine's Vision*, pp. 87–8. For Christine's awareness of the more problematic aspect of fame, infamy, see Thelma Fenster, 'La Fama, la femme, et la Dame de la Tour', in *Au champ des escriptures*, ed. Eric Hicks (Paris: Champion, 2000), pp. 461–77.

[3] Christine de Pizan, *Oeuvres poétiques de Christine de Pisan*, ed. Maurice Roy, 3 vols. (Paris: Librairie de Firmin Didot et Cie, 1886; reprint, New York: Johnson Reprints, 1965); Thelma Fenster and Mary Carpenter Erler (eds.), *Poems of Cupid, God of Love* (Leiden: Brill, 1990).

[4] Christine de Pizan, *Epistre Othea*, ed. Gabriella Parussa (Geneva: Librairie Droz, 1999); *Christine de Pizan's Letter of Othea to Hector*, trans. Jane Chance (Newburyport, MA: Focus Information

during which Christine produced two long allegorical poems and her now most famous works, *The Book of the City of Ladies* (1405) and *The Book of Three Virtues* (1406). In the first, she constructs an allegorical city to defend women, and in the second she exhorts them to populate her city by leading practical lives of political virtue.[5] Directing her advice at potential 'citoyennes' (female citizens)[6] of the city of ladies, Christine, by her usage, suggests a claim to female citizenship not generally articulated until the eighteenth century. These feminist works were complemented by *The Long Path of Learning* (1402), *The Book of the Mutation of Fortune* (1403), *The Feats and Mores of the Good King Charles, V of that Name* (1404), *The Book of the Body Politic* (1407), and *The Book of Peace* (1412–14). All of these are variously devoted to articulating Christine's vision of the means for bringing about peace and the common good.[7]

I

It is, indeed, in *Christine's Vision* of 1405 that one sees Christine at her most original and philosophical. We therefore begin our account of her political outlook with this work, which will develop three interconnected themes: the influence of Dante on her work, her 'political epistemology' (her theory of the grounds of political knowledge) and her defence of

Group, 1990). The surviving manuscripts of this work are described in Gianni Mombello, *La tradizione manoscritta dell' 'Epistre Othéa' di Christine de Pizan* (Turin: Accademia delle Scienze, 1967). Not only were English translations printed, but John Lydgate's *Troy Book* shows evidence of Christine's influence. See David Benson, *The History of Troy in Middle English Literature* (Woodbridge: D. S. Brewer, 1980), pp. 124–5; and P. G. C. Campbell, 'Christine de Pisan en Angleterre', *Revue de Littérature Comparée* 5 (1925), 659–70.

5 Christine de Pizan, *La Città delle dame*, trans. Patrizia Caraffi, ed. Earl Jeffrey Richards (Milan and Trento: Luni Editrice, 1997); *The Book of the City of Ladies*, trans. Earl Jeffrey Richards (London: Picador, 1983); *Trois Vertus*, ed. Charity Cannon Willard and Eric Hicks (Paris: Champion, 1989); *The Treasure of the City of Ladies*, trans. Sarah Lawson (Harmondsworth: Penguin, 1985); Maureen Quilligan, *The Allegory of Female Authority: Christine de Pizan's Cité des Dames* (Ithaca: Cornell University Press, 1991).

6 Christine de Pizan, *Trois Vertus*, I.I, p. 9.

7 Christine de Pizan, *Le Chemin de longue étude*, ed. Andrea Tarnowski (Paris: Le Livre de Poche, 2000); *Le Livre de la mutacion de fortune*, ed. Suzanne Solente, 4 vols. (Paris: Editions A & J Picard, 1959); *Le Livre des fais et bonnes meurs du sage roy Charles V*, ed. Suzanne Solente, 2 vols. (Paris: Champion, 1936–40; reprint, Geneva: Slatkine, 1975); *Le Livre du corps de policie*, ed. Angus J. Kennedy (Paris: Champion, 1998); *The Book of the Body Politic*, ed. and trans. Kate Langdon Forhan (Cambridge University Press, 1994); *The Book of Peace*, ed. and trans. Karen Green, Constant J. Mews, and Janice Pinder (University Park, PA: Penn State University Press, 2008). Selections from these and other works of Christine's are available in Charity Cannon Willard (ed.), *The Writings of Christine de Pizan* (New York: Persea, 1994); and Renate Blumenfeld-Kosinski (ed.), *The Selected Writings of Christine de Pizan* (New York: W. W. Norton & Co., 1998).

women's claim to authority as both political advisers and actors.[8] One might equally well introduce Christine's political thought with the metaphor of the body politic that she borrows from John of Salisbury (*fl.* 1120–80) and this metaphor is certainly a guiding thread in her political philosophy.[9] However, by focusing initially on *Christine's Vision* we are led to consider some of the more alien and 'prophetic' aspects of her political voice. As we will see in subsequent chapters, political prophecy has a perennial influence in Europe: not only do women who enter the realm of political speech exploit the image of the prophetess, they also treat political virtue and salvation as intertwined.

We know about Christine's life story largely from *Christine's Vision*, and as others have noted, here and in other works she demonstrates her commitment to establishing an authoritative identity, for herself and other women.[10] Her account of her tribulations is 'a highly selective and stylized self-representation' in which she positions herself as the heir of a

---

[8] For an argument for seeing this as a political work, see Rosalind Brown-Grant, '*L'Avision Christine*: Autobiographical Narrative or Mirror for the Prince?', in *Politics, Gender, and Genre: The Political Thought of Christine de Pizan*, ed. Margaret Brabant (Boulder: Westview, 1992). For a convincing argument that it should be read on many levels, see also Liliane Dulac and Christine M. Reno, 'The *Livre de l'advision Cristine*', in Altmann and McGrady (eds.), *Christine de Pizan: A Casebook*, pp. 199–214.

[9] For a study of Christine's political thinking which begins from this image, see Langdon Forhan, *The Political Theory of Christine de Pizan* and the essays in Karen Green and Constant J. Mews (eds.), *Healing the Body Politic: The Political Thought of Christine de Pizan* (Turnhout: Brepols, 2005), particularly Cary Nederman, 'The Living Body Politic: The Diversification of Organic Metaphors in Nicole Oresme and Christine de Pizan', pp. 19–33.

[10] Renate Blumenfeld-Kosinski, 'Christine de Pizan and Classical Mythology. Some Examples from the *Mutation de Fortune*', in *The City of Scholars: New Approaches to Christine de Pizan*, ed. Margarete Zimmerman and Dina De Rentiis (Berlin: Walter de Gruyter, 1994), pp. 3–14; Diane Bornstein (ed.), *Ideals for Women in the Works of Christine de Pizan* (Detroit: Michigan Consortium for Medieval and Early Modern Studies, 1981); Rosalind Brown-Grant, '"Hee! Quel honneur au feminin sexe!" Female Heroism in Christine de Pizan's *Ditié de Jehanne d'Arc*', *Journal of the Institute of Romance Studies* 5 (1997), 123–33; Kevin Brownlee, 'Discourses of the Self: Christine de Pizan and the *Roman de la rose*', *Romanic Review* 79 (1988), 199–221; Kevin Brownlee, 'Structures of Authority in Christine de Pizan's *Ditié de Jehanne d'Arc*', in *Discourse of Authority in Medieval and Renaissance Literature*, ed. Kevin Brownlee and Walter Stephens (Dartmouth, NH: University Press of New England, 1989), pp. 131–150; Liliane Dulac, 'Authority in the Prose Treatises of Christine de Pizan: The Writer's Discourse and the Prince's Word', in Brabant (ed.), *Politics, Gender, and Genre*, pp. 129–40; Liliane Dulac, 'L'Autorité dans les traités en prose de Christine de Pizan: discours d' écrivain, parole de prince', in *Une Femme de lettres au Moyen Age*, ed. Liliane Dulac and Bernard Ribémont (Orléans: Paradigme, 1995), pp. 15–24; Patricia Phillippy, 'Establishing Authority: Boccaccio's *De Claris Mulieribus* and Christine de Pizan's *Le Livre de la cité des dames*', in Blumenfeld-Kosinski (ed.), *The Selected Writings of Christine de Pizan*, pp. 329–61; Quilligan, *The Allegory of Female Authority*; Christine M. Reno, 'Autobiography and Authorship in Christine's Manuscripts', *Romance Languages Annual* 9 (1997), xxi–xxiv; Christine M. Reno, 'Feminist Aspects of Christine de Pizan's *Epistre d'Othea*', *Studi Francesi* 71 (1980), 271–6; and Earl Jeffrey Richards, 'Virile Woman and Womanchrist: The Meaning of Gender Metamorphosis in Christine', in *'Riens ne m'est seur que la chose incertaine': Etudes sur l'art d'écrire au*

tradition of exiled and persecuted philosopher-poets.[11] In an early verse, she speaks of France's tradition of welcoming exiles, and invites the reader to compare her widowed state, far from her native Italy, with the exile of Dante, who spent much of his life travelling throughout Italy following his expulsion from Florence in March 1302.[12] Her exclusion, as a woman, from a position of civil authority is thus represented as similar to the unjust civic exile of the virtuous poet. Even more explicitly, in *Christine's Vision*, she casts herself in the role of a female Boethius. In Boethius she finds a powerful image with which to identify the exclusion of virtuous women from civic power and moral authority, and she turns to him for consolation and inspiration.

Christine's identification with Boethius, and her indebtedness to his philosophy, are most explicit in the third part of *Christine's Vision*. There Christine recounts her misfortunes to a beautiful and noble woman with a glowing face, who introduces herself as 'she who appeared clearly and visibly in the time of his exile and tribulation to my dear son Boethius the most satisfactory philosopher'.[13] Like Boethius, Christine learns the lesson that true happiness is to be found in God; and the trials that she has been through have benefited her by forcing her to study and to acquire the wisdom necessary for the recognition of this truth.[14] She intends this lesson to apply, not only to herself, but also – following the idea of a correspondence between microcosm and macrocosm – to a princely reader who ought to conclude that his or her happiness, as well as that of the people, is to be found in the exercise of virtue in this world and salvation in the next.

Boethius' Stoic philosophy also profoundly influenced Dante, a writer whose political outlook and world vision permeate Christine's writings. In the early fifteenth century, Dante was little known in France. Philippe de Mézières, who was instrumental in encouraging Christine's father to go to Paris, mentions him in his *Dream of the Old Pilgrim*.[15] But it is Christine, in her poem *The Long Path of Learning*, who is the first person in France to imitate Dante and to appropriate elements of his political

Moyen Age offertes à Eric Hicks par ses élèves, collègues, amies et amis, ed. Jean-Claude Mühlethaler (Genevea: Slatkine, 2001), pp. 239–52.
[11] Kevin Brownlee, 'Literary Genealogy and the Problem of the Father: Christine and Dante', *Journal of Medieval and Renaissance Studies* 23 (1993), 366, 376, and 385.
[12] Christine de Pizan, *Christine's Vision*, III.6, pp. 115–16; *L'advision*, pp. 105–6.
[13] *Christine's Vision*, III.1, p. 107; *L'advision*, p. 94.
[14] *Christine's Vision*, III.26, p. 140; *L'advision*, p. 138.
[15] Philippe de Mézières, *Le Songe du vieil pelerin*, ed. G. W. Coopland, 2 vols. (Cambridge University Press, 1969).

thought.[16] Two interconnected aspects of Dante's outlook influence Christine. The first is his attitude to women, and his idealised conception of women's moral role. The second is his political optimism and faith that peace and happiness are possible within the temporal realm. These two aspects of Dante's thought are connected through a theory of the interpenetration of divine and human love.

Some feminist philosophers complain that the history of philosophy is replete with images and metaphors that tend to debase women, identifying them with the body and carnal desire. They argue that these metaphorical associations provide for a problematic relationship between women and philosophy.[17] Yet in Dante's poetry we find a tradition of allegory that is much more positive for women, and which may have eased Christine's path to staking a claim as a philosophical authority. Central to Dante's world is Beatrice, a woman who inspires his love and intercedes to allow him to enjoy the vision of hell, Purgatory, and heaven that he sets out in the *Divine Comedy*. Dante's Beatrice was of course a real woman, but she is also a personification of charity or the love of God. Dante's understanding of Christian wisdom, and the place that he represents women as occupying in men's spiritual world, derives from a strand of philosophical literature that is a more fertile source for women than the unabashed sexism of Aristotle.

The roots of this more positive tradition for women stretch back to Plato's *Symposium*, in which the wise Diotima is represented as having taught Socrates the truth about love. Diotima represents love as the child of poverty and contrivance, and as the desire to reproduce beauty. Ordinary physical love is the desire to bring into existence bodily beauty,

[16] Gertrude H. Merkle, 'Martin Le Franc's Commentary on Jean Gerson's Treatise on Joan of Arc', in *Fresh Verdicts on Joan of Arc*, ed. Bonnie Wheeler and Charles T. Wood (New York: Garland, 1996), pp. 177–204. Christine's debt to Dante in this poem is also discussed in Kevin Brownlee, 'Le moi "lyrique" et généalogie littéraire: Christine de Pizan et Dante dans le *Chemin de long estude*', in 'Musique naturele'. *Interpretationen zur französischen Lyrik des Spätmittelalters*, ed. Wolf-Dieter Stempel (Munich: Fink, 1995), pp. 105–39; Brownlee, 'Literary Genealogy and the Problem of the Father', 365–87; Arturo Farinelli, *Dante e la Francia dall'età media al secolo di Voltaire*, 2 vols. (Milan: Hoepli, 1908), vol. 11; Arturo Farinelli, *Dante nelle opere di Christine de Pisan* (Halle: Niemeyer, 1905); Earl Jeffrey Richards, 'Christine de Pizan and Dante: A Reexamination', *Archiv für das Studium der neueren Sprachen und Literaturen* 222 (1985), 100–11; Anna Slerca, 'Le *Livre du chemin de long estude* (1402–1403): Christine au pays des merveilles', in *Sur le chemin de longue étude . . . Actes du colloque d'Orléans – juillet 1995*, ed. Bernard Ribemont (Paris: Champion, 1998), pp. 135–74.
[17] Susan Bordo, *The Flight to Objectivity: Essays on Cartesianism and Culture* (Albany: State University of New York Press, 1987); Genevieve Lloyd, *The Man of Reason: 'Male' and 'Female' in Western Philosophy* (London: Methuen, 1984); and Genevieve Lloyd, 'Texts, Metaphors and the Pretensions of Philosophy', *Monist* 69 (1986), 87–102.

while a higher form of love is the desire to bring into existence beautiful cities, deeds, and words. In many later readings of this myth, Diotima's distinction between a lower reproductive love and a higher love, which is ultimately love of beauty and truth, is conjoined with the Platonic idea that the soul is trapped in a debased body from which it yearns to escape. It thus contributes to that strand of dualist thinking which contemporary feminists have argued has served to exclude women from philosophy. But in Dante's hands, following both Boethius and elements of chivalric love poetry such as that written by his contemporary Guido Cavalcanti, we find a more positive set of images.[18] In Boethius' *Consolation*, Diotima transforms into *Philosophia*, the personification of philosophic wisdom, who appears to Boethius and later to Christine; in Dante's *œuvre*, in which Beatrice and *Philosophia* merge, love for a particular virtuous and beautiful woman comes to be seen as continuous with the love of God. Thus, at the climax of Dante's *Paradiso*, Dante sees the enthroned Beatrice, elsewhere identified with the theological virtue Charity (identified as the love of God) and invests her with great theological authority.[19] With his poems to Laura, Petrarch continued the tradition of representing an idealised feminine object of love who is an allegory of virtue.

These allegories are aspects of a well-established medieval tradition in which the theological virtues (faith, hope, and charity) and the civic virtues (prudence, justice, temperance and fortitude) are given a feminine

---

[18] This more positive early Renaissance representation of women is discussed in Sister Prudence Allen, *The Concept of Woman: The Early Humanist Reformation 1250–1500*, 2 vols. (Grand Rapids, Michigan: Erdmans Publishing, 2002), vol. II, pp. 223–320. On p. 227, Allen implies that this positive representation of women was instrumental in the slightly later increase in women who entered into intellectual dialogue with men. Allen includes Christine de Pizan among those women who may have been influenced by this development, and she mentions Dante's influence on Christine (p. 562); however, she does not develop the theme at great length when she later outlines Christine's thought (pp. 537–658).

[19] Beatrice's allegorical significance is a hotly debated topic in Dante studies, but there is substantial evidence that she represents Charity both in the *Vita nuova* and the *Divine Comedy*. See Robert Pogue Harrison, *The Body of Beatrice* (London and Baltimore: Johns Hopkins University Press, 1988). Harrison argues that at the climax of the *Vita nuova* Dante discovers that Beatrice is Charity; and he examines the many other allegorical interpretations of Beatrice. For a review of this work, see Winthrop Wetherbee, 'The Body of Beatrice', review in *Modern Philology* 88 (1991), 299–301; Jefferson B. Fletcher, 'The Allegory of the *Vita nuova*', *Modern Philology* II (1913), 21–2. Fletcher states that '*Charity*, infused by grace of God, (is) reflected in Beatrice' (p. 22). See also Owen C. Thomas, 'Beatrice or Iseult? The Debate about Romantic Love', *Anglican Theological Review* 79 (1997), 571–87; Charles Williams, *The Figure of Beatrice: A Study in Dante* (Woodbridge and Rochester, NY: D. S. Brewer, 1994; originally published, London: Faber and Faber, 1943); and Joan Ferrante, 'Dante's Beatrice. Priest of an Androgynous God', in *Occasional Papers*, Center for Medieval and Early Renaissance Studies, No. 2 (Binghamton: Medieval & Renaissance Texts & Studies, 1992), p. 11.

bodily form.[20] This metaphorical association has positive implications for women. Just as the metaphorical association of the mind with masculine rule militates against real women's philosophical participation, this older metaphorical imagery arguably serves to elevate the feminine and paves the way for philosophically inclined women, such as Christine, to identify themselves with the wise feminine philosophical voice.[21] Certainly, Christine was quick to exploit such tropes in the service of elevating women's authority. Other images of wise women, for example the sibyls (believed to have prophesied Christ's coming), the Christian saints and martyrs, the muses, and various figures from antiquity were also exploited by Christine in the construction of an authoritative philosophical persona. Dante undoubtedly played a significant role in this refashioning of woman's image. Christine was also acquainted with the writings of Dante's admirers Giovanni Boccaccio (1313–75) and Petrarch.[22] Echoing a formulation of Petrarch's, in *Christine's Vision* Christine explains that she found in these 'theological poets' a style that was congenial to her. And in her writing she continued to develop the tradition of the feminine personification of the virtues, thus supplementing at a metaphorical level her explicit arguments for women's capacities and moral excellence.

Like much medieval political philosophy, Dante's political thought was deeply indebted to Aristotle, and to the elaboration of Aristotelian themes in the works of Cicero, Seneca, Boethius, and ultimately Aquinas. Dante begins his *Monarchia* (most likely composed between 1310 and 1313) with a reference to God's infusion of a love of truth into all human beings, and Christine extends this love of truth and desire for knowledge to include women.[23] Christine challenges Aristotle's assessment of women's

---

[20] The famous fresco by Ambroglio Lorenzetti at Siena, which represents good and bad government, demonstrates this tendency, as well as the contrary tendency to represent the vices as also taking a feminine form.

[21] See Karen Green and Jacqueline Broad, 'Fictions of a Feminine Philosophical Persona: Christine de Pizan, Margaret Cavendish, and Philosophia Lost', in *The Philosopher in Early Modern Europe: The Nature of a Contested Identity*, ed. Conal Condren, Stephen Gaukroger, and Ian Hunter, Ideas in Context (Cambridge University Press, 2006), pp. 229–53. It may well be objected that the vices are also often represented as women, even by Christine; but while this is certainly the case, it does not detract from the fact that the feminine character of *Philosophia* provides a ready-made persona for Christine to adopt.

[22] For a brief account of the connections between these authors, see Anthony Levi, *Renaissance and Reformation: The Intellectual Genesis* (New Haven: Yale University Press, 2002), pp. 86–9.

[23] The opening sentence of the *Monarchia* is 'For all men whom the Higher Nature has endowed with a love of truth, this above all seems to be a matter of concern' (1.1). Here Dante is speaking of the desire to work for the amelioration of society. For an English translation of *Monarchia*, see Dante Alighieri, *Monarchy*, ed. and trans. Prue Shaw (Cambridge University Press, 1996).

capacities, but she also inherited much from the tradition that descended from him. She was sufficiently indebted to Boethius to record the date, 15 October 1402, when a copy of his *Consolation* came into her hands. She frames her dream vision, *The Long Path of Learning*, with a brief outline of the *Consolation*, which she represents herself as reading just before the fictional experiences that she recounts. Aristotle began his *Ethics* with a proof that there must be a single highest good, which is desired for its own sake and which he called *eudaimonia*, and which in Christine's works is called *félicité humaine*. The Hellenistic period saw vigorous debate over the nature of the highest good. Should it be identified with pleasure, as the Epicureans claimed, or with virtue, as the Cynics and Stoics asserted? In Boethius, one finds a Christian transformation of the Stoic view that happiness is identical with virtue. The highest good is God, so that human happiness becomes identified with participation in God. God is here thought of in Platonic fashion as a form rather than as an individual substance.[24] Following the identification of God with the highest good, Aquinas identifies the desire for truth (pursued in the study of metaphysics) with the desire to understand God (theology). Christine's political ideas emerge out of this background.

Implicitly including women among those whose happiness consists in participation in Godliness, Christine brings her own interview with *Philosophia* to a climax by quoting a passage from Boethius in which philosophy and theology merge.[25] In this context, the passage also serves to extend Aquinas' identification of theology with metaphysics – conceived as the study of the highest being – to include ethics, conceived as the search for the highest good. She thus makes it clear that she thinks of politics, like ethics, as part of theology. Biblical history and prophecy are thus relevant for understanding why states fail, and Christine makes clear that she believes that this is largely the consequence of vice: fraud, greed, and luxury. In the introductory explanation added to at least one manuscript of *Christine's Vision*, she shows that she intends this work to have a triple reading which involves a political as well as a personal and a cosmic import.[26] It is easiest to understand the nature of this political

[24] Boethius, *The Consolation of Philosophy*, trans. Victor Watts (Harmondsworth: Penguin, 1999), III.10–12; John Marenbon, *Boethius*, ed. Brian Davies (Oxford University Press, 2003), pp. 106–14.

[25] Christine de Pizan, *Christine's Vision*, III.26, p. 140; *L'advision*, pp. 137–8; Boethius, *The Consolation of Philosophy*, III.10, pp. 72–3. Glynnis Cropp identifies the French translation which Christine used in 'Boèce et Christine de Pizan', *Moyen Age* 87 (1981), 387–417.

[26] Christine M. Reno, 'The Preface to the *Avision-Christine*', in *Reinterpreting Christine de Pizan*, ed. Earl Jeffrey Richards with Joan Williamson, Nadia Margolis, and Christine M. Reno (Athens,

import by returning to *The Long Path of Learning* and examining its indebtedness to Dante's theological politics.

Departing from Augustine's pessimism concerning the temporal realm, Dante had argued in *Monarchia* that the Romans ruled their empire by right and that, during the rule of Augustus, at the time of the birth of Christ, 'a perfect monarchy existed' and peace reigned throughout the world.[27] Dante looks forward to a time when the world will again experience peace by being united under the rule of a single emperor. This emperor will derive his authority directly from God, and will not be subject to the Pope, for, according to Dante, the Pope is supreme in spiritual matters only, and should keep out of temporal affairs.[28] The result is an optimism on Dante's behalf concerning the possibility of just temporal government, and this is an optimism that Christine shares. In particular, in *The Long Path of Learning*, she recounts Nature's complaint about the strife and sinfulness of people on earth. Then she relates how in the court of Reason, where Nobility, Chivalry, Wisdom, and Wealth sat in counsel, it was determined that to overcome greed, and the wars that result from it, a single monarch should govern the earth.[29] Here Christine exactly echoes Dante's argument.[30]

It is widely recognised that Christine was familiar with Dante's *Commedia* but less widely acknowledged that she was also in all probability familiar with his *Monarchia* or *Convivio* or possibly both. Arturo Farinelli, in his now quite dated and condescending account of Dante's influence on Christine, traces the influence of the *Commedia* on her thought, but asserts that 'the noble woman could not have obtained *De Monarchia*: the political confession and all of Dante's minor works were

GA: The University of Georgia Press, 1992), pp. 207–27. Dulac and Reno suggest that this is only intended as a guide to reading the first part of the work in their 'The *Livre de l'advision Cristine*', p. 205. However, once the interpretative schema is applied to the first part it naturally suggests a triple reading of the later parts as well.

[27] For Dante's belief that Rome was ordained by God to rule over the holy and secular empires, see *Monarchia*, II.4, III.1; *Convivio*, IV.5, and *Inferno*, II, lines 20–24. In *Monarchia*, I.16, Dante expresses his belief that the world was at peace under Augustus. For Dante's *Monarchia* and *Convivio*, see F. Chiapelli (ed.), *Dante Alighieri: tutte le opere*, 3rd edn (Milan: Mursia, 1965).

[28] See, *Monarchia*, III.6–7, where Dante argues that God's vicar should not hold authority over temporal powers.

[29] Christine de Pizan, *Le Chemin de longue étude*, lines 2811–3066. Anna Slerca outlines the Platonic background, and in particular the influence of Alan of Lille behind Christine's use of the story of Nature's complaint, in 'Le *Livre du chemin de longue estude* (1402–1403): Christine au pays des merveilles', pp. 135–74.

[30] Dante states that the world is best disposed when it is under the rule of one single monarch in *Convivio*, IV.5.

not yet available in France'.[31] Nevertheless, others have noted the striking parallels between Book II of *Monarchia* and the debate on the subject of a universal monarch developed by Christine in *The Long Path of Learning*.[32] It seems quite possible that Christine's father possessed copies of works by Dante, which may not have remained in France, but returned to Italy with his sons. Such an eventuality would explain both Christine's familiarity with the substance of Dante's arguments and her failure, apart from a few scattered phrases, to quote his texts verbatim. There are many features of Christine's political outlook that recall Dante and *The Long Path of Learning* is clearly a reprise of the *Commedia*. Since Dante there refers obliquely to the political theses developed in *Monarchia*, showing in *Paradiso*, III that he believes Henry VII could have come to Italy as a new Augustus, Christine's knowledge of his works could indeed have been limited to the *Commedia*.[33] Nevertheless, the proposal discussed in *The Long Path of Learning* is quite likely informed by the more fully developed argumentative style of Dante's prose works.

Another feature of Christine's political outlook that echoes Dante, but has not been much remarked upon, is a respect for a prophetic tradition of history initiated by the Italian abbot Joachim of Fiore. Marjorie Reeves has demonstrated that Dante's optimistic argument in *Monarchia*, which looks forward to an age of peace and justice under a single ruler, betrays an outlook on history influenced by Joachim, and she shows that Dante exploits Joachim's images in *Paradiso*, XVIII and XXXIII.[34] Christine also clearly indicates that she is familiar with the substance of Joachim's writings. In the explanatory introduction, intended to help the reader interpret *Christine's Vision*, she explains:

In the XIIIth chapter and what is said in the following and other chapters, one should note what is meant by the ancient prophecies of Merlin, the sibyls, of Joachim and John concerning the plagues to come to the world as much to the realm of France as elsewhere, because of the sins occurring there which is to say

---

[31] Farinelli, *Dante e la Francia*, vol. I, p. 191.

[32] Slerca, 'Le *Livre du chemin de longue estude*', 139, n. 13.

[33] See Dante, *Paradiso*, XXX, lines 133–41. Here Dante predicts Henry VII's death in 1313 from the fictional date of his journey (1300) and states that Henry VII came to save Italy before it was ready to be saved. Three of Dante's Epistles refer to Henry VII. Epistle V is addressed to the people and princes of Italy, urging them to receive and welcome Henry VII. Epistle VI is addressed to the Florentines as they opposed his coming, and the third (Epistle VII) is addressed to Henry VII, imploring him to come to Tuscany and set the Florentines straight.

[34] See Marjorie Reeves, 'Dante and the Prophetic View of History', in *The World of Dante: Essays on Dante and His Times*, ed. Cecil Grayson (Oxford: Clarendon Press, 1980), pp. 44–60.

because of the pride of the rich and powerful and the lasciviousness, fraud, greed, and lack of faith found in the world.[35]

In the chapters alluded to here, Christine tells the story of a Crowned Lady who is, on the most obvious allegorical interpretation, France. This Lady had been protected by two birds of prey, but the first of these was flung to the earth and rendered weak and dependent. This image, Christine explains, represents the madness of Charles VI after his first breakdown in 1392. Thereafter France's misfortunes began to multiply:

> After these events larcenous spirits came, creatures of the woods, who said it was their business to partake of personal and private things. They made closed houses places of common use and appropriated them for themselves so that even the wild beasts cried against them.
> During this time the cry of the chameleon woke an illbred kind of person who said that they could not in the slightest suffer the injurious clamour of female voices.[36]

After these rather obscure events, which will be interpreted below, a flood arrived, and Christine represents these occurrences as together embodying the birth of the pestilence.

In the chapters that follow, which Christine explains are inspired by the prophecies of Merlin, the sibyls, Joachim, and John, Christine sees Reason with her mirror imprisoned and dulled by Fraud, Justice, with measuring cup and ruler, falling sick, and Chivalry put to sleep by Luxury. The monster Fraud, she says, which infects the whole world, had been seen by Dante in the form of a horrible serpent when he was shown through hell by Virgil.[37] The Crowned Lady goes on to relate the fates of Nebuchadnezzar, Saul, and other biblical and historical figures whose realms were punished because their people had variously succumbed to lasciviousness, fraud, greed, and lack of faith. She laments, 'Alas, considering what my subjects deserve, have I not cause to fear my ruin?'[38] Clearly, Christine intends her audience to read the fate of France as paralleling these biblical events – immorality is being punished by war – and in doing so she follows a

---

[35] *Christine's Vision*, p. 9; *L'advision*, p. 10.

[36] *Christine's Vision*, 1.13, p. 21; *L'advision*, p. 24.

[37] *Christine's Vision*, 1.16, p. 25; *L'advision*, p. 30. Geryon, Dante's image of Fraud, appears in *Inferno* XVI, lines 127–36 and XVII, 1–42 and 79–136, where Dante refers to him as 'colei che tutto'l mondo apuzza' [the one that makes the whole world stink] (*Inferno* XVII, 3). For the text and translation of *Inferno*, see Dante Alighieri, *The Divine Comedy of Dante Alighieri: Inferno*, ed. Robert M. Durling and Ronald L. Martinez (New York: Oxford University Press, 1996), vol. 1.

[38] *Christine's Vision*, 1.23, p. 34; *L'advision*, p. 40.

method of political prophecy derived from Joachim, who expounded the Apocalyptic writings of John. Joachim claimed to predict both the coming of the Anti-Christ and the eventual arrival of a third age, the age of the Holy Spirit, which would follow the Age of the Father (before Christ) and the Age of the Son.[39] Christine shares with Joachim a love of the Trinity and of tripartite structures, and she concludes the third book of her vision with an obscure image of three precious stones. However, she refrains from spelling out Joachim's prophecies, or those of Merlin and the sibyls, because, as she says, some claim them to be apocryphal. Yet the import of her vision implies that she accepts Joachim's method of finding parallels between ancient and modern times. And in contemporary manuscripts, the prophecies of Joachim are often found collected together with prophecies attributed to the sibyls and Merlin, suggesting that Christine was familiar with some such collection.[40]

In *The Long Path of Learning*, there are further allusions to prophecies associated with Joachim. The Cumean sibyl, who takes Christine on a journey through the known world before allowing her to climb the ladder of speculation into the fifth firmament, shows Christine the Caspian Sea; close by Gog and Magog are confined, waiting the coming of the Anti-Christ, at whose appearance they will descend on humanity.[41] Christine claims that after she was led down from the fifth firmament into the realm of air, she came to understand the destinies of things and in particular the prophecies of the sibyls and Merlin.[42] She thus underscores her claim to authority in the role of handmaiden to the sibyl, whose prophetic words about the punishment of vice, and the virtuous character required in a universal prince, should be taken seriously.[43] Here Christine

---

[39] Marjorie Reeves, *Joachim of Fiore and the Prophetic Future* (London: SPCK, 1976), p. 6.

[40] Marjorie Reeves, *The Influence of Prophecy in the Later Middle Ages: A Study in Joachimism* (Oxford: Clarendon Press, 1969).

[41] Christine de Pizan, *Le Chemin de longue étude*, lines 1467–70.

[42] Ibid., lines 2049–256.

[43] Dante uses a similar tactic to assert his poetic and prophetic authority. His journey is willed on high: as Beatrice explains to Virgil, the Virgin Mary in heaven called upon Saint Lucy, who beseeched Beatrice to ensure that Dante undertook the journey to Truth in order to free himself and the world from the bondage of sin; see Dante, *Inferno*, II, lines 70–117. See also ibid., line 32, where Dante states: 'I am not Aeneas, I am not Paul; neither I nor others / believe me worthy of that.' While Dante is ostensibly expressing his fear that he is not worthy of the journey, rhetorically he is aligning himself with those great figures, for indeed he will undertake the journey successfully. Thus, he is accentuating the magnitude of the journey he will accomplish: from the outset we are to understand that Dante is presenting his journey as equivalent to the journeys of Aeneas (the Forefather of the Romans) and Saint Paul, 'Vas d'elezïone' [the chosen vessel] (ibid., II, line 28).

seems to anticipate the theme of *Christine's Vision*, which she did not complete until three years later.

To modern thinkers, Christine's interest in the prophetic tradition may appear to detract from the seriousness of her political thought. However, there is a sense in which the optimism concerning the possibility of just temporal rule, which she inherits from Dante, underlies her faith that in a world ordered by the knowable principles of a totally good God, virtuous government is possible and will be rewarded with peace.

Following these threads we can interpret the political message of *Christine's Vision* in which, according to the explanatory introduction, Christine's own fate is to be read as a microcosm of the fate of France and of the universe.[44] Just as Christine's individual tribulations, recounted in the third book, lead her to understand the true nature of happiness, which is participation in God and hence in the Holy Trinity of Faith, Hope, and Charity, so the tribulations of France – similarly represented as an abandoned widow – are to be read as punishments designed to bring the realm to its moral perfection.

At the end of the third book, Christine addresses Philosophy, who now appears to her in the form of Saint Theology and who encompasses all knowledge, including physics, logic, ethics, and politics.[45] In the second book, Christine discourses with Opinion, who was created after Philosophy in order to allow the enlightened to discover Philosophy.[46] Opinion explains to Christine that the troubles of the world are not due to Fortune, as Christine represents in her *Mutation of Fortune*, but to the diversity of false opinions generated in men by the desire for knowledge.[47] In the first book, Christine looks back to the origin of the universe, of France, and of herself. In the second book, she draws heavily on Aquinas' *Commentary on the Metaphysics of Aristotle* for her representation of the partial and false opinions of the ancient philosophers.[48]

[44] *Christine's Vision*, pp. 3–5; *L'advision*, pp. 3–5.
[45] *Christine's Vision*, III.27, pp. 142–3; *L'advision*, pp. 140–1. See Glynnis Cropp, 'Philosophy, the Liberal Arts, and Theology in *Le Livre de la mutacion de Fortune* and *Le Livre de l'advision Cristine*', in Green and Mews (eds.), *Healing the Body Politic*, pp. 139–59.
[46] *Christine's Vision*, II.3, p. 61; *L'advision*, pp. 54–5.
[47] *Christine's Vision*, II.14–22, pp. 76–88; *L'advision*, pp. 75–90.
[48] Liliane Dulac and Christine M. Reno, 'Traduction et adaptation dans l'*Advision Christine* de Christine de Pizan', in *Traduction et adaptation en France à la fin du Moyen Age et à la Renaissance: Actes du Colloque organisé par l'Université de Nancy II (23–24 mars 1995)*, ed. Charles Brucker (Paris: Champion, 1997), pp. 121–31. Liliane Dulac and Christine M. Reno, 'L'humanisme vers 1400, essai d'exploration à partir d'un cas marginal: Christine de Pizan traductrice de Thomas d'Aquin' (paper presented at the conference 'Pratiques de la culture écrite en France au xvme siècle', Louvain-La-Neuve, 1994).

Following Aquinas' identification of metaphysics with theology, and Dante's reference to God's infusion of a love of truth in all human beings, Christine also represents the political knowledge that is required to solve France's problems as a form of the understanding of God's nature. Once prince and people universally participate in God through the exercise of virtue, the aim of political organisation, the common good, will be achieved and peace will follow.

In her political works directed to the young prince Louis of Guyenne, such as *The Book of the Body Politic* and *The Book of Peace*, and in *The Book of Three Virtues*, dedicated to his young wife Marguerite of Burgundy, the prophetic elements found in Christine's earlier works recede into the background. In these later works, she directs her efforts towards practical advice on how to govern. Yet, even in these texts, prudent government is represented as an exercise in charity, or love of God. And in *The Book of Peace*, she draws on events in biblical history to draw conclusions concerning God's punishment of both rebellious subjects and tyrannical princes.

In her last work, her *Ditty of Joan of Arc*, written in 1429 a few days after the coronation of Charles VII, we see Christine explicitly returning to her prophetic voice.[49] Here she announces that in Joan the prophecies of Merlin, the sibyls, and Bede have finally been fulfilled. Christine hails Charles as the fulfilment of the Charlemagne prophecy, which promised a Charles, son of Charles, who according to well-known prophecies would conquer Rome and occupy the place of the just Christian emperor that Dante thought could have been filled by Henry VII.[50] In this poem, she appeals to the biblical heroines Judith, Esther, and Deborah as precursors to Joan, anticipating, as we will see, many later women who point to these examples to authorise their political interventions.

There are other connected aspects of Christine's political thinking that are highly reminiscent of Dante. Like Dante, she has a rather rosy perception of Roman virtue and chivalry. Drawing heavily on Valerius Maximus and Vegetius, Christine repeatedly turns to the Romans for

---

[49] Christine de Pizan, *Le Ditié de Jehanne d'Arc*, trans. Angus J. Kennedy and Kenneth Varty (Oxford: Medium Aevum Monographs, 1977). Earl Jeffrey Richards has raised with us the question as to whether 'ditty' appropriately translates the title of Christine's poem. Blumenfeld-Kosinski translates the title as 'The Tale of Joan of Arc', in *The Selected Writings of Christine de Pizan*, pp. 252–62, while Willard prefers 'The Poem of Joan of Arc', in *The Writings of Christine de Pizan*, pp. 352–62. However, 'ditty' is the closest English word etymologically to 'ditié' and carries some of the connotations of a light and celebratory song, conveyed by the diminutive element in the French title, so we are prepared to argue that 'ditty' is an appropriate translation.

[50] Dante, *Paradiso*, XXX, lines 133–41.

examples of the virtues. Fabricius, whom Dante also mentions, is praised
for his disdain of worldly goods and devotion to the common good, as is
Scipio Africanus.[51] And even when she is concerned at a more practical
level to give advice to a prince or a princess, Christine assumes that peace,
justice, and prosperity are possible just so long as the prince or princess is
sufficiently wise and virtuous to be able to follow God's commands and
bring about the common good.

Christine's source for a guiding metaphor for the polity, 'the body
politic', derives from John of Salisbury's *Policraticus*. She names one of
her works *The Body Politic* after the image he helped to make famous, and
she captures the essence of the medical analogy for the art of good
government in the following lines:

> The Policraticus maintains
> In his book, that it appertains
> To a prince to be grave
> In manners, he should behave
> Temperately and in council
> Wisely listen to counsel,
> And he should know how to govern
> Like a doctor, knowing the prescription
> Of every kind of medicine.
> Drinks from roots or other things
> He gives to purge our sufferings;
> To others for nature's fostering,
> He readies many various syrups,
> And where there already gallops
> Putrefaction which will cost dear,
> He knows the bad from good to shear.[52]

Nevertheless, in her attitude to the clergy Christine shows herself closer to
Dante than to John of Salisbury. Salisbury made the clergy the heart and
soul of the body politic. Christine treats them as simply a part of the body,
which is ruled like the rest by the prince. Here too she is surely influenced

---

[51] Christine de Pizan, *Corps de policie*, 1.12, 1.13, 1.29, 11. 4, 11.9 and 11.17, pp. 19–22, 23, 48–50, 61–2,
69–71 and 82–3; *Book of the Body Politic*, pp. 21–4, 25, 49–52, 62–3, 69–73, and 81–3; *Le Chemin de
longue étude*, lines 4806, 3815 and 4481. Fabricius is cited as an example of liberality, the virtue
opposed to avarice, in *Purgatorio*, XX, lines 25–7. Dante also speaks of Fabricius' virtue in
Monarchia 11.5, where he describes him as having refused bribes, despite his poverty, out of loyalty
to Rome. Fabricius is mentioned in the context of those who ignore personal advantage for the
sake of the greater good.

[52] Christine de Pizan, *Le Chemin de longue étude*, lines 5705–20.

by Dante, who was among those who insisted that the church had no place in temporal affairs.

Although Christine imagines virtue as participation in Godliness, she is far more optimistic about the possibility of exercising virtue in the temporal realm than were earlier medieval authors. Her attitudes are thus justly described as humanist. Her humanism manifests itself in her belief that an active life devoted to bringing about temporal good for others, while it may not be the highest life (which she admits is the life of contemplation of God), is nevertheless a worthy expression of one's charity or love of God.[53] And her high regard for the active virtues, so manifest in the Romans, leads her at times even to disagree with her hero Boethius. She sees the desire for glory and good reputation as fundamentally beneficial, believing that the Romans' virtue was motivated by their custom of performing public acts of recognition, which fostered the desire to acquire renown for good deeds. She is led to conclude that 'despite the fact that Boethius argues in his third book, not to quest too ardently for glory in this world . . .', that '. . . for those who live morally in the active life, to desire glory in a just cause is not a vice'.[54] Yet, as we will see, she did not slavishly follow the ancients either, for she perceived, rightly, that their texts were the source of much medieval misogyny.

II

In the preceding section, we saw how Christine exploits Dante, Boethius, and the biblical tradition to underscore her authority as a writer, as well as Joan of Arc's authority as a political actor. In both cases, women's authority can be traced back to God, since if God has revealed his truth to a woman, there can be an appeal to no higher justification for accepting her right to be believed. In this second section, we turn to Christine's explicit defence of women's right to exercise political authority, touch on the way in which her love debate poetry anticipates the themes of her later political works, and broach the question of the contemporary political purpose of Christine's works defending women. We argue that she was responding to the way in which contemporary women, such as Valentina Visconti and Isabeau de Bavière, had been treated and that, in particular, she intended to support Isabeau's right to operate as regent during the periods of her husband's madness.

[53] Christine de Pizan, *Treasure*, 1.5–6, pp. 43–6; *Trois vertus*, 1.6–7, pp. 22–8.
[54] Christine de Pizan, *Book of the Body Politic*, 11.17, pp. 82–3; *Corps de policie*, p. 83.

Much has been written on Christine's defence of women, and the question of whether her contribution to the *querelle des femmes* entitles her to be considered a precursor of feminism.[55] Leaving aside this issue, which depends largely on one's definition of feminism, it is more relevant to point out that Christine's works on women were inspired by the political circumstances in which she found herself. They were intended to support the claims of Isabeau de Bavière, Charles VI's wife, to govern France as regent, and were developed against the background of the exclusion of women from inheriting the French crown, which had been effected during the previous century.[56] At the same time, by crafting a citadel from which the 'citoyennes' could never be dislodged, Christine provides a source of images of prudent female government, which were known to and exploited by princesses for at least two centuries after she wrote. In *The Book of the City of Ladies*, Christine announces what she calls 'un nouvel royaume de Femenie' [a new kingdom of womanhood]. This realm is to replace the old 'royaume et la seigneurie des femmes' [kingdom and dominion of women] maintained by the Amazons, which Christine describes as having lasted for many centuries. Her new realm, Reason promises her, will last even longer.[57] In the new realm of womanhood, women's prudence and capacity for governing themselves and others will

[55] Sheila Delany, 'History, Politics and Christine Studies: A Polemical Reply', in Brabant (ed.), *Politics, Gender, and Genre*, pp. 193–206; Sheila Delany, '"Mothers to Think Back Through": Who Are They? The Ambiguous Example of Christine de Pizan', in *Medieval Texts and Contemporary Readers*, ed. Laurie A. Finke and Martin B. Shichtman (Ithaca, NY: Cornell University Press, 1987), pp. 177–97; Christine M. Reno, 'Christine de Pizan: "At Best a Contradictory Figure?"', in Brabant (ed.), *Politics, Gender, and Genre*, pp. 171–91; Susan Schibanoff, 'Taking the Gold out of Egypt: The Art of Reading as a Woman', in *Gender and Reading*, ed. Elizabeth A. Flynn and Patrocinio P. Schweickart (Baltimore: Johns Hopkins University Press, 1986), pp. 83–106.

[56] For a more extended argument to this effect, see Karen Green, 'Isabeau de Bavière and the Political Philosophy of Christine de Pizan', *Historical Reflections/Réflexions Historiques* 32 (2006), 247–72. For the background to the exclusion of women from the French crown, see Earl Jeffrey Richards, 'Political Thought as Improvisation: Female Regency and Mariology in Late Medieval French Thought', in Broad and Green (eds.), *Virtue, Liberty, and Toleration*, pp. 1–22; M. Paul Viollet, 'Comment les femmes ont été exclues en France, de la succession à la couronne', *Mémoires de l'Institut de France, Académie des Inscriptions et Belles-Lettres* 34 (1893), 125–78; Sarah Hanley, 'The Politics of Identity and Monarchic Governance in France: The Debate over Female Exclusion', in Smith (ed.), *Women Writers*, pp. 289–304.

[57] Christine de Pizan, *La Città delle dame*, 11.12, p. 250, 1.19, p. 130, and 1.4, p. 56; *Book of the City of Ladies*, pp. 117, 51 and 12. In *The Creation of Feminist Consciousness: From the Middle Ages to Eighteen-Seventy* (Oxford University Press, 1993), Gerda Lerner sees the frequent representation of strong women as Amazons during the early modern period as fundamentally negative, but Christine's exploitation of the Amazonian stories operates in a very direct way to show that women's lack of power is merely conventional, not natural. At a period during which the accounts of the Amazons were accepted as historically accurate they provided a potent example to women of what was possible.

be celebrated. Women, as equal participants in God's plans for humanity, will be included as equals in the quest for the common good.

It has not been usual to interpret Christine as defending Isabeau's right to rule as regent during her husband's absence, although it is not unprecedented.[58] This is largely because Isabeau has been the victim of a campaign of character assassination, in which she has been depicted as a venal, vain, promiscuous, and overweight Eve. It has seemed impossible to readers of Christine that the moralistic and pious widow could have done anything other than disapprove of the adulterous queen.[59] But since the 1960s, Isabeau has been largely rehabilitated.[60] This allows us to read Christine's defence of women rulers, particularly her accounts of female regents such as Fredegund and Blanche of Castile, who figure prominently in *The Book of the City of Ladies*, as bolstering Isabeau's right to rule as regent during the periods of her husband's madness. Indeed, chapters 13–15 of the first part of *The City of Ladies* are entirely taken up with examples of widows from ancient history, and from more recent French experience, who have governed their countries or estates well. Christine

[58] See Thelma Fenster, 'Who's a Heroine? The Example of Christine de Pizan', in Altmann and McGrady (eds.), *Christine de Pizan: A Casebook*, pp. 115–28 (p. 122); and Tracy Adams, '*Moyenneresse de Traictié de Paix:* Christine de Pizan's Mediators', in Green and Mews (eds.), *Healing the Body Politic*, pp. 177–200. Both Fenster and Adams rehabilitate Isabeau and see Christine's attitude to her as positive.

[59] See e.g. Marie-Josèphe Pinet, *Christine de Pisan* (Geneva: Slatkine Reprints, 1974), p. 117; Charity Cannon Willard, *Christine de Pisan: Her Life and Works* (New York: Persea, 1984), p. 143. More recently Julia M. Walker has referred to the 'implicit and explicit critiques offered by Christine de Pizan' of 'a queen whose conduct could be called honorable in only the most conventional discourse'; see Julia M. Walker, 'Re-politicizing the *Book of the Three Virtues*', in Hicks (ed.), *Au champ des escriptures*, pp. 533–48 (p. 533).

[60] Yann Grandeau must be credited with the impetus for this rehabilitation, and his research uncovered much of the detail of Isabeau's court: Yann Grandeau, 'Isabeau de Bavière ou l'amour conjugal' (paper presented at the Congrès National des Sociétés Savantes, Limoges, 1977); *Jeanne insultée: procès en diffamation* (Paris: Editions Albin Michel, 1973); 'L'exercice de la piété à la cour de France: les dévotions d'Isabeau de Bavière' (paper presented at the conference 'Jeanne d'Arc: une époque, un rayonnement'. Colloque d'histoire médiévale', Orléans, 1979); 'Le Dauphin Jean duc de Touraine', *Bulletin Philologique et Historique du Comité des Travaux Historiques et Scientifiques* (1968), 665–728; 'De quelques dames qui ont servi la reine Isabeau de Bavière', *Bulletin Philologique et Historique du Comité des Travaux Historiques et Scientifiques* (1975), 129–239; 'Les enfants de Charles VI: essai sur la vie privée des princes et de princesses de la maison de France à la fin du Moyen Age', *Bulletin Philologique et Historique du Comité des Travaux Historiques et Scientifiques* (1967), 809–50. See also R. C. Famiglietti, *Royal Intrigue: Crisis at the Court of Charles VI* (New York: AMS Press, 1986); Rachel Gibbons, 'Isabeau of Bavaria, Queen of France (1385–1422), The Creation of an Historical Villainess', *Transactions of the Royal Historical Society* series 6.6 (1996), 51–73; 'Les conciliatrices au bas Moyen Age: Isabeau de Bavière et la guerre civile (1401–1415)', in *La guerre, la violence et les gens au Moyen Age*, ed. Pierre Contamine and Olivier Guyotjeannin (Paris: Comité des Travaux Historiques et Scientifiques, 1996), pp. 23–33; and 'The Piety of Isabeau of Bavaria, Queen of France, 1385–1422', in *Courts, Counties and the Capital in the Later Middle Ages*, ed. Diana Dunn (Stroud: Sutton Publishing, 1996), pp. 205–224.

thus demonstrates the falseness of the view that women do not plead cases at law because of a past woman who governed unwisely. This series of stories ends with the example of Semiramis and at the end of her account of this widow's expansion of the Babylonian empire, Reason announces that 'now the first stone is set in the foundation of our city'.[61]

At various junctures during the struggle between the Burgundians and Armagnacs which resulted from the incompetence of Charles VI, Isabeau attempted to assert her authority as regent.[62] Yet, as Christine well understood, clerical representations of women as untrustworthy, changeable, and defective examples of humanity undermined the queen's authority as well as that of the 'chambermaid' who proposed to defend her. It is surely no coincidence, then, that Isabeau requested the sumptuously illuminated collection of Christine's works which culminates in *The Book of the City of Ladies* and which is now Harley MS 4431 of the British Library, in time for it to be presented to her at the beginning of 1414.[63] For it was during exactly this period that her chancellor, Robert le Maçon, was arguing in the royal council, faced with the failure of Louis of Guyenne to fulfil the hope that he would govern – expressed by Christine in her *Book of Peace* – that Isabeau should lead the government. For the direction of the government during the king's absences had initially been consigned to her.[64]

When we read *Christine's Vision* in conjunction with the nearly contemporary *Book of the City of Ladies*, we can see, as it were, the negative and positive sides of a single vision. In the first Reason, Chivalry, and Justice are dulled and disarmed by Fraud, Greed, and Luxury. In the second, Reason, Righteousness, and Justice are active, helping Christine to dig the foundations of her edifice, planning its streets and defences, and peopling it with prudent and virtuous women. The work moves from memory of the past, to an understanding of the reality of women, and towards the desire for godliness represented by the Virgin Mary and Christian saints and martyrs of the third book.

---

[61] Christine de Pizan, *Book of the City of Ladies*, 1.15, p. 40; *La Città delle dame*, p. 110.

[62] M. L. Bellaguet (ed.), *Chronique du Religieux de Saint-Denys*, 6 vols. (Paris: Editions du Comité des Travaux Historiques et Scientifiques, 1994), IV.91 and V.237.

[63] James Laidlaw argues that in the 'Autres Ballades' found in the queen's manuscript there are references to Jean of Bourbon's victory at Soubisse and so it must have been presented to her early in 1414. See James Laidlaw, 'Christine de Pizan, le duc de Bourbon et le manuscrit de la reine (Londres, British Library, Harley MS 4431)', in *La Chevalerie du Moyen Age à nos jours: mélanges offerts à Michel Stanesco*, ed. Mihaela Voicu and Victor-Dinu Vladulesco (Bucharest: Editura Universitătii din Bucuresti, 2003), pp. 332–44; the English version of this is James Laidlaw, 'The Date of the Queen's MS (London, British Library, MS 4431)', 2005, www.pizan.lib.ed.ac.uk/harley4431date.pdf, accessed 6 August 2007.

[64] Bellaguet, *Religieux de Saint-Denys*, V.237.

Here, more than anywhere, Christine demonstrates the limits of her respect for classical models. In chapter eighteen of the third part of the work, when the city is nearly complete and the Virgin Mary and Christian saints and martyrs have been welcomed into it, Justice returns to question the way in which women have been represented:

> while as you said previously, certain authors criticise women so much, I say that whatever you have found in the writings of pagan authors, I believe that you will find little criticism of women in the holy legends and the stories of Jesus Christ and his Apostles.[65]

The implied criticism of pagan authorities, whose beliefs were formed without the benefit of Christian revelation, is reinforced by reading the *City of Ladies* in conjunction with *Christine's Vision*, where Theology is represented as true knowledge, in contrast to pre-Christian Philosophy, which is at best wisdom's propaedeutic.

Nevertheless, it would be a mistake to take this criticism of classical misogyny to imply that Christine was not indebted to a fundamentally classical and Aristotelian concept of the purpose of political organisation. When Christine says that the common good of a city is a general good in which all members, women as well as men, participate, she presupposes a fundamentally Aristotelian conception of the subject of politics.[66] Ethics and politics are concerned with the flourishing life, and the best political organisation is that which is conducive to such flourishing. However, as we have seen, the classical idea that happiness is the highest good was transformed by early Christians so as to equate goodness with participation in God. Christine clearly thinks that women's good involves their development as virtuous beings and, as we will see, many later women share this presupposition. Virtues are those excellences of character which are conducive to flourishing, and Christine inherits an approach to political thought which therefore concentrates on detailed description of the development of virtue.

III

The virtues of an ideal prince constitute the core of most medieval political texts. In this last section, we examine Christine's contribution to this literature and the way in which her development of the image of the good

---

[65] *Book of the City of Ladies*, III.18, pp. 251–2; *La Città delle dame*, p. 492.
[66] *Book of the City of Ladies*, II.54, p. 187; *La Città delle dame*, p. 376.

prince is compatible with her argument for women's political authority. While many of the virtues that she describes as necessary for good princely rule are common to her male contemporaries, in *The Book of Peace* her extension of the four cardinal virtues to seven (including clemency, liberality, and truthfulness) goes beyond her sources. She offers a compassionate and caring conception of the legitimate monarch that differs considerably from earlier and later models, both in its lack of emphasis on the importance of male descent as the origin of legitimacy and in its distrust of the use of brute force.

After 1403, when Christine was commissioned by the Duke of Burgundy to write a history of the life of his brother, the late Charles V, she increasingly adopted a more practical, didactic style, designed to teach the young prince, princess, knight, or baroness the nature of prudence. Prudence is for Christine the fundamental political virtue, and 'mother and guide of all the virtues'.[67] It is personified in *The Letter of Othea*, as the Goddess Othea who stands for prudence and wisdom. And the teachings of prudence are variously laid out in Christine's *Book of Prudence*, her *Book of Three Virtues*, and her *Book of Peace*. It is important, in order to understand Christine as a political thinker, not to be misled by the modern connotations of the term 'prudence'. Since the time of Hobbes, prudence has come to be identified with rational self-interest. And while this is part of the meaning of prudence in Christine's mouth, such self-interest has to be understood in the light of her adoption of the identification of true happiness with participation in God, which she took from Boethius. Therefore, prudence has a much wider meaning for Christine than narrow self-interest. In fact, it is the standard contemporary translation of Aristotle's *phronesis* and thus encompasses practical understanding of how to bring about the good of the state, the household, and the self.

In these writings, Christine develops her own ideal conception of the just polity ruled by a virtuous and prudent prince, an ideal that also extends to rule by women in certain situations. Aristotle discusses *phronesis* at length

[67] Christine de Pizan, *Letter of Othea to Hector*, p. 38; *Epistre Othea*, pp. 201–2. See also Christine de Pizan, *Prudence*, 236ʳ and 238ʳ. References to Christine de Pizan's *Prudence* are to Brussels, Bibliothèque Royale de Belgique, MS 5698. Christine de Pizan, *The Book of Deeds of Arms and of Chivalry*, trans. Sumner Willard (University Park: Pennsylvania State University Press, 1999), 1.22, p. 59. For a more extended discussion of this trope, and a longer discussion of Christine's understanding of prudence, see Karen Green, 'On Translating Christine de Pizan as a Philosopher', in Green and Mews (eds.), *Healing the Body Politic*, pp. 117–37; Green, '*Phronesis* Feminised: Prudence from Christine de Pizan to Elizabeth I', in Broad and Green (eds.), *Virtue, Liberty, and Toleration*, pp. 23–38.

in the sixth book of the *Nicomachean Ethics* and makes clear that it is the central political virtue.[68] *Phronesis* is knowledge in an applied and practical sense, and to gain it requires experience. Aristotle distinguishes it from *sophia*, the theoretical wisdom of an unworldly Anaximander or Thales, and represents it as an active virtue.[69] The idea that prudence is the mother of the virtues, so often utilised by Christine, derives from the fact that, according to Aristotle, the possession of *phronesis* implies possession of all the virtues, for 'if a man have the one moral virtue of prudence he will also have all the moral virtues along with it'.[70]

A prudent prince accepts the counsel of the old and wise, avoids flatterers, and loves justice. Christine sees the appointment of experienced advisers as essential for princely government, and while she insists on the importance of taking advice she is also very aware of the danger of corrupt or incompetent counsellors. These must be avoided. Christine advises that the king will need the counsel provided by experienced individuals from all estates who are experts in their fields and have shown themselves to be honest and intelligent.[71] He has a moral obligation to heed such counsellors, but she never invokes the right of parliament or even the Royal Council to impose its advice on the king.

Christine is very aware of the importance of the appearance of majesty and the dangers of defamatory loose talk that undermines royal authority.[72]

---

[68] It is still not clear how much Aristotle Christine knew first hand. Angus Kennedy has shown that Christine relied heavily on a glossed translation of Valerius Maximus' *Memorable Words and Deeds* (produced by Nicholas Gonesse and Simon Hesdin) for quotations from Aristotle, Cicero, and others; see Christine de Pizan, *Corps de policie*, pp. xxvi–xxxii. Many commentators assume that Christine must have read the French translations of Aristotle's *Ethics* and *Politics* commissioned by Charles V from Nicholas Oresme; see A. D. Menut, 'Le *Livre des politiques d'Aristote* de Nicole Oresme', *Transactions of the American Philosophical Society* n.s, 60 (1970), 3–392. Christine mentions these translations briefly in *Le Chemin de longue étude*, line 5020; and in greater detail in *Le Livre des fais et bonnes meurs*, vol. II, III.12, p. 43 and *Book of Peace*, II.18. Christine's familiarity with at least the *Ethics* has more recently been argued for in Kate Langdon Forhan, 'Reading Backward: Aristotelianism in the Political Thought of Christine de Pizan', in Hicks (ed.), *Au champ des escriptures*, pp. 359–481; and Sylvie Lefèvre, 'Christine de Pizan et l'Aristote oresmien', in ibid., pp. 231–43. Some doubts concerning the strength of this evidence are raised in Karen Green, 'Philosophy and Metaphor: The Significance of Christine's Blunders', *Parergon* 22 (2005), 119–36; and Green, 'On Translating Christine de Pizan as a Philosopher', pp. 109–28. However, Green provides evidence of Christine's familiarity with Oresme's translation of the *Politics* in ''*Phronesis* Feminised'.

[69] Aristotle, *The Nicomachean Ethics*, trans. H. Rackham, Loeb Classical Library (London: Heinemann, 1982), book XIX, 1141b8; A. D. Menut (ed.), *Maistre Nicole Oresme, Le Livre de ethiques d'Aristote, Published from the Text of Ms 2902, Bibliothèque Royale de Belgique* (New York: G. E. Stechart, 1940), p. 344.

[70] Aristotle, *Nicomachean Ethics*, VI.10, 1144b32, p. 158; Menut, *Maistre Nicole Oresme*, p. 360.

[71] Christine de Pizan, *Book of Peace*, I.7–12, pp. 72–86 and 212–23.

[72] Ibid., 1.6–7; *Le Livre des fais et bonnes meurs*, vol. I, II.18, pp. 182–3.

A prince should administer justice promptly and with firmness, make himself a worthy example of the dignity of his office. He should avoid anger and cruelty, be liberal, clement, and truthful. He should make himself available to his subjects and always dress in a manner appropriate to his station. She is particularly aware of the need for what we would now call 'good governance' as a precondition for the economic prosperity of the realm. Magistrates must not be corrupt, they should be elected to their offices on merit, and she advises that the practice of allowing positions to be bought, common in France, should cease. The consequence of good governance is increased economic activity and the encouragement of trade by foreign merchants, who will know that their commercial activities and property rights are secure.[73]

A prince should be careful not to engage in unjust war, and where war is just and necessary should ensure that he is served by experienced generals. She advises him not to go into battle himself, since the loss or ransom of the king may lead to the ruin of the kingdom. He should pay his troops well, in order to prevent them from pillaging the people, and she advises him to establish a system to train and equip knights and soldiers so that there are always well-trained troops to be had in time of need.[74] Christine's prince is more of an administrator than a warrior. He must be economically responsible, but economic responsibility does not imply meanness. She points out that Charles V, who is her model of what a ruler should be, engaged in many building projects, which stimulated the economy and provided employment for the artisans of Paris. He also encouraged learning, fostered the freedoms of the university of Paris, and endowed monasteries, thus stimulating the growth of science and culture.[75] Prudence thus consists largely in good management, and this virtue is essential for political stability.

Prudence of this kind, which according to Aristotle is involved equally in governing a state and running a household, can be exercised by women as well as men.[76] In chapter forty-three of the first book of the *City of Ladies,* hard on the heels of her accounts of historical female rulers, Amazons, poetesses, and philosophers, Christine asks Reason whether it is part of woman's intellectual nature to be prudent. 'Are they equally

---

[73] *Book of Peace,* 11.6–8, pp. 102–6 and 237–41.
[74] Christine de Pizan, *The Book of Deeds of Arms and of Chivalry,* 1.6, p. 23; *Book of Peace,* iii.13, pp. 144–5 and 275–6.
[75] Ibid., iii.27–8, pp. 168–71 and 297–9.
[76] Aristotle, *Nicomachean Ethics,* 1141a20 and 1141b23, pp. 345 and 347; Menut, *Maistre Nicole Oresme,* p. 344.

prompt and clever in those matters which prudence teaches, that is can women reflect on what is best to do and what is better to be avoided, learning from the examples they have seen, are they wise in managing current circumstances, and do they possess foresight concerning those to come?'[77] Here she echoes a standard characterisation of Prudence, which as she says elsewhere, works by means of circumspection with regard to which 'three other points are pertinent: one is to take account of what happened in similar past cases by way of example, the second, what will come about in order to make provision for it and the third, how things are presently in order to make good use of them'.[78] Reason answers that of course women have prudence, and they demonstrate it in the way in which they manage their households as well as (in the case of Dido, discussed in chapter forty-six as a paragon of prudence) in the way in which they manage affairs in general and govern states.

In the *Book of Three Virtues*, Christine represents her task as that of a bird catcher, who, having built her city of ladies, must populate it with honourable women. Reason, Rectitude, and Justice return to her side, castigating her for her fatigue and laziness after having completed the city, saying 'Blessed will be those who inhabit our city and increase the number of citizens of virtue. To all the female collegiate and to their religious devotion the sermon and lesson of wisdom should be preach-ed.'[79] Christine thus promises the women who read her advice the blessed happiness that comes from participation in the good expounded by Boethius. But, as Charity Willard has remarked, Christine does not see this blessedness as deriving only from the life of contemplation, but also as the reward of the active life.[80] Prudence is the guiding virtue of the active life of practical charity, and Christine thus structures her work as a series of teachings by Prudence. In reading it, one needs to keep in mind that this Prudence is the descendant of Aristotle's *phronesis* and that while it includes caution and circumspection, it is not, as the modern connota-tions suggest, a pusillanimous virtue, but the acknowledged source of good princely government. Thus Christine not only points to the capacity that women have shown in the past to exercise the central virtue of the good prince, but also looks towards a future in which women are encouraged to continue to govern those for whom they have responsibility.

[77] *Book of the City of Ladies*, 1.43, p. 87; *La Città delle dame*, p. 196.
[78] *Book of Peace*, 1.5, pp. 70 and 210.   [79] *Treasure*, p. 32; *Trois vertus*, p. 9.
[80] Willard, *Christine de Pisan: Her Life and Works*, p. 145.

The body politic that Christine paints is one in which, ideally, each element fills its God-given place, mirroring the peaceable concord of the heavens: 'The stars have their movements ordained by good proportion, concord and peace, and similarly the elements and things here below; by this reasoning it is clear that without peace we cannot live properly nor according to virtue.'[81] The result is a conservative acceptance of the hierarchies of society, including those within marriage, a result that is alien to modern feminism.[82] Christine did not approve of the popular uprisings of her time, and in her *Book of Peace* she refers to the attempts by the tradespeople of Paris to interfere in political events as the 'mad government of the low-born and bestial rabble'.[83] While she advocates clemency to the prince, and warns that God will punish a tyrannical monarch, she also warns the common people that God will strike down rebellious subjects, whose punishment for their uprisings will ultimately be subjection to a foreign power.[84] Similarly, in *The Book of Three Virtues*, Christine advocates that a wife show the patience of an Esther, being humble and obedient towards her husband. She considers the plight of a woman who suffers from a tyrannical husband and asserts that prudence advises that she make the best of her lot.[85]

In the following chapters, we see how the tensions in this picture of society work themselves out in various ways in the works of subsequent authors. Christine writes in opposition to a clerical misogyny that tends to attack marriage, hence her defence of women includes a defence of the estate of marriage, which she sees as a good institution perverted by the immorality of individual men. She similarly represents monarchy as a just institution, perverted by human vice. Christine nevertheless has faith that the tribulations of earthly government are part of God's plan, and that a moral reformation on the part of human beings will usher in a time of peace, as she announces in her *Ditty of Joan of Arc*.

For the next two hundred years, and in many cases beyond, many of the women whose texts we examine shared Christine's faith in the two political institutions of marriage and monarchy. Yet the premises she accepted would also lead to their being challenged. If the aim of political theory is to determine the most effective means of bringing about the common good, both monarchy and marriage are only justifiable in so far

---

[81] *Book of Peace*, III.2, pp. 127 and 260.
[82] On this topic see Delany, 'History, Politics and Christine Studies'; and Delany, ' "Mothers to Think Back Through" ', pp. 177–97.
[83] *Book of Peace*, II.1., pp. 95 and 231. [84] Ibid., III.4–15, pp. 129–49 and 261–79.
[85] *Treasure*, I.13, pp. 62–4; *Trois vertus*, pp. 52–5.

as they effectively promote this good. In the following centuries, both institutions would come under scrutiny, and we shall trace women's contributions to this process – a process that would ultimately result in modern political theory, in which the family and the state are no longer conceived as analogous, as they were by Christine. We should acknowledge, however, that Christine made a powerful case for women's participation in the body politic, and for their capacity to govern when necessary, which was known by and influenced noble women for at least a century after her death. Many men would continue to blast on their discordant trumpets of misogyny. Ordinary women would continue to live in subjection to their husbands. Yet an elite of educated noble women, fortified by Christine's texts, would govern themselves and their estates in very much the manner she prescribed. Some among them would continue the debate about love, governance, and male–female relations which she had begun.

Christine's arguments for women's equality with men in prudence and blessedness were intended to justify the legitimacy of women rulers in a fairly limited set of circumstances. Most clearly she accepted a queen's right to act as regent for her infant son; a wife's duty to manage her husband's estate while he was away; and a widow's right to govern the domains left to her as her dower, or in trust for her children. Yet her arguments and outlook provided a cogent ideology for the appropriateness of women governing as queens in their own right. In light of her emphasis on a monarch's duty to care for their subjects, their God-given role of bringing about the common good, and her faith that the exercise of virtue will secure the love of a monarch's subjects, one might ascribe a maternalist monarchism to her. However, we prefer to use the term 'parentalist' to characterise this conception of the duties of a monarch. If monarchists are automatically assumed to conceive of power as paternal, then a feminist monarchism seems contradictory. Yet we will see that almost all early female defenders of women were monarchists. It is due to the fact that they emphasise those strands of the monarchist tradition that represent the duties of a monarch as those of a parent, whether male or female, that these early women writers do not recognise any incompatibility between their monarchism and their defence of women's prudence and capacity to exercise power.

In *Christine's Vision*, Opinion encourages Christine to have faith in her well-founded opinions, and explains to her that she is not appreciated in her own time because science and learning are in their infancy. She promises Christine that in the future a prince will emerge who, having read her volumes, will have a great desire to have lived in her times and to have met her.[86] We like to imagine that this prince was in fact Elizabeth I of England. For, as we will see, Elizabeth was one of the last in a line of Renaissance princesses who knew Christine's works, and in many ways she emphasised the parental aspects of her rule and epitomised the feminine *phronimos* that Christine believed in and desired to promote. However, before arriving at Elizabeth we will make a detour through developments in Italy and France, which illustrate the participation and hesitations of women in undertaking the first step towards political authority, that which involved securing lasting recognition as legitimate aspirants to the authority and self-fashioning of an authorial voice.

---

[86] *Christine's Vision*, III.22, p. 88; *L'advision*, pp. 89–90.

CHAPTER 2

Women of the Italian Renaissance

Italy is universally acknowledged as the source of the European Renaissance, yet when one considers the trajectory of women's thought, France appears to have provided a more fertile intellectual context for women. This fact is paradoxical, for in the Italian city-states and principalities a significant number of women were provided with an excellent education that included training in Latin and occasionally even Greek and Hebrew.[1] The numbers of such women were greater in Italy than in other European countries, and though women in France were literate in the vernacular, few wrote in Latin, perhaps because vernacular learning was established earlier in France.[2] Christine de Pizan's father, Tomasso, may well have been following something of a Bolognese tradition when he gave his daughter an education approaching that of her brothers. In the north of Italy, and in Venice, Bologna, and Verona in particular, it was not completely unusual for the daughters of well-established noble and bourgeois families to be educated, and during the fifteenth century a good number of learned Italian women published letters, dialogues, and treatises. Christine reports that Novella Andrea, the daughter of a Bolognese legist, lectured at the university. This story is confirmed by other sources.[3] Yet, from the point of view of the advancement of political themes, the known work of fifteenth-century Italian women is far less developed than Christine's.

It is worth examining this period, however, both because of the enormous influence of intellectual developments in Italy in general, and because it is only in the light of earlier thinkers that one can appreciate what is innovative in the thinking of the far more varied and prolific late

---

[1] For an excellent overview, see Margaret L. King, 'Book-Lined Cells: Women and Humanism in the Early Italian Renaissance', in *Beyond their Sex: Learned Women of the European Past*, ed. Patricia H. Labalme (New York: New York University Press, 1980), pp. 66–90.
[2] Jane Stevenson, *Women Latin Poets: Language, Gender and Authority from Antiquity to the Eighteenth Century* (Oxford University Press, 2005), p. 141.
[3] Ibid., p. 151.

sixteenth and seventeenth-century women writers. In the previous chapter, we saw how Christine's arguments for women's political authority went hand in hand with a set of complex strategies intended to bolster her own authority as a female writer. In Italy no single female both exercised political influence and attempted to play the role of a learned authority. Rather, two distinct groups of women can be discerned. The first belong to ducal families, who had developed a tradition of educating daughters. These women had little need to justify their learning, since it contributed to the prestige of their families. The second group came from families with slightly less status, and it is among this group that the question of the justification of their desire to write becomes political. For if women are not expected to take up a position of authority, their adoption of the status of author already challenges the widely held view that it is women's lot to weep, and spin, and sew.

The fifteenth-century Italian women whose texts have survived, and whose ideas we examine here, wrote in classical Latin. Their orations and letters were designed to show off their learning and erudition, and they sought and received praise from the most learned men of their time. Many were prodigies whose greatest literary activity was in their teens. For them, learning was a kind of adornment, a route to fame, and an expression of personal excellence. Many were to become famous and lavishly praised, their names repeated in later catalogues of learned women. Their excellence 'beyond their sex' was seen to bring glory to their families and cities, but their ambition to acquire lasting fame through the production of great intellectual works was ultimately thwarted by the fact that nothing of any great substance has survived from their pens.[4] Some scholars have claimed that in the very act of writing and publicly circulating letters these women were being politically transgressive. According to this account, 'Women who wrote and read Latin were thought deviant and

[4] Stevenson makes the point that these women were seen as reflecting well on the culture (ibid., pp. 142–3), quoting Poliziano's description of Cassandra Fedele, 'O virgin ornament of Italy' which she takes from Margaret L. King and Albert Rabil (eds.), *Her Immaculate Hand: Selected Works by and about the Women Humanists of Quattrocento Italy* (Binghamton: Medieval & Renaissance Texts & Studies, 1992), pp. 126–7. King suggests that while juvenile precocity was acceptable in girls, in adulthood they had to choose between marriage or the convent, neither of which was compatible with continuing participation in intellectual life, and it was this which led to their ambitions being thwarted. See King, 'Book-Lined Cells', pp. 66–71; and Margaret L. King, 'Thwarted Ambitions: Six Learned Women of the Early Italian Renaissance', *Soundings* 59 (1976), 280–304. King observes that Poliziano's greeting to Fedele uses words that Virgil addressed to Camilla, the warrior maid of the *Aeneid*, 'O decus Italiae virgo', and interprets this as implicitly expressing a fear of learning in women ('Book-Lined Cells', p. 79). But here perhaps King is projecting a later suspicion of the Amazons back on to the Renaissance.

were seen as a threat to society, whether in the public or private domain.'[5] However, Jane Stevenson has recently cast doubt on this generalisation, since men often expressed pride in their learned female compatriots. We suggest that while some women, whose learning and writing were seen as enhancing the authority of their family or state, were not particularly transgressive, others whose aim in writing was to enhance the authority of women in general did challenge widely held prejudices.

By the late fourteenth century, it is clear that a group of noble families, who were related by marriage, routinely gave their daughters a thorough humanist education, so that they could help with the government of their husbands' lands. Many of these were related to the Montefeltro of Urbino. One of the earliest was Battista da Montefeltro, who married Galeazzo Malatesta. Her name was to appear often in later works listing illustrious women. According to Antoine Dufour, who wrote *Les Vies des dames célèbres* for Anne of Brittany in 1505, Battista wrote at least three books, including 'le livre des passions humaines' (the book of human passions), and she corresponded with Petrarch.[6] Another woman famous for her oratory was Battista's great-granddaughter, Battista Sforza. The Montefeltro family married into the Gonzaga of Mantua, the Malatesta of Pesaro, the Sforza, and the Varano of Camino.[7]

Wives and daughters of the d'Este were also highly educated. These women wrote occasional orations and letters, usually pleading some specific cause. Their attitudes were conventional for their time and class. They praised the nobility of the wise and prudent prince in discourses heavily laden with compliments and classical allusions. Their political discourse was an active exercise in persuasion, and as such involved little reflection on political institutions or practice. Nevertheless, as we show at the end of this chapter, these women were instrumental in encouraging the production of books that combated misogyny and promoted the positive representation of women.[8] The now most famous and widely read defence of women from this period, Book 3 of Baldassare Castiglione's *The Book of*

---

[5] Diana Robin, 'Cassandra Fedele's *Epistolae* (1488–1521): Biography as Ef-facement', in *The Rhetorics of Life Writing in Early Modern Europe*, ed. Thomas F. Mayer and D. R. Woolf (Ann Arbor: The University of Michigan Press, 1995), p. 191.

[6] Antoine Dufour, *Les Vies des dames célèbres (1505)* (Geneva: Librairie Droz, 1970), p. 159. Dufour probably derived this information from Jacobi Philippi Bergomensis, *De Claris Mulieribus*, discussed below.

[7] For a full account of the women related to this family, see Cecil H. Clough, 'Daughters and Wives of the Montefeltro: Outstanding Bluestockings of the Quattrocento', *Renaissance Studies* 10 (1996), 31–55.

[8] Stevenson, *Women Latin Poets*, pp. 169–73.

the Courtier, describes a series of conversations that took place in the court of Guidubaldo of Montefeltro, who was the son of Battista Sforza. His wife, Elizabetta Gonzaga, was also descended from a family related to the Montefeltro, and Castiglione pays homage to the learned women and competent princesses of these dynasties in his book.[9] Guidubaldo's granddaughter, Vittoria Colonna, would in her turn become one of the most famous female poets of the sixteenth century.

A group of women whose surviving works are, from our perspective, more interesting, because they show the diffusion of learning beyond the highest nobility, are a select few who took advantage of their education to devote themselves to a life of study. The best documented of these are Isotta Nogarola (1418–1466), Cassandra Fedele (1465–1558), and Laura Cereta (1469–1499). The first two became immensely famous, yet their surviving *œuvre* is disappointingly slender. It is worth lingering a while over these early steps in the development of the self-consciousness of women, because the politics of their reception indicates the resistance contemporaries felt to accepting women who wished to engage as equals in scholarly intercourse with men. The work of Cereta, in particular, can be read as a failed attempt by a woman to justify the pursuit, by women, of classical erudition, from the perspective of the assumption that women's virtue is as much the aim of political organisation as is men's.

Following Greek and Roman models, a classical education during the Renaissance aimed to equip a man for public office, public speaking, and service to the state. Yet a significant proportion of the population saw a complete incompatibility between feminine modesty and the public exposure which was the goal of male education. This implied that women's education should differ from men's. In arguing for the proper education of women, Leonardo Bruni famously asserted that 'rhetoric in all its forms [was and should remain] absolutely outside the province of women'.[10] And while it is not clear that Bruni intended to exclude all forms of women's public speaking, since plain non-rhetorical speech is not necessarily excluded, Francesco Barbaro claimed 'not only the [bare] arms but indeed also the speech of a woman should never be made public'.[11] It is true that not everybody shared his view, and the idea that oratory was inappropriate for women was publicly rejected in the funeral

[9] Baldassare Castiglione, *The Book of the Courtier*, trans. Thomas Hoby (London: Everyman, 1994), III.34–6, pp. 243–6.
[10] King, 'Book-lined Cells', p. 77.
[11] Quoted in King and Rabil (eds.), *Her Immaculate Hand*, p. 13.

oration given for Battista Sforza in 1472.[12] However, the views expressed by Bruni and Barbaro indicate that learned women faced conflicting pressures. On the one hand, modesty was essential to women's honour. On the other, women's culture could be appreciated only if it was on display, and there were many who were happy to laud the elegant productions of learned virgins whose precocity brought fame to their families and cities.[13]

Cassandra Fedele, in particular, received copious admiring letters from humanists and nobles who read or received her letters.[14] These men were soon boasting of their female compatriot's accomplishments. Like singing, dancing, and playing musical instruments, rhetorical performances, whether spoken orations or letters made available to be read in public, might not have been modest, but they were entertaining, unusual, and perhaps even erotic.[15] Thus the public display of learning and the pursuit of fame was simultaneously lavishly lauded and implicitly problematic.

By the time Cassandra Fedele was communicating with nobles and humanists in the latter half of the fifteenth century, the idea that an exceptional woman brought glory to a nation was well established. Ludovico Maria Sforza, writing in January 1490, says:

> Fortunate is your father, who chanced to procreate a daughter blessed with such gifts of mind and nature. Happiest is the city of Venice, which has obtained in its citizen Cassandra an ornament for the greatness of its empire and heroic deeds, because nature wanted to test in her what was possible in the female sex.[16]

Renaissance men, having determined that they lived in a new and glorious age in which the learning, heroism, and glory of classical Greece and Rome were being revived, were happy to imagine that even their women were reviving the excellence that ancient authors ascribed to certain famous examples – Sappho, Camilla, and Hortensia. In a similar vein to

[12] Clough, 'Daughters and Wives of the Montefeltro', 39.
[13] Stevenson, *Women Latin Poets*, pp. 152–6.
[14] Cassandra Fedele's letters and orations were not printed until the seventeenth century, in Cassandra Fedele, *Clarissimæ Feminæ Cassandrae Fidelis Venetæ Epistolæ & Orationes*, ed. Jacobo Philippo Tomasino (Padua: Franciscus Bolzetta, 1636). Cassandra Fedele, *Oratio pro Bertucio Lamberto* (Modena, 1487; Venice, 1488; Nuremberg, 1489) is the only work by her that was printed during her lifetime. There is an English translation of the published letters and orations: Cassandra Fedele, *Letters and Orations*, ed. and trans. Diana Robin (Chicago: University of Chicago Press, 2000). Robin asserts that Fedele is also claimed to have written a book called *Ordo Scientiarum* and Latin poetry that has not survived (p. 3).
[15] It is no accident that in the coming centuries the 'cortegiane honeste' of Venice would be among the most prolific women writers in Italy.
[16] *Letters and Orations*, p. 54; *Clarissimæ Feminæ*, p. 188.

Ludovico Sforza, Ludovico da Schio of Vicenza writes to Cassandra, after her famous public oration in Padua:

I used to think that the glory of the Muses, the eloquence of women and every kind of rhetoric that was womanly (if one is allowed to use that word) had all but disappeared in our modern age, and I didn't believe that there was any woman now who could match either Hortensia's skill at composition and her talent as an orator or, for that matter, any of the ancient Roman women orators. But when I think of your not simply human but divine eloquence, when I consider your physical gestures suitable to oratory, when I ponder your constantly ornate style, I don't know what else to say about you unless I may adapt the following verse from Virgil to describe you: 'I believe – nor are these empty words – that you are descended from the race of the Gods.'[17]

The exceptional woman was evidence that even members of the inferior sex from Italy outshone ordinary mortals and were descended from gods.

A story from the seventeenth century provides a revealing illustration of the limitations for women of this tendency to exploit the exceptional few as adornments of a noble town or family. In June 1678, Elena Lucrezia Piscopia was awarded a doctorate from the University of Padua and is thus the first fully attested case of a woman receiving this quali- fication. In order to acquire her doctorate and become one of the *laureati* she publicly discoursed on Aristotle in a ceremonial *viva*. Soon afterwards the father of another learned woman, Gabriella Patino, attempted to make his daughter a laureate as well. But both the Cardinal Gregorio Barbarigo and Piscopia's father were horrified at the thought that this unique and exceptional woman laureate might lead the way to a general acceptance of women's right to take degrees.[18] Piscopia's success did not open the way for further female *laureate*.

Early fifteenth-century attitudes were even less hospitable to women, and the implicit contradiction in the status of 'learned maid' is clearest in the legacy of Isotta Nogarola.[19] Her correspondence and experience bring out, far more clearly than those of Fedele, the contradiction between the

[17] *Letters and Orations*, p. 65; *Clarissimæ Feminæ*, pp. 144–5.

[18] Stevenson, *Women Latin Poets*, pp. 302–9.

[19] Nogarola's surviving works, with those of her aunt Angela and sister Genevieve, have been published in two volumes: *Isotæ Nogarolæ Veronensis Opera Quæ Supersunt Omnia Accedunt Angelæ et Zenever Nogarolæ Epistolæ et Carmina*, ed. Eugenius Abel, 2 vols. (Budapest: Gerold et Socii, 1886). Abel gives details of his manuscript sources in vol. 1, pp. clvii–clxi. The most important collections are Vienna 3481, Vatican 5127, and Verona 256, but individual letters are scattered through other manuscripts. English translations of Nogarola's works are available in Isotta Nogarola, *Complete Writings: Letterbook, Dialogue on Adam and Eve, Orations*, ed. and trans. Margaret L. King and Diana Robin (Chicago: University of Chicago Press, 2004).

pursuit of eloquence and learning by women, and their usual status as subordinates who were not expected to claim independent authority.[20] Nogarola, who had chosen to neither marry nor enter a convent, defended her pursuit of eloquence and Latin letters with a passage from Cicero to which she alludes in a number of places:

For what is more lasting than eloquence, which among every free people and in every republic is held in the highest esteem when it is strengthened by good customs? For eloquence is the companion of peace and tranquillity and the daughter of the well-governed city, one might say.[21]

But of course, Cicero was thinking of the eloquence of free men, called to speak in public political fora. He did not expect this eloquence to extend to slaves or women, whose virtues were silence and obedience. Because she attempted to engage in written and spoken debate with men, Nogarola was attacked in 1439 in an invective that asserted, along with the accusation of incest, that 'an eloquent woman is never chaste'.[22]

The incompatibility of the pursuit of public fame, power, and learning with feminine modesty was to bedevil women for many centuries. Women writers were faced with the complex task of reconciling their desire for fame and influence with the construction of a virtuous and modest persona. This juggling act was perhaps inevitable given the contemporary structure of the debate over women's nature. The misogynists invariably associated woman's lack of virtue with her lustfulness, greed, lack of self-control, and sexual rapaciousness. In the face of such attacks, women and their defenders were virtually forced to offer a contrary picture that emphasised women's chastity, modesty, constancy, and virginity. But how could these virtues coincide with the public and promiscuous exchange of laudatory letters, free and easy mixing in public company, the vicious invective of academic dispute, and the unashamed self-promotion that was characteristic of the Renaissance man of letters?

Isotta Nogarola was the victim of this set of contradictions when she was attacked in the pamphlet, mentioned above, and accused of being a whore who had had incestuous relations with her brother. It is suggested

---

[20] Lisa Jardine, 'Isotta Nogarola: Women Humanists – Education for What?' *History of Education* 12 (1983), 231–44.

[21] Nogarola, *Complete Writings*, p. 35; Abel (ed.), *Isotæ Nogarolæ*, 1:8–9 (repeated in essence on pp. 61 and 62), quoting Cicero, *Brutus* 45, 'Pacis est comes otiique socia et iam bene constitutae civitatis quasi alumna quaedam eloquentia.'

[22] Nogarola, *Complete Writings*, p. 68. See A. Segarizzi, 'Niccolò Barbo, patrizio veneziano del sec. xv e le accuse contro Isotta Nogarola', *Giornale storico della letteratura italiana* 43 (1904), 39–54.

that after this bruising attack, and as a consequence of it, she left Venice and retired to live with her mother.[23] So far as we know she never publicly defended herself against these libels, and the men who praised her defended her only implicitly, by constantly referring to her piety and virginity. She does not challenge the demands of feminine decorum, but excuses herself for transgressing them: 'I however, lured by the sweetness and loveliness of your poems, am unable to be silent, although this goes against feminine decorum.'[24]

Even in her most sustained and interesting piece of writing, the dialogue over the relative sinfulness of Adam and Eve, Nogarola fails to question women's fundamental inferiority. So, while Christine de Pizan asserts that Eve did not deceive Adam, but repeated to him innocently the words of the Devil,[25] Nogarola defends Eve by accepting that, 'where there is less intellect and less constancy there is less sin'.[26] This works perhaps as an *ad hominem* argument against those who would place all the responsibility for human suffering on women's shoulders, but it admits the characterisation of women as defective, something that Christine would not allow.

The contradiction between the subordination of women in marriage, the demands of feminine modesty, and the increasing desire on behalf of women for education and a public voice could only be solved by the development of new conceptions of the marriage relation, new characterisations of the virtue of modesty, and a reformulation of the place of women in society. Models of civic friendship between men did not easily extend to include women. However, during the sixteenth and seventeenth centuries, courtly women, and later those associated with the rise of salon culture, would increasingly develop models of mixed-sex civic friendship, culminating in the conversations of Madeleine de Scudéry.

In medieval discourse, love has a far clearer political role to play than it does in later political writing in which it is accepted, following Machiavelli, that politics is a matter of the balance of power. We have already seen Christine's appeal to Boethius' synthesis of Stoic and Christian thought, in which love of virtue and love of God are identified with happiness. In her *Book of Peace*, she exclaims, 'Oh, you men of France, you will be so blessed if you desire it, that is to say if you are governed by

---

[23] Nogarola, *Complete Writings*, p. 6.   [24] Ibid., p. 60; Abel (ed.), *Isotæ Nogarolæ*, 1:130.
[25] Christine de Pizan, *Letter of the God of Love*, in Blumenfeld-Kosinski (ed.), *Selected Writings of Christine de Pizan*, p. 26.
[26] Nogarola, *Complete Writings*, p. 146; Abel (ed.), *Isotæ Nogarolæ*, 11:188.

the love, that holds up the heavens and without which nothing is stable.'[27] Love, which keeps the heavens revolving, was also conceived of as a force that promoted political harmony. The good prince who understood this harmony could thus rule through love. Nogarola shared this understanding. In a letter to Ludovico Foscarini she praises him thus:

So Vicenza considers herself, which you governed with such wisdom, prudence, justice, and kindness that the Vicentines love you no less than the Sicilians loved Timoleon of Corinth, who reigned with the approval of all, for he preferred to be loved than to be feared.[28]

Nogarola also openly expresses her love for the learned humanists who graced Venice, and courts their love, as she indulges her love of fame. But love, once women were involved, was an ambiguous notion. How could men and women participate in the civic friendship that ideally united men, without transforming it into an erotic intercourse that threatened marriage and transgressed modesty? The problem is implicit in an exchange of letters between Nogarola and Damiano dal Borgo in which, as Diana Robin points out, the man's friendly greetings and expressions of love and admiration, characteristic of humanist expressions of civic friendship, transform into passages that are easily read as declarations of physical desire.[29] We will see how the difficult negotiation of sociable intellectual relations between people of the opposite sex, anticipated in Nogarola's letters, comes clearly into focus during the seventeenth century.

The implicit politics of the discourse on love is explored in greater detail in the following chapters. We now turn to the writings of Laura Cereta, who shows a greater awareness than her more lauded contemporaries of the contradictions involved in the feminine pursuit of eloquence and fame.[30] She was born in Brescia, a town half way between Milan and Verona, just two years after her more famous compatriot Cassandra Fedele.

[27] Christine de Pizan, *The Book of Peace*, III.6, pp. 134 and 265.
[28] Nogarola, *Complete Writings*, pp. 129–30; Abel (ed.), *Isotæ Nogarolæ*, 11:31.
[29] Nogarola, *Complete Writings*, pp. 83–9.
[30] In 1640, seventy-one of Laura Cereta's letters were published in *Laurae Ceretae Brixiensis Feminae Clarissimae Epistolae Iam Primum e MS in Lucem Productae*, ed. Jacobo Philippo Tomasino (Padua: Sebastiano Sardi, 1640). The remainder of the total of eighty-three letters and orations that are known in manuscript are in *Laura Cereta: Quattrocento Humanist*, ed. Albert Rabil (Binghamton: Medieval & Renaissance Texts & Studies, 1981) from Vat. lat. 3176. cart. 3. XVI and Venice, Marc. cod. Lat. XI, 28 [4186]mbr. XV. Fifty-six of the letters and orations are translated into English by Diana Robin in *Collected Letters of a Renaissance Feminist* (Chicago: University of Chicago Press, 1997).

Cereta has left us a collection of letters, written during a mere two years between the ages of sixteen and eighteen, during which time she was also married and then widowed. Although she lived until she was thirty, and it is alleged that she later taught at the university, no works are known to survive from this later period. This is a pity, because the letters that do survive show an acute mind and sharp wit that contrast favourably with the vanity and sycophantic flattery so characteristic of the slightly older Fedele.

Cereta prepared her letter-book with care. Many of the most interesting pieces were probably never sent as letters, but are addressed to fictional characters. By writing to fictional addressees who are caricatures of the prejudices of her time, Cereta was able to craft a series of responses to those who she knew disapproved of her literary ambitions. 'Bibulus Sempronius', the constant tippler who is the alleged recipient of her defence of women's learning, and 'Lucilia Vernacula', the recipient of an invective against uneducated women who slander those women who pursue learning, are surely imaginary.[31] So too is 'Lupus Cynicus', the addressee of a letter against avarice.[32] Even 'Nazaria Olympica', to whom she dedicates a carefully constructed autobiography, is probably not a real woman but invented.[33]

In the case of Laura Cereta we can see an influence descending from Petrarch, similar to that which operated with regard to Christine de Pizan and Dante. In a letter to her uncle Ludovico that occurs reasonably early in the sequence, Cereta claims: 'I took all this work on myself so that the name of Laura, so wondrously celebrated by Petrarch, might be preserved in a second and quite new immortality – in me.'[34] Thus the possibly imaginary Laura, an ideal feminine type and the epitome of virtue, is transformed into an ideal to which a real woman might aspire. In her biographical letter to Nazaria Olympica, Cereta explains how she was named after a laurel tree that had shrivelled in the frost. She describes how the house of her childhood echoed with the name 'Laura' so that it seemed that her destiny was to pursue the laurels after which she had been named.[35] In her earliest letters, she evinces a faith both in astrology and in the pursuit of fame, but the later letters question both the attempt to know the future through the study of the stars and the value of the pagan

[31] Cereta, *Collected Letters*, pp. 74 and 81; *Laurae Ceretae*, pp. 187 and 122.
[32] Cereta, *Collected Letters*, p. 165; *Laurae Ceretae*, p. 199.
[33] Cereta, *Collected Letters*, p. 23; *Laurae Ceretae*, p. 145.
[34] Cereta, *Collected Letters*, p. 49; *Laurae Ceretae*, p. 20.
[35] Cereta, *Collected Letters*, p. 24; *Laurae Ceretae*, p. 146.

pursuit of temporal immortality through fame. These letters can be read as a justification for the renunciation of the pursuit of worldly glory, in favour of Christian spirituality.[36]

A persistent questioning of temporal values is common in educated women during the early modern period. We will meet it again in various guises, particularly in the writings of Marguerite de Navarre. Women understand the point of education as a means to the development of a virtuous life. But they also come to question the relationship between a complex classical education and genuine virtue. If happiness is to be found in a simple knowledge of God's love or in caring for others, heights of intellectual achievement are unnecessary. And if this is the right way to read the overall purport of Cereta's letter-book, it explains why there is nothing from her more mature years.

In the dedication of her work to Cardinal Maria Ascanius Sforza, the son of Francesco Sforza and Maria Bianca Visconti, which dates from March 1488 and so is one of her later productions, Cereta says,

I have found contentment in contemplation. Now that I have availed myself of the counsel of religious texts, wherein writings about morality combine profundity with utility, I have found satisfaction in literature that would give me not smoke and darkness but something perfect, secure and lasting. Since men receive an education in literature and other studies, however, so they may benefit from the example of their forebears, the most elect of men of diverse orders have said publicly that education has been wasted on me because it has benefited only me and not others.[37]

While not absolutely clear, this seems to admit that her learning can be of benefit only to herself, and that it is the religious texts, not classical pagan writings, that will provide her with a secure and lasting good. And yet the conclusion of her dedication, and the tone of the epilogue to her collection, also dedicated to the Cardinal Sforza, belie this sense of renunciation:

Therefore this your little book, on which I have spent sleepless nights and long labors, although it is sterile in itself, will grow nonetheless more fertile in your hands. It will germinate, bear fruit, and flow with juices. For who would not live secure from every slander if he entrusted himself to the integrity of a man who regards all things with the objectivity of an excellent mind, and who sees all and knows all things? Both future generations and men of the current age will know

---

[36] For a reading of her correspondence with Brother Thomas which suggests this development, see *Laura Cereta*, pp. 16–20.

[37] Cereta, *Collected Letters*, p. 39; *Laurae Ceretae*, p. 3.

you as a man most highly educated in the whole of literature, and they will sing this torn invention of mine which will exalt and venerate your memory honorably and for a long time to come.[38]

The cardinal's renown becomes entwined with Cereta's own, his protection ensuring the fruition of her ambitions, while enhancing his own reputation.

The problem of feminine adornment runs throughout Cereta's letters, and she develops a sophisticated interplay between the adornment of literary virtuosity and women's more usual commitment to jewels and dress. In her letter to Sigismundo de Buccis, she claims to have been embroidering an incredible shawl. But the shawl, the fruit of her nightly labours, becomes a metaphor for the collection of letters to which she is putting the finishing touches. In her letter, she is critical of women's love of adornment:

But the demand by women for luxury items and their fascination with the exotic – and neither India with its pearls nor Arabia can satisfy these cravings – has increased to such an extent in our society that there is no end today to the public display of such merchandise. An aversion to moderation is characteristic of women everywhere – and by their own doing.[39]

But by the end of the letter one cannot help but feel that Cereta's real intention is to excuse her own pursuit of literary adornment by pointing out how acceptable it has become for women to show off less elevated treasures. With tongue in cheek, she declaims:

But, ah, these are the meaningless concerns of women. What is it about our desires and our era that has caused us to reject the Oppian law, in which garments embellished with this kind of artfulness were characterized as 'wantonly painted' as though those garments might, in all their proliferation of color – their golds, silver and blazing purple – run amuck under the weight of so much useless erudition. Scipio Africanus castigated Suplicius Gaulus for this, and Lucius Torquatus denigrated Hortensius as a mere actor for this. But so be it: the decadent manners of this age of ours may well demand such laws. These then are the things I have made with my own hands before the first rays of the dawning day. This grand volume of epistles, for which the final draft is now being copied out, bears witness, letter by letter, to whatever muses I have managed to muster in the dead of night. I have placed all my hope in the love of literature.[40]

---

[38] Cereta, *Collected Letters*, pp. 42–3; *Laurae Ceretae*, p. 10.
[39] Cereta, *Collected Letters*, p. 32; *Laurae Ceretae*, pp. 13–14.
[40] Cereta, *Collected Letters*, pp. 33–4; *Laurae Ceretae*, p. 16.

It was her oration against the Oppian laws banning women from wearing sumptuous clothes that made Hortensia famous. Cereta is happy to give up the meaningless feminine adornment that women have won the right to wear, but she asserts the right to another kind of adornment: literature and oratory, for which Hortensia was criticised.

Letters are not, however, merely an adornment, they are a path to virtue. And one finds in Cereta's early letters the repeated demand that women be educated in order to become more virtuous:

> Do be aware, though, that you are going to see a little woman who is humble in both her appearance and her dress, since I am more concerned with letters than with adornment, having committed myself to the care of virtue, which can indeed confer honor on me not only during my lifetime but when I am dead.[41]

This is a theme that will become a staple of later female writers. In Cereta's correspondence the nature of the virtue to which one should aspire becomes the dominant theme of the second half of the collection. Given the nature of Christian virtue, this attitude to learning leads directly towards the renunciation of the pursuit of glory. Nevertheless, we argue that Cereta's original conception of virtue should not be equated with the sort of monastic withdrawal from society that Margaret King has suggested was forced on learned Renaissance women.

The keys to understanding Cereta's letter collection lie in her exchange with Brother Thomas, a Milanese monk. In the Tomasino edition there are three letters to Thomas; in the Vatican manuscript they are accompanied by three letters from him to Cereta, the only letters from anyone other than her in the collection. There is also a letter from him to her father. In an early letter, Thomas accuses Cereta of pride, criticises the pursuit of glory, and encourages her to read the Church Fathers.[42] In her second letter to him, Cereta appears persuaded; she unequivocally rejects the pursuit of glory, which had been the initial impetus for her late-night 'embroidering', and puts in place of a transitory temporal immortality a meditation on death: 'I have established a life obedient not to other people's opinions but to my own death.'[43] The thought that we should meditate on and prepare for our own death will become the insistent conclusion of a series of letters, which come towards the end of the collection and which reject certain false goals in life as not truly virtuous. It is not surprising to find that this is the conclusion of her invective

---

[41] Cereta, *Collected Letters*, p. 83; *Laurae Ceretae*, p. 67.   [42] *Laurae Ceretae*, pp. 97–9.
[43] Cereta, *Collected Letters*, p. 107; *Laurae Ceretae*, p. 130.

against avarice, the letter to Lupus Cynicus.[44] Nor is it surprising to find that it is the core of her advice to Barbara Alberti, to whom she writes a letter on the occasion of her marriage, concerning the instability of fortune.[45] It is more surprising to find that it is the conclusion of her letter to Solitaria Europa, where the attempt to find tranquillity in this life, through retreat to the country, is rejected as resting on false pagan values.[46] The meditation on death leads to the conclusion that charity (which should be understood as love of God) is quite different from the pursuit of human glory:

But charity, not ill-will or enviousness, is the object of the well-ordered mind; nor can charity be fed on smoke. Aimless and empty are the paltry rewards of human glory. Our transitory journey through this fleeting life tells me to relinquish desire, trampling it underfoot.[47]

What then is the positive characterisation of the virtuous life that Cereta has extracted from her nightly studies and the experience of her husband's untimely death?

One might conclude, from the following passage, which also comes from the second letter to Brother Thomas, that it is a life of religious retreat and that Cereta, thwarted in her ambition to cover herself in glory by engaging in philosophical debate, sees no other path to virtue than solitary study in her book-lined cell:

Since I, a mere female, inept at literary matters and deficient in talent, cannot cover myself with glory by making public my talent in the areas of debate, I shall declaim my arguments against you in my small and humble cell, with Christ.[48]

It seems pretty clear from a letter to her sister Diana, and from another to another female relation, Deodorata di Leno, that religious retreat is seen by Cereta as one acceptable form of the virtuous life. She tells her sister that

The delight in study should not come from the reward of being praised, but should be exercised for the sake of virtue. I think it is enough that those who embark upon the road to learning are the winners of their own wisdom and glory.[49]

[44] Cereta, *Collected Letters*, pp. 165–9; *Laurae Ceretae*, pp. 199–204.
[45] Cereta, *Collected Letters*, pp. 134–6; *Laurae Ceretae*, pp. 154–8.
[46] Cereta, *Collected Letters*, pp. 123–8; *Laurae Ceretae*, pp. 214–20.
[47] Cereta, *Collected Letters*, p. 108; *Laurae Ceretae*, p. 131.
[48] Cereta, *Collected Letters*, p. 108; *Laurae Ceretae*, p. 132.
[49] Cereta, *Collected Letters*, p. 149; *Laurae Ceretae*, p. 34.

In her letter to Deodorata, Cereta offers a partial defence of Epicurus, but implicitly criticises his limited notion of virtue, which looks only to this life. In a passage reminiscent of Boethius, true pleasure is represented as the reward of a virtue that looks to God and immortality:

A pleasure that lives and endures is a thing not generally known; for disdaining that which belongs to this world, it purchases that which is immortal with the currency of virtue. This pleasure delights and cares for our minds in its nurturing bosom; it inhabits the fortress of respected religion. And it is protected, free from care, and blessed, even among the Syrtes and the most difficult terrain of our life. This one pleasure represents the highest fulfilment of the contented mind, the most tranquil satiety of our solace, by which we are led by the safe path to God. For the right-thinking mind is the companion of the gods; and in this mind neither idleness, nor darkness, nor ghosts, nor any emotion shall hold dominion.[50]

Nevertheless, the conception of virtue which Cereta develops, and which her epilogue shows she hopes will be spread abroad through the agency of the cardinal, is not limited to solitary self-improvement.

Coining a happy phrase, she asserts that 'Ethics is that state of being useful which is also honorable.'[51] This occurs in a letter concerning friendship in which she hopes that a difference of opinion will not spoil her friendship, based on mutual love and respect, with another woman. Cereta had strong opinions as to lives that were not really virtuous, but her conception of the ways in which women might pursue virtue was also quite pluralistic. In her third letter to Brother Thomas, she claims to have learned from him that we should follow conscience:

Therefore when I learned from you that this body is empty, that the promises of the heart and mind are deceptive, and that the most precious pearl of the wandering souls of humans is the conscience, I abandoned my plan to seek fame through human letters, lest my mind, bereft, unhappy and unaware of the future should seek happiness through diligence. What is more, since too great a concern for knowledge raises the suspicion that one leads a prodigal life, our all-night sessions of study ought not to continue, as if we were born solely for the sake of literature.[52]

A life of honest usefulness, in which one follows one's conscience, can be led in many ways. It is compatible with the public dissemination of the doctrine, and even with the receipt of a certain amount of recognition.

---

[50] Cereta, *Collected Letters*, pp. 121–2; *Laurae Ceretae*, p. 177.
[51] Cereta, *Collected Letters*, p. 137; *Laurae Ceretae*, p. 105.
[52] Cereta, *Collected Letters*, p. 112; *Laurae Ceretae*, p. 225.

Thus Cereta's decision to publish her letters, and her hope that they will be fruitful and even famous, no longer appears to conflict with her renunciation of the pursuit of glory for its own sake. Cereta has seen that honour is only really valuable as the reward of honourable acts, and she publishes her letters in the hope of making people, and women in general, more honourable.

This outlook potentially brought her into collision with her more famous contemporary Cassandra Fedele. Fedele was surely clever enough to read the letter that Cereta sent her, which begins with a long description of a dream about hell, as implicitly critical of Fedele's obsession with fame, and as warning her to commend her soul to God.[53] If Fedele did as a consequence criticise Cereta in return, as Cereta's letter to Bonifacio Bembo claims, she was perhaps justly piqued at Cereta's implicit questioning of her motives. Cereta's letter to Bembo is most interesting for the evidence that it contains of her sensitivity to the dangers for women of the cult of exceptionalism. In her letter to Bibulus Sempronius, she rejects the thought that her learning is exceptional,

as if you had reached the conclusion, on the facts of the case, that a similar girl had seldom been seen among the peoples of the world. You are wrong on both counts, Semproni, and now you've abandoned the truth, you are going to spread information abroad that is clearly false.[54]

And in the case that she makes for her lack of exceptionality, Cereta mentions Cassandra:

I will not mention here Cicero's daughter Tulliola or Terentia or Cornelia, Roman women who reached the pinnacle of fame for their learning; and accompanying them in the shimmering light of silence will be Nicolosa of Bologna, Isotta of Verona, and Cassandra of Venice.[55]

Cereta asserts that nature grants the freedom to learn equally to all, and elsewhere she insists that it is within any woman's capacity to be learned, so long as she does the requisite work.[56] She states her intention to fight to defend the republic of women, thus suggesting that she sees herself as

---

[53] Cereta, *Collected Letters*, pp. 145–8; *Laurae Ceretae*, pp. 117–22. There is a slight puzzle about this letter. In Tomasino and in the Venice manuscript the letter is addressed to Lorenzo Capreolo, and the learned woman who is alleged to have criticised Cereta is called Gismunda. In the Vatican manuscript, it is Cassandra who is named. Rabil argues that the version naming Cassandra is the original and Robin translates this version. See *Laura Cereta*, pp. 89–90.

[54] Cereta, *Collected Letters*, p. 75; *Laurae Ceretae*, p. 187.

[55] Cereta, *Collected Letters*, p. 78; *Laurae Ceretae*, p. 191.

[56] Cereta, *Collected Letters*, p. 82; *Laurae Ceretae*, p. 125.

part of an imaginary female community. It is the lack of evidence of reciprocal friendship and support from Fedele that galls her. Cereta is also perceptive in her analysis of the causes of this example of the phenomenon of 'exceptional' women who belittle other women who present a challenge to their dominance:

And so it would appear that she either has contempt for her peers or heaps more abuse on people who are more knowledgeable than she. But the appearance of deceptiveness in a person's speech is often the cover for a fearful heart. This woman doesn't impair the firmly rooted trust that my all-night sessions of study have strengthened in the eyes of everyone regarding me, does she? . . . where does the old compassion for one's fellow humans lie sleeping? No longer is there a show of friendship among people but only darkness. This sister, whom I praised with such reverence so many times, insinuates that I am a person whose learning is specious.[57]

Cereta implies that insecurity, jealousy, and contempt for her own kind are the basis for Fedele's reaction to an implicit critique, and she regrets the lack of any evidence of friendship in her apparent response. This thwarted correspondence suggests a reason for women's so often thwarted ambitions different from any that Margaret King has considered: the difficulty that women faced developing a female community of scholars. The insecurity that arises from an 'exceptional' status, and fear of being shown up as a merely ordinary example of the 'inferior' sex, makes it particularly difficult for women to take and receive criticism from other women. Nevertheless, as we will see, by the seventeenth century in France, courts centred on noble women interested in literature had developed into intellectual salons, and the women who participated in them could, up to a point, see themselves as part of a feminine intellectual community.

While Cereta's thought does not broach such central political issues as the nature of power, political organisation, or even the character of the good ruler, it does focus on the nature of the good life for women, struggling with the problem that for those who do not fulfil a useful public role, eloquent erudition may be mere vanity. There is also a broadly political agenda to her collection, which includes descriptions of the horrors of war and vaguely prophetic warnings that war may come again. Like Christine, Cereta represents war as the consequence of human vice, greed, and short-sightedness, implicitly offering her model of human excellence as virtuous usefulness as an appropriate model for men as well as women.

---

[57] Cereta, *Collected Letters*, p. 145; *Laurae Ceretae*, pp. 117–18.

Cereta also represents marriage as a blessed natural state involving reward for hard labour:

Birds have learned to build nests for the purpose of laying eggs for their off-spring. Nature inclines towards the propagation of her species. She teaches us to hope for heirs to perpetuate our name and our deeds. The church, moreover, has instituted a sacrament that allows us to enter joyously into a sweet oath to beget children. The unbroken probity of conjugal love beckons us to fulfill this oath, and it is this probity content with toil and duty that enables us to rear up children amid wailing and all night vigils.[58]

Cereta praises women for their loyalty and constancy and represents them as peacemakers who care for and mourn for others. From Cereta's description it appears that she accepts the normal active life of the good woman as being as worthy and virtuous as any other.

It may well be that we are intended to read her otherwise puzzling funeral oration, the 'Dialogue on the Death of an Ass', as a metaphor for the life of a woman, the indispensable and reliable hard worker who is abused and treated cruelly while alive, only to be mourned in death, when all the benefits that she has brought are recognised and their absence felt.[59] Whether or not it was Cereta's intention that one should appreciate this parallel, her letters as a whole bring to the fore a paradox that will dog learned women's representation of economic and political realities. Lisa Jardine has asked, with regard to learned women of this period, 'education for what?'[60] Laura Cereta would have had no hesitation in answering, 'education for the acquisition of virtue'. But if one denies that the vanities of intellectual precocity, and the withdrawal to the appreciation of art or nature for their own sake, are truly virtuous, as Cereta does, and puts in their place an honest usefulness that heeds the voice of conscience, it is not clear that learning is necessary for virtue at all. It might even impede the exercise of virtue, as Cereta suggests in her last letter to Thomas, by being mistaken as an end in itself, rather than just the means to a virtuous life.[61]

This was not, however, a problem for the many noblewomen whose learning was clearly intended to allow them to function as the governors of their husbands' estates, as deputies and regents. Many pious, well-educated princesses took to heart the traditions of virtuous princely rule

[58] Cereta, *Collected Letters*, p. 71; *Laurae Ceretae*, p. 185.
[59] Cereta, *Collected Letters*, pp. 180–202; *Laura Ceretae*, pp. 118–34.
[60] Jardine, 'Isotta Nogarola: Women Humanists'.
[61] Cereta, *Collected Letters*, p. 112; *Laurae Ceretae*, p. 225.

and governed as effectively as, or even better than, their husbands. Of Eleonora of Aragon, who was married to Ercole I d'Este, Duke of Ferrara, in 1473, it was said, 'She listened to the people, heard their pleas, and was accepted by the Ferrarese people. And the duke devoted himself to having a good time and playing [cards] and riding around the park.'[62] Her eldest daughter, the more famous Isabella d'Este, marchioness of Mantua, took a similar attitude to her responsibilities as marchioness, and was more active than her mother in attempting to construct images of her intellectual excellence and political authority.[63]

It is noteworthy that, although such women did not usually write or publish works themselves, their courts were often the origin of the works in praise of women which began to appear regularly in both Italy and France from the second half of the fifteenth century. It was for Eleonora of Aragon that Bartolomeo Goggio wrote his 'De Laudibus Mulierum', a work that he addresses to her, and in which he sets out to demonstrate women's superiority over men.[64] As well as having a copy of this work in her library, Eleonora possessed other works relevant to women's status: the works of St Catherine of Siena, as well as a life of this saint, and the works of St Jerome, often cited for their praise of early Christian virgins.

Goggio's 'De Laudibus Mulierum' was not influential: a single manuscript survives, most probably the one owned by Eleonora.[65] Nevertheless, its appearance in Eleonora's library is evidence of a tendency for the existence of women in power to encourage the production of texts that implicitly or explicitly justified women's exercise of power. Goggio's discussion of Semiramis, and other women to whom the foundation of states is attributed, operates as an implicit endorsement of Eleonora's political activities.[66] In *The Book of the Courtier*, Castiglione represents Margaret of Gonzaga as encouraging Giuliano de' Medici to retell the stories about noble women, 'For although these our enemies have heard

[62] Caleffini, quoted in Werner L. Gundersheimer, 'Women, Learning, and Power: Eleonora of Aragon and the Court of Ferrara', in Labalme (ed.), *Beyond their Sex*, p. 53. Stephen Kolsky briefly discusses her administrative role in *The Ghost of Boccaccio: Writings on Famous Women in Renaissance Italy* (Turnhout: Brepols, 2005), p. 112.

[63] See Kolsky, *Ghost of Boccaccio*, pp. 113–15; Carolyn James, '"Machiavelli in Skirts": Isabella d'Este and Politics', in Broad and Green (eds.), *Virtue, Liberty, and Toleration*, pp. 57–75.

[64] Werner L. Gundersheimer, 'Bartolomeo Goggio: A Feminist in Renaissance Ferrara', *Renaissance Studies* 33 (1980), 175–200, contains a full description of this work. For more recent discussions, see Pamela Joseph Benson, *The Invention of the Renaissance Woman: The Challenge of Female Independence in the Literature and Thought of Italy and England* (University Park, PA: The Pennsylvania State University Press, 1992); Kolsky, *Ghost of Boccaccio*, pp. 175–90.

[65] Bartolomeo Goggio, 'De Laudibus Mulierum', in British Library, London, MS Add. 17415.

[66] Kolsky, *Ghost of Boccaccio*, pp. 175–6.

them and read them, yet they make wise not to know them, and would fain the memory of them were lost.'[67] Books retelling such stories were to appear regularly from the middle of the fifteenth century. In almost every case they were dedicated to a noblewoman or princess who shared Margaret's aspiration that women's capacities and contribution to society should not be forgotten. In 1497, soon after Eleonora's death, the influential *De Plurimis Claris Selectisque Mulieribus*, by Jacopo Foresti Bergamo of Brescia, was printed in Ferrara and dedicated to Eleonora's sister Beatrice, queen of Hungary.[68] Its image of female excellence is arguably conservative, for Foresti praises women who instance the Christian virtues and depicts Semiramis as obscene and debauched.[69] It was, however, soon followed in 1501 by Equicola's *De Mulieribus* and Strozzi's *Defensio Mulierum*, which both represent powerful women in a more positive light and were encouraged by Isabella d'Este's patronage.[70]

In these late fifteenth-century works, Boccaccio's stories are supplemented with the lives of biblical women, Christian saints, and contemporary women in a manner reminiscent of Christine's *City of Ladies*. This raises the question whether Christine's text could have influenced the development of works praising women in Italy. Eleonora of Aragon possessed a number of French works, tantalisingly underdescribed. Her husband owned a copy of Christine's life of Charles V in French, and this leads one to wonder whether perhaps a copy of Christine's *City of Ladies* might not also have arrived at the court of Ferrara, which Goggio was able to use as inspiration for his work.[71] Like Christine, he adds the stories of the Christian saints to Boccaccio's women from antiquity, and implies like her, and in opposition to Boccaccio, that nobility is not confined to the heroines of the classical past. While it has so far been impossible for us to establish the diffusion of Christine's more feminist texts into the Italian states, it has been established that her influence was felt in the Iberian peninsula.[72]

[67] Castiglione, *Book of the Courtier*, p. 232.   [68] Kolsky, *Ghost of Boccaccio*, pp. 116–17.
[69] Ibid., pp. 117–21.   [70] Ibid., p. 115.
[71] Giulio Bertoni, *La biblioteca estense e la cultura ferrarese ai tempi del duca Ercole I, 1471–1505* (Turin: Loescher, 1903). In her edition of *Le Livre des fais et bonnes meurs du sage roy Charles V*, vol. 1, pp. lxxxix–xci, Suzanne Solente discusses the manuscript of this work (Modena, bibl. d'Este, α. n. 8. 7), claiming that it does not appear in Ercole's inventory, but this is mistaken.
[72] Charity Cannon Willard, 'The Manuscript Tradition of the *Livre des Trois Vertus* and Christine de Pisan's Audience', *Journal of the History of Ideas* 27 (1966), 433–44; 'The Patronage of Isabel of Portugal', in *The Cultural Patronage of Medieval Women*, ed. June Hall McCash (Athens, GA: University of Georgia Press, 1996), pp. 306–20; 'A Portuguese Translation of Christine de Pizan's *Livre de Trois Vertus*', *PMLA* 78 (1963), 459–64.

Noblewomen like Eleonora and her daughters, who were models of female prudence and virtue, were also obvious potential patrons for educated women of a slightly less elevated social status. Cassandra Fedele corresponded with Eleonora and with one of her daughters, Beatrice d'Este, who was married to Ludovico Sforza who, we have seen, praised Fedele warmly.[73] Fedele also corresponded with Francisco Gonzaga and was invited to the court of Isabella and Ferdinand in Spain. Laura Cereta addressed a letter to Pietro Bembo, one of the participants in the dialogues recorded in *The Book of the Courtier*, suggesting that these dialogues reflected a genuine sense, among a small group of women, of their participation in a cultural interchange that was redefining women's role.

In turn these women were included in catalogues that provided new models of excellence to which women could aspire. During the decade prior to 1490, Giovanni Sabadino degli Arienti wrote his *Gynevera de le clare donne*, dedicated to Gynevera Bentivoglio, sister of Battista Sforza, as well as to Eleonora and her daughter.[74] This work included biographies of contemporary women, which were then borrowed by Jacopo Foresti, who combined many of the classical, biblical, and saintly examples familiar from Boccaccio and Christine de Pizan with such recent exemplars as Eleonora herself, Battista da Montefeltro/Malatesta, Angela and Isotta Nogarola, Cassandra Fedele, and Joan of Arc.[75] This Latin text was reprinted in 1521 in Paris as part of a collection that also included Plutarch's *De Claris Mulieribus*, Joannis Pini Tolosani's *Epistola* (which is a life of St Catherine of Siena), an anonymous *De Illustribus Foeminis*, and Valerandi Varanii's *Gesta Joannae Gallicae*. In 1647, when F. Hilarion de Coste compiled *Les Eloges et les Vies des Reynes, des Princesses, et des Dames Illustres en Piété*, Foresti's collection of lives was still influential and is named by de Coste as one of his sources.[76]

During the fifteenth century, Italy was not the only place where women who were actively exercising political power were associated with

[73] Fedele, *Letters and Orations*, p. 5.
[74] Giovanni Sabadino degli Arienti, *Gynevera de le clare donne*, ed. Corrado Ricci and Alberto Bacchi (Bologna: Gaetano Romagnoli, 1888; reprint, Bologna, 1968).
[75] Jacobi Philippi Bergomensis *De Claris Mulieribus* (Ferrara: Magistri Laurentii de rubeis Valentia, 1497); Eleonora of Aragon, Ch. 177, f. 161v–168r; Battista Malatesta, Ch. 152, f. 140r; Angela Nogarola, Ch. 159, f. 149r; Isotta Nogarola, Ch. 163, f. 151r; Cassandra Fedele, Ch. 179, f. 164v–165r.
[76] F. Hilarion de Coste, *Les Eloges et les Vies des Reynes, des Princesses, et des Dames Illustres en Piété, en Courage et en Doctrine, qui ont fleury en nostre temps, et du temps de nos Pères* (Paris: Sebastien Cramoisy et Gabriel Cramoisy, 1647).

a growing literature that justified their public political role – both by refuting the arguments of women's critics, and by offering examples of women's prudence. In France too, there was a proliferation of such texts, and in France, the recent example of Joan of Arc served as a particularly outstanding example, for women and their defenders, of the fact that heroic and inspired women were not just a thing of the past, but existed also in the present.

CHAPTER 3

From Anne de Beaujeu to Marguerite de Navarre

The debate that took place from the fifteenth to the seventeenth century about the relative worth and capacities of men and women has come to be known as the *querelle des femmes*. This phrase can evoke images of querulous, quarrelsome women. Some dismiss the debate as nothing but an academic dispute among scholars, of no social relevance. According to Simone de Beauvoir, it 'was a secondary phenomenon reflecting social attitudes but not changing them'.[1] Yet, for all the polemical and satirical aspects of some of this literature, the fifteenth century saw the consolidation of a set of arguments and strategies, initially collected by Christine in *The Book of the City of Ladies*, which together refuted the Aristotelian view that women lacked prudence and were incapable of governing. Once noblewomen's fitness to rule as prudent monarchs was established, at least in the minds of educated women, it was a small step to conclude that women in general had a perfectly sound capacity for self-determination, and thus women's subjection to their husbands was ultimately open to question. The evolution of such arguments would be spread over the next three centuries, and would sometimes take surprising turns. The first

---

[1] Simone de Beauvoir, *The Second Sex*, trans. H. M. Parshley (Harmondsworth: Penguin, 1983), p. 136. For a survey of the debate prior to and up to Christine, see Alcuin Blamires, *The Case for Women in Medieval Culture* (Oxford: Clarendon Press, 1997). The view that this remained a literary debate with little influence on either social attitudes or women's self-representation or men's beliefs about women is found in Patricia Francis Cholakian, *Women and the Politics of Self-Representation in Seventeenth Century France* (Newark: University of Delaware Press, 2000), p. 19, and Evelyne Berriot-Salvadore, *Les Femmes dans la société française de la Renaissance* (Geneva: Librairie Droz, 1990), p. 45. Berriot-Salvadore claims this view was established by E.V. Telle, *L'Oeuvre de Marguerite d'Angoulême reine de Navarre et la Querelle des femmes* (Toulouse: Lion, 1937; reprint, Geneva: Slatkine Reprints, 1969). Telle implies that the origins of feminism are to be found in Marguerite de Navarre, who is the first who brings reason into the debate between men and women (pp. 29 and 147). This judgement can have been based only on a superficial knowledge of Christine and her influence.

sixteenth-century woman whose thought we shall look at in detail, Marguerite de Navarre (1492–1549), was a defender rather than a critic of marriage, though she demonstrated in her actions women's capacity as prudent governors of their realms.

The evolution that we track is an evolution in women's thought that did not necessarily go hand in hand with an improvement in women's social status.[2] In the late fifteenth century, we see two developments that, from the point of view of the status of women, seem to pull in opposite directions. On the one hand, the late fifteenth to sixteenth century is the period during which the witch-hunts escalated. On the other hand, books and poems praising women also began to proliferate, while increasing numbers of courtly women began to write poetry as a pastime. Christine comments that one reason why her poems were well received was that it was unusual for a woman to write poetry. Fifty years later there was considerable poetic production in the courtly circles associated at Tours with Margaret of Scotland, Louis XI's first wife, and at Blois with Marie of Clèves, Charles of Orléans's third wife.[3] While this activity was regarded with some suspicion, and in the case of Margaret of Scotland blamed for her ill-health, it foreshadowed the increasing participation of women in literary production during the next century.

In the early fifteenth century, Christine had argued against the misogynists, and called on women to strive to demonstrate their virtue. Joan of Arc then appeared and showed that heroines such as Judith, Esther, and Deborah were not confined to the biblical past. In the texts praising women produced in France during the last decades of the fifteenth century and the early decades of the sixteenth, both Joan of Arc and Christine are often added to lists of historical women, as examples of contemporary female excellence. One of the earliest examples of this, *The Ladies' Champion* (*Le Champion des dames*), by Martin le Franc, was

[2] See Joan Kelly, 'Did Women have a Renaissance?', in *Women, History and Theory: The Essays of Joan Kelly* (Chicago: University of Chicago Press, 1984), pp. 19–50. Kelly famously argues for a deterioration in women's situation. Her analysis has been accepted rather unquestioningly by many, including Alan P. Barr, 'Christine de Pizan's *Ditié de Jehanne d'Arc*: A Feminist Exemplum for the Querelle des femmes', *Fifteenth-Century Studies* 14 (1988), 1–12.

[3] Catherine Müller, 'Autour de Marguerite d'Ecosse: quelques poétesses françaises méconnues du xve siècle', in *Contexts and Continuities: Proceedings of the IVth International Colloquium on Christine de Pizan (Glasgow 21–27 July 2000), published in honour of Liliane Dulac*, ed. Angus J. Kennedy, Rosalind Brown-Grant, James C. Laidlaw, and Catherine M. Müller, Glasgow University Medieval French Texts and Studies, 3 vols. (Glasgow: University of Glasgow Press, 2002), vol. 11, pp. 603–19; Catherine Müller, 'Marie de Clèves, poétesse et mécène du xve siècle', *Le Moyen Français* 48 (2001), 57–76.

written in 1441.[4] It was dedicated to Isabella of Portugal, third wife of Philip the Good, Duke of Burgundy. Later examples of the genre had noble dedicatees, some of whose grandparents or great-grandparents had fought with Joan. Echoing the sentiments of Margaret of Gonzaga, such patrons were determined that the memory of this exceptional woman's contribution to the political fate of France would not be lost.

Among such texts we find Antoine Dufour's *Vies des dames célèbres*, produced in 1505 for Anne of Brittany, the wife of Charles VIII and, later, Louis XII, which begins with a life of the Virgin Mary and ends with an account of Joan's exploits.[5] This is illuminated by an elegant image of Joan mounted on a white charger, wearing beautiful, figured armour that may have been modelled on the actual armour made for her, which was allegedly preserved at Moulins. Anne of Brittany was also the recipient of Jean Marot's *La Vraye Disant advocate des dames*, which adds both Christine and 'la pucelle' Joan of Arc to its typical list of valiant Amazons and wise women.[6]

Anne de Beaujeu, Charles VIII's older sister, and her daughter Suzanne of Bourbon were dedicatees of another similar text, Symphorien Champier's collection *La Nef des dames vertueuses*, which was published in Lyons in 1503 and Paris in 1515.[7] This too adds Joan to a catalogue of noble women whose deeds should not be forgotten. Likewise, a series of works by Jean Bouchet add both Joan and Christine to the ancient and biblical examples of noble women. The earliest of these is *Le Temple de Bonne Renommee*, where Bouchet's account of Christine is almost certainly derived from Martin le Franc's *The Ladies' Champion*.[8] Bouchet was associated with the household of Louis II de Trémouille, whose

---

[4] Martin le Franc, *Le Champion des dames*, edited by Robert Deschaux, 5 vols. (Paris: Champion, 1999).

[5] Dufour, *Les Vies des dames célèbres* (1505). For the account of Joan, see pp. 162–5.

[6] Jehan Marot, *Les Deux Recueils*, ed. Gérard Defaux and Thierry Mantovani (Geneva: Droz, 1999), pp. 108 and 10. For an account of Anne of Brittany's patronage of Jean Marot, see also Laurent Bozard, 'Le poète et la princesse. Jean Molinet, Jean Lemaire de Belge, Jean Marot et leurs "muses" Marguerite d'Autriche et Anne de Bretagne', *Le Moyen Français* 57–58 (2005–6), 27–40.

[7] Symphorien Champier, *La Nef des dames vertueuses* (Lyon: Jacques Arnollet, 1503; Paris: Jehan de Lagarde, 1515). The more famous Cornelius Agrippa appears to have been a friend of Champier: in his *De Nobilitate et Praecellentia Foeminae Sexus*, written in 1509 and intended for Margaret of Austria, he too evokes Joan. See Charles G. Nauert, *Agrippa and the Crisis of Renaissance Thought* (Urbana: University of Illinois Press, 1965), pp. 22–3.

[8] See Jean Bouchet, *Le Temple de Bonne Renommee* (Milan: Vita e Pensiero, 1992), pp. 338 and 341, for his praise of Joan and Christine. The first edition was *Le Temple de Bonne Renommee* (Paris: Galliot du Pré, 1516). The reason for thinking that he follows Martin le Franc consists in the similarity in what is said and in the fact that he moves directly from Christine to Jamette Nesson, as does le Franc.

grandfather, Georges de la Trémouille, had known Joan, and whose wife, Gabrielle de Bourbon, an author in her own right, was the daughter of a bibliophile mother, Gabrielle de la Tour, and of Louis of Montpensier who was one of Joan's companions in arms.[9] Bouchet later published a *Jugement poétique de l'honneur féminin*, which commemorated the death of Louise of Savoy. In this work, Louise faces the judgement of Minos and is welcomed into the company of virtuous women.[10] Thus in the seventy years after her death, Joan functioned as a potent reminder that female honour, and women's active participation in political events, were not a thing of the past, as Boccaccio implied in his *Of Noble Women*, but could be achieved in the present, as Christine claimed in her *Book of Three Virtues*. As late as the early seventeenth century, Marie le Jars de Gournay, in her *Equality of Men and Women*, cited Joan, along with Judith, as evidence of the favour shown by God to women.[11]

Anne de Beaujeu, Anne of Brittany, and Louise of Savoy, who in one way or another are connected with these texts in praise of female prudence, virtue, and courage, lived lives patterned on the aspirations that Christine held out when she wrote her *Book of Three Virtues*, and hoped to entice women to inhabit the 'nouvel royaume de Femenie' (new kingdom of womanhood) that she had constructed in *The Book of the City of Ladies*.[12] This was surely no accident. Anne de Beaujeu, the eldest surviving daughter of Louis XII, inherited from her mother, Charlotte of Savoy, a library which contained among its more than 100 volumes

[9] See Colette Beaune and Elodie Lequain, 'Femme et histoire en France au xvme siècle: Gabrielle de la Tour et ses contemporaines', *Médiévales: Langue, Textes, Histoire* 38 (2000), special number on 'L'Invention de l'histoire', 111–36. For Gabrielle de la Tour's library, see M. A. de Boislisle, 'Inventaire des bijoux, vêtements, manuscrits et objets précieux appartenant à la comtesse de Montpensier, 1474', *Annuaire-Bulletin de la Société de l'Histoire de France* 17 (1880), 269–309; Sophie Léger, 'Gabrielle de Bourbon: une grande dame de la France de l'Ouest à la fin du Moyen Age. Etude de son cadre de vie à partir de l'inventaire après décès de ses biens demeurés au château de Thouars (1516)', in *Autour de Marguerite d'Ecosse. Reines, princesses et dames du XVᵉ siècle. Actes du Colloque de Thouars (23 et 24 mai 1997)*, ed. Geneviève and Philippe Contamine (Paris: Champion, 1999), pp. 181–99. Two of Gabrielle de Bourbon's works are to be found in Paris, MS Bibliothèque Mazarine 978, another in the Archives Nationales (1AP 220*), and have been edited in Gabrielle Bourbon, *Oeuvres spirituelles 1510–1516*, ed. Evelyne Berriot-Salvadore (Paris: Champion, 1999).

[10] Jean Bouchet, *Jugement poétique de l'honneur féminin* (Poitiers: Jehan et Enguilbert de Marnef Frères, 1538).

[11] Marie le Jars de Gournay, *Apology for the Woman Writing and Other Works*, ed. and trans. Richard Hillman and Colette Quesnel (Chicago: University of Chicago Press, 2002), p. 92.

[12] Christine de Pizan, *La Città delle dame*, 11.12, p. 250, 1.19, p. 130, and 1.4, p. 56; *Book of the City of Ladies*, pp. 117, 51 and 12. For a detailed account of the interconnected lives of these women, see Pauline Matarasso, *Queen's Mate: Three Women of Power in France on the Eve of the Renaissance* (Aldershot: Ashgate, 2001).

not only many devotional works, such as Boethius' *Consolation* and Boccaccio's *Of Noble Women*, but also Christine's *Letter of Othea*, *City of Ladies*, and *Book of Three Virtues*.[13] Anne's husband, Pierre de Beaujeu, was the youngest son of Charles I of Bourbon and Agnes of Burgundy and thus the grandson of Mary of Berry, who inherited a considerable collection of Christine's works from her father Jean de Berry. On the death of his brother, Jean II of Bourbon, in 1488, Pierre de Beaujeu and Anne of France became duke and duchess of Bourbon, and in turn inherited Jean de Berry's library, which then passed to Suzanne when she married her cousin Charles of Montpensier (whose grandmother was Gabrielle de la Tour, and whose mother was Chiara Gonzaga).[14] An inventory, made at Moulins in 1523, shows that by then they possessed multiple copies of *The City of Ladies*, *The Book of Three Virtues*, and *The Letter of Othea*, as well as the bulk of Christine's other works, including the volumes that make up the duke's manuscript of her collected works, which the inventory notes had been retrieved from Paris.[15]

After the death of her father in 1483, Anne of France and her husband acted as regents for Charles VIII. Anne carried out her duties in this regard so successfully that there was only muted opposition when, twenty years later, François I designated his mother Louise of Savoy regent of France during his wars. In her *Enseignements*, written for her daughter, Anne left a manual of good behaviour that stresses the importance of modesty and good reputation. Her advice is conservative: her daughter should love God, obey her mother, father, and husband, and not be ostentatious or idle. Anne's model is clearly the work written by her famous ancestor, St Louis, for his daughter Elizabeth, rather than Christine's more recent manual. But it shows a strong awareness of the considerable, if constrained, power and responsibility that highly placed noblewomen possessed. And it recommends reading as an appropriate means for noblewomen to avoid idleness.

At Moulins, Anne de Beaujeu was responsible for the education of a number of young women who would later be queens or regents, and who

---

[13] See Anne-Marie Legaré, 'Charlotte de Savoie's Library and Illuminators', *Journal of the Early Book Society* 4 (2001), 32–68. Legaré comments that 'Christine was the most frequently represented fifteenth-century author in women's libraries at the end of the Middle Ages' (p. 42). See also Alexandre Tuetey, 'Inventaire des biens de Charlotte de Savoie', *Bibliothèque de l'Ecole des Chartes* 26 (1865), 338–66 and 423–42; and Léopold Deslisle, *Le Cabinet des manuscrits de la Bibliothèque Impériale* (Paris: Imprimerie Impériale, 1868), vol. 1, pp. 91–3.

[14] Matarasso, *Queen's Mate*, fig. 1, p. ix.

[15] Anne de Beaujeu, *Les Enseignements d'Anne de France à sa fille Susanne de Bourbon*, ed. A.-M. Chazaud (Moulins: C. Desrosiers, 1878), pp. 222–314.

would continue to encourage the production of works that promoted women's prudence and capacity to rule. One of these was Louise of Savoy, born in 1476, whose mother died before she was seven, when Louise was placed in Anne's care.[16] Louise was the great-granddaughter of Amadeus VIII of Savoy; her great aunt Charlotte was the second wife of Louis XI and she was therefore Anne's cousin. She was educated in the company of Margaret of Austria, who as a child was betrothed to Charles VIII, until this engagement was humiliatingly broken off to allow the marriage between Anne of Brittany and Charles. The general awareness in this milieu of Christine's work can be seen from the fact that two of these princesses, Anne of Brittany and Margaret of Austria, acquired suites of tapestries called the *City of Ladies*, which used images extracted from Christine's book to reflect their noble status.[17]

Thus, although 130 years separate the birth of Louise's daughter, Marguerite de Navarre, from that of Christine de Pizan, if one looks at the generations between them one sees that they were more closely connected than one might expect. Marguerite was the sister of King François I of France and her brother's claim to the French throne derived from his grandfather, Jean d'Angoulême, the youngest son of Louis of Orléans and Valentina Visconti. In 1413, just after the peace that Christine celebrated in her *Book of Peace*, when Jean was little more than a child, he was sent to England as a hostage, and was not able to return to France until the 1440s. In 1449, at the age of forty-five, he married Marguerite of Rohan, who did not die until 1497. Their only son, Charles d'Angoulême, was born in 1459, but it was not until 1488 that he married Louise of Savoy, who gave him two children before his death in 1496: Marguerite, born in 1492, and François, who would become king of France.

Marguerite grew up in a household dominated by her widowed mother, who devoted all her energies to the care of her two children, overseeing their education and providing them with the freedom both to play and to grow, as well as with a thorough humanist training. Louise of Savoy stands out as a remarkable woman who provided an environment that allowed Marguerite to flourish and gave her the skills to become, not just an author, but also a woman who ruled as a duke in her own right.[18] It is generally believed, however, that Louise's aim was not to educate

---

[16] Matarasso, *Queen's Mate*, pp. 36–7.
[17] Susan Groag Bell, *The Lost Tapestries of the City of Ladies: Christine de Pizan's Renaissance Legacy* (Berkeley, CA: University of California Press, 2004).
[18] See Stephenson, *The Power and Patronage of Marguerite de Navarre*, pp. 79–111. Stephenson discusses François's gift of the duchy of Berry to Marguerite and his elevation of her to the peerage

her daughter for her own sake. Rather, the education that Marguerite received was the fortuitous result of a programme devised by her mother to prepare François for the crown, which Louise firmly believed, on the basis of a prophecy, would come to him. She held on to this faith despite the fact that at his birth François's position as cousin to King Louis XII made him rather unlikely to succeed. It has been observed that Louise rarely mentions her daughter in her journal, and this has been taken as evidence that Marguerite played a subservient role in the 'Trinity' which united them. But, whether deliberately or not, Louise brought her daughter up in the belief that prudence, constancy, and the capacity to rule were as likely to be found in a female body as in a male one.

An examination of the illuminated manuscripts that were produced for Louise of Savoy indicates her conscious participation in the dissemination of works that show women in various positions of power. BNF fr. 599 is a copy of Boccaccio's *Cleres et Nobles Femmes* decorated with Louise of Savoy's arms and illustrated with very realistic images of women painting, sculpting, and ruling. BNF fr. 143, a volume containing *Les Eschez amoureux* and *L'Archiologe Sophie* of Jacques le Grand, which are not particularly feminist works, is nevertheless beautifully illuminated, and full of images of classical gods and goddesses. At the beginning of BNF fr. 5715, the *Gestes de Blanche de Castile* by Etienne le Blanc, Louise herself is illustrated as Blanche of Castile, who calmly holds the rudder of the ship of state, the author prostrate at her feet. This work, which tells the story of one of the most successful queens of France to rule during her son's minority, clearly contributes to an ideological programme intended to support Louise's own regency, and indicates that she must have brought up her daughter in the expectation that she would herself potentially exercise considerable power. Louise's prudence is further underscored in manuscripts in which she is portrayed as the incarnation of this primary political virtue.[19] And by commissioning a heavily illuminated life of Mary Magdalene, Louise did her part to emphasise the importance of women in the story of Christ's life and passion.[20]

of France, and argues convincingly that Marguerite exercised power in her own right in the territories under her jurisdiction.

[19] BNF fr. 2285, *Le Compas du Dauphin*, BNF fr. 12247, *Traité des vertus*, and other texts in which Louise is identified with Dame Prudence are discussed in Anne-Marie Lecoq, *François Ier imaginaire* (Paris: Macula, 1987), pp. 69–117; and more briefly in Elizabeth McCartney, 'The King's Mother and Royal Prerogative in Early Sixteenth-Century France', in *Medieval Queenship*, ed. John Carmi Parsons (New York: St. Martin's Press, 1993), pp. 119–20.

[20] BNF fr. 24955, *Vie de Ste Madeleine*.

We can assume, then, that Marguerite benefited from being born at a time when her mother and others had considerably undermined the tradition that was opposed to women exercising power. After her brother became king, Marguerite was made duke of Berry in her own right, and a peer of France. She governed these lands independently, wielding the same power as any feudal lord, without any apparent opposition. Yet her concerns were very different to Christine's and in some ways, from a feminist point of view, might be considered a step backwards.

It may be for this reason that it is only recently that Marguerite's work has been read as influenced by Christine. Doing so allows us to recognise the continuities in the development of women's ideas, for we have every reason to believe that Marguerite was familiar with some of Christine's works, and it is certain that they were well known to others in the milieu in which Marguerite moved.[21] Marguerite's father, Charles d'Angoulême, inherited a copy of *The Book of the City of Ladies* from his father, Jean d'Angoulême. This was inventoried at Cognac in 1467 at Jean's death. Although François inherited most of his father's library, this particular copy of *The Book of the City of Ladies* did not end up in the royal library with his other works, and Maureen Curnow surmises that it might have been given to his sister Marguerite.[22] Jean d'Angoulême also owned a copy of Christine's *Book of the Body Politic*.[23]

It is, nevertheless, the generation prior to Marguerite that can be more easily shown to have had direct knowledge of Christine's texts. Anne of Brittany could not have been unaware of Antoine Vérard's printed edition of *The Book of Three Virtues* (called in this instance *Le Tresor de la cité des dames*), for he presented her with a special vellum copy with a frontispiece depicting the publisher presenting his book to her.[24]

---

[21] See Paula Sommers, 'Marguerite de Navarre as Reader of Christine de Pizan', in *The Reception of Christine de Pizan from the Fifteenth through the Nineteenth Centuries*, ed. Glenda K. McLeod (Lewiston, NY: Edwin Mellen Press, 1992), pp. 71–82.

[22] Maureen Cheney Curnow, 'The *Livre de la Cité des Dames* of Christine de Pisan: A Critical Edition' (PhD dissertation, Vanderbilt University, 1975), pp. 550–3. For the inventory of Jean d'Angoulême's library, see Gustave Dupont-Ferrier, 'Jean d'Orléans, comte d'Angoulême, d'après sa bibliothèque (1467)', *Mélanges d'Histoire du Moyen Age* 1 (1897), 39–72. For that of Charles d'Angoulême, see Edmond Sénemaud, 'La bibliothèque de Charles d'Orléans, comte d'Angoulême, au château de Cognac (1496)', *Bulletin de la Société Archéologique et Historique de la Charente*, 3rd ser., 2 (1862), 130–87.

[23] This is Christine de Pizan, *Le Livre du corps de policie*, BNF, Paris, fr. 1197. Christine de Pizan, *Le Livre du corps de policie*, p. xiii.

[24] Cynthia Brown, 'The Reconstruction of an Author in Print', in *Christine de Pizan and the Categories of Difference*, ed. Marilynn Desmond (Minneapolis: University of Minnesota Press, 1998), pp. 215–35. Louise of Savoy also had considerable dealings with this publisher, who appears to have sent her mostly didactic texts thought appropriate for her son's edification; see Mary Beth

This work was reprinted in 1503, 1518, 1521, and 1536, by which time Marguerite's own first publication had appeared. Three editions of the *Letter of Othea* were also printed during this period. This work, in which the Goddess Othea is presented as an allegory of prudence, most likely influenced the representation of Louise of Savoy as the incarnation of this virtue. In the *Letter of Othea*, Othea/Prudence offers a letter of moral advice to the fifteen-year-old Hector, who epitomises the young French prince. In the *Compas du Dauphin*, a book of moral advice for her son, Louise/Prudence holds a huge gold compass over the Dauphin, whom she appears to protect. That the compass is intended to symbolise her prudence is clear from Jean Bouchet's *Triomphes de la noble et amoureuse dame et l'art de honnestement aymer* (*Triumphs of the Noble and Amorous Woman and the Art of Honourable Love*).[25]

Marguerite could hardly have been unaware of Christine's works, but she belonged to a new generation and demonstrated her originality by moving beyond the concerns of her immediate foremother. In fact, her political epistemology is diametrically opposed to that accepted by Christine. Christine, as we saw, was fundamentally a humanist, and grounded her political beliefs on a faith that those who are wise can know the good. Marguerite's sensibility reflects the mood of the early Reformation, and is profoundly pessimistic about humanity's capacity to know and achieve any genuine good. Christine uses the figure of the Virgin Mary as queen of justice to validate women's exercise of temporal power. Marguerite questions all forms of temporal achievement, replacing them with a mystical revelation of God's love.

In adopting a mystical faith in the power of God's love and the gratuitous benevolence of his grace, Marguerite was at least partly inspired by an earlier woman writer, the mystic and beguine Marguerite de Porete, burned for heresy in 1310.[26] In turning to Porete, Marguerite expresses a

Winn, 'Books for a Princess and her Son: Louise de Savoie, François d'Angoulême and the Parisian libraire Anthoine Véraud', *Bibliothèque d'Humanisme et Renaissance* 46 (1984), 604–17.

[25] Jean Bouchet, *Triomphes de la noble et amoureuse dame et l'art de honnestement aymer* (Poitiers: Jehan le Marnef, 1530), f. 4v. This image is discussed and reproduced in McCartney, 'The King's Mother and Royal Prerogative'. For a more detailed discussion of Louise's self-conscious self-construction as Prudence, see Green, '*Phronesis* Feminised'.

[26] Marguerite de Porete, *Speculum Simplicium Animarum*, ed. Romana Guarnieri and Paul Verdeyen (Turnhout: Brepols, 1986); Marguerite de Porete, *The Mirror of Simple Souls*, trans. Ellen Babinsky (New York: Paulist Press, 1993). The influence of Porete on Marguerite de Navarre is discussed in Carol Thysell, *The Pleasure of Discernment: Marguerite de Navarre as Theologian* (Oxford University Press, 2000), pp. 20–4; Catherine M. Müller, '"La lettre et la figure": lecture allégorique du *Mirouer* de Marguerite Porete dans *Les Prisons* de Marguerite de Navarre', *Versants* 38 (2000), 153–67.

thought that anticipates later feminisms of difference when she questions
the value of masculine scholarship, and intimates that the simplicity of a
woman's love of God is more authentic than all the quibbles of the
scholars. In her late poem *Les Prisons*, where she most explicitly alludes to
Porete, Marguerite describes how love of worldly things at first seduced
her into believing that happiness could be found by the soul still trapped
in the prison of the flesh, and how spiritual illumination came to liberate
her from this false belief (*cuyder*).[27] During the last stage of her journey
towards liberation, she falsely believed herself to have been made free
through the pursuit of wisdom. She enumerates the kinds of book that
she read: books of poetry, law, history, science, mathematics, and theology, which she piled into pillars, and which she at first failed to recognise constituted a new prison. But one book suddenly liberated her
from this last worldly illusion, and her heart was illuminated by the 'stone
knife' of revelation:

> With merciful clean killing instrument,
> Most quietly the lord omnipotent,
> Who, through eye to heart so swiftly enters,
> Struck mine to the heart where its depth centers
> In this fashion: As I was reading text
> Where Jesus, manifesting goodness, next
> Tells God, "My Father, thanks I give to thee,
> Who to the small and those of low degree
> Thy treasures and thy secrets hast revealed
> And from the learnéd these things has concealed;
> For such is the bounty that doth please thee."[28]

Human books, she realises, can be judged only by means of the revelation
of the Holy Spirit, and everything that is good in them comes from God.

Having recognised that it is not the word of man but Scripture, read
through the illumination of the Holy Spirit, which reveals the truth,
Marguerite is able to recognise a greater truth in the revelations of the
unlettered Marguerite Porete than in the arguments of better-schooled
women and men:

> So I judged these books with penetration
> And gave each my heart's consideration.
> I saw a book that bore a maiden's name.

---

[27] Marguerite de Navarre, *Les Prisons*, ed. and trans. Claire Lynch Wade (New York: Peter Lang,
1989).
[28] Ibid., lines 2193–203, p. 46.

Composed a hundred years ago, aflame
With kindness and with warmth to the extent
That loving was her total argument,
Commencement and the end; all else she spurned.
One felt, in reading it, that from the heart
Was burned false and vain belief
By this love, burning so suddenly
That makes living water spring from the rock.[29]

Marguerite finds the loving faith of the simple woman superior to the subtle arguments of the theologians, who sow the seeds of doubt and division. This implies that she questions that form of the pursuit of equality with men which would see women attempting to equal them in power, glory, and learning. The direction of Christine's thought led her to rehabilitate even the Babylonian queen, Semiramis, and the warlike Amazons. Marguerite, rather than arguing that women can equal men even in their questionable capacity to exercise force, implies that they are superior to men in their simple capacity for a pure and true love.

Nevertheless, when one considers their sexual politics, one sees a continuity between the thought of Marguerite and that of Christine. Both work to undermine the clerical, misogynistic representation of women as particularly corporeal. But Marguerite goes further than Christine, and implies the spiritual superiority of women, cementing in place a way of thinking about sexual difference that ultimately led some women to reject the exercise of power by women and to question the virtue of queens. By the time Marguerite was writing, the burgeoning literature defending women was becoming repetitive and tedious. She retreated both from the worldliness of Christine's appeal to classical virtue, and from the artificiality of rhetorical embellishment. Her spiritual poems reject the idea that it is within human power to deserve salvation through active good works, and she places all her hope in Christ's saving grace. Her most famous secular work, *The Heptameron*, avoids rhetoric and, in proclaiming the literal truth of its stories, seems to move in the direction of naturalism. Nevertheless, it can also be read as an allegory that reveals God's purpose by means of new parables.

Although Christine is not explicitly mentioned by Marguerite, there are echoes of her writings throughout Marguerite's works. The overarching conception of *The Heptameron*, which is to rewrite Boccaccio's *Decameron* in order to replace fiction with truth, is remarkably similar to

---

[29] Ibid., lines 3027–37, p. 63. The last three lines of the translation have been modified.

that of *The Book of the City of Ladies*, which also involved rewriting one of Boccaccio's texts, *Of Noble Women*, in order to replace the lies told by women's detractors with the truth revealed by reason. The themes that connect Marguerite's stories, the relative virtue of men and women and the nature and possibility of true love, also continue the debate that Christine began with her *Letters on the Romance of the Rose*, her *Letter of the God of Love*, and her love-debate poems. Marguerite's late poem *The coach* (*La coche*) returns rhetorically to the scene of Christine's love-debate poetry, and, with the appearance of three ladies who engage the narrator in conversation, hearkens back to the opening scenes of the *City of Ladies* and *Three Virtues*. It is also a noteworthy coincidence that Marguerite's last great spiritual poem, *Les Prisons*, echoes in its title and theme one of Christine's last works, *La Prison de la vie humaine*. It therefore seems justifiable to read Marguerite's works as engaged in the debates initiated by Christine, whose conclusions she modifies in line with her greater attraction to the thought of the male evangelicals who were her contemporaries, and to Porete's more manifest spirituality.

As aforementioned, Marguerite's political epistemology and her anthropology differ fundamentally from Christine's. As well as the clear influence of Porete, there is a purely coincidental similarity between her thought and that of Laura Cereta. While we saw in Cereta a move from the pursuit of fame to a Christian concern with the afterlife and true virtue, Marguerite moves in what looks like the opposite direction. She begins to write in order to express her very personal faith and mystical spirituality, and only later turns to combining her spiritual thinking with secular stories that explore the politics of sexuality, love, and marriage. But even these later works by Marguerite question all temporal goods. In what follows we first touch briefly on the nature of Marguerite's spirituality and then concentrate on a reading of her *Heptameron* as a central contribution to the sexual politics of the Reformation.[30]

The imperial ideal, of a Christianity united under a French monarch, that we saw surfacing in Christine's thought re-emerged during the reigns of Charles VIII and François I and helped to justify their attempts to conquer Italy.[31] This ideal was particularly evident in 1517, when François I entered Rouen as the new king. There he was greeted with a stage which

[30] See also Patricia Francis Cholakian, *Rape and Writing in the 'Heptaméron' of Marguerite de Navarre* (Carbondale: Southern Illinois University Press, 1991). Cholakian offers a selective reading of the *Heptaméron* as it relates to the sexual politics of rape.
[31] Lecoq, *François Ier imaginaire*, p. 17.

was at first lit with silver, denoting the age of silver. Pallas Minerva, carrying the shield of prudence, was seated opposite an immense star, which opened to reveal a boy dressed as the king; as he descended, the scene turned to gold, denoting the coming of the golden age of justice.[32] Many other books and pageants produced during his reign evoke this same imperial theme.

Despite the failure of François's Italian enterprises, which resulted in the death of Marguerite's first husband and her own famous journey to Spain to save her ailing brother, she never explicitly rejected this imperial ideal; she represented her brother in her published epistolary poems as the perfect prince, a second Abraham or David, elect and loved by God.[33] Yet, implicitly, her acts and words show a distrust of such dreams of earthly grandeur. The fear and impotence she expresses in one of her poems to her brother, as she waits to hear news of a distant battle, make comprehensible her intense need for God and her attraction to the doctrine of salvation through grace. Waiting, she describes the very sound of the words 'battle', 'war', and 'harness' as drawing tears. She is a woman, far away, powerless to do anything but pray to the Lord begging him to remember his David, who, she promises, loves God better than himself.[34] And although she does not explicitly criticise her brother, what she says in the fourth poem addressed to him, and published in her *Suyte des Marguerites* (1547), implies that she believes him to have been guilty of hubris, too wedded to things of this world, and too confident in his own beliefs. Here she praises him for what she represents as a new turn towards a faith in God's love, similar to her own,

> Since I see that sure and sweet repose
> Like nothing else proposed for our travails
> Where your spirit is consoled and rests,
> I, who have desired so much this thing
> Who so wished a like good for you,
> And prayed sighing before God
> Wishing your sleep-filled eyes opened,
> To the discovery of his secret beauty.[35]

[32] Ibid., pp. 113–15.
[33] Marguerite de Navarre, *Suyte des Marguerites de la Marguerite des princesses* (Lyon: Jean de Tournes, 1547; reprint, The Hague: Johnson Reprint and Mouton, 1970), pp. 40–1, 46–53. A similar description of François appears in *The coach*, lines 1055–108; see Marguerite de Navarre, *The Coach and the Triumph of the Lamb*, trans. Hilda Dale (Exeter: Elm Bank Publications, 1999), pp. 58–9.
[34] Marguerite de Navarre, *Suyte des Marguerites*, pp. 60–1.
[35] Ibid., pp. 65–6.

Marguerite praises God for having removed from her brother all vain desires, and promises God that his heart will leave behind bitterness and understand how to truly love as he appreciates the joy of loving God better than himself.[36]

As with Cereta, it is therefore initially difficult to read Marguerite's writing as political. Her immediate concerns appear to be centrally religious. But we should remember that Marguerite was writing during the first years of the Reformation, when the political issues of spiritual liberty and subjection to authority were being intensely debated in a religious context. The schism in the Catholic church, which had finally been healed by the 1430s, nevertheless raised many issues concerning the authority of the Pope relative to the Council of the bishops of the church. Nicholas of Cusa articulated the position that the authority of the community of Christians overrode the authority of the Pope. Against this, the Pope asserted his absolute authority within the church, but this brought into focus an issue that had been central for Dante: the relationship between secular and church power. At this time, secular and church authority were not clearly distinguished, and it was seen as part of the responsibility of 'the very Christian king of France' to uphold the authority of the church in his realm. At the same time, the French ecclesiastical community would from time to time appeal to the authority of the king to preserve the traditional liberty and autonomy of the church in France.[37]

In the next century, the Protestant challenge to the authority of the Pope in spiritual matters would result in widespread challenges to the authority of the monarch in the state. And already in the first years of the sixteenth century, the challenge that Lutheranism posed to the church implicitly involved the monarchy. Those who believed in the authority of the church required the temporal power of the king to persecute heresy. For the French king to fail to uphold orthodox Christianity was to betray his sacred inheritance as defender of the church. Dante's imperial dream involved a king divinely sanctioned as the ultimate temporal authority, working in partnership with a Pope who held absolute spiritual authority. With Protestant challenges to the Pope's authority, this dream began to fracture. Ultimately, the image of the peaceful polity as a body governed by a prudent head would itself be undermined, as the king's privileged access to knowledge of the common good came into question.

---

[36] Ibid., pp. 68–9.
[37] Nancy Lyman Roelker, *One King, One Faith: The Parlement of Paris and the Religious Reformations of the Sixteenth Century* (Berkeley, CA: University of California Press, 1996), pp. 161–88.

The philosophical currents which led in this direction can be detected even in the literature in praise of prudence associated with Louise of Savoy. In the years after his return from a pilgrimage to the Holy Land, which he undertook at Louise's behest, the Franciscan Jean Thenaud wrote for his patroness a series of 'triumphs' of the virtues prudence, force (or fortitude), justice, and temperance.[38] Incorporated into the first of these is a translation of Erasmus' *In Praise of Folly*, altered to conform to Louise's taste by removing Erasmus' misogyny. Following Erasmus, Thenaud distinguishes sharply between the 'folly' of merely worldly prudence and the true wisdom of the evangelical 'folly' of the soul liberated from things of this world. Christine asserted with regard to prudence, 'This prudence serves our spiritual just as much as our physical welfare, for by her man desires to know God, to love and fear him, and to know the things which lead to salvation and to live by them. For without this knowledge all other prudence is nothing but folly.'[39] Yet she never adequately confronted the potential conflict between worldly and spiritual prudence. Once this conflict is brought to the fore, particularly in the figure of the hypocritical prelate who lines his pockets and pursues the satisfaction of bodily desires, the ideal of prudence itself bifurcates. We are left either with the worldly prudence – intelligent self-interest – for which Hobbes will provide the canonical development, or with the saintly prudence of evangelical folly. Marguerite pursues the second form of prudence and recommends it to her brother, but it is not obvious how a prudence of this kind coheres with the responsibilities of a king.

Not only were there currents of Erasmus' thought in Louise's court, Marguerite was also abreast with the moves towards reform within France and coming from Germany. She received Luther's *De Votis Monasticis* from Antoine Papillon, and she herself translated into French Luther's *Explication du Pater Noster*.[40] However, she was most closely allied with the evangelical movement within France, which sought a return to the authority of Scripture and reform within the church and monasteries without challenging the Pope's supremacy. During the 1520s, she entered into an intense correspondence with Guillaume Briçonnet (1470–1533),

[38] Jean Thenaud, *Le Triomphe des vertus. Premier Traité, le Triomphe de Prudence*, ed. Titia J. Schuurs-Janssen (Geneva: Droz, 1997).This text is discussed at length in Lecoq, *François I*er *imaginaire*, pp. 101–112.
[39] Christine de Pizan, *The Book of Peace*, 1.5, pp. 69 and 209.
[40] Will G. Moore, *La Réforme allemande et la littérature française. Recherches sur la notoriété de Luther en France* (Strasbourg: La Faculté des Lettres à l'Université, 1930), pp. 431–41.

the reformist Bishop of Meaux.[41] It is from him that she is generally thought to have acquired the theology that she expresses in her first published work, *The Mirror of the Sinful Soul (Le Miroir de l'âme pécheresse)*.[42]

This poem expresses a profound pessimism concerning any human ability to do good. Thus it implicitly rejects worldly prudence altogether, and theologically speaking, is diametrically opposed to Christine's outlook. The earlier writer implicitly accepted our capacity to deserve salvation through good works, she assumed that we could know the good, and she accepted the ideal of a universal monarch who could, at least theoretically, establish peace on earth through his prudent rule. Marguerite believes that we are incapable of bringing about the good out of our own power. We are completely dependent on God's grace for our salvation, and we can achieve happiness only through an intense appreciation and reciprocation of the completely undeserved love that God manifests towards us in this grace.

It is not clear that there is anything contradictory to Catholic teaching in this outlook; nevertheless, in October 1533 the theology faculty of the Sorbonne attempted to ban Marguerite's poem. For a short while it was included in a list of prohibited works. The intervention of the king soon resulted in the lifting of this ban, but clearly some felt that Marguerite was too close to Protestantism. This may have been more to do with the people that she promoted and protected than with anything in the actual text. Her almoner, Gérard Roussel, preaching in Paris at Easter the same year, aroused the anger of the syndic of the faculty, Noël Beda. The disruptions which resulted from this led to the king sacking Beda, but this was a pyrrhic victory for the cause of reform. A year later, in October 1534, when placards attacking the Mass and the sacraments were posted in Paris, Orléans, and Blois, François I was compelled to allow the *parlement* and the faculty of theology to pursue the perpetrators of heresy. As defender of the church he could not do otherwise. Simon du Bois and Antoine Augereau, the men who had printed Marguerite's poem along with other more obviously Protestant works, were among those targeted.

---

[41] For an edition of this correspondence, see Guillaume Briçonnet and Marguerite d'Angoulême, *Correspondence*, ed. Christine Martineau and Michel Veissière (Geneva: Droz, 1975). On the influence of the French evangelicals and reformers of Meaux, and in particular Lefèvre d'Etaples, see Henri Heller, 'Marguerite of Navarre and the Reformers of Meaux', *Bibliothèque d'Humanisme et Renaissance* 33 (1971), 271–310.

[42] There are a number of modern editions of this poem. Marguerite de Navarre, *Le Miroir de l'âme pécheresse*, ed. Renja Salminen (Helsinki: Soulalainen Tiedeakatemia, 1979) contains a useful introduction and includes Elizabeth I's translation of the poem.

The former mysteriously disappeared. The latter was condemned and executed. The poet Clément Marot fled to Nérac in Marguerite's domain of Navarre, and Marguerite also left the court for her own domains, where Roussel was to survive many years employed by her in the position of almoner. She, however, returned to the court and remained close to her brother for many years despite growing tensions due to conflicts of interest between her husband, Henri d'Albret, and the king, which came to a head over the issue of her daughter Jeanne's marriage.[43]

Although experts are divided as to whether Marguerite's poem does in fact contain anything that is contrary to the Catholic faith, it was perceived as sufficiently Protestant for it to be thought an appropriate subject as a translation exercise for the young Protestant Princess Elizabeth in England.[44] During the 1520s, Elizabeth's mother Anne Boleyn was one of the ladies in waiting of Claude, François I's wife, during a period when Marguerite was heavily involved in court affairs. Elizabeth's governess, Catherine Champernowne, was married to John Ashley, a cousin of Anne Boleyn, and it may have been through this conduit that Marguerite's poem came into Elizabeth's schoolroom. Elizabeth's translation, made at the age of eleven, was presented to her stepmother, Katherine Parr, in 1544, and five later revised versions were published during her reign.[45] Clearly those who taught Elizabeth, who would become the epitome of the learned, prudent, Renaissance monarch, felt that the example of the learned pious princess in France was an image to be emulated. Elizabeth excuses herself in her prologue, addressed to Parr, for the mistakes and roughness of her translation, but she gives as good a *précis* of the content of Marguerite's work as could be desired, describing it thus:

wherein is conteyned, how she doth perceue how, of herself, and of her own strength, she can do nothing that good is, or prevayleth for her salvation: onles it be through the grace of god: whose mother daughter, syster, and wife, by the scriptures she proueth herselfe to be: Trusting also that through his incomprehensible love, grace and mercy she doth faithfully hope to be saved.[46]

It is therefore against the background of the doctrine that we are completely dependent on God's grace that the apparently secular stories of the *Heptameron* should be read.

---

[43] For a full account of Marguerite's relationship with her daughter, see Nancy Lyman Roelker, *Queen of Navarre: Jeanne d'Albret (1528–1572)* (Cambridge, MA: Harvard University Press, 1968).
[44] Marguerite de Navarre, *Le Miroir de l'âme pécheresse*, pp. 71–84.
[45] Ibid., pp. 251–63.   [46] Ibid., pp. 286–7.

From the outset, the stories of the *Heptameron* are set in a frame that evokes the Old Testament flood, and God's promise of redemption.[47] Having each escaped from various perils, including drowning, bandits, and bears, the ten story-tellers, five men and five women, find themselves stranded at the monastery of Notre-Dame de Serrance waiting for a bridge over the river to be built. In the prologue, the oldest female participant, Oisille, suggests that in order to pass the time they should read Scripture, and take spiritual flight. Hircan, generally supposed to be modelled on Henri d'Albret, Marguerite's second husband, expresses his interest in private pleasures of the flesh. But Parlamente, who (we assume with others) is Marguerite's mouthpiece, proposes that they tell true stories.[48] The pastime she proposes, telling true tales, is suspended between the corporeal and the spiritual. It takes place as a conversation between men and women, whose opinions are equally represented in the informal parliament that will meet for seven days in the meadow of the monastery.

One can already read into this utopian scene an implicit politics, and a dream of a different social organisation. Christine's allegory the *City of Ladies* was a fortress, built by reason, law, and justice to defend womankind and establish a new realm of female authority to replace the Amazons. In *The Ladies' Champion*, Martin le Franc imagines the defence of women as a joust. But Marguerite's allegory is a dialogue, a discourse, a parliament of men and women, in whom the most authoritative figure is a woman who leads them each morning through a reading of Scripture, the word of God, and thus helps them to understand the deeper truth revealed in the 'true' stories that they share.[49]

Running through the dialogues, interspersed between the daily stories, two levels of political commentary can be discerned. The most obvious is the politics of male/female relations. More subtle is the question of the discernment of truth and the political implications that follow from the limit to what can be known by rational inquiry.

There emerges out of the interactions between the men and women gathered at Notre-Dame de Serrance, and the stories they tell, a powerful recasting of sexual difference which has been enormously influential in

[47] Robert D. Cottrell, 'Inmost Cravings: The Logic of Desire in the *Heptameron*', in *Critical Tales: New Studies of the 'Heptameron' and Early Modern Culture*, ed. John D. Lyons and Mary B. McKinley (Philadelphia: University of Pennsylvania Press, 1993), p. 4.

[48] See Donald Stone, ' "La malice des hommes": "L'Histoire des satyres" and the *Heptameron*', in Lyons and McKinley (eds.), *Critical Tales*, pp. 53–64.

[49] Thysell, *The Pleasure of Discernment*, pp. 97–126.

the West. Because it is never didactically forced on the reader, the lesson of these stories is subtle, and is accepted as merely a description of the way things are. It is a measure of Marguerite's genius that the description of the difference between the sexes that she allows to emerge from her stories is now taken very much for granted. But its novelty can be seen by comparing it to what had gone before. Marguerite appears to be the first to propose that in general what men want is sex, while what women offer is love. She is never so crude as to assert outright the superiority of women over men in matters of love. She is careful to have her participants warn against hasty generalisations and to acknowledge the fundamental sinfulness of both sexes. Nevertheless, she cleverly allows the weight of evidence to establish her case, while leaving open space for other views and interpretations.[50]

Without any heavy-handed didacticism, Marguerite turns the clerical representation of women as purely sexual beings on its head, and levels the accusation of sexual voracity squarely at men. But she never accuses men directly. She allows her male characters to make their own confession. Gerburon, in particular, is cast as an older man, keen to warn women of men's true desires. He compares men in love with hunters chasing deer, saying 'our one pride and joy, our one true delight, is to see you caught, and to take from you that which you prize more than life itself'.[51] At the conclusion of a story of attempted rape, the origin of which is believed to have involved Marguerite herself and the admiral Guillaume de Bonnivet, Hircan asserts, 'the tall lord of your story lacked nerve and didn't deserve to have his memory preserved'.[52] Again, at the conclusion of the story of Amadour and Floride, which also involves an attempted but unsuccessful rape, both Hircan and Saffredent express the view that Amadour was incompetent and would have been a more admirable man if he had managed to get Floride to submit to him.[53] Thus, by their own confession, men are exposed as rapists and callous seducers.

---

[50] We therefore disagree with Marcel Tetel, 'Marguerite of Navarre: The *Heptameron*, a Simulacrum of Love', in *Women Writers of the Renaissance and Reformation*, ed. Katharina M. Wilson (Athens, GA: University of Georgia Press, 1987), pp. 99–131. Tetel suggests that Marguerite simply allows a plurality of points of view to vie with each other. By contrast, the reading offered here is largely in accord with that in Telle, *L'Œuvre de Marguerite d'Angoulême*, pp. 93–147.

[51] Marguerite de Navarre, *The Heptameron*, ed. and trans. P. A. Chilton (Harmondsworth: Penguin, 1984), p. 208; Marguerite de Navarre, *Heptaméron*, ed. Renja Salminen (Geneva: Droz, 1999), p. 164.

[52] Marguerite de Navarre, *The Heptameron*, p. 96 ; *Heptaméron*, p. 41. In Michel François's edition, the source of the claim that Bonnivet was the unsuccessful rapist is identified as Brantôme. See Marguerite de Navarre, *L'Heptaméron*, ed. Michel François (Paris: Garnier, 1967), p. 453, note 125. Renja Salminen, however, calls Brantôme's claim a 'legend' (*Heptaméron*, p. 685).

[53] Marguerite de Navarre, *The Heptameron*, p. 153; *Heptaméron*, p. 103.

One writer, commenting on Marguerite, observes that 'Moving in the immediacy of appetitive time, males represent, in one sense at least, the old Adam. On the other hand, the drive that propels the human creature toward the only "things" that can be properly "enjoyed" is figured primarily in those females whose overwhelming desire is for chastity.'[54] But another moral is to be read in these stories. This is the perversity of the sexual double standard. Ironically, Hircan, as a figure of Henri d'Albret, is made to assert, in his response to the story apparently involving Bonnivet and Marguerite, that the man should have gone so far as to kill the woman's companion and carry through his rape. Here the inconsistency of men's attitudes is implicitly exposed, since Hircan could, one must assume, hardly have wanted his own wife raped and her long-time friend and companion murdered.

In other stories the sexual double standard is explicitly criticised. In the fifteenth story a young bride deceives her husband, who has neglected her because of his love for a woman who is the king's mistress. She forcefully defends her right to an equal sexual liberty, pointing out that what she has done, which is to enter into a friendship with an unmarried man, is far less reprehensible than what her husband has done, since he has both neglected his wife and betrayed his lover's husband, as well as his king.[55] All that the husband can say to this is that a woman's honour is different from a man's. Despite her husband's best endeavours, this woman gets away with her affairs. The female story-tellers disapprove of her behaviour, but the men are impressed. Simontault remarks: 'the woman in the story completely forgot she was a woman for a while, for even a man could not have taken his revenge so well'.[56] One is left to conclude for oneself that if women in general had the morals of men, men would be much worse off, while Oisille reminds the audience, echoing Christine's *Letter of the God of Love*, 'Because one woman is not virtuous ... one should not think that all others are like her.'[57]

While the men are often portrayed as rejecting the sexual double standard, in the sense that they claim that women are just as much sexual beings as men, the stories expose the inconsistency of this perspective

[54] Cottrell, 'Inmost Cravings', p. 17.
[55] Marguerite de Navarre, *The Heptameron*, p. 197; *Heptaméron*, pp. 152–3.
[56] *The Heptameron*, p. 202; *Heptaméron*, p. 159.
[57] *The Heptameron*, p. 202; *Heptaméron*, p. 159. One of Marguerite's female characters, Nomerfide, also warns against over-generalisation (p. 46; p. 101). For Christine's formulation, see *The Selected Writings of Christine de Pizan*, ed. Blumenfeld-Kosinski, p. 19; *Oeuvres poétiques de Christine de Pisan*, vol. 11, p. 7.

from the male point of view. Hircan rejects the idea that the hearts of
men and women are different.[58] And Saffredent twice quotes Jean de
Meun, first repeating the Old Lady's claim that men and maids are made
for each other, and then quoting him on the equivalence of all women
in matters of love.[59] However, Parlamente points out that the man who
pursues his sexual desires, believing women to be equally carnal, will
always be insecure: 'It's impossible for men who do wrong themselves not
to be suspicious of others. But it's a happy man who gives no cause for
others to be suspicious of him.'[60]

Men are not only represented as, in general, more carnal than women;
the reliability of the stories they tell, in which women are criticised, is
undermined by their self-confessed desire to be revenged on the virtuous
women who have spurned them. In her *Letter of the God of Love*, Christine
claims that men spurned by virtuous women then slander them. Simontault begins the very first story by confessing that he is similarly motivated:

Ladies, I have been so ill rewarded for my long and devoted service, that, in order
to avenge myself on Love and on the woman who is so cruel to me, I shall do my
utmost to collect together all the accounts of foul deeds perpetrated by women
on us poor men. And every single one will be the unadulterated truth.[61]

At the end of this story, Simontault expresses the standard misogynistic
assessment of women, 'I think that you will agree that ever since Eve
made Adam sin, women have taken it upon themselves to torture men,
kill them and damn them to Hell.'[62] In this way, Simontault's veracity
and motives are exposed as questionable. When Saffredent tells the story
of a hypocritical woman who refuses to give in to her noble lover's desire
for sex, but is then discovered having sex with the stable-boy, he too
confesses that he is motivated by revenge.[63]

By contrast, the credibility of those who tell stories that demonstrate
women's virtue is never undermined. Among these are a number of
stories that illustrate how those of a low and base degree understand
virtue more clearly than the sophisticated. The simple muleteer's wife,
who allows herself to be killed rather than give in to her would-be rapist,
sets a standard for all women: 'Can any woman regard herself as virtuous
unless she has, like this woman, resisted to the last?'[64]

---

[58] *The Heptameron*, p. 254; *Heptaméron*, p. 217.
[59] *The Heptameron*, pp. 120 and 315; *Heptaméron*, pp. 65 and 279.
[60] *The Heptameron*, pp. 106–7; *Heptaméron*, p. 51.   [61] *The Heptameron*, p. 70; *Heptaméron*, p. 13.
[62] *The Heptameron*, p. 78; *Heptaméron*, p. 21.   [63] *The Heptameron*, p. 234; *Heptaméron*, pp. 192–3.
[64] *The Heptameron*, p. 88; *Heptaméron*, p. 25.

By contrast, the sophisticated, who believe that they can achieve the good through their own intelligence, are shown to be deluded. The thirtieth story brings to a conclusion a series of tales which all tend to emphasise that 'there is nothing more foolish than a man who thinks he's clever, and nothing more wise than a man who knows that he is nothing', a thought that Parlamente immediately endorses with the paradox that 'the man knows something ... who knows that he does not'.[65] This moral is driven home by the bizarre story of a widow who, by attempting to keep her son innocent, causes him to commit incest both with her and with the daughter born from her incestuous encounter with him. This story leads Hircan to conclude: 'There, Ladies, that is what becomes of those women who presume by their own strength and virtue to overcome love and nature.'[66]

A number of key stories allow Parlamente to develop her particular adaptation of the Neoplatonic theory of love made popular by Ficino's translation of Plato's *Symposium*. However, we need to be careful in treating the question of Neoplatonism, for there appear to be a number of different characterisations of Platonic love running through the commentaries that are not at all equivalent. Saffredent argues for the innocence, or at least venality, of actions caused by love, which he claims do not anger God, since corporeal passion 'is one step in the ascent to perfect love of Him'.[67] He quotes the first Epistle of John, verse 20, 'How shall you love God, whom you see not, unless you love him whom you see?' This is a text which Parlamente also seems to have in mind when she says 'Furthermore ... I hold the view that no man will ever perfectly love God, unless he has perfectly loved some creature in this world.'[68] However, the women reject Saffredent's Ficinian interpretation of this text and Oisille accuses Saffredent of distorting the words of Scripture. It is not corporeal love which should be understood here, and no excuse for sexual promiscuity is to be found in the Bible.

Thus, the view that sexual passion is forgivable because it is a step on the path to love of God is rejected. Yet Marguerite does appear to subscribe to some version of the view that love for other human beings is related to the love of God, which derives from her understanding of the immanence of God in all things. In *Les Prisons*, she goes so far as to assert that 'there is no figure of love in which I fail to find the living portrait of

---

[65] *The Heptameron*, p. 312; *Heptaméron*, p. 276. [66] *The Heptameron*, p. 321; *Heptaméron*, p. 285.
[67] *The Heptameron*, p. 356; *Heptaméron*, p. 322. [68] *The Heptameron*, p. 228; *Heptaméron*, p. 187.

the true lover and the single perfect love'.[69] She recognises a form of perfect love that can exist in human relations and which is an image of the love of God, though it is insufficient without faith, which enables us to distinguish the image from its true original. She puts the following explanation into Parlamente's mouth:

> Those whom I call perfect lovers . . . are those who seek in what they love some perfection . . . Yet if God does not open the eyes of faith, they will be in danger of leaving ignorance behind only to become infidel philosophers. For only faith can reveal and make the soul receive that Good which carnal and animal man cannot understand.[70]

It is this love that her mouthpiece Parlamente suggests is more characteristic of women than men:

> A woman's love is rooted in God and founded on honour, and is so just and reasonable that any man who is untrue to such love must be considered base and wicked in the sight of God and in the eyes of all [good] men. But most [men's] love is based on pleasure, so much so that women not being aware of men's evil intentions, sometimes allow themselves to be drawn too far. But when God makes them see the wickedness in the heart of the man of whom they had previously thought nothing but good, they can still break it off with their honour and reputation intact.[71]

Yet it is not only women who can feel this more perfect love. In the story of Pauline and her lover, a couple who are truly in love but not permitted to marry, it is the man who first becomes a monk and who shows Pauline how they can convert their honourable love into love of God. Hircan calls such behaviour 'folly', to which Oisille responds, 'Do you call it folly if one loves with an honourable love in one's youth, and then converts this love entirely to God?'[72] If this is folly, it is the folly of true wisdom.

However, Marguerite never encourages the view that women are without blemish. She puts into Hircan's mouth the accusation that women's chastity is cruel and based on pride, so that one vice, lust, is simply replaced by another. The accusation of pride is not denied, yet she also suggests that women's sins are less harmful than men's.

> I know well . . . we are all in need of God's grace, since we all incline to sin. Yet the fact is that our temptations are not the same as yours, and if we sin through

[69] Marguerite de Navarre, *Les Prisons*, lines 2611–13, p. 54.
[70] *The Heptameron*, p. 229; *Heptaméron*, pp. 187–8.
[71] *The Heptameron*, pp. 253–4; *Heptaméron*, p. 216.
[72] *The Heptameron*, p. 228; *Heptaméron*, p. 186.

pride no-one suffers for it, and neither our body nor our hands are tainted by it. But all your pleasure is derived from dishonouring women, and your honour depends on killing other men in war. These are two things that are expressly contrary to the law of God.[73]

Women are thus not exempt from the need for God's grace, but they do not descend as far into sin as men. Implicitly, this discussion of women's cruelty and pride refers back to a popular debate, set in train by Alain Chartier's *La Belle Dame sans merci*, which initiated a debate over whether women who reject men's amorous advances are cruel.[74]

Although the stories told during the first three days of the sojourn at Notre-Dame de Serrance seem to attribute to women, and to some men, a love of the creature which can lead to love of the Creator, the stories told during the latter days place a significant restriction on this view, and introduce Marguerite's philosophy of marriage. Prior to Ficino's rediscovery of the Plato of the *Symposium*, a rather different doctrine of Platonic love from the one that he developed was already quite common. This was the idea of a perfect love, offered by a man to a married woman, which inspired him to pursue virtue in order to deserve her love, but demanded nothing dishonourable in return. In the *Heptameron*, Dagoucin is represented as a believer in this kind of love.[75] This love might appear less problematic for women than the carnal love glorified in Ovid's *The Art of Love*, Capellanus' book of nearly the same name, and Meun's *Romance of the Rose*. But Christine questioned its benefits for women, particularly in her *Duke of True Lovers* and in the *Book of Three Virtues*, in which she reproduced a letter, included in the earlier work, explaining why a married woman could not afford to engage even in such 'Platonic' affairs without endangering her marriage, honour, and reputation. Marguerite shows a similar suspicion of this form of Platonic love, implying that it typically masks carnal passion. This turns out to be the situation in the case of Amadour and Floride. At the point when Floride has decided to accept Amadour as a 'true lover' he reveals his carnal intentions.[76] Even more dangerous is such apparently 'spiritual' love, which disguises the flames of passion, when it is felt by a woman.[77] It appears, therefore, that it

---

[73] *The Heptameron*, p. 305; *Heptaméron*, p. 270.
[74] Alain Chartier, *The Quarrel of the Belle dame sans mercy*, ed. and trans. Joan E. McRae (New York and London; Routledge, 2004).
[75] *The Heptameron*, p. 113; *Heptaméron*, pp. 57–8.
[76] *The Heptameron*, pp. 142–3; *Heptaméron*, pp. 97–8.
[77] *The Heptameron*, pp. 346–7; *Heptaméron*, p. 311.

is in only a restricted set of circumstances that the love that human beings feel for each other is a step towards the love of God.

Marguerite's understanding of the circumstances in which human love and love of God can co-operate are revealed in the contrast between her appraisal of Rolandine's behaviour, the subject of story twenty-one, and that of her aunt, told in the fortieth story. These two stories are strikingly similar, since in both a young woman is prevented from marrying and then marries secretly. In the case of Rolandine, the marriage is not consummated, yet she remains true to her husband even after his infidelity towards her is exposed. She refuses to have her marriage annulled, arguing that 'if love and honest intent founded on the fear of God were the true and sure bonds of marriage', then she was indissolubly married.[78] In the case of the aunt, there is a secret marriage which the lovers persuade themselves will be forgiven, which in fact leads to the death of the husband, killed by his wife's brother, who is unaware that the couple are in fact man and wife. Parlamente draws from this story the moral that no one should marry for their own pleasure without the consent of those to whom they owe obedience.[79] The situation leads to a discussion of imperfect marriages and Parlamente's assertion that praiseworthy marriage is not concerned with glory, greed, or sensual enjoyment but is grounded in virtuous love and obedience to one's parents' wishes. Marguerite's intention appears to be to imply that Rolandine's marriage was grounded in her love for her husband's perceived perfections, not on sexual desire, and so was acceptable despite not being endorsed by her family. In general, however, a pure spiritual love is impossible for corrupt human beings. Hence it is only within marriage that love between men and women, which will inevitably be partly corporeal, can, with the help of faith, promote the love of God. Alternatively, love of the creature can be renounced entirely in favour of love of the Creator, as happens in the case of Pauline and her lover, and as the lady of Vergy, whose love is pure but still human, is led to wish she had done.[80]

Marguerite confines acceptable human love within the bounds of marriage and the family. She thus helps to pave the way for the later sentimentalisation of married love, and begins the process which was to see marriage transformed in the Western consciousness, from a contract grounded in economic and social requirements, only fortuitously accompanied by love, to a relationship purely dependent on love.

---

[78] *The Heptameron*, p. 250; *Heptaméron*, p. 212.   [79] *The Heptameron*, p. 370; *Heptaméron*, p. 341.
[80] *The Heptameron*, p. 528; *Heptaméron*, p. 493.

Marguerite clearly rejects marriages grounded merely in the passions of individuals, thinking marriage good only if it both conforms to the economic and social demands of the family and involves love. Yet by emphasising the importance of love within marriage, and the destructive character of even the most seemingly elevated forms of love outside marriage, she contributes to the spiritual elevation of married love characteristic of Protestantism.

Erasmus praised marriage in a short work, the *Encomium Matrimonii*, which had been translated into French by Berquin and published in 1525, four years before Berquin became one of the earliest victims of persecution of the reformers.[81] It is in her similar preference for marriage, and her repeated exposure of the hypocrisy of the Franciscan friars, that Marguerite shows herself closest to Protestantism. Her stories thus contribute to a representation of marriage that was to be extremely influential in the development of the modern conception of married love.

Political theory in the modern period has been so heavily influenced by the fiction that the family is a natural institution, which grounds the political edifice of the state, that discourse like Marguerite's is not generally thought of as political. However, the family is not simply natural, since, although reproduction takes place in nature, much of the political structure of any society is bound up with the laws and customs that regulate reproduction, inheritance, property rights, and marriage. It is in this sphere also that the basic power relations between the sexes are constituted. The fact that the word *economy* has its roots in the Greek word *oikos*, meaning 'hearth', should remind us that the economy of a society is inextricably bound up with the nature of the household, household production, expenditure, the transmission of property, the circulation of commodities, and consumption, which are all mediated by family structures. Transformations in the understanding of marriage and the family are therefore inextricably linked to the growth of modern society, in which the family is not so obviously a nexus of political power as it was in the late feudal and monarchist world in which Marguerite lived. Thus, Marguerite's stories, which may initially appear to be about sexual morality, individual passion, and religious transformation, also operate as blueprints for a social structure that allows for the reconciliation of human sinfulness and carnal passion with the maintenance of female honour and obedience to God's will. They contribute to the evolution of our understanding of the

[81] Le Chevalier de Berquin, *Déclamation des louanges de mariage*, ed. Emile Telle (Geneva: Droz, 1976).

female subject, her relationship to her husband, and the place of the married couple within the wider political organisation.

Marguerite does not question the fundamental proposition that a woman's honour consists in chastity before marriage and faithfulness within it. She could hardly do so, since the whole tenor of medieval clerical misogyny was to depict women as dishonourable because inconstant. Taking up a critique of courtly love in both its older form and its newer Ficinian manifestations, the stories of the *Heptameron* expose the danger that men's sexual passions and deceptive 'true love' hold for women. They reject the old endorsement of lifelong chastity as too rigorous for average human beings, and show celibacy (that is, the failure to marry) to be the cause of the hypocrisy and vice of many Franciscans. They rehabilitate marriage grounded in love for another's perfections and love of God, and elevate women as naturally more inclined to participate in that human love which is the pale image of divine love immanent in the world.

What emerges as required for a society in which women's honour is preserved is a new marriage in which the faithfulness of the husband is as important as the faithfulness of the wife. Parlamente is quite censorious of the patient wives who forgive their husbands' infidelities, arguing that since true love is grounded in that appreciation of another's perfections, immorality in a husband will lead to a loss of love.[82] She also reacts with approval to a number of stories in which a husband punishes his wife in a manner that seems to modern sentiments to be quite barbarous and cruel. For example, she endorses the actions of the husband who makes his wife drink from her dead lover's skull, and seems in general to approve of death as a penalty for adulterers.[83] While it may be tendentious to equate every utterance of Parlamente's with Marguerite's own views, this attitude is commensurate with her assertion in *Les Prisons* that those who are led by the Holy Spirit are neither seducer nor seduced.[84]

The *Heptameron* was undoubtedly influential, first appearing in a form close to its current one in 1559, and then being reprinted regularly throughout the sixteenth and seventeenth centuries. It was partly translated into English during Queen Elizabeth's reign, while the first complete English translation by Robert Codrington appeared during Cromwell's Commonwealth.[85] Marguerite's very visible and authoritative

---

[82] *The Heptameron*, p. 360; *Heptaméron*, p. 330.   [83] *The Heptameron*, p. 335; *Heptaméron*, p. 299.
[84] *Les Prisons*, line 2909, p. 60.
[85] A list of manuscripts and editions is provided in François's edition of Marguerite de Navarre's *Heptaméron*, pp. xxi–xxvi. The English translations are outlined in *The Heptameron*, pp. 22–6.

entry into print was part of a proliferation of women's writing which took up the theme of love and exposed the dangers from a female point of view of succumbing to passion. Under the pseudonym 'Helisenne de Crenne', Marguerite de Beit had previously developed the theme in her *Angoysses douloureuses qui procedent d'amours*, first published in 1538. She also praised her near contemporary, Marguerite, in her *Lettres invectives*.[86] We will discuss later how Mme de Lafayette harks back to the period of the writing of the *Heptameron* in her novel *The Princess of Cleves*.

In order to discern the more subtle implications that Marguerite's outlook has for political organisation in general we need to look beyond the *Heptameron*. As previously mentioned, Marguerite's epistemology emphasises the limits of reason and the arrogance of those who believe that they can achieve the good through their own power. There are times when she sounds like a sceptic, for example when (echoing Socrates) she avers that we know simply that we know nothing. Yet she is not a moral sceptic, at least not on the interpretation of her work offered here. Faith and Scripture can reveal the truth, but people who arrogantly presuppose that they have knowledge will face humiliation. This epistemological humility suggests a politics of toleration and open-mindedness and an ideal of a community like that which is formed at Notre-Dame de Serrance, in which a diversity of opinions are exchanged and criticised with a view to the emergence of truth. It is noteworthy that such a politics is entirely commensurate with Marguerite's practice. Not only did she endow the University of Bourges, helping to make it a centre of humanistic learning, she also protected a range of individuals, including Calvin, whose beliefs did not necessarily coincide with her own.[87]

It has been shown that the metaphysical and epistemological doctrines imparted to Marguerite by Briçonnet owe a good deal to Nicholas of Cusa.[88] And it is tempting to conclude that his political outlook may also have been absorbed by her. However, we have no real evidence that the utopian and democratic gathering that Marguerite depicted at Notre-Dame

---

[86] Helisenne de Crenne, *Les Angoysses douloureuses qui procedent d'amours* (1538), ed. Paul Demats (Paris: Belles Lettres, 1968); *Les Epistres familieres et invectives de ma dame Helisenne* (Montreal: Les Presses de l'Université de Montréal, 1995); *Oeuvres* (Geneva: Slatkine Reprints, 1977); *A Renaissance Woman: Helisenne's Personal and Invective Letters*, trans. Marianna M. Mustacchi and Paul J. Archambault (Syracuse, NY: Syracuse University Press, 1986); *The Torments of Love*, trans. Lisa Neall and Steven Rendall (Minneapolis: University of Minnesota Press, 1996).

[87] Felix Frank, 'Marguerite d'Angoulême, sœur de François Iᵉʳ, reine de Navarre, et l'esprit nouveau en France au xvιᵉ siècle', *Revue Moderne* 38 (1866), 220–42.

[88] Glori Cappello, 'Nicolò Cusano nella corrispondenza de Briçonnet con Margherita di Navarra', *Medioeva. Rivista di storia della filosofia medievale* 1 (1975), 96–128.

de Serrance was one that she imagined might be transported into the real world. In her poems to her brother she never questions his exceptional and divinely appointed role as king, though she emphasises his duty to love God more than himself. We do, however, have evidence of a political caution and generally tolerant attitude on Marguerite's behalf which is consistent with the doctrine of ignorance that is found in Cusa. For example, Marie Dentière addressed to Marguerite a letter which is patently Protestant, filled with rhetoric decrying idolators and criticisms of the Mass, unlike anything to be found in Marguerite's writing. She accuses Marguerite of being too soft and kind, and of supporting evangelicals who had remained subservient to the Pope.[89] Similarly, Calvin's letter criticising the Spiritual Libertines implicitly opposes Marguerite's toleration, since she supported those whom Calvin attacked.[90] Marguerite's reaction was not to impose her opinions on others, nor to break officially with the church; rather she and Henri d'Albret accepted a *de facto* diversity of belief and practice within their realm.[91] Had others followed the caution implied by her epistemological humility, and focused as she did on the centrality of love in the message of the Gospel, the religious wars which were soon to sweep through Europe might have been averted. But it would take some time for the tolerant attitude at least implicit in her philosophy to acquire an explicit articulation.

During this period some French women from circles outside the court also began to commit their works to publication. In Poitiers, Madeleine des Roches (1520–87) and her daughter Catherine (1542–87) were at the centre of a literary circle that in some ways prefigured the later development of the salon.[92] They defended women's right to an education and, in a dedicatory poem to the king, give a summary of the virtues of the monarch that would have been equally approved by Christine de Pizan:

> The greatness of a King, his honour and his nobility,
> Come from loving virtue much more than wealth,
> Loving good counsel much more than a great gift,
> More than fickle pleasure, loving Temperance,

---

[89] Marie Dentière, *Epistle to Marguerite de Navarre and Preface to a Sermon by John Calvin*, ed. and trans. Mary B. McKinley (Chicago: University of Chicago Press, 2004), pp. 78–82.

[90] See Thysell, *The Pleasure of Discernment*, pp. 19–20. Thysell points out that Marguerite's tolerant attitude led to her being accused of heresy by Calvin's supporters.

[91] Roelker, *Queen of Navarre*, p. 265.

[92] See Diana Robin, Anne R. Larsen, and Carole Levin (eds.), *Encyclopedia of Women in the Renaissance: Italy, France and England* (Santa Barbara: ABC-CLIO, 2007), pp. 109–11, for a brief biography, and p. 204 for a description of their salon.

> Having before one's eyes the eyes of Prudence
> Which sees times past, future and present.[93]

In Lyons, as well, women were asserting their right to display their literary merits. Louise Labé was only one of a number of young women whose poetry and prose asserted women's right to an education, and examined love, folly, and male–female relations.[94] Her collected works, which included the *Débat de Folie et Amour*, were published by Jean de Tournes, also the publisher of Marguerite's *Suyte des Marguerites*.

Meanwhile, in Italy the first tentative steps towards the development of women's self-consciousness, which we sketched in Chapter 2, had burst forth into a torrent of female-authored poetry, which it is beyond the bounds of this work to examine. To give a sense of the extent of this poetic production it is sufficient to note that in 1559, when Ludovico Dominichi published *Rime diverse d'alcune nobilissime e virtuossime donne*, he was able to include 331 pieces by fifty-three women poets.[95] Of these, Vittoria Colonna (1492–1547), who was partly responsible for the publication of Castiglione's *The Book of the Courtier*, was one of the most famous.[96] Like her exact contemporary Marguerite de Navarre, she was attracted to Reformation ideas and came under suspicion of heresy. Marguerite was sufficiently interested in her work to request a copy of her poems, evidence of the growing sense among women of belonging to the female republic of letters that Cereta had imagined. In her book *Publishing Women*, Diana Robin provides a vivid glimpse of the interconnected literary salons and political intrigues which provided the background to Marguerite and Vittoria's brief correspondence, and to a society which was the precursor to the more famous literary salons of the seventeenth century.[97]

---

[93] Madeleine and Catherine des Roches, *Les Oeuvres* (Geneva: Droz, 1993), p. 299; *From Mother and Daughter: Poems, Dialogues, and Letters of Les Dames des Roches*, trans. Anne R. Larsen (Chicago: Chicago University Press, 2006), p. 115.

[94] Louise Labé, *Complete Poetry and Prose: A Bilingual Edition*, ed. Deborah Lesko Baker, trans. Deborah Lesko Baker and Annie Finch (Chicago: Chicago University Press, 2006); Louise Labé, *Oeuvres complètes*, ed. François Rigolot (Paris: Flammarion, 2004); Ingrid Åkerlund, *Sixteenth Century French Women Writers* (Lewiston: The Edwin Mellen Press, 2003); Robin, Larsen, and Levin (eds.), *Encyclopedia of Women*, pp. 195–8.

[95] Mentioned in Evelyne Beriot-Salvadore, 'La problématique histoire des textes féminins', *Atlantis* 19 (1993), 10.

[96] Joseph Gibaldi, 'Child, Woman, Poet: Vittoria Colonna', in Wilson (ed.), *Women Writers of the Renaissance and Reformation*, pp. 22–46.

[97] Diana Robin, *Publishing Women: Salons, the Presses, and the Counter-Reformation in Sixteenth-Century Italy* (Chicago: University of Chicago Press, 2007) p. 29; see also Barry Collett, *A Long and Troubled Pilgrimage: The Correspondence of Marguerite d'Angoulême and Vittoria Colonna, 1540–1545* (Princeton, NJ: Princeton Theological Seminary, 2000).

CHAPTER 4

Queen Elizabeth I of England

Queen Elizabeth I (1533–1603) is one of the best-known political figures of England, but she is not generally studied as a political thinker. Commentators on Elizabeth's politics examine such topics as Elizabethan state and foreign policy, the internal politics of court and council, Elizabeth's various conflicts with parliament about marriage and the succession, and the conscious construction of the queen's public persona. Few scholars attempt to define Elizabeth's abstract political thought or the political ideas espoused in her speeches, letters, prayers, and poems.[1] When Elizabeth's writings are studied, they are studied first and foremost as the productions of an important historical figure, rather than those of an intellectual; and scholars concentrate on what Elizabeth's speeches *do*, rather than merely what they say.[2] If one looks closely, however, it is possible to discern a distinctive political outlook in Elizabeth's written pieces. Generally speaking, her political thought is representative of a standard sixteenth-century view that princely authority is ultimately founded in God, and that active rebellion against an anointed prince constitutes unlawful rebellion against divine authority.

---

[1] For Elizabeth's collected writings, see *Elizabeth I: Collected Works*, ed. Leah S. Marcus, Janel Mueller, and Mary Beth Rose (Chicago and London: The University of Chicago Press, 2000). This volume includes almost all of Elizabeth's written pieces, except for her translations of other authors' works. In the Preface, the editors remind us that many of Elizabeth's written pieces were collaborations or co-productions with others (p. xii).

[2] It is in fact quite difficult to divorce Elizabeth's written pieces from their historical-political context: her statements on authority (as well as obedience, divine providence, and so on) were often strategic devices designed to achieve certain concrete political ends, rather than to make a theoretical point. See, for example, Mary Thomas Crane, ' "Video et Taceo": Elizabeth I and the Rhetoric of Counsel', *Studies in English Literature 1500–1900* 28 (1988), 1–15. On the politics of Elizabeth's marriage negotiations, see Ilona Bell, 'Elizabeth and the Politics of Elizabethan Courtship', in *Elizabeth I: Always Her Own Free Woman*, ed. Carole Levin, Jo Eldridge Carney, and Debra Barrett-Graves (Aldershot: Ashgate, 2003), pp. 179–91; and Ilona Bell, 'Elizabeth I – Always Her Own Free Woman', in *Political Rhetoric, Power, and Renaissance Women*, ed. Carole Levin and Patricia A. Sullivan (Albany, NY: State University of New York Press, 1995), pp. 57–82.

For a few feminist theorists, it is disappointing that Elizabeth simply promotes the masculine values of the patriarchal order that she represents, and that she does not subvert that tradition, or make any attempt to further the status of women as a social class.[3] Elizabeth presents herself as an exception in nature, a woman above and 'beyond her sex'; and her success is attributed to her status as a symbolic figurehead rather than a woman *per se*. Allison Heisch observes that 'the Queen, having established herself as an exceptional woman, did nothing to upset or interfere with male notions of how the world was or should be organised'. According to this interpretation, Elizabeth was, in effect, 'absorbed into the existing patriarchal system, de-sexed, elevated and hence transformed into a figure both above and distinct from other women'.[4]

In this chapter, however, we argue that although Elizabeth I was not an obvious champion of her sex, she did not merely appropriate the tradition of masculine princely rule. We examine the content of Elizabeth's writings in an effort to establish Elizabeth's own independent political viewpoint, and we focus on those texts in which Elizabeth attributes her prudential management of the kingdom to her virtues as a loving 'mother' and 'wife' of the realm. In light of the ideological programme begun by Christine de Pizan, Elizabeth can be seen as part of a tradition of female political thinkers who oppose the exclusion of women from power and authority on the basis of their supposed lack of prudence or capacity to discern between good and bad.

I

In her writings, Elizabeth emphasises that her rule is ordained by God, and that all subjects (especially the nobility) have a religious duty to provide their service to the realm. Elizabeth first articulates this view in her maiden speech, on 20 November 1558:

My lords, the law of nature moveth me to sorrow for my sister; the burden that is fallen upon me maketh me amazed; and yet, considering I am God's creature, ordained to obey his appointment, I will thereto yield, desiring from the bottom of my heart that I may have assistance of His grace to be the minister of His heavenly will in this office now committed to me. And as I am but one body naturally considered, though by His permission a body politic to govern, so I

---

[3] See Allison Heisch, 'Queen Elizabeth I and the Persistence of Patriarchy', *Feminist Review* 4 (1980), 45–54.
[4] Ibid., 53, 54.

shall desire you all, my lords (chiefly you of the nobility, everyone in his degree and power), to be assistant to me, that I with my ruling and you with your service may make a good account to almighty God and leave some comfort to our posterity in earth.[5]

Upon her accession, it is understandable that Elizabeth was at pains to emphasise the divine nature of her political authority: she was not only a young female, but also one who had been denounced as illegitimate. (Throughout her reign, she would be especially concerned about overcoming her father Henry VIII's slanders against her mother, Anne Boleyn.) The opening line of her first speech implicitly draws on the biblical injunction to 'Let every soul be subject unto higher powers. For there is no power but of God: the powers that be are ordained of God' (Romans 13.1). According to this influential precept, whoever resists the powers that be resists the ordinance of God, and is therefore subject to punishment by eternal damnation. Like Mary Tudor before her, Elizabeth thus justifies her right to demand obedience regardless of the inferiority of her sex. The traditional legal distinction between the 'body natural' and the 'body politic' is a useful way of asserting this right. According to the figurative distinction, the body politic is representative of the monarch's immortal power and authority, conferred by God. The body politic consists 'of Policy and Government, and [is] constituted for the Direction of the People, and the Management of the publick-weal'; it is 'utterly devoid of Infancy, and old Age, and other natural Defects and Imbecilities which the Body Natural is subject to'.[6] The body politic is, in other words, devoid of any physical imperfections or weaknesses, such as femaleness. Although the body politic is contained within the queen's natural body during her lifetime, it is not identical with it; the body politic will continue to exist even after the queen's physical body is deceased. For this reason, the body politic is not subject to the same laws as the body natural, and hence the common law does not apply to the monarch.

In other speeches, Elizabeth exploits a different but closely related metaphor: the metaphor of the realm as a single human body,[7] which

---

[5] 'Queen Elizabeth's first speech', Hatfield, 20 November 1558; Speech 1, *Elizabeth I: Collected Works*, pp. 51–2.

[6] Edmund Plowden, *The Commentaries and Reports of Edmund Plowden* (1779), p. 217, quoted in Marie Axton, *The Queen's Two Bodies: Drama and the Elizabethan Succession* (London: Royal Historical Society, 1977), p. 17; see also Ernst Kantorowicz, *The King's Two Bodies: A Study in Mediaeval Political Theology* (Princeton University Press, 1957).

[7] Diana Saco explains the difference as one between 'corporal' and 'corporational' entities: the 'body politic' metaphor refers to the person of the king, rather than a collective organisation, whereas the single body metaphor includes heads and limbs. See Diana Saco, 'Gendering Sovereignty: Marriage

was also favoured by Christine de Pizan, following John of Salisbury. According to Elizabeth, the monarch represents the head of this body and parliament represents the subservient feet. The entire body functions harmoniously only when mind and reason (the head) rule the body and its members. This metaphor figures prominently in Elizabeth's responses to pressures for her to marry or to declare a successor. In several key speeches before parliament, Elizabeth asserted that it was her role to direct her subjects, and not the other way around. She would decide the question of her marriage and the succession, and not them. It was, she said in 1566, 'A strange thing that the foot should direct the head in so weighty a cause, which cause hath been so diligently weighted by us that it toucheth us more than them.'[8] When parliament threatened to with-hold her subsidy until Elizabeth declared a successor, Elizabeth responded that 'I am your anointed queen. I will never be by violence constrained to do anything . . . I will deal therefore in your safety and offer it unto you as your prince and head, without request. For it is monstrous that the feet should direct the head.'[9] In 1567, Elizabeth likewise reproached the House of Commons for challenging her decision to forbid debate concerning the succession (the Commons saw this as a violation of the House's liberty of free speech). 'As to liberties', Elizabeth said, 'who is so simple that doubts whether a prince that is head of all the body may not command the feet not to stray when they would slip? God forbid that your liberty should make my bondage or that your lawful liberties should any ways have been infringed.'[10] With this figurative language, Elizabeth implicitly justifies her right to be obeyed by drawing parallels between head–body and prince–subject relations. Just as it is natural and proper that only one head should rule the body, so too must one entity, the prince, control the realm. Any other state of affairs – such as multiple heads, a headless body, or the feet ruling the head – is 'monstrous' and a violation of God's natural order.

Elizabeth consistently applied this doctrine of royal supremacy to monarchs in countries other than England – even to those countries that were ruled by a tyrannical or 'irreligious' prince. Early in her reign, she

---

and International Relations in Elizabethan Times', *European Journal of International Relations* 3 (1997), 309.

[8] 'Elizabeth to a joint delegation of Lords and Commons', 5 November 1566; Speech 9, version 2, *Elizabeth I: Collected Works*, p. 96.

[9] Ibid., pp. 97–8.

[10] 'Elizabeth's speech dissolving Parliament', 2 January 1567; Speech 10, *Elizabeth I: Collected Works*, p. 105.

refused to offer support to the Scottish rebels against the Catholic Mary, Queen of Scots. In Elizabeth's view, these rebels were challenging God's order by rebelling against their natural sovereign. Likewise, later in her reign, Elizabeth expressed a deep reluctance to have Mary executed for treason. Rather than have Mary tried by common law, Elizabeth chose to proceed according to the Act for the Queen's Safety, a parliamentary statute. Before parliament, on 12 November 1586, Elizabeth said:

> I will tell you the cause of the manner of my proceedings with the Scottish queen and why I did not deal by the course of the common law of the realm . . . For if I should have followed that course of the common law, forsooth, she must have been indicted by a jury of twelve men in Staffordshire. She must have held up her hand and openly been arraigned at a bar, which had been a proper manner of proceeding with a woman of her quality! (I mean her quality by birth and not by conditions.) . . . But I thought it much better and more fit to have her tried by the most honorable and ancient nobility of the realm, against whom and whose proceedings no exceptions might or can be taken.[11]

For Elizabeth, it is simply not fitting that ordinary subjects should pass judgement on Mary Stuart.[12] However barbarous or tyrannical princes may be, they gain their authority from God, and are therefore above the common law. Elizabeth articulated a similar view in a Latin speech made to the heads of Oxford University in 1592:

> Know that I would be dead before I command you to do anything that is forbidden by the Holy Scriptures. If, indeed, I have always taken care of your bodies, shall I abandon the care of your souls? God forbid! Shall I neglect the care of souls, for the neglect of which my own soul will be judged? Far from it. I admonish you, therefore, not to go before the laws but to follow them, nor dispute whether better ones could be prescribed but observe what the divine law commands and ours compels. *And henceforth remember that each and every person is to obey his superior in rank, not by prescribing what things ought to be, but by following what has been prescribed, bearing this in mind: that if superiors begin to do that which is unfitting, they will have another superior by whom they are ruled, who both ought and is willing to punish them.*[13]

Elizabeth asserts that it is not for subjects to question God's order, but simply to obey his representatives on earth. This duty of obedience

---

[11] 'Elizabeth's first reply to the Parliamentary petitions urging the execution of Mary, Queen of Scots', 12 November 1586; Speech 17, version 1, *Elizabeth I: Collected Works*, pp. 188–9.

[12] On this topic, see Wallace MacCaffrey, *Elizabeth I* (London: Edward Arnold, 1993), p. 143.

[13] 'Elizabeth's Latin speech to Oxford', 28 September 1592; Speech 20, *Elizabeth I: Collected Works*, p. 328; our italics.

extends even to those superiors who do what is unfitting. Every member of the realm has his or her duty; one duty of princes is to protect the spiritual welfare of their subjects; if they fail to meet this duty, they will be accountable to *their* superior, and not to their subjects.

II

As her speeches show, Elizabeth subscribed to the widespread sixteenth-century view that the social order is providentially arranged by God in order to bring about the harmonious functioning of society. For some writers of the time, far from providing support for Elizabeth's reign, this hierarchical world view raised an implicit problem for female rulership in general.[14] Women, in the traditional view, have a duty of obedience to the divinely ordained authority of *men*; for women to rebel against, or usurp the authority of, their masculine superiors is to challenge God's natural order. Due to their natural political subordination, women who rule over men are thus 'monsters in nature'; and in so far as this unnatural state of affairs is accepted in the state, it also threatens to undermine the husband's natural authority over his wife.[15] In previous chapters, we observed that Aristotle also challenges female leadership on the grounds of women's natural inferiority. In his view, women cannot have political authority because they lack the prime political virtue of *prudence*, or the deliberative capacity to distinguish between good and bad when deciding upon a course of action for the well-being of the community.

  Both before and during Elizabeth's lifetime, the question of women's capacity for virtue was fiercely debated in print. We have seen that the literature defending and defaming women was highly relevant to the situation of European queens, regents, and other women exercising power in the fifteenth and sixteenth centuries. In England in 1521, by which time it was evident that Catherine of Aragon was unlikely to produce a male heir to Henry VIII, an anonymous English translation of Christine's *Book of the City of Ladies* appeared.[16] Shortly thereafter, in 1540, Sir Thomas Elyot published his *Defence of Good Women* (written between 1531 and

---

[14] On sixteenth-century arguments for and against female rule, see Constance Jordan, 'Women's Rule in Sixteenth-Century British Political Thought', *Renaissance Quarterly* 40 (1987), 421–51.

[15] In the sixteenth century, this line of reasoning is particularly clear in Jean Bodin, *Les Six Livres de la République* (Paris: Jacques du Puis, 1583; republished London: Scientia Aalen, 1961), pp. 1001–3.

[16] On this work, see Maureen Cheney Curnow, '*The Boke of the Cyte of Ladyes*, an English Translation of Christine de Pisan's *Le Livre de la Cité des dames*', *Les Bonnes Feuilles* 3 (1974), 116–37; Stephanie Downes, 'Fashioning Christine de Pizan in Tudor Defences of Women', *Parergon* 23 (2006), 71–92; and Cristina Malcolmson, 'Christine de Pizan's *City of Ladies* in Early Modern

1538), a work explicitly defending Catherine and her daughter Mary's legitimacy and right of succession. At about the same time, David Clapham published an English prose translation of Cornelius Agrippa's *De nobilitate et praecellencia foeminei sexus*, titled *A Treatise of the Nobilitie and Excellencye of Woman Kynde* (1542). The appearance of such works defending female virtue was highly political. When Mary I finally succeeded to the throne, becoming the first woman ruler of England, there was an intemperate backlash in some quarters.

In 1558, two months before Elizabeth's accession to the throne, the Protestant reformer John Knox (c. 1514–72) published *The First Blast of the Trumpet Against the Monstrous Regiment of Women*. This work was specifically directed against the Catholic rule of Mary[17] – but its implications were apparently broad enough to earn Elizabeth's disapproval. In *The First Blast*, Knox argues that rebellion against constituted authority is sometimes lawful; in particular, he advocates a duty of resistance to those monarchs who threaten true religion. He says that 'To promote a woman to bear rule, superiority, dominion, or empire above any realm, nation, or city is repugnant to nature, contumely to God, a thing most contrarious to his revealed will and approved ordinance, and, finally, it is the subversion of good order, of all equity and justice.'[18] The people, therefore (and the nobility in particular), have a duty to resist female rule. 'If any man be afraid to violate the oath of obedience which they have made to such monsters,' Knox adds, 'let them be most assuredly persuaded that, as the beginning of their oaths, proceeding from ignorance, was sin, so is the obstinate purpose to keep the same nothing but plain rebellion against God.'[19]

Knox's argument in favour of rebellion against women rulers begins with the premise that God has endowed human beings with an ability to discern between the natural and unnatural order of things. Our intuitions, according to Knox, tell us that it is repugnant to nature that the weak shall lead the strong, or that the foolish and mad shall govern the 'sober of mind'. Yet nature informs us that women are physically frail, mentally feeble, and generally lacking in the necessary princely virtues.

England', in *Debating Gender in Early Modern England 1500–1700*, ed. Cristina Malcolmson and Mihoko Suzuki (New York: Palgrave, 2002).
[17] Knox conveniently ignored the fact that Scotland was also ruled by a woman, Mary of Guise (regent for Mary Stuart).
[18] John Knox, *The Political Writings of John Knox: The First Blast of the Trumpet Against the Monstrous Regiment of Women, and Other Selected Works*, edited with an introduction by Marvin A. Breslow (Washington: The Folger Shakespeare Library, 1985), p. 42.
[19] Ibid., p. 75.

Thus 'it is more than a monster in nature that a woman shall reign and have empire above man'.[20] Knox supports this view with reference to authorities such as ancient writers, the civil law, and Scripture. In the second part of his *Politics*, Aristotle claims that when women bear authority over men, injustice and disorder necessarily follow.[21] Likewise, Chrysostom, the Bishop of Constantinople (c. 354–407), suggested that women are unfit to rule because they 'lack prudence and right reason to judge the things that be spoken'.[22] Good rulers exhibit the virtues of constancy, prudence, discretion, and rationality – virtues that 'women cannot have in equality with men'.[23] Instead, according to Basil of Caesarea (c. 329–79), women excel in tenderness, softness, and compassion – natural traits that God has given them so that they 'may be apt to nourish children'.[24] The civil law (a reflection of human reason) informs us that women should not hold public office; they are not legally permitted to speak for others, or to occupy the roles of judge and magistrate. Finally, the Scriptures tell us that it is a virtue for women to be submissive and subject to men. It is, after all, part of the legacy of Eve's transgression that man 'shall be lord and governor' over woman.[25]

An obvious problem for Knox's argument is that the Scriptures also tell us that there have been exceptional and noble women rulers of the past – women such as Deborah and the prophetess Huldah. To forestall this objection, Knox allows that God has occasionally exempted a few women from the common rank. But these historical examples do not show that women rulers are part of the natural order, only that God can work miraculously and give 'most singular grace and privilege' to a few chosen individuals.[26] If one wants to defend a particular female ruler as exceptional, then one must first demonstrate that she resembles a Deborah or a Huldah in godliness and virtue.[27] Knox also suggests that exceptional women rulers do not themselves possess political authority, and that they are merely passive instruments of God's will.

In *An Harborowe for Faithful and Trewe Subjects* (1559), John Aylmer came to Elizabeth's defence against such arguments. But is there any

---

[20] Ibid., p. 38.   [21] Ibid., p. 43.   [22] Ibid., p. 53.
[23] Ibid. In his *Les Six Livres de la République* (1583), Jean Bodin returns to Knox's theme: 'La Monarchie doit seulement estre devolué aux males, attendu que la Gynecocratie est droitement contre les loix de nature, qui a donné aux hommes la force, la prudence, les armes, le commandement, & la osté aux femmes' [The monarchy should only ever be inherited by men, given that gynocracy is directly against the laws of nature, which have given force, prudence, arms and command to men and taken them from women] (see Bodin, *Les Six Livres de la République*, p. 1001).
[24] Knox, *First Blast*, p. 54.   [25] Ibid., p. 46.   [26] Ibid., p. 65.   [27] Ibid., p. 66.

evidence, we might ask, that Elizabeth herself developed a position contrary to Knox's views, to justify her rule as a woman? As a single female, Elizabeth was compelled to present a defence of her right to be obeyed without a man by her side. Although Mary Tudor had ruled before her, Mary had married early in her reign and (despite safeguards to the contrary) had subsequently failed to limit the power of her husband, Philip (later Philip II of Spain). As a result, there was some apprehension about Elizabeth's marriage prospects: on the one hand, there was an expectation that she could not remain single – anxiety about the succession had convinced her counsellors that she must marry, and marry quickly at that. On the other hand, any marriage to a foreign prince threatened to diminish Elizabeth's authority as sole sovereign, and place the nation in danger of foreign takeover.[28] Alternatively, it was thought that if Elizabeth married an English subject, she would be marrying beneath her, and that a show of favouritism might lead to tensions among the nobility. But as long as Elizabeth remained single, her authority was also somewhat weakened. Knox's views about a woman's natural defects were, after all, widely accepted at the time; and women in general were thought to be lacking the qualities expected of a good governor.

In the early part of her reign, Elizabeth placed a distinct emphasis on the fact that although she was a woman, she was a woman of extraordinary ability and, more importantly, a woman who received her special gifts by the grace of God. In her public prayers, Elizabeth put forward the view that, although her natural body was that of a weak and feeble woman, her power as a body politic was derived entirely from God. She is among the 'highest rank of honour among mortals', she said, not because of her own merit, but because of God's goodness.[29] In a 1563 prayer, she said:

Eternal God, Creator and Accomplisher of all things, and the same most merciful Father to those who are faithful to Thee, when I think how of late I was altogether nothing – without body, without soul, without life, without sense and understanding – and when I think that at this point I was as clay in the hand of the potter, so that by Thy will Thou mightst make me a vessel of honor or of disgrace, Thou hast willed me to be not some wretched girl from the meanest rank of the commonest people, who would pass her life miserably in poverty and squalor, but to a kingdom Thou hast destined me, born of royal parents and

---

[28] On this topic, see Saco, 'Gendering Sovereignty', 291–318.

[29] See 'Thanksgiving for recovered health', from 'Private Prayers of Queen Elizabeth at Court', 1563; Prayer 7, *Elizabeth I: Collected Works*, p. 139; and 'Elizabeth's speech at the close of parliamentary session', 15 March 1576; Speech 13, *Elizabeth I: Collected Works*, p. 168.

nurtured and educated at court. When I was surrounded and thrown about by various snares of enemies, Thou hast preserved me with Thy constant protection from prison and the most extreme danger; and though I was freed only at the very last moment, Thou hast entrusted me on earth with royal sovereignty and majesty.

Beyond this, indeed, when I consider how many – not only from among the common people but also from the nobility as well as royal blood, by Thy hidden but just judgment – some are miserably deformed in body, others (more miserably by far) destitute of wit and intelligence, still others (by far the most miserable) disordered in their mind and reason, and finally how many were and are, even today, insane and raging. Indeed, I am unimpaired in body, with a good form, a healthy and substantial wit, prudence even beyond other women, and beyond this, distinguished and superior in the knowledge and use of literature and languages, which is highly esteemed because unusual in my sex. Finally, I have been endowed with all royal qualities and gifts worthy of a kingdom, and have been given these freely by Thee. I perceive how much I owe to Thy goodness, most merciful Father, for other things that are from Thee, even though of these other things I have not at all been deserving beforehand.[30]

Here Elizabeth emphasises her fitness to govern: although she is a woman, she is not disordered in her mind, or altogether without reason. She might have been an ordinary woman, poverty-stricken in both mind and body; but due to God's special intervention, she has prudence 'beyond other women', she is superior in learning and knowledge, and, in these respects, entirely unusual for her sex. In similar prayers, she compares herself to male rulers, such as Solomon, who also attributed their success to God. 'How much less am I, Thy handmaid, my unwarlike sex and feminine nature,' she says, 'adequate to administer these Thy kingdoms of England and of Ireland, and to govern an innumerable and warlike people, or able to bear the immense magnitude of such a burden, if Thou, most merciful Father, didst not provide for me (undeserving of a kingdom) freely and against the opinion of many men.'[31] The implication, of course, is that she *is* deserving of such a kingdom, despite the weakness of her sex, because God has so ordained it.

But in no instance does Elizabeth claim that women are not weak or feeble by nature, or not capable of exemplifying the princely virtues *as women*. In fact, she cannot ascribe her success to her own virtues, she says,

---

[30] 'Thanksgiving for benefits conferred', from 'Private Prayers of Queen Elizabeth at Court', 1563; Prayer 8, *Elizabeth I: Collected Works*, p. 141.

[31] 'Prayer for wisdom in the administration of the kingdom', from 'Private Prayers of Queen Elizabeth at Court', 1563; Prayer 9, *Elizabeth I: Collected Works*, pp. 142–3.

precisely because she is a woman and therefore naturally inferior.[32] Instead she emphasises her weakness, thanking God that

Thou hast done me so special and rare a mercy that, being a woman by my nature weak, timid, and delicate, as are all women, Thou hast caused me to be vigorous, brave, and strong in order to resist such a multitude of Idumeneans, Ishmaelites, Moabites, Muhammadans, and other infinite of peoples and nations who have conjoined, plotted, conspired and made league against Thee, against Thy Son, and against all those who confess Thy name and hold to Thy holy Word as the only rule of salvation.

O my God, O my Father, whose goodness is infinite and whose power is immense, who art accustomed to choose the weak things of this world in order to confound and destroy the strong, persist – persist for the glory of Thy name, for the honor of Thy Son, for the repose and quietude of Thine afflicted Church – in giving me strength so that I, like another Deborah, like another Judith, like another Esther, may free Thy people of Israel from the hands of Thy enemies.[33]

In this passage, it is possible to recognise that strand of Protestant humility that was so central for Marguerite de Navarre. (There is also evidence of the same imperial themes that Christine de Pizan uses in her representation of Joan of Arc, and Elizabeth's biblical heroines are exactly those used one hundred years earlier to justify Joan's intervention in the political crises of France.[34]) Elizabeth possesses the princely virtues, but only by the grace of God. She is especially capable of courage, but as a prince (a sexless body politic) and not a female (a body natural): 'though I be a woman,' she says, 'yet I have as good a courage answerable to my place as ever my father had.'[35] In the famous Armada Speech, Elizabeth reminds the troops that 'I have the body of a weak and feeble woman, but I have the heart and stomach of a king and a king of England too.'[36]

---

[32] In one speech, Elizabeth says that 'To be a king and wear a crown is a thing more glorious to them that see it than it is pleasant to them that bear it. For myself, I was never so much enticed with the glorious name of a king or royal authority of a queen as delighted that God had made me His instrument to maintain His truth and glory, and to defend this kingdom from dishonor, damage, tyranny, and oppression. But should I ascribe anything of this to myself, or my sexly weakness, I were not worthy to live, and of all, most unworthy of the mercies I have had from God. But to God only and wholly, all is to be given and ascribed'; Speech 23, version 2, *Elizabeth I: Collected Works*, p. 342.

[33] 'Third prayer' from 'The Spanish Versicles and Prayers'; Prayer 22, *Elizabeth I: Collected Works*, p. 157.

[34] For the importance of imperial imagery in the reign of Elizabeth I, see Frances A. Yates, *Astraea: The Imperial Theme in the Sixteenth Century* (London: Routledge and Kegan Paul, 1975).

[35] 'Elizabeth to a joint delegation of Lords and Commons', 5 November 1566; Speech 9, version 2, *Elizabeth I: Collected Works*, p. 97.

[36] 'Elizabeth's Armada speech to the troops at Tilbury', 9 August 1588; Speech 19, *Elizabeth I: Collected Works*, p. 326.

In short, Elizabeth is capable of shouldering the heavy weight of office, but only because God lightens the load.[37] In other prayers, she suggests that it is not really she who governs or administers the kingdom, but God himself: 'Expressly, in truth, since I am feminine and feeble, and only Thou art worthy to sit in governance of this kingdom and this administration . . . it befits me to give an accounting in the presence of Christ.'[38] She is, as she often says, merely an instrument of God.[39]

Elizabeth thus justifies her supreme authority, and her right to be obeyed, without challenging the idea of female weakness. We might therefore conclude that she agrees with the common perception (promoted by Knox and others) of women as naturally inferior, while affirming that she represents one of those exceptional women rulers ordained by God, women such as Deborah and Judith. Elizabeth does not seem to endorse the view that women themselves are capable of prudential government; femaleness, on her view, is synonymous with weakness.

III

Nevertheless, despite Elizabeth's explicit statements about the inferiority of her sex, it is possible to find a positive conception of female rule, and an implicit rejection of the Aristotelian claim that women lack prudence, both in Elizabeth's portraits and in her writings.

In the portraits that were produced during her reign, Elizabeth consciously worked to undermine the tradition that women lacked prudence. Well aware of the need for monarchs to be perceived as regal, Elizabeth exercised a careful control over the production of her portraits, as they constituted the most direct way in which her image was disseminated to the public. She had herself painted holding the sword of justice, the palm of peace, the rainbow, and quite often – and more perplexingly – holding a large and rather domestic-looking sieve.[40] Frances Yates interprets this image as a symbol of her virginity, but a closer look at other manuscripts in which a woman is represented as carrying a sieve shows that it is in fact

---

[37] 'It was Thy kindness, Thine alone, and my enthroned office – a heavy weight, surely, for a woman's shoulder, but light with Thee making it light': 'The Queen's prayer' from 'The Latin Prayers'; Prayer 23, *Elizabeth I: Collected Works*, p. 158.

[38] From 'The Latin Prayers'; Prayer 24, *Elizabeth I: Collected Works*, p. 159.

[39] Prayer 30, p. 313; Speech 23, version 2, p. 34, *Elizabeth I: Collected Works*.

[40] See Roy Strong, *Gloriana: The Portraits of Queen Elizabeth I* (New York: Thames and Hudson, 1987); Roy Strong, *Portraits of Elizabeth I* (Oxford: Clarendon Press, 1963).

a symbol of prudence or discernment.[41] There can be no doubt that the sieve is intended to represent Elizabeth's prudent capacity to distinguish the good from the bad. In case the point is not immediately grasped, some of the sieves in her portraits are inscribed with words to the effect that 'the good remains in the seat while the bad falls to the ground', an obvious reference to the monarch's capacity to sift good from evil in the pursuit of good. Like Louise of Savoy before her, Elizabeth had herself represented as Prudence, the first of the virtues, and the one virtue that Aristotle claims is both essential to a political leader and deficient in women.

In Elizabeth's written pieces there is also a positive conception of prudent female leadership, much like that of Christine de Pizan. We have seen that, in some of her statements on political authority, Elizabeth appeals to Scripture, and to the metaphors of the body politic and the 'king's two bodies', in defence of her leadership as a (sexless) body artificial rather than a body natural. But in this period, there were other figurative political models available for Elizabeth to exploit – among them, the parental and conjugal paradigms of government.[42] In her many speeches and prayers, Elizabeth appeals to a parentalist or conjugal conception of her queenship, in which she highlights the traditional virtues of mothers and wives: their unwarlike nature and love of peace, their care and concern for others, their instinct to provide nourishment and protection for their families, and their supreme loyalty.

First, Elizabeth adopts the traditional metaphor of queens as mothers of their people: 'I will never in that matter [the succession],' she said in 1558, 'conclude anything that shall be prejudicial to the realm, for the weal and safety whereof I, as a good mother of my country, will never shun to spend my life.'[43] And so, she warns, 'reproach me so no more . . . that I have no children: for every one of you, and as many as are English, are my children and kinsfolks, of whom, so long as I am not deprived and God shall preserve me, you cannot charge me, without offense, to be

---

[41] See Yates, *Astraea*; Green, '*Phronesis* Feminised'.

[42] On the conjugal paradigm, see Donald R. Kelley, 'Elizabethan Political Thought', in *The Varieties of British Political Thought, 1500–1800*, ed. J. G. A. Pocock with the assistance of Gordon J. Schochet and Lois G. Schwoerer (Cambridge University Press, 1993), pp. 47–79 (esp. pp. 51–2).

[43] 'Cambridge MS version of first speech', in *Elizabeth I: Collected Works*, p. 58. Elizabeth's sister Mary also said that 'a prince or governor may as naturally love her subjects as the mother doth love the child', and this has been take to contrast with Elizabeth, yet here we see Elizabeth using the same imagery. See Kathi Vosevich, 'The Education of a Prince(ss)', in *Women, Writing and the Reproduction of Culture in Tudor and Stuart Britain*, ed. Mary E. Burke, Jane Donawerth, Linda Dove, and Karen Nelson (Syracuse, NY: Syracuse University Press, 2000), pp. 61–76, esp. p. 66.

destitute'.[44] Elizabeth also uses the maternal metaphor to emphasise her legitimacy as a natural ruler of her country, or a hereditary sovereign rather than a ruler by marriage: 'And so I assure you all that though after my death you may have many stepdames,' she says, 'yet shall you never have any a more mother than I mean to be unto you all.'[45] Similarly, in one prayer, she alludes to Isaiah 49:23 when she asks God to 'give me the grace to be a true nourisher and nurse of Thy people';[46] and in another, she thanks God that he has given her 'the honor of being mother and nurse of Thy dear children'.[47]

Along similar lines, Elizabeth exploits the idea that, as sovereign, she is married to the kingdom (the conjugal paradigm):

And therefore it is that I have made choice of this kind of life, which is most free and agreeable for such human affairs as may tend to His service only. From which, if either the marriages which have been offered me by diverse puissant princes or the danger of attempts made against my life could no whit divert me, it is long since I had any joy in the honor of a husband; and this is that I thought, then that I was a private person. But when the public charge of governing the kingdom came upon me, it seemed unto me an inconsiderate folly to draw upon myself the cares which might proceed of marriage. To conclude, I am already bound unto an husband, which is the kingdom of England, and that may suffice you.[48]

I am married already to the realm of England when I was crowned with this ring . . . I am sworn when I was married to the realm not to alter the laws of it.[49]

In these passages, Elizabeth subtly transforms the traditional metaphor of sovereigns being married to their realms. In many versions of the marriage metaphor, the sovereign symbolically represents the husband, whereas the subjects occupy the subordinate position of the wife.[50] But Elizabeth conceives of herself as a wife loyally serving her kingdom, rather than the other way around. She thus combines the marriage metaphor with an image much closer to the parentalist conception of monarchy.

[44] Speech 3, version 2, *Elizabeth I: Collected Works*, p. 59.
[45] 'Elizabeth's answer to the Commons' petition that she marry', 28 January 1563; Speech 5, *Elizabeth I: Collected Works*, p. 72.
[46] Prayer 13, *Elizabeth I: Collected Works*, p. 149.
[47] *Elizabeth I: Collected Works*, p. 314.
[48] Speech 3, version 2, *Elizabeth I: Collected Works*, p. 59.
[49] 'Elizabeth's conversations with Maitland', September and October 1561; Speech 4, *Elizabeth I: Collected Works*, p. 65.
[50] Saco, 'Gendering Sovereignty', 302. See also Sarah Hanley, 'The Monarchic State: Marital Regime Government and Male Right', in *Politics, Ideology, and the Law in Early Modern Europe*, ed. Adrianna Bakos (Rochester, NY: Rochester University Press, 1994), p. 110.

She demonstrates herself to be committed to a conception of monarchical authority in which the duty of the sovereign is to love and care for the people, one that we saw Christine de Pizan attributing to Charles V.

In these respects, Elizabeth does not adopt an entirely androgynous or sexless conception of princely virtue: she exploits the motherly and wifely virtues of the female sex to affirm her rule. In a recent paper, Cynthia Herrup argues that even before the Elizabethan period, good government required the monarch to possess both masculine and feminine traits: 'Kings male and female were supposed to nurture their subjects, to act as scripture said, as "nursing fathers".'[51] On this view, the key to good governance was about striking the proper balance between masculine and feminine characteristics, not about being exclusively masculine. So it might be argued that Elizabeth was merely appealing to a well-established tradition by highlighting her feminine excellencies. Herrup says that 'Elizabeth I's insistence that courtiers use the language of love to describe the relationship between her and her subjects was not an innovation born of her femaleness, but a continuation of earlier male attempts to rethink loyalties once expressed in feudal terms.'[52]

Nevertheless, while it might have been acceptable for a male monarch to exhibit femininity (in due proportion), it was another matter altogether for a female monarch to suggest that she had prudence – a masculine capacity that women were supposedly lacking. In some speeches and prayers, Elizabeth emphasises that God is responsible for her possessing prudence 'beyond other women'; but on other occasions, she reconceptualises the masculine virtue of prudence as a feminine excellence associated with care or carefulness. 'For although perhaps you may have after me one better learned or wise,' she says in 1567, 'yet I assure you, none more careful over you.'[53] These words become a familiar refrain in Elizabeth's orations. In a 1593 speech, she said, 'This kingdom hath had many noble and victorious princes. I will not compare with any of them in wisdom, fortitude, and other virtues; but (saving the duty of a child that is not to compare with her father) in love, care, sincerity, and justice, I will compare with any prince that ever you had or ever you shall have.'[54]

[51] Cynthia Herrup, 'The King's Two Genders', *Journal of British Studies* 45 (2006), 493–510 (esp. 498).
[52] Ibid., 502.
[53] 'Elizabeth's speech dissolving Parliament', 2 January 1567; Speech 10, version 2, *Elizabeth I: Collected Works*, p. 108.
[54] 'Elizabeth's speech at the closing of Parliament', 10 April 1593; Speech 21, *Elizabeth I: Collected Works*, p. 329.

In the famous Golden Speech of November 1601, Elizabeth again affirmed that 'though you have had and may have many princes more mighty and wise sitting in this seat, yet you never had or shall have any that will be more careful and loving'.[55] Although her natural female body may rob her of some of the masculine princely virtues such as wisdom, Elizabeth suggests, she makes up for this with her loving and caring nature (the stereotypical traits of a mother and wife). In short, Elizabeth suggests that love and care dictate her prudential deliberations on the good of subjects. As a female ruler, Elizabeth is capable of epitomising prudence, and looking out for the interests of others; but she does so not by considering the consequences of her actions from a disinterested point of view, but as a loving caretaker. Her deliberative judgement, she implies, is chiefly directed toward achieving the good of her people, out of love rather than wisdom. In one version of the Golden Speech, Elizabeth says:

I do assure you that there is no prince that loveth his subjects better, or whose love can countervail our love. There is no jewel, be it of never so rich a price, which I set before this jewel – I mean your loves. For I do more esteem it than any treasure or riches, for that we know how to prize. But love and thanks I count unvaluable [invaluable], and though God hath raised me high, yet this I count the glory of my crown: that I have reigned with your loves . . . Of myself I must say this: I never was any greedy, scraping grasper, nor a strait, fast-holding prince, nor yet a waster. My heart was never set on worldly goods, but only for my subjects' good. What you bestow on me, I will not hoard it up, but receive it to bestow on you again. Yea, my own properties I account yours to be expended for your good, and your eyes shall see the bestowing of all for your good.[56]

Then in her final speech to parliament, in December 1601, Elizabeth said, 'This testimony I would have you carry hence for the world to know: that your sovereign is more careful of your conservation than of herself, and will daily crave of God that they that wish you best may never wish in vain.'[57]

Following a long tradition of representing queens as peace-loving mediators, Elizabeth also exploits the typical feminine virtue of peacefulness:

It may be thought simplicity in me that all this time of my reign [I] have not sought to advance my territories and enlarge my dominions, for both opportunity

[55] 'Elizabeth's Golden Speech', 30 November 1601; Speech 23, version 1, *Elizabeth I: Collected Works*, p. 340.
[56] Ibid., pp. 337–8.
[57] 'Elizabeth's final speech before Parliament', 19 December 1601; Speech 24, version 1, *Elizabeth I: Collected Works*, p. 351.

hath served me to do it, and my strength was able to have done it. I acknowledge my womanhood and weakness in that respect, but it hath not been fear to obtain or doubt how to keep the things so obtained that hath withholden me from these attempts; only, my mind was never to invade my neighbors, nor to usurp upon any, only contented to reign over my own and to rule as a just prince.[58]

'From the beginning of my reign,' she said in an earlier speech at Oxford, 'my greatest and special concern, care, and watchfulness has been that the realm be kept free as much from external enemies as from internal tumults, that it, long flourishing for many ages, might not be enfeebled under my hand.'[59]

In such statements on her prudential management of the realm, Elizabeth departs from John Knox's view that 'in the nature of all women lurketh suche vices as in good governors are not tolerable'. Elizabeth presents prudence as a trait that women can possess: her motherly and wifely care and concern for her subjects has led to political actions that have ensured peace, security, and prosperity for England. Whether Elizabeth intended to do so or not, she promoted the idea that the female sex as a whole is capable of acting with prudence and therefore capable of good government.

Contrary to modern feminist opinion, it seems that Elizabeth does in fact challenge certain 'male notions' about how the world ought to be governed. Although she explicitly supports customary views about the prince's supreme authority being ordained by God, and attributes her success to God's grace rather than to any natural merit of her own, this should not be taken as evidence that she supports an entirely androgynous or sexless conception of princely rule. In some writings, Elizabeth appeals to the parentalist and conjugal paradigms of monarchical authority: she conceives of herself as a 'mother' and a 'wife' to her subjects. By drawing on these paradigms, Elizabeth formulates a feminised conception of the virtuous ruler, one that emphasises a woman's capacity for prudence in contradistinction to the Aristotelian tradition that makes prudence a purely masculine trait. A female ruler, Elizabeth suggests, may not excel in the typical princely virtues of courage, temperance, magnanimity, and wisdom; or, if she does exhibit these virtues, then it is entirely due to the grace of God, and not to her own merit. But, somewhat paradoxically,

---

[58] 'Elizabeth's speech at the closing of Parliament', 10 April 1593; Speech 21, *Elizabeth I: Collected Works*, p. 329.
[59] 'Elizabeth's Latin speech to Oxford', 28 September 1592; Speech 20, *Elizabeth I: Collected Works*, p. 327.

Elizabeth suggests that a woman ruler compensates for her natural deficiencies with other virtues, such as her compassion, clemency, peacefulness, care, and love of her subjects. These traits – the stereotypical characteristics of mothers and wives – can assist a monarch in deciding what is good or best for the kingdom; they can, in other words, assist her in the prudential management of the realm. Women have certain virtues, she suggests, that make them worthy governors and caretakers of the people – as women, and *not* as 'honorary men' or as a sexless body politic.

We conclude this chapter with an observation about Elizabeth's place in the history of women's political thought, as a 'bridge' between the post-medieval and early modern women. Though there is no explicit evidence that Elizabeth had read the works of Christine de Pizan, it is entirely possible that Elizabeth's conception of monarchical authority was influenced by Christine. In Christine's works, prudence is also closely connected with care and concern,[60] and in her feminist writings she exploits the fact that the Bible recognises the prudence of the good housewife. In 1521, the same year as the English version of her *Book of the City of Ladies* appeared, an English translation of Christine's *Book of the Body Politic* was also printed.[61] In this work, Christine develops John of Salisbury's metaphor of the polity as a body ruled by the king, and emphasises the role of the prince as a good shepherd of his people. There is also evidence that Elizabeth had access to copies of Christine's manuscripts and possessed tapestries illustrating her works. In the Old Royal Library there was a copy of Christine's *Livre de la Cité des Dames*, believed to have belonged to Edward IV's father, Richard the third Duke of York.[62] Edward IV also possessed a manuscript of Christine's *L'Epistre d'Othea*, of which there were two copies in the royal collection.[63] And Christine's *Fais d'armes et chevallerie* was included in a collection presented to Henry VI and his wife, Margaret of Anjou, as a wedding gift. This text was subsequently translated into English and printed by Caxton

[60] On this topic, see Green, 'On Translating Christine as a Philosopher', esp. p. 137.
[61] Christine de Pizan, *The boke of the body of Polycye* (London: John Skot, 1521).
[62] Now British Library, London, MS Royal 19 A xix. See George F. Warner and Julius P. Gilson (eds.), *British Museum, Catalogue of Western Manuscripts in the Old Royal and King's Collection*, 4 vols. (London: British Museum, 1921), vol. 11, pp. 322–3.
[63] Now British Library, London, MS Royal 14 E ii and MS Royal 17 E iv. See Janet Backhouse, 'Founders of the Royal Library: Edward IV and Henry VII as Collectors of Illuminated Manuscripts', in *England in the Fifteenth Century: Proceedings of the 1986 Harlaxton Symposium*, ed. Daniel Williams (Woodbridge: The Boydell Press, 1987), pp. 39 and 40.

at the behest of Elizabeth's grandfather, Henry VII.[64] These texts would have been considered appropriate reading material for a princess who, unlike her sister Mary, was educated to possess all the intellectual virtues and eloquence of a prince.[65]

In addition, Susan Groag Bell discusses at length the implications of a 1547 reference to a set of tapestries depicting Christine's *City of Ladies*, in the possession of fourteen-year-old Elizabeth.[66] These tapestries included imagery associated with Christine's defence of women's prudence and capacity to rule, and could be found throughout the courts of Renaissance princesses who exercised a governing function. (We have already noted that Margaret of Austria and Anne of Brittany owned copies of these same tapestries.) Again, we might speculate about the influence that these tapestries had on Elizabeth's thinking about female rule.

In the century following Elizabeth's reign, the Renaissance concern for female political virtue occupied only a small part of women's political writings. Nevertheless, in 1704, Mary Astell was compelled to defend both Queen Elizabeth and Queen Anne's natural capacity for discernment. In his *Essays upon Peace at Home and War Abroad* (1704), Charles Davenant praises Elizabeth I for surmounting all the difficulties of her reign with 'a Mind above her Sex'.[67] In response to Davenant, Mary Astell laments that whenever a woman does a great or good action, the male historians remark that she 'acted above her sex'.[68] A woman is not permitted to do a heroic or virtuous action without first unsexing herself and shedding her womanly inferiority. In defence of Anne, Astell points out that

If therefore these Men would leave Her Majesty to Her own Superior Judgement, and the integrity of Her *own English Heart*, would they let Her exert Her Self, according to Her own Good Sense, Right Principles, and Generous

---

[64] See Michel-André Bossy, 'Arms and the Bride: Christine de Pizan's Military Treatise as a Wedding Gift for Margaret of Anjou', in Desmond (ed.), *Christine de Pizan and the Categories of Difference*, pp. 236–56; Christine de Pizan, *The Book of Deeds of Arms and of Chivalry*.

[65] Vosevich, 'The Education of a Prince(ss)'.

[66] Susan Groag Bell, 'A New Approach to the Influence of Christine de Pizan: The Lost Tapestries of *The City of Ladies*', in Ribemont (ed.), *Sur le Chemin de longue étude*, pp. 7–12; *The Lost Tapestries of the City of Ladies*; and 'A Lost Tapestry: Margaret of Austria's Cité des Dames', in Dulac and Ribemont (eds.), *Une Femme de lettres au Moyen Age*, pp. 449–67.

[67] Charles Davenant, *Essays upon Peace at Home, and War Abroad. In Two Parts*, second edition (London: James Knapton, 1704), p. 180.

[68] In *Moderation truly Stated*, Astell says that 'if Women do any thing well, nay should a hundred thousand Women do the Greatest and most Glorious Actions, presently it must be *with a Mind* (for sooth) *above their Sex!*'. See Mary Astell, prefatory discourse to *Moderation truly Stated: Or, A Review of a Late Pamphlet, Entitul'd. Moderation a Vertue. With a Prefatory Discourse to Dr. D'Aveanant, concerning His late Essays on Peace and War* (London: R. Wilkin, 1704), pp. lii–liii.

Inclinations, with that undaunted Courage and Royal Magnanimity, that has never been wanting to those Ladies that have adorn'd the English Throne, I make no question but we shall be a most Happy People.[69]

Left to her own judgement, Anne could prove to them, once and for all, that 'there's nothing either Wise, or Good, or Great that is above Her Sex'.[70] We have seen that the same sentiment – albeit in slightly less explicit language – marks some of the speeches of Elizabeth herself, speeches that Mary Astell may have been familiar with. Here, then, we can discern a positive view of female political authority that may have descended from Christine de Pizan to Elizabeth I to Mary Astell.

There is, of course, another respect in which Elizabeth I exerted an influence on women political thinkers: as a historical precedent for an unmarried queen regnant. For the sixteenth-century political thinker Jean Bodin, the challenge that a reigning queen poses to the structure of patriarchal marriage constitutes a good part of his opposition to accepting a female monarch. In a tirade against the unnaturalness of 'gynecocratie', he argues that if a woman rules in her own right without marrying, the majesty of the monarchy will be in danger. A decent, 'manly' active populace will be impatient when subject to a woman, while a populace that is so cowardly as to suffer being ruled in public by a female will soon be ruled by women in their own homes.[71] If the queen marries, however, all the standard assumptions of patriarchal marriage will be called into question. For thinkers such as Bodin, a woman who rules implicitly threatens every man's dignity. If Bodin was right, then Elizabeth I's authoritative example of female virtue might have inspired later women to write against their subordination in the home. In the previous chapters we saw that for Marguerite de Navarre and Christine de Pizan marriage and monarchy were both divinely ordained institutions in which the needs of the weak were to be defended by the power of the strong. In the seventeenth century, we start to see greater complexity in the parallels that writers draw between marriage and monarchy, amidst growing criticism of both institutions.

[69] Ibid., pp. liv–lv.   [70] Ibid.   [71] Bodin, *Les Six Livres de la République*, p. 1002.

CHAPTER 5

From the Reformation to Marie le Jars de Gournay

By the middle of the sixteenth century, two of the features of Christine de Pizan's political thought, which had been innovative and distinctive when she wrote, had become staples of Protestantism. The first of these was the defence of marriage, which in Christine's writing was intimately connected with the defence of women. The second was the idea that temporal authority comes directly from God and is not mediated by the Pope; elements of which doctrine, we argued, Christine had absorbed from Dante. This latter doctrine was subsequently reflected in the view, characteristic of Elizabeth I and her heir James I, that monarchs are accountable to God alone, deriving their authority, and the duty to care for their subjects, directly from this source. It was expressed also by Marguerite de Navarre's daughter, Jeanne d'Albret (1528–72), who introduced the reformed religion into Navarre, and who, like Elizabeth, was consequently threatened with invasion by Philip II of Spain.

During the next hundred years, a new focus emerged in women's political writing. Rather than defending marriage against the attacks of clerical misogynists, the most outspoken and radical female writers increasingly attack marriage as an institution that makes women slaves who are tyrannised over by men. This pre-Enlightenment critique of women's subjection in marriage arose first in the writings of Venetian women, and was taken up later in France. We examine it in the second part of this chapter. In the third section, we outline the political ideas of Marie le Jars de Gournay (1565–1645), a French contemporary of the Italian writers. However, first we briefly outline the political legacy of Marguerite de Navarre's sympathy for reform, and in particular, sketch its consequences for the political outlook and activities of her daughter, Jeanne d'Albret.

I

As Nancy Roelker demonstrates, many of the women who spearheaded the political movement to establish a reformed church in France, and in certain associated territories, were connected to Marguerite de Navarre, or were descendants of women connected with her.[1] At the court of Ferrara, Marguerite de Navarre's sister-in-law, the second daughter of Anne of Brittany, Renée of France, Duchess of Ferrara (1510–74), promoted and protected reformist writers and preachers. Following her husband's death, Renée returned to France and resided at Montargis, whence she exchanged letters with Calvin. Her position was somewhat ambiguous, however, since her daughter was married to the Duke of Guise, who was a leader of the Catholic faction at the French court.

After Marguerite's death, Jeanne d'Albret was to become a far more dramatic defender of the Protestant cause than either her mother or Renée. When young, Jeanne publicly adopted the same equivocal attitude to reform that her mother had done, but in a letter, apparently written by her shortly after her father's death, and five years before 1560 when she publicly confessed her adherence to Protestantism, she asserts that she followed this course of action only out of consideration for her father's feelings, mixed with fear of his wrath. For, when she was young, he had violently insisted that she and her mother refrain from meddling in matters of doctrine.[2] In this missive she partly attributes her resolve to equivocate no more over her faith, following the example and urging of her cousin Renée, thus identifying herself as belonging to a group of women who owed their initiation into Protestantism to the early circle around Marguerite. However, this feature of the letter is one that should perhaps cast doubt on its authenticity, for in a letter written by Renée to Calvin nine years later, Renée represents herself as a follower, rather than an instigator of reform, and says she wishes to follow Jeanne's example, though she disagrees with the tendency of the reformers to malign the

---

[1] Nancy Lyman Roelker, 'The Appeal of Calvinism to French Noblewomen in the Sixteenth Century', *Journal of Interdisciplinary History* 2 (1972), 391–418; 'The Role of Noblewomen in the French Reformation', *Archive for Reformation History* 63 (1972), 168–95. David Bryson reports that Imbart de la Tour attributes the move towards Protestantism in Guyenne to the wives and other female members of the nobility: *Queen Jeanne and the Promised Land* (Leiden: Brill, 1999), p. 131.

[2] See Roelker, *Queen of Navarre*, p. 127; and Bryson, *Queen Jeanne*, pp. 77–84 and 317–18. There is some question as to the authenticity of this letter, and we are not entirely satisfied by Bryson's case for accepting its veracity. Nevertheless, even if it is not genuine it shows that this is the way in which near-contemporaries understood Jeanne's situation.

reputations of members of the Catholic party, to whom she was related by marriage.[3]

While possibly not genuine, the letter in which Jeanne d'Albret discusses her turn to Protestantism is interesting in so far as it illustrates the way in which the claim by Protestant women to worship independently – that is, their claim to spiritual freedom and liberty of conscience – posed, and was seen to pose, a potential threat to paternal and husbandly authority. Both Marguerite and her daughter Jeanne accepted the legitimate authority of their husbands, as well as that of their rulers, and this forced them to adopt complex and equivocal strategies when their own firmly held beliefs were opposed to the wills of their recognised superiors. Marguerite is represented in the letter as submitting to her husband's demands. However, it contains an implicit critique of Marguerite and justification of Jeanne's later behaviour, for, unlike her mother and her childish self, who are represented as cowed into acquiescence with a religious practice with which they did not concur, Jeanne would later openly oppose her husband in the defence of reform.

Neither Jeanne nor Marguerite clearly articulates any principled right to resistance, nor any notion of the limits of legitimate parental or monarchical authority. But the conflicts in which they were embroiled are illustrative of the tensions that led to the articulation of such principles. While still a child, Jeanne was forced into her first, subsequently annulled, marriage by her mother, who acted in obedience to her brother the king's wishes against her own.[4] With regard to Jeanne's second marriage to Antoine de Bourbon, Marguerite was forced to acquiesce in the command of her nephew, Henri II, though this time the marriage concurred with Jeanne's desires.[5] And while Jeanne ultimately broke with her husband, and defied him by continuing openly to practise the reformed religion against his wishes, she suggested by way of excuse that he had been tempted to 'give up certainty for lack of certainty' by the false promises of Cardinal Charles de Lorraine.[6] Despite having defied her husband in this case, Jeanne did not articulate any clear right of rebellion against higher authority. Although she increasingly adopted an independent political stance and joined her brother-in-law, Condé, in his attempt to

---

[3] Ibid., p. 228.
[4] Carla Freccero, 'Marguerite de Navarre and the Politics of Maternal Sovereignty', in *Women and Sovereignty*, ed. Louise Olga Fradenburg (Edinburgh University Press, 1992), pp. 132–49; Roelker, *Queen of Navarre*, pp. 41–66.
[5] Roelker, *Queen of Navarre*, pp. 71–5.
[6] Jeanne d'Albret, *Mémoires et Poésies*, ed. Le Baron de Ruble (Geneva: Slatkine Reprints, 1970), p. 5.

conquer Guyenne for the reformers, she continued to represent herself as loyal to Catherine de Medici and Charles IX, whom she painted as forced and even tricked by the Guises into their opposition to the reformers.[7]

Nevertheless, in the perceived conflict between duty to God and duty to temporal superiors, it would not always be the earthly authorities that would prevail. In her memoir, written from La Rochelle in 1568, after she had decided that the only way to protect reform was by force of arms, Jeanne explains how, just before his death in 1562, her husband had sent his secretary, Jean Lescrivain (called 'Boulogne'), to Béarn, to suppress the reformed religion against her wishes:

When I discovered this, I used the natural power which God had given me over my subjects, which I had ceded to a husband for the sake of the obedience that God commands we show them: but when I saw that he strayed from the glory of my God and his pure service, I had the said Boulogne put in prison.[8]

In this instance Jeanne exploits the divine right of monarchs to invest herself with an authority sufficient to oppose her husband, despite the general religious injunction to wifely obedience.

Showing herself aware of just war theory, Jeanne insists that in the years that separated the death of her husband and her flight to La Rochelle to join the Protestant rebellion, she did everything possible to avert war, and she implies that Queen Catherine de Medici's desire to tolerate the reformed religion had been treacherously undermined by the Cardinal of Lorraine and others of the Catholic Guise faction, whose real intention was the destruction of France.[9] Jeanne is not a rebel:

But are not the true rebels those who violate the King's proclamations, and those who wish to overturn his edicts, massacring his people, communicating with and being paid by foreigners, and who, in order to be able to more freely carry out their evil, wish to exterminate the princes of the blood and faithful officers of the crown?[10]

---

[7] For a detailed account of this campaign, see Bryson, *Queen Jeanne*.

[8] D'Albret, *Mémoires et Poésies*, pp. 29–30.

[9] Bryson notes that this was the way most Protestant nobles presented the case. His suggestion that the strategy was hypocritical seems to be unfair to Jeanne, who clearly believed that her opponents were the hypocrites. See Bryson, *Queen Jeanne*, p. 131. Catherine does not seem to have been able to maintain a coherent policy. It has been beyond our scope to consider her as a thinker who may have had a clear political agenda. For discussions of her reputation, see Nicola M. Sutherland, 'Catherine de' Medici: The Legend of the Wicked Italian Queen', *Sixteenth Century Journal* 9 (1978), 45–56; Sheila ffolliott, 'Exemplarity and Gender: Three Lives of Queen Catherine de' Medici', in Mayer and Woolf (eds.), *The Rhetorics of Life Writing*, pp. 321–40.

[10] D'Albret, *Mémoires et Poésies*, p. 53.

Jeanne refers here to the edict of 17 January 1562 which followed the Colloque de Poissy held in September of the previous year, and which allowed in principle freedom of conscience and a restricted freedom of worship for Protestants in France.[11] Despite the continuing persecution of Protestants after this edict, and what she represents as the skulduggery of the Guise faction, Jeanne insists that she continued for a long time to cry out 'peace! peace!' in letters addressed to all involved, but her intelligent proposals towards this end were ignored.[12] In a letter to Elizabeth I of England, sent at the same period, she succinctly puts her case, insisting that neither she nor her son are 'guilty of divine or human lèse-majesté' but are faithful to God and king. However, others have forced the king to break his own oaths and to perjure himself.[13]

Jeanne represents her decision to go to join up with the army, led by her brother-in-law Condé, who was also forced to take up arms in self-defence, as prompted 'by the feeling of my conscience taught by the word of God'.[14] She recalls that some 'worldly wise people' advised her to prevaricate and 'swim between conscience and the world, supporting the cause, but nevertheless retaining enough credit with the adversaries'.[15] But echoing her mother, she dubs these prudent worldly people foolish for 'the wisdom of the world is deemed folly before God'.[16] Ultimately, she implies, she will have to justify her actions before God, whose edicts are eternal, in contrast to the transient edicts of temporal rulers.

The military attempt to secure Guyenne for the Protestant cause, which Jeanne had backed, did not succeed. Nevertheless, after the Edict of Pacification of 1570, Jeanne negotiated the marriage of her son Henri (the future Henri IV of France) to Marguerite de Valois, and Jeanne had her lands restored to her. In her last years, she drew up orders for the imposition of Protestant government in Navarre and Béarn, which proclaimed her duty to procure the salvation of her subjects:

There is no monarch alive who is not obligated to use his full powers to place his subjects under the rule of Jesus Christ, since the Eternal Father has given Him all power in Heaven and earth and commanded all his creatures to seek Him above all things. How much greater is the obligation of princes whom He has saved from sin and death by his grace and goodness alone to procure the complete establishment and advancement of [Christ's] kingdom.[17]

---

[11] For a recent description, see Bryson, *Queen Jeanne*, pp. 132–9.
[12] D'Albret, *Mémoires et Poésies*, pp. 55–64.   [13] Ibid., pp. 219–22.   [14] Ibid., p. 82.
[15] Ibid., p. 84.   [16] Ibid., p. 85.   [17] Quoted in Roelker, *Queen of Navarre*, p. 430.

Jeanne's edicts show a particular concern with morality and the married state. She provides wives with legal redress against delinquent husbands, and attempts to protect widows, orphans, and the poor.[18] In asserting her duty to impose 'the complete establishment and advancement of [Christ's] kingdom' on her people, she unwittingly indicates a tension that soon rose in all Protestant theocracies. She accepts the authority of her own conscience over that of the Pope. Soon, members of Protestant sects would be insisting on the authority of their consciences against Protestant rulers. This would not be the case in Béarn, which was absorbed into France after Henri IV's succession to the French crown. But, as we will see in the next chapter, English sectarian women would soon be moving in the direction of arguing for definite limits to the authority of both husbands and rulers over individual conscience.

II

The fundamental ideas of the reformed church – that the word of God is comprehensible to simple souls, and that each individual has a duty to follow their own conscience – imply the possibility of conflict with any power, whether marital or monarchical, that stands in opposition to conscience. Yet few women who followed the Protestant injunction to read the Scripture saw this kind of conflict as justifying an out-and-out critique of marriage or of husbandly authority, no doubt because these are both explicitly endorsed in the Bible. It was rather, so far as we can determine, in Italy, where the reform movement was suppressed, that female texts explicitly attacking marriage and men's dominion over women first appeared.

Venice and the surrounding region continued in the tradition of providing a thorough education for its daughters, while continuing to exclude them from political power. Three women from this period made explicit contributions to the debate over women's role in society: Moderata Fonte (the pseudonym of Modesta dal Pozzo, 1555–92), Lucrezia Marinella (1571–1653), and Arcangela Tarabotti (1604–52). Various reasons might be suggested for the rhetorical bite of Venetian women's discussion of their place in society in the first years of the seventeenth century. Virginia Cox has argued that Venetian women suffered a diminution in their financial freedom in the latter part of the

---

[18] Bryson, *Queen Jeanne*, p. 288.

sixteenth century, associated with a rise in the cost of dowries, and increased levels of forced claustration.[19] This is certainly an issue that motivated Tarabotti, whose attack on male tyranny is focused on the practice of forcing 'excess' daughters, who were quite lacking in religious vocation, to take the veil.[20] The earlier writing of Fonte and Marinella is not, however, dominated by this issue, and while sociological explanations of their writing are worth considering, we are more interested in their overtly declared intentions. Both these women established themselves as writers before they were married, and their works include heroic poems, plays, and, in the case of Marinella, biographies.[21] Here we largely confine ourselves to their texts criticising

---

[19] Virginia Cox, 'The Single Self: Feminist Thought and the Marriage Market in Early Modern Venice', *Renaissance Quarterly* 48 (1995), 528.

[20] Arcangela Tarabotti, *Paternal Tyranny*, trans. Letizia Panizza (Chicago and London: The University of Chicago Press, 2004). Cox reports that 'Tiepolo reflects, if the two thousand or more Venetian noblewomen stored in convents "as though in a public warehouse" were to have insisted on remaining in the world, their action would have plunged the whole of Venetian society into a maelstrom of disorder and scandal': 'The Single Self', p. 540. See also Arcangela Tarabotti, 'Antisatira', in *Contro il lusso donnesco, satira menippea con l'Antisatira di d.A..T. in risposta*, ed. F. Buoninsegni (Siena: Bonetti, 1646); Arcangela Tarabotti, *Lettere familiari e di complimento* (Venice: Guerigli, 1650); *Lettere familiari e di complimento*, ed. Meredith Ray and Lynn Westwater (Turin: Rosenberg and Sellier, 2005); *Le lagrime d'Arcangela Tarabotti per la morte dell'Illustriss. signora Regina Donati* (Venice: Guerigli, 1650); *Che le donne siano della spetie degli huomini. Difesa delle donne di Galerana Barcitotti [pseud.] contro Horatio Plata* (Nuremberg: J. Chercherberger, 1651); 'Women are of the Human Species', in *"Women are not Human"*, ed. and trans. Theresa M. Kenney (New York: Crossroad Publishing, 1998), pp. 89–159; *La semplicità ingannata* (Leiden: Gio. Sambix [Elzevier], 1654); *Il paradiso monacale* (Venice: Gugliemo Oddoni, 1663); 'L' inferno monacale', in *L' 'inferno monacale' di Arcangela Tarabotti*, ed. Francesca Medioli (Turin: Rosenberg & Sellier, 1990); *Che le donne siano della spezie degli uomini: Women Are No Less Rational Than Men*, ed. Letizia Panizza (London: Institute of Romance Studies, 1994).

[21] During her lifetime, Fonte published *La feste. Rappresentazione avanti il Serenissimo Prencipe di Venetia Nicolò Ponte il giorno di S. Stefano* (Venice: Guerra, 1581); *La Passione di Christo descritta in ottava rima da Moderata Fonte* (Venice: Guerra, 1582); *La Resurrezione de Gesù nostro Signore che segue alla Santissima Passione in ottava rima da Moderata Fonte* (Venice: Imberti, 1592); and *Tredici canti del Floridoro di Mad. Moderata Fonte* (Venice: 1581). Marinella was even more prolific, publishing *Amore innamorato ed impazzato*. *Poema di Lucrezia Marinella* (Venice: 1598); *Arcadia felice di Lucrezia Marinella* (Venice: Ciotti, 1605); *De' gesti heroici e della vita meravigliosa della serafica Santa Caterina da Siena, di Lucrezia Marinella. Libri sei* (Venice: B. Barezzi, 1624); *Holocausto d'amore della vergine Santa Giustina* (Venice: Leni, 1648); *L'Enrico overo Bisantio conquistato. Poema heroico* (Venice: 1635); *La colomba sacra. Poema eroico di Lucrezia Marinella* (Venice: Ciotto, 1595); *La nobiltà et eccellenza delle donne co' diffetti et mancamenti de gli huomini* (Venice: Ciotti Senese, 1600; all short references will be to this 1600 version unless otherwise indicated); *La nobiltà et eccellenza delle donne co' diffetti et mancamenti de gli huomini* (Venice: Ciottti Senese, 1601); *La vita di Maria Vergine imperatrice dell'universo* (Venice: B. Barezzi, 1602); *Le vittorie di Francesco il serafico. Li passi gloriosi della diva Chiara* (Padua: Crivellari, 1647); *Rime sacre* (Venice: 1603); *Vita del serafico et glorioso San Francesco. Descritto in ottava rima da Lucrezia Marinella. Ove si spiegano le attioni, le astinenze e i miracoli di esso* (Venice: Bertano, 1597); and *Vita di Santa Giustina in ottava rima* (Florence: 1606).

the contemporary treatment and representation of women, for it is here that we see them applying the political concepts of liberty and tyranny to women's situation.[22]

Moderata Fonte's *The Worth of Women* was not published during her lifetime, but appeared with a dedication by her daughter in 1600, eight years after her death.[23] Its opening suggests that Fonte was motivated to write it by the contradiction between the explicit rhetoric of civic liberty, associated with the republican traditions of Venice, and the restraints imposed on Venetian women's lives. She begins her dialogue with a description of Venice, a sumptuous city whose inhabitants enjoy remarkable freedom: 'Money flows here as nowhere else and ours is a city as free as the sea itself; without needing legislation itself, it legislates for others.'[24] In this city live a group of women, whose conversation will be the subject of her book. These women 'would often steal some time together for a quiet conversation, and on those occasions, safe from any fear of being spied on by men or constrained by their presence, they would speak freely on whatever subject they pleased'.[25]

It is only when they are free from men that they experience liberty, and Fonte makes Lucrezia, the older married woman in the dialogue, exclaim: 'we are only ever really happy when we are alone with other women, and the best thing that can happen to any woman is to be able to live alone, without the company of men'.[26] While Venice's men may live without the imposition of laws, it is clear from Fonte's introduction that women are not among those who live 'senza leggi' (without laws) and that men make laws which unduly constrain women. Near the end of the dialogue Leonora protests:

What on earth do magistrates, law courts, and all this other nonsense have to do with us women? Are not all these official functions exercised by men, against our interests? Do they not make claims on us, whether we are obliged to them or not?

[22] Virginia Cox observes that 'In its basic outlines these two writers' conception of the relations between the sexes is consistent with that of at least the more "political" of their male predecessors. Men's dominance over women is represented as a tyranny that seeks to legitimate itself by spurious claims of male superiority' ('The Single Self', 520).

[23] Moderata Fonte, *Il merito delle donne*, ed. Adriana Chemello (Venice: Eidos, 1988); *Il merito delle donne scritto da Moderata Fonte in due giornate ove chiaramente si scopre quanto siano elle degne e più perfette de gli huomini* (Venice: Imberti, 1600), *The Worth of Women*, ed. and trans. Virginia Cox (Chicago and London: The University of Chicago Press, 1997).

[24] *Worth of Women*, p. 44; *Il merito delle donne*, p. 14.

[25] *Worth of Women*, p. 45; *Il merito delle donne*, p. 14.

[26] *Worth of Women*, p. 47; *Il merito delle donne*, p. 17.

Do they not act in their own interests and against ours? Do they not treat us as though we were aliens? Do they not usurp our property?[27]

The vaunted freedom of the Venetian city clearly does not extend to its women, who are shut away if unmarried, and if married, are dependent for their liberty on husbands who may be jealous, fickle, or even violent.

Lucrezia Marinella is also aware of the constrained lives of Venetian women and in her feminist tract, *The Nobility and Excellence of Women and the Defects and Vices of Men* (1600), she implies that, in comparison to French women of the period, they are unjustly treated. Arguably, this perceived injustice, as much as the recent scurrilous attack on women published by Giuseppe Passi, motivates her audacious 'turning of the tables' on men, whom she describes as the inferior sex.[28] She points to the fact that in France and Flanders women inherit estates, and even duchies, and participate in business.[29] It is noteworthy, in this context, that Fonte dedicated her *Tredici canti del Floridoro* (*Thirty Songs of Floridoro*, 1581) to the Venetian Bianca Capello, who had recently married Francesco de Medici. This epic poem, written in the style of Ariosto's *Orlando Furioso*, purports to recount the heroic origins of the Medici family, whose daughters Catherine and Marie were both queens of France.[30] Stephen Kolsky observes that, in the *Tredici canti*, 'Fonte is making a determined effort to rewrite myth; to valorise female achievement in the context of a universal story.'[31] Her refashioning of heroic myth involves imagining a female knight, Risamante, whose quest to win back the kingdom that is rightfully hers can be read as an allegory of women's quest to regain an imagined noble past. Similarly, Fonte's *Worth of Women* concludes with a

[27] *Worth of Women*, p. 204; *Il merito delle donne*, p. 143.

[28] For a short discussion of Passi's work and its importance in prompting Marinella's response, see Lucrezia Marinella, *The Nobility and Excellence of Women, and the Defects and Vices of Men*, ed. and trans. Anne Dunhill, with an introduction by Letizia Panizza (Chicago and London: Chicago University Press, 1999), pp. 15–18. It is also discussed in Patricia H. Labalme, 'Venetian Women on Women: Three Early Modern Feminists', *Archivo Veneto* 5 (1981), 103–4. A deeper and more illuminating account is provided by Stephen Kolsky, who argues convincingly that the support of the second Venetian Academy was instrumental in the appearance of these works: 'Moderata Fonte, Lucrezia Marinella, Giuseppe Passi: An Early Seventeenth-Century Feminist Controversy', *The Modern Language Review* 96 (2001), 973–89. Cox points out that the passage describing the freedoms of women elsewhere in Europe suggests that Marinella sees women's greater freedom as a realistic aspiration ('The Single Self', 523–4).

[29] Marinella, *Nobility and Excellence of Women*, p. 74; *La nobiltà et eccellenza delle donne* (1601 edition), p. 29.

[30] *Tredici canti del Floridoro di Mad. Moderata Fonte*. This work is available in a modern edition: *Tredici canti del Floridoro*, ed. Valeria Finucci (Bologna: Mucchi, 1995).

[31] Stephen Kolsky, 'Moderata Fonte's *Tredici canti del Floridoro*: Women in a Man's Genre', *Rivista di Studi Italiani* 17 (1999), 171.

poem that imagines a past when love ruled, lovers were true, and the relations between the sexes were not corrupted by avarice and pride.[32]

Another reason for the boldness of these women's ideas is that they do not feel that their learning is exceptional, since they are aware of those who preceded them. In order to do something new, they must go beyond the women of the previous century. In the catalogue of noble women that makes up the fifth chapter of Marinella's tract, and which demonstrates women's participation in the cardinal virtues – wisdom, temperance, fortitude, and prudence – she includes among the stock examples of classical, mythological, and Christian heroines the names of Laura Cereta (who she claims wrote letters to Girolamo Savonarola), Cassandra Fedele (whose lost book on the sciences she seems to have known), as well as Marguerite de Navarre, Vittoria Colonna, Veronica Gambara, and Isotta Nogarola.[33] She also quotes approvingly passages from Fonte's *Tredici canti del Floridoro*, which argue that, with the same education as men, women would be as capable in all areas as men are.[34]

Equal capacity is not enough for Marinella, however, and in her work the superiority of women, which was subtly implied by Marguerite de Navarre, is boldly defended, using all the resources of scholastic logic and Renaissance rhetoric. Marinella exploits to the full the positive implications for women of the Platonic theory of love, discussed in our first chapter, and she refers extensively to Dante, Petrarch, and a host of other Neoplatonic poets to demonstrate that women participate in God's divine beauty.[35] In developing her arguments, she shows her familiarity with Aristotle's theories of causation and generation, as well as a thorough acquaintance with scholastic texts. She shows, more clearly than any of the earlier women we have discussed, a delight in philosophical argumentation, bordering on sophistry, as is evident in the case she makes for women's superiority. She argues that while the efficient cause of all creation is God, he is capable of creating things of greater or lesser nobility according to the nature of the Idea in his mind. Referring to Plato's theory of forms, she then demonstrates that the Idea, or form, of woman is more noble than that of man, by virtue of women's beauty and goodness:

I say that the Idea of women is nobler than that of men. This can be seen by their beauty and goodness, which is known to everybody. There is not a philosopher

---

[32] Fonte, *Worth of Women*, pp. 241–60; *Il merito delle donne*, pp. 173–81.
[33] *Nobility and Excellence of Women*, pp. 85, 87, 88, and 89; *La nobiltà et eccellenza delle donne*, pp. 14–15.
[34] *Nobility and Excellence of Women*, pp. 78–9; *La nobiltà et eccellenza delle donne*, p. 12.
[35] *Nobility and Excellence of Women*, pp. 53–62; *La nobiltà et eccellenza delle donne*, pp. 5–8.

or poet who fails to attribute these qualities to them, rather than to men. I can confirm, furthermore, that the idea of a charming woman adorned with beauty is nobler than that of a less beautiful and pleasing one, because Ideas exist of particular people, as Marsilio Ficino and many holy doctors confirm.[36]

But not only is the efficient cause of women more noble than that of men, so too is the material cause, since man was made of mud, whereas woman was made from man's rib.[37]

Marinella then refers to Fonte's argument in the *Tredici canti del Floridoro*, according to which women are as noble as men because they are members of the same species and hence of the same substance. But Marinella disagrees with Fonte, further developing her case that in fact women's souls are nobler than men's. First, she uses Peter Lombard's *Sentences* 2.32 as her authority for the possibility that some souls may be superior to others. Since the soul is the form of the body, and women's bodies are more delicate, temperate, and beautiful than men's, women's souls must be more perfect. This is because 'the soul . . . is the cause and origin of physical beauty' and 'the corporeal beauty which shines in bodies is a shadow and image of incorporeal beauty'.[38]

Following the logic of the theory of forms and the Platonic theory of love, Marinella further argues that

the beauty of women is the way by which men, who are moderate creatures, are able to raise themselves to the knowledge and contemplation of the divine essence. Everybody will be convinced of these matters one day, and the obstinate oppressors of women who trample on their dignity with greater insolence each day will be overcome.[39]

One can hear echoes in this passage of Ficino's version of the Platonic theory of the stair that leads from corporeal to divine love. But Marinella adds her own twist, saying, 'I would not merely call beauty a staircase. I believe it to be the golden chain referred to by Homer that can always raise minds toward God and can never for any reason be dragged down toward earth.'[40]

---

[36] *Nobility and Excellence of Women*, p. 53; *La nobiltà et eccellenza delle donne*, p. 5.
[37] *Nobility and Excellence of Women*, p. 54; *La nobiltà et eccellenza delle donne*, pp. 5–6. This argument, well known in the medieval period, was also used by Fonte; see Fonte, *Il merito delle donne*, pp. 26–7; *Worth of Women*, p. 60.
[38] *Nobility and Excellence of Women*, pp. 58–9; *La nobiltà et eccellenza delle donne*, p. 7.
[39] *Nobility and Excellence of Women*, p. 62; *La nobiltà et eccellenza delle donne*, p. 8.
[40] *Nobility and Excellence of Women*, p. 66; *La nobiltà et eccellenza delle donne*, p. 10.

The idea that men are raised up by women, while women are debased through intercourse with men, is also found in Fonte's dialogue, and provides ammunition for those speakers who conclude that women are best off when they avoid male company. Leonora, for example, argues that since men boast of their affairs with women, while women are ashamed of their affairs with men, one should conclude that women are noble and dignified whereas men are not. It is because there is a gulf between the perfection of women and the imperfection of men that 'it *is* a very shameful thing when we, who are so far superior to them, stoop so far as to have anything to do with these inferior creatures'.[41] Leonora, who has inherited the fine property where these discussants meet, voices some of the sharpest rejections of marriage, saying, 'I'd rather drown than submit again to a man! I've just escaped from servitude and suffering and you're asking me to go back again of my own free will and get tangled up in all that again? God preserve me.'[42]

Corinna also exclaims that she would rather die than submit to a great rough man who would want to rule her life.[43] Her situation is represented as the happiest possible, since she is free to study and achieve immortal fame. Marriage, she argues, at least as organised in Venice, is of no benefit to women:

You've got it all wrong . . . On the contrary, the woman when she marries has to take on the expense of children and other worries; she's more in need of acquiring money than giving it away. Because if she were alone, without a husband, she could live like a queen on her dowry (more or less so, of course, according to her social position). But when she takes a husband, especially if he's poor, as is often the case, what exactly does she gain from it, except that instead of being her own mistress and the mistress of her own money, she becomes a slave, and loses her liberty and, along with her liberty, her control over her own property, surrendering all she has to the man whom she has bought.[44]

The slavery of Venetian women in marriage stands in stark contrast to the liberty of Venetian men.

Yet while the unmarried Corinna and the young virgin Leonora are represented as happy in choosing the best life, one that does not involve

---

[41] Fonte, *Worth of Women*, p. 91; *Il merito delle donne*, p. 54.
[42] *Worth of Women*, p. 53; *Il merito delle donne*, p. 21.
[43] *Worth of Women*, p. 48; *Il merito delle donne*, p. 18.
[44] *Worth of Women*, pp. 113–14; *Il merito delle donne*, p. 69. Cox translates 'colui che ella ha comprato' to 'man who has bought her'. We translate it as 'the man whom she has bought'. This makes more sense, as we are talking about the irony of the fact that a woman is made to pay money to become a 'slave' to her husband.

marriage, the dialogue form allows other views to be aired, and marriage is represented as good for men. Adriana, who is their elected queen for the period spanning the discussion, asserts that 'a man without a woman is like a fly without a head'.[45] She is unconvinced by the arguments that her daughter Virginia should not marry, but promises to attempt to find a husband who is not too proud, whose nobility encompasses humility, and who may be brought around by reason.[46]

Neither Fonte nor Marinella voices clear prescriptions as to how society ought to be organised in order to deliver justice for women. Both assert that women's rights have been usurped by men. Leonora asserts that women ought to speak up about this:

If men usurp our rights, should we not complain and declare that they have wronged us? For if we are their inferiors in status, but not in worth, this is an abuse that has been introduced into the world and that men have then, over time, gradually translated into law and custom; and it has become so entrenched that they claim (and actually believe) that the status they have gained through their bullying is theirs by right.[47]

Leonora's prescription for improving the world, which is to follow the example of the Amazons, seems unrealistic, though it is interesting to see that the myth of the Amazons functions for Fonte, as it did for Christine, as offering the prospect of a different social organisation:

I'd like to see us women arming ourselves like those Amazons of old and going into battle against these men. At any rate, it's generally believed that there are more women than men in the world, so our greater numbers would compensate for the disadvantage of our physical weakness, which results from our lack of military training.[48]

Adriana the queen demurs, citing her love of peace, and the dialogue turns to a joking discussion of the devices that the women should wear into battle, indicating Fonte's lack of seriousness in advancing this course of action.

Marinella argues that it is men's brute strength that has kept women in subjection, and she too looks forward to a time when women will do something about their situation: 'But if women, as I hope, wake themselves from the long sleep that oppresses them, their ungrateful and proud

---

[45] *Worth of Women*, p. 116; *Il merito delle donne*, p. 71.
[46] *Worth of Women*, pp. 238–40; *Il merito delle donne*, pp. 170–1.
[47] *Worth of Women*, p. 61; *Il merito delle donne*, p. 27.
[48] *Worth of Women*, p. 230; *Il merito delle donne*, p. 163.

oppressors will be humbled and tamed.'[49] She too imagines women taking up arms, not against men, but rather with them:

Would to God that in our times it were permitted for women to be skilled at arms and letters! What marvellous feats we should see, the like of which were never heard, in maintaining and expanding kingdoms.[50]

However, Marinella does not outline any concrete proposals for the amelioration of women's social position. After completing this text, she returned to writing biographies, some of them dealing with the virtuous women she mentions in her defence of women, possibly demonstrating that she hoped that by continuing to bring the lives of illustrious women to the world's attention, she would contribute to the process of awakening women. And, while it is difficult to determine the extent of the influence of these texts, we will see that many of the themes developed by these Venetian women recur in works written in France and England later in the seventeenth century.

Arcangela Tarabotti, by contrast, had one very concrete proposal for improving the social situation of Venetian women. She wrote with the aim of combating the practice of the involuntary enclosure of young women in convents, a fate that she herself had suffered. Grounding her invective in the doctrine that God has endowed both men and women with intellect, memory, and will, so that they may 'shun avoidable evil and pursue the good of their own choice by their own voluntary inclination', Tarabotti condemns forced enclosure because it prevents women from developing themselves as free moral agents.[51] Like Moderata Fonte, to whom she refers, she begins her work by contrasting the reputation of Venice, a city famed for its liberty, with its treatment of women. For there, more than elsewhere, the abuse of forcing young girls to take the veil is rampant.[52] Like Lucrezia Marinella, whom she also mentions, she contrasts the greed, duplicity, and injustice of men with the loyalty, fortitude, and compassion of women. She compares the tyranny of Venetian men with the patience and kindness of Christ, who met many women and 'was never scandalized to see them on the street', but freely gave them salvation when it was requested.[53] Assuming, as she does, that the exercise of free will requires freedom from external constraint, Tarabotti underscores the political potential of the metaphysical doctrine of

---

[49] Marinella, *Nobility and Excellence of Women*, pp. 131–2; *La nobiltà et eccellenza delle donne*, p. 46.
[50] *Nobility and Excellence of Women*, p. 80; *La nobiltà et eccellenza delle donne*, p. 12.
[51] Tarabotti, *Paternal Tyranny*, p. 44.   [52] Ibid., p. 37.   [53] Ibid., pp. 131–2.

free will. Although her aim is not directly to defend women's right to
political power, she argues that were women educated they would out-
strip men as lawyers and administer greater justice.[54] She goes on to
mention a tradition according to which women once attended the
meetings of the Senate in Athens, a tradition mentioned later in the
century by Gabrielle Suchon. As we will see, Suchon develops the connection between the exercise of free will and the need for freedom from
external constraint even more explicitly than Tarabotti. Like her predecessor, Suchon was a nun who drew on orthodox Christian doctrine to
deplore women's lack of education, liberty, and authority, and she used
arguments which are sufficiently similar to suggest some influence.[55]

III

Although no one at the time appears to have explicitly drawn this conclusion, women's growing critique of marital authority subtly undermined the traditional parentalist and marital metaphors that were so
important for legitimising monarchy in the sixteenth century.[56] By itself,
the parental metaphor is insufficient to justify absolutism, for a parent's
power is limited to that required for the nurture of offspring, and,
arguably, is limited once children come of age.[57] The marital metaphor is
more pertinent, so long as the absolute authority of the husband over his
wife is accepted. But once the justice of a husband's absolute authority
over his wife is called into question, so too is the justice of a king's
absolute authority over his realm.

   We have seen that Christine de Pizan and Elizabeth I tended to conceive of the relationship between sovereign and subject as parental. The
monarch has a duty to care for his or her subjects, and while rebellion is
not endorsed, when caused by an unjust monarch it takes on an aspect of

---

[54] Ibid., p. 101.
[55] In an unpublished paper, 'Arcangela Tarabotti's attempts to publish her *Tirannia Paterna* through
   her "illustrious" networks', delivered at the First NEER International Conference in Perth, July
   2007, Julie Robarts discusses Tarabotti's French connections. However, so far we have not found
   definite proof that Suchon had read Tarabotti.
[56] Elaine Viennot justly comments that, given the interconnections between the *querelle* and
   developments that lead to the modern state, scholars of French history are strangely silent concerning the way in which the *querelle des femmes* flourished during the period of the development
   of the modern state. See Marguerite de Valois, *Mémoires et autres écrits, 1574–1614*, ed. Elaine
   Viennot, 2 vols. (Paris: Champion, 1999), vol. 1, p. 254.
[57] John Locke makes these arguments explicit in his *Two Treatises of Government* (1689). For a
   modern edition, see *Two Treatises of Government*, ed. Peter Laslett (Cambridge University Press,
   1988).

just punishment for a duty to God not fulfilled. The tyrant is a monster, an unnatural parent, who cares nothing for the good of the people with which he or she has been entrusted by God. Jean Bodin, by contrast, like many other authorities, thinks of the analogy between family and state as marital. As well as opposing women's rule, Bodin was the first political thinker to represent sovereignty explicitly as indivisible, and he was thus instrumental in the development of absolutism. Because he likened the husband's rule of his wife to the sovereign's power over the people, his opposition to gynocracy, mentioned at the end of Chapter 4, flows logically from his claim that sovereignty is indivisible. A woman could not be sovereign and married. He worried that, if unmarried, a queen would undermine the marital authority of men, by making an exception to the general principle that men rule.[58] The contrasting implications of the image of the caring and shared power of parents, as against the indivisible and absolute power of a sovereign/husband, helps to explain how female monarchists could easily expect the institution to adapt to allow for a female sovereign. On the parental model, the difference between male and female is no more than the difference between the mother and the father of a family.[59] By contrast, if the king is the husband of the state, and his authority is conceived as analogous to that of a husband, a female 'husband' appears monstrous and a perversion of the natural order of man and wife.

By the end of the seventeenth century, both the marital and the parental metaphors for monarchical authority were being contested, and many political theorists preferred to ground political authority in a social contract. Oddly, few women seem to have shared this preference. Often, as with the Venetian writers discussed in the previous section, women's criticisms of marriage develop independently of any explicit discussion of monarchism. And Marie le Jars de Gournay, the first to propose the equality of men and women, assumes the justice of divinely appointed monarchy.

When Gournay discusses good government, she, like earlier women, uses parental language. Gournay, the editor of Michel de Montaigne's

---

[58] For Bodin's views on sovereignty, see Jean Bodin, *On Sovereignty*, trans. Julian H. Franklin (Cambridge University Press, 1992).

[59] Sarah Hanley suggests that during this period there was a decline from a 'medieval marriage metaphor', in which the marriage of monarch and realm is conceived along the lines of the marriage of church and prelate, to a 'political state marriage metaphor' in which the king is equated with a husband: 'The Monarchic State'. For the earlier, more reciprocal image see Kantorowicz, *The King's Two Bodies*, pp. 207–23. We, however, do not find evidence of this 'deterioration' in women's writing.

essays, and his 'adoptive' daughter, devoted her life to disseminating his wisdom, and helped, through the preparation of many editions of the *Essays*, to establish his reputation.[60] Publishing in the last decades of the sixteenth century and the first decades of the seventeenth, she was one of the few women of her period to write an explicitly political text on the art of good government in a manner similar to Christine. In a number of essays, including her 'Institution du Prince' (Instruction of the Prince) and 'Adieu de l'ame du Roy' (Farewell of the Soul of the King) and other works that make up her collected essays, *Les Advis ou, Les Presens de la demoiselle de Gournay* (1610), she develops her ideas on the importance of princely education and her conception of monarchical duty.[61]

Gournay's commitment to a parental conception of monarchical authority is clear throughout her writing. Although she often uses the combined image of 'husband and father' to speak of kings, it is clear that she makes little distinction between the king's role as father and the queen's role as mother. In her essay 'De l'education des enfans de France' (The Education of the Royal Children of France), she addresses herself to 'Henry IV, the most august and victorious King in the universe, and Marie de Medici the most august and beautiful queen':

God is pleased and obliged SIRE to see that man knows how to properly manage the gift whereby he is made man, which is his Reason: and is doubly obliged, when he recognises a prince who, through a more ample exercise of that light, makes himself worthy of the name of the father of the People, since he imparts to him a paternal authority over them.[62]

---

[60] Giovanni Dotoli, 'Montaigne et les libertins via Mlle de Gournay', *Journal of Medieval and Renaissance Studies* 25 (1995), 389. Dotoli justly overturns the judgement of Maurice Rat, who suggests that Gournay caused a reaction against Montaigne.

[61] The 'Adieu de l'ame du Roy' was first published as Marie le Jars de Gournay, *Adieu de l'Ame du Roy de France et de Navarre Henry le Grand à la royne, avec, La Défence des Pères Iésuites* (Paris: Fleury Bourriquant, 1610). It was reprinted by the author in *Les Advis ou Les Présens de la Demoiselle de Gournay* (reprint, Paris: Toussainct Du-Bray, 1634; reprinted with additions, 1641). This work also contains the 'Institution du Prince'. Various modern editions of Gournay's essays are available, including *Les Advis, ou, les Presens de la Demoiselle de Gournay* (1641), ed. Jean-Philippe Beaulieu and Hannah Fournier (Amsterdam: Rodopi, 1997), pp. 102–17. The two versions of 'Adieu de l'ame du Roy' and the 'Institution du Prince' are available in Marie le Jars de Gournay, *Oeuvres complètes*, ed. Jean-Claude Arnould, Evelyne Berriot, Claude Blum, Anna Lia Franchetti, Marie-Claire Thomine, and Valerie Worth-Stylianou, 2 vols. (Paris: Champion, 2002), vol. 1, pp. 191–236, 653–86, and 818–41. All references to Gournay's works will be to this edition, and the reader is referred to it for the complexities of Gournay's publishing practices. For an overview of Gournay's life and works, see Marjorie H. Ilsley, *A Daughter of the Renaissance: Marie le Jars de Gournay, Her Life and Works* (The Hague: Mouton, 1963). For a more recent biography, see Michèle Fogel, *Marie de Gournay* (Paris: Fayard, 2004).

[62] Gournay, *Oeuvres*, vol. 1, p. 577.

Lamenting the murder of this king, some years later, she declaims, 'Oh parricidal murderer, what fury carries you away . . . do you wish to render your desolate homeland orphan and widow?'[63] In her 'L'Ame du Roy' the parental metaphor reappears, this time in a bisexual form. The soul of the dead king, addressing his wife, tells her that 'From now on you are King, Queen, and Father and Mother: and just as you begin to represent the prudence of both in conducting your affairs, you must also represent constancy in your consolation.'[64] Following the logic of the parental image, Gournay emphasises the duties of kingship rather than its powers and rights.

The king's responsibility towards his people places on him a particularly important duty to educate his children who will be monarchs after him. Gournay insists that good birth is insufficient to assure virtue, and a proper education is of the utmost importance:

Despite being natural, the rainbow shimmer of a pigeon's neck only appears when the sun shines on it: thus the soul of a well-born man is nothing unless the Sun of education, coming to shine on it, makes it disclose its inner goodness, as the fire does to the incense.[65]

The education that will disclose virtue has to be a practical one, designed to teach the prince moral and political understanding, and its execution requires a tutor of the highest moral probity, who is possessed of practical experience as well as a capacity to pass on his virtues.

For her understanding of the character of a good education, Gournay takes much from Montaigne.[66] He rejects pedantry and advocates an education directed towards the practical. Gournay does not emphasise, as Montaigne does, the need for physical training and rough exercise, but takes him to be advocating the development of reason and moral understanding which is oriented towards life and self-knowledge. She advises the prince to study ethics, politics, and history, but considers other knowledge inessential, fearing lest an excess of book-learning should diminish his willingness to study.[67] Contrasting the methods she proposes to those of others, who follow an academic and inadequate method, she says 'Those others show how to discourse and comment on doctrine: these

[63] Ibid., p. 640.   [64] Ibid., p. 654.   [65] Ibid., p. 580.
[66] Michel de Montaigne, *Essais*, ed. Maurice Rat, 3 vols. (Paris: Garnier Frères, 1958), 1.26, pp. 154–92; *The Essays of Michel de Montaigne*, trans. and ed. M. A. Screech (London: Allen Lane, 1991), pp. 163–99.
[67] Gournay, *Oeuvres*, vol. 1, p. 828.

to discourse and reason about our own conduct and about the conduct of others, when it is necessary.'[68]

Pursuing the logic of parental obligation, Gournay is led, in a sense, to limit the freedom of the monarch in ways that are reminiscent of constitutional monarchies, without, however, employing any explicit theory of the limits of a monarch's sovereignty. In order to exercise the duty of caring for his people a monarch must show both prudence and justice:

Prudence and justice are, to those that master them, mothers of liberty, of contentment and good fortune, which are never found where these virtues are lacking. Of liberty, because imprudent and unjust princes are forced, in order to repair their mistakes, to make worse ones, and constrained, in order to protect themselves against rebellions, to stoop shamefully and servilely to worse than they fear, following that true saying: that one abyss brings another.[69]

Gournay is led to the conclusion that under certain circumstances, a prince should be prepared to abdicate, if it is necessary to do so in order to secure the good of the people. She also provides the example of the emperors of China, as reported by the Jesuits, who would disinherit their own children if there were others more capable of governing.[70]

Regarding the possibility of abdication, however, she makes a rather inconsistent exception, which reveals her deep partiality for the mythic trappings with which the French invested their kings. The eldest of the royal house, she insists, is exempt by nature from any requirement to abdicate, since the peace and prosperity of his subjects depend on the stability of the hereditary crown.[71] Elsewhere she alludes to descendants of the same prophetic tradition that Christine exploits, suggesting that astrological signs indicate that at last France is to achieve the great heights promised by Virgil. The astrologers believe that the current constellation

brings after it a comet which presages ill for the Turkish States, by virtue of the ancient Prophecies: which are seen by all according to common belief, whether those of its own people or those of the Christians, to predict the overthrow of his throne at the hand of the French. *To what heights of glory will the Gauls arise?*[72]

Gournay thus looks back to the same prophetic tradition that inspired Christine and shares her political attitudes. Although she insists on the duty of monarchs to care for the well-being and freedom of the people, she never explicitly mentions limits to sovereignty, nor does she acknowledge the

[68] Ibid., p. 593.   [69] Ibid., pp. 596–7.   [70] Ibid., pp. 615–16.   [71] Ibid., p. 616.
[72] Ibid., pp. 621–2, quoting Virgil, *Aeneid* IV, 49.

people's right of resistance. Her political attitudes seem to have evolved little from those expressed by Christine, yet she wrote at a time when France had recently suffered a Huguenot revolt, and during which many were urging resistance and contesting the authority of the sovereign. In order to make better sense of Gournay's outlook, one needs to bring out the close relationship of her political ideas to those of Montaigne.

In late 1588, Montaigne passed some months at his adoptive daughter's family estate at Gournay. During this period, they worked together on the enlargement and correction of chapters 22 and 23 of the first book of the *Essays*, and on chapter 21 of the second book.[73] Of these, Montaigne's essay 'On Habit: and on Never Easily Changing a Traditional Law' contains the fullest development of the sceptical conservatism that characterises his political outlook, and this sceptical conservatism surely influenced Gournay, although she appears at first blush to have followed Montaigne's conservatism rather more readily than his scepticism.[74]

Montaigne's political thought derived from both his wide reading and his immediate circumstances. In his introduction to Jean Bodin's essay on sovereignty, Julian Franklin suggests that

in the aftermath of the St. Bartholomew's Day massacre and the recurrent civil war, Bodin feared for the very existence of the state. He agreed with the Huguenots that the war had been provoked by the tyrannical tactics of the crown, for which Machiavellianism could be blamed. But the right of resistance, which was publicly asserted by the Huguenots as a right against the king himself, left him thoroughly alarmed. It seemed to him nothing less than a recipe for anarchy.[75]

Similarly moved by the same historical events, Montaigne's reaction was to emphasise the limits of the human capacity to know the truth, the variability of human custom, and the wisdom of following the laws and customs of one's own society. Anticipating Edmund Burke, he decries those who are so vain, presumptuous, and fond of their own opinions that they are prepared to overthrow an established peace in order to attempt to enforce them on others, and thus to impose the horrors of civil war on themselves and the community.[76]

---

[73] Fogel, *Marie de Gournay*, pp. 47 and 51.

[74] For Montaigne's scepticism, see Anne Hartle, 'Montaigne and Scepticism', in *The Cambridge Companion to Montaigne*, ed. Ullrich Langer (Cambridge University Press, 2005), pp. 183–206. Even in those places where she emphasises the fallibility of human reason, as in her essay 'Des vertus vicieuses', Gournay accepts the possibile existence of those with higher intellectual powers who can recognise the truth: *Oeuvres*, vol. 1, p. 993.

[75] In Bodin, *On Sovereignty*, p. xxiii.　　[76] Montaigne, *Essays*, 1.23, p. 135; *Essais*, p. 127.

Montaigne's erudite compilation of the variety of human custom, gleaned from contemporary travellers and ancient sources, culminates in the conclusion that one is at a loss to justify human behaviour on rational grounds. Montaigne defends freedom of belief, saying 'a wise man should withdraw his soul from the crowd, maintaining its power and freedom freely to make judgements'.[77] But he goes on to insist that it is 'the Rule of rules, the general Law of laws' that one observes the laws of the place where one resides.[78]

This conservatism placed Montaigne in an awkward intellectual position, for his professed closest intellectual friend, Etienne de La Boëtie, had written in his youth a text, the *Contr'un*, that seemed to oppose all customary acceptance of tyranny. Tyranny, La Boëtie suggests, survives only because of the implicit consent of the people. He argues that since the people outnumber the tyrant they are free to withdraw their consent, and thus the text can be read as endorsing resistance.[79] In Montaigne's eulogy of friendship, in which he describes the irreplaceable and special friendship that he enjoyed with La Boëtie, Montaigne distances himself from this reading and expresses distress at the fact that the essay was included in a collection of Huguenot tracts. He defends his friend, arguing that while he must have believed what he wrote when he wrote it, 'he had another maxim supremely imprinted upon his soul: to obey, and most scrupulously submit to, the laws under which he was born'.[80] By attributing his 'law of laws' to his friend, Montaigne underscores its actual importance in his own philosophy. Gournay also mentions La Boëtie's text, and the lack of esteem from which La Boëtie suffered. Going even further than Montaigne, she argues that the work was not written in opposition to kingship:

As much and worse happened to La Boëtie, reputed such a great man according to the *Essays*: who, in detestation of tyranny, of which insolence is the ugly consequence, wrote that delightful and perspicacious work the *Contr'un*: which was, however, very far from being written in hatred of kings, an intention which certain Protestants formerly wanted to attribute to him.[81]

It is difficult to believe that Montaigne was being entirely candid with regard to his friend's text. La Boëtie's work was originally written at the

---

[77] *Essays*, 1.23, p. 133; *Essais*, p. 125.   [78] Ibid.
[79] Etienne de La Boëtie, *De la servitude volontaire ou Contr'un*, ed. Malcolm Smith (Geneva: Droz, 1987), and *The Politics of Obedience: The Discourse of Voluntary Servitude*, ed. Murray N. Rothbard, trans. Harry Kurz (New York: Free Life Editions, 1975). The *Contr'un* was published in *Mémoires sur l'Estat de France sous Charles IX* (1576).
[80] Montaigne, *Essays*, 1.28, p. 219; *Essais*, p. 211.   [81] Gournay, *Oeuvres*, vol. 1, p. 786.

time of the uprising in Bordeaux that was suppressed by Henry II in 1548.[82] It is thus very easy to read the work as endorsing resistance to unjust regimes, and so arguing directly counter to the beliefs that Montaigne attributes to his friend.

Reading Gournay's political essays in the light of her comments on the *Contr'un* suggests that she was just as conservative as, but rather less sceptical than, Montaigne. Gournay maintains that reason can deliver more than simply the injunction that one should obey the laws under which one is born.[83] The passage above makes it clear that Gournay reads La Boëtie as writing, not against kingship in general, but against tyranny. He represents tyranny as being upheld by habit, but also by a hierarchy of the greedy and ambitious who benefit from the tyrant and who are allowed, under tyranny, to exploit the people.[84] Gournay's instructions to the prince, and her advice to Marie de Medici, in effect, attempt to teach monarchs to govern without becoming tyrants. They must care for the good of the people, avoiding flatterers and all those whose attempts to gain their ear are founded on mere self-interest. They must be models of virtue so that their subjects will be models of virtue. Far from showing Montaigne's scepticism with regard to the possibility of providing a rational justification for the law, Gournay asserts: 'The true secret, in a word, of reigning happily, is to reign worthily: and to reign or command worthily is nothing other than to serve Reason and practise Virtue.'[85] And just as Christine saw the security of the prince as residing in the love of the people, so too Gournay takes issue with Machiavelli and asserts that

Machiavelli's advice to his Prince, to make himself feared rather than loved, if he is reduced to one of these two options (men, he says, being so ungrateful that the ease with which they free themselves from the causes of friendship is matched only by the difficulty they have in escaping those of fear) shows his conscience too mocking, indeed even imprudent. Inasmuch as there is no Grandeur which a Prince ought to accept, for the price of the ills, the anxieties and spiritual torments which he must suffer, nor the evils he must commit, in order to reign by terror . . . Moreover, he will never be reduced to the necessity of choosing the aid of only love or fear: since if he reigns by love, which is to say, by justice and

[82] La Boëtie, *De la servitude volontaire*, p. 8.
[83] This follows the judgement of René Pintard, *Le Libertinage érudit dans la première moitié du XVIIe siècle* (Paris: Slatkine, 1983). Pintard calls Gournay the inheritor of Montaigne's pyrrhonism, and points out that she associated with many of the libertine school, but was not irreligious (p. 135). Elsewhere it has been argued that she was in fact a concealed libertine; see Dotoli, 'Montaigne et les libertins via Mlle de Gournay', 397.
[84] La Boëtie, *The Politics of Obedience*, pp. 77–81.
[85] Gournay, *Oeuvres*, vol. 1, p. 888; see also p. 660.

goodness, nothing prevents him from making it apparent that he has the power and vigour to chastise those who would abuse it.[86]

In one place, in support of the proposition that goodness, prudence, and justice are necessary for reigning well, Gournay turns from the parental to the marital metaphor for the relationship of prince and people. She concludes her imaginary discourse by the soul of Henry IV, addressed to Marie de Medici, with the following Adieu:

this is the eternal reproach of the false policy of certain writers who ground the safety of Potentates on rigour and violence; which you will find in the domestic example of a spouse who reigned as gently as nobly, powerfully and triumphantly.[87]

Here the model of a gentle but authoritative husband/spouse becomes indistinguishable from that of the virtuous and prudent prince.

The gentle prince protects the weak against the strong by ensuring equitable justice. He or she is 'the counterweight of the feeble against the strong'.[88] Implicitly he or she upholds the liberties of the people, and Gournay advises Marie de Medici, through the voice of her dead husband, to uphold his edicts of Mantes and Nantes, which had brought to an end the wars of religion in France.[89] However, Gournay does not explicitly discuss religious toleration at any great length, seeming to believe that personal animosity, insults, duelling, and resultant faction are what really cause discord and the dissolution of states.

For Gournay, one of the greatest threats to justice and peace is posed by libel, slander, rumour, and the destruction of reputation, and this is closely followed by the danger of flattery and falsehood. The first version of 'L'Ame du Roy', published in 1610, while partly written to lament the loss of Henry IV, is also intended to prevent his murder from resulting in further discord. Gournay perceives that the Jesuits are being unjustly maligned, and this motivates her to defend them, in line with her general observation that campaigns of slander of this sort ultimately lead to civil disturbance. The Jesuits were in danger of persecution because a member of their company had assassinated the king. Gournay compares the slanderer to the cannibals of the New World:

For my part, the man who by means of the ear or the tongue, and particularly the latter, devours the honour of the unblemished, full of life and feeling, is far more

---

[86] Ibid., pp. 886–7.   [87] Ibid., p. 678.
[88] Ibid., p. 661. On the importance of upholding justice, see also pp. 842–4.   [89] Ibid., p. 673.

Cannibalistic, and a true Anthropophage, than those people there, where they feed only on the dead bodies of their enemies.[90]

Anyone familiar with Montaigne's work would be reminded by this analogy of his essays 'On Cannibalism' (1: 31) and 'On Custom' (1: 23), in the first of which he deals at length with cannibalism, and in the second mentions it in passing. On first reading, Gournay seems to be simply quoting these passages in order to suggest an analogy and pass an adverse moral judgement on the slanderer. But on a deeper reading, her invitation to the reader to remember these sections of the *Essays* suggests that her dislike of slanderers derives, at least in part, from an application of a scepticism not unlike Montaigne's. If it is an arrogant presumption to attempt to enforce one's opinions on others, it is equally pernicious to presume, on the basis of ill-grounded opinion, to rob others of their honour, when it is as important to them as their life. Thus, although Gournay's writing does not focus explicitly on toleration, her insistence that one not slander or destroy another's reputation involves an implicit toleration of others, in the commitment to protecting the reputation of even those with whom one does not agree. Scepticism is conducive to toleration, since sceptics cannot be certain either that others are wrong or that they themselves are correct. By contrast, for the fervent believer, to tolerate what one 'knows' to be evil can appear to be little better than promoting vice.

At the same time, as others have observed, there is a clear connection between Gournay's experiences as a woman and her near-obsession with the damage done to society and to individuals by the practice of slander, mockery, and gossip. She acutely felt the effects of the general disdain meted out to women who attempted to write, publish, or be taken seriously, and she bitterly attempted to defend her reputation against such dismissal in her 'Apology for the Woman Writing'.[91] Likewise, her short 'Ladies' Complaint' is an eloquent outburst against the vulgar despising of intellectual women. You men, she says, find yourselves in the happy position of being permitted the freedom to pursue all the virtues proper to public office, which are prohibited to women. You are 'blessed again . . . since you can be wise without offence, your masculinity allowing you – as much as one forbids these to women – every action of lofty purpose, every

[90] Ibid., pp. 193–4. She later reuses this image in her essay on slander, which is included in the *Advis* (a work that omits the defence of the Jesuits); see ibid., p. 711.
[91] Gournay, *Apology for the Woman Writing*, pp. 111–54; *Oeuvres*, vol. 11, pp. 1375–429.

preeminent judgement, and every expression of subtle speculation'.[92] She vents her frustration at all those men who responded to her contribution to conversations with a dismissive smile, a barrage of irrelevant pedantry, or a simple refusal to accept a point. And while one can hope that 400 years have improved the situation, and that now women's opinions are allowed the same authority as men's, only half a century ago Montaigne's later editor, Maurice Rat, could unblushingly write of his precursor, 'With her old maid's enthusiasm and white hair, Mlle de Gournay, who made the mistake of living too long, appeared rather ridiculous to the regulars at the hotel Rambouillet; she had always been a pedant, but she had become terribly so, and her peevish or aggressive attitude did great damage to her "father".'[93] The attitude against which Gournay complained in 1641 – that a beard is essential in order to be taken seriously, and guarantees the right to disdain one half of the population – was still alive and well in 1958.[94]

Gournay extols a virtuous monarchism, but, although she remained single, she does not explicitly criticise marriage. Her sexual politics is strangely difficult to fathom. Her most famous 'feminist' essay, 'The Equality of Men and Women' was dedicated to Anne of Austria in 1624 when the young queen was twenty-one. Although it may be the first essay to propose the equality of the sexes in exactly those terms, given the period during which it was written it seems to be a rather conventional defence of women. Gournay insists on women's spiritual equality with men, but she does not make any clear demand for social change. She praises what had become the French custom of female regency, and refers to Joan of Arc and Judith as examples that demonstrate God's favour to women. However, when it is read in conjunction with an essay of Montaigne's to which it refers, Gournay's essay might be thought to be more radical and to contain a hidden defence of some of the doctrines associated with Montaigne's sexual libertinism.

We have seen that Marguerite de Navarre both criticises the sexual double standard and proposes the moral superiority of women in relation to love and sex. Following Montaigne, Gournay distances herself from any such position at the beginning of her essay: 'For my part, I fly all

[92] Gournay, *Apology*, p. 101; *Oeuvres*, vol. 1, pp. 1074–5.
[93] Montaigne, *Essais*, p. xiii. To which one might respond that as expressing the self-satisfaction of a former student of the Ecole Normale Supérieure, Rat's professed disdain of Gournay's pedantry might have been ridiculous when first penned, but has had the misfortune to survive long enough to become hilariously so, and to have brought severely into question the good judgement of his sex.
[94] Gournay, *Apology*, p. 103; *Oeuvres*, vol. 1, p. 1077.

extremes, I am content to make them equal to men, given that nature, too, is as greatly opposed, in this respect, to superiority as to inferiority.'[95] In making this assertion, Gournay may have been responding to Marguerite de Navarre's great-niece, Marguerite de Valois, whose more explicit defence of the superiority of women had been published a decade earlier.[96] Gournay may also have known Cornelius Agrippa's text, or Lucrezia Marinella's more recent and provocative assertion of women's superiority. In more modestly arguing for the equality of the sexes, Gournay is once again following Montaigne, though placing a certain (not entirely justified) gloss on his words. He asserts that 'male and female are cast in the same mould: save for education and custom the difference between them is not great'.[97] Gournay refers to the essay in which this assertion is made in her 'Equality', saying that he reports that 'Antisthenes denies all difference in ability and in virtue between the two sexes.'[98] Yet in citing Montaigne in this way, Gournay is either being disingenuous, or slyly proposing a rather more radical sexual libertinism than appears on the surface. Montaigne says nothing to defend women's equality with regard to ability, and in asserting women's equality in virtue he asserts (in opposition to Marguerite de Navarre's opinion, for example) that women are not morally superior to men with regard to sexual passion.[99]

It has been pointed out that for some years Gournay frequented the libertine circle surrounding Marguerite de Valois, which included, among others, Brantôme and Honoré d'Urfé.[100] In his collection of bawdy tales about women, Brantôme (whose grandmother had been the model for one of the participants in the *Heptameron*) makes it clear that while he, like the author of the *Heptameron*, deplores the sexual double standard, he believes that women are just as sexual as men and that their infidelities do not justify death.[101] Montaigne concurs in this judgement about male and female equality in sexual desire. Discussing the burning fires of

[95] Gournay, *Apology*, p. 75; *Oeuvres*, vol. 1, p. 965.
[96] Marguerite de Valois, *Mémoires et autres écrits*.
[97] Montaigne, *Essays*, III.5, p. 1016; *Essais*, p. 124.
[98] Gournay, *Apology*, p. 82; *Oeuvres*, vol. 1, p. 973.
[99] Abraham C. Keller, 'Montaigne on Women', in *Onze nouvelles études sur l'image de la femme dans la littérature française du dix-septième siècle*, ed. Wolfgang Leiner (Tübingen: Gunter Marr Verlag, 1984), pp. 33–7.
[100] Dotoli, 'Montaigne et les libertins via Mlle de Gournay', 396; Valois, *Mémoires et autres écrits*, vol. 1, pp. 260–1.
[101] For a discussion of Brantôme's grandmother, see Pierre Jourda, *Marguerite d'Angoulême, duchesse d'Alençon, reine de Navarre (1492–1549): Etude biographique et littéraire*, 2 vols. (Paris: Champion, 1930; reprint, Geneva: Slatkine Reprints, 1978), vol. 1, p. 289.

passion that motivate the young, he concludes that 'It is therefore madness to assay restraining so blazing a desire, so natural to women. And when I hear them boasting that their very wills are coldly chaste and virginal I laugh at them.'[102] However, it is difficult to determine with any certainty whether or not Gournay concurred with this judgement. Her recent French biographer speculates that she may have had a carnal affair with Montaigne, but there is very little to justify such speculation.[103]

In the long preface to the *Essays*, which Gournay initially repressed and then reinstated, she defends Montaigne against the charge of indecency, while at the same time distancing herself from his relaxed sexual mores. She defends his honest discussion of sexuality, his confession of his early sexual escapades, and his claims for the naturalness of sexual desire, saying, 'Is it reasonable to condemn the theory of Love as guilty and infamous, while accepting its practice as made honest, legitimate, and sacramental by marriage?'[104] This comment certainly implies, at least indirectly, that sex is not intrinsically bad. Yet in her defence of Montaigne, Gournay also accepts that it would be a bad thing were young people to become more licentious. She asserts that 'It is not frank and speculative discussions of Love which are dangerous; it is those which are soft and delicate, the artistic and arousing stories of love's passions and effects which one sees in novels, the poets, and that kind of writer.'[105] Gournay also blames court ceremony for raising the profile of love and making it more highly valued.

In her introduction, Gournay distances herself from the frank pleasure with which Montaigne expresses his delight in the pursuit of love, even though Montaigne had rejected sex, where there is insufficient attraction, as unsatisfying:[106]

I don't, however, approve of the licence of these poets, nor of the allegiance that my Father sometimes shows to them, nor yet a certain freedom in his belief; as much because I find them distasteful, as because I am totally of the view that each should, as far as he can, contain his acts and deeds within the limits of customary form and ceremony. However, I deplore far more than these errors, the error of those who accuse them of being worse than they are.[107]

In this, one of the few passages in which Gournay explicitly distances herself from Montaigne, she cleverly turns his own thoughts against him,

---

[102] Montaigne, *Essays*, III.5, p. 979; *Essais*, p. 89.   [103] Fogel, *Marie de Gournay*, pp. 47–51.
[104] Gournay, *Oeuvres*, vol. 1, p. 291.   [105] Ibid., p. 295.
[106] See Montaigne, *Essays*, III.3, p. 931; *Essais*, pp. 42–3.   [107] Gournay, *Oeuvres*, vol. 1, p. 294.

suggesting that, in matters of sexual relations as much as in matters of government, one should follow the customs of one's time and place. At the same time, if Montaigne's error consisted mainly in being more frank about his sexual passions and youthful affairs than was the common custom, it was not a serious error. Gournay's concluding comment is therefore compatible with the attribution to her of a sceptical conservatism similar in substance to Montaigne's, though differing from his in some of its detail.

Although she complained of the difficulty that women had in being taken seriously, Gournay lived at the dawn of a period of French civilisation during which women were, for a time, to play an increasingly prominent role. Her own small salon, where she entertained a coterie of educated men and women (although, as she complained, many of whom came more for a good feed than out of genuine intellectual friendship), was a pale reflection of the intellectual court that Marguerite de Valois presided over in her residence opposite the Louvre.[108] Both were precursors of the salon society that was to flourish in Paris for the next century and a half, and that would lead to the production of immense numbers of letters, novels, maxims, memoirs, and other reflections on society and its mores. Even during her lifetime Gournay was aware of the works of other intellectual women, and it is worth considering her reaction to, and relations with, them, for it helps to bring out what is distinctive in her outlook as well as reinforcing the conservatism of her ideas.

It is fair to say that Gournay's fundamental aspiration was to be accepted as the intellectual equal of her adopted father and to stand to him in the same relationship of intellectual equality and respect as he had stood to La Boëtie.[109] From a modern point of view, this feature of Gournay's self-image has certain disadvantages. In her attempt to write seriously, Gournay adopts a style that is complex and full of erudite allusions, which unashamedly display the extent of her learning. Her taste was formed when trends that were partly associated with Protestantism, and partly with the idea of the 'modern', were in their infancy. She was led to defend the 'old-fashioned' poets and writers, who had dominated the decades before her birth, against the moderns who would impose a simpler style on literature during the decades that preceded her death.

---

[108] For a brief account of her court, see Valois, *Mémoires et autres écrits*, pp. 259–61.
[109] Patricia Francis Cholakian, 'The Economics of Friendship: Gournay's *Apologie pour celle qui escrit*', *Journal of Medieval and Renaissance Studies* 25 (1995), 407–17.

Her *Défense de la poésie et du langage des poètes* is dedicated to Madame des Loges, a woman who presided over an influential Protestant salon frequented by the principal critic of old-fashioned usage, Malherbe. Gournay concludes this work with the amusing suggestion that she will be happy if she is successful in imparting a love of antiquity, given her own great age.[110] Perhaps, inadvertently, this defence shows Gournay expressing a certain disdain for courtly women as well as for the moderns' demand that one's writing include nothing that would not fall from the lips of courtly ladies, referred to by Gournay as 'paidagoguesses poupines' (baby-doll teachers).[111] Like later women who aspire to equality with men, Gournay seems at times to feel a certain disdain for more feminine females.

Gournay does not, for example, offer any warm support to Marguerite de Valois, a princess excluded from the throne by the Salic law. Indeed, Gournay's attitude to the Salic law is equivocal. By contrast with Brantôme, who argues explicitly against the law and points out the injustice of Marguerite's exclusion from the throne, Gournay's comments do not amount to an explicit rejection of the French custom, but follow contemporary monarchical ideology in locating its origins (erroneously) in the period of Pharamond and the need for a strong military leader.[112] This could be taken to imply that the law's justification is obsolete, but Gournay does not explicitly draw that conclusion. In making his case, Brantôme mentions Isabeau and other queens who acted as regents. While Gournay points to France's tradition of female regents, accepting it as an established custom, she never regrets the exclusion of Marguerite from the throne.[113] In fact, Gournay partly blames Marguerite for some of the troubles of the period, accusing her of having relayed to her husband, the future Henry IV, the way that he was mocked by Henry III.[114] Although Gournay is familiar with the queen's own memoirs, first published in 1628, she does not bother to recount Marguerite's claims that she was slandered and falsely accused of infidelity.[115] A more forceful

[110] Gournay, *Oeuvres*, vol. 1, p. 1200.
[111] Ibid., p. 1123. The passage is discussed in Linda Timmermans, *L'accès des femmes à la culture (1598–1715)* (Paris: Champion, 1993), pp. 134–5.
[112] Gournay, *Apology*, p. 84; *Oeuvres*, vol. 1, pp. 975–6. For the history of this law, see Craig Taylor, 'The Salic Law and the Valois Succession to the French Crown', *French History* 15 (2001), 358–77.
[113] For Brantôme's discussion of the Salic law, see Pierre de Bourdeille, Seigneur de Brantôme, *Oeuvres*, 9 vols. (Paris: Jules Renouard, 1866), vol. VIII, pp. 54–5.
[114] Gournay, *Oeuvres*, vol. 1, pp. 722–3.
[115] In an interesting passage, Marguerite relates how her mother Catherine de Medici, having been convinced that Marguerite was falsely accused of infidelity, compared the tendency to slander in

writer could easily have used this memoir as the basis of a thorough critique of the insidiousness of women's political situation, but Gournay is hampered by her own conservative respect for custom, her distrust of harsh criticism, and her hero worship of Henry IV.

In the years just before Gournay's death, women's participation in learning had increased significantly. From Utrecht, the young Anna Maria van Schurman (1607–78) sent her a Latin poem singing her praises.[116] Gournay returned the compliment, praising Schurman in the 1634 and subsequent editions of the 'Equality'.[117] Schurman was herself to become a friend and beneficiary of Princess Elisabeth of Bohemia, Descartes's famous correspondent.[118] Subsequently, Schurman's fame led Madeleine de Scudéry to attempt to initiate a correspondence.[119] Yet, like many of the highly educated women whose works we have looked at, Schurman was to turn away from classical erudition as a training ground in virtue, replacing it with a deep spiritual calling. Scudéry by contrast would come to offer a powerful new characterisation of the role of educated women in polite society, which combined worldly sociability with feminine virtue.

the present period unfavourably with the time that she had spent at court with Marguerite de Navarre during the reign of François I. During this period, the sexes had mixed freely without being subject to gossip. See Valois, *Mémoires et autres écrits*, pp. 117–18.

[116] Mario Schiff, *La Fille d'alliance de Montaigne, Marie de Gournay* (Paris: Champion, 1910), Appendix C, p. 117.

[117] Gournay, *Apology*, p. 78; *Oeuvres*, vol. 1, p. 969.

[118] Joyce Irwin, 'Learned Woman of Utrecht: Anna-Maria van Schurman', in *Women Writers of the Seventeenth Century*, ed. Katharina M. Wilson and Frank Warnke (Athens and London: University of Georgia Press, 1989), p. 168. The early friendship between Elisabeth and Schurman was not without tensions, however. On this topic, see Jacqueline Broad, *Women Philosophers of the Seventeenth Century* (Cambridge University Press, 2002), pp. 18–19.

[119] See Edouard Barthélmy and René Kerviler (eds.), *Un Tournoi de trois pucelles en l'honneur de Jeanne d'Arc. Lettres inédites de Conrart, de Mlle de Scudéry et de Mlle du Moulin* (Paris: Alphonse Picard, 1878).

CHAPTER 6

Women of the English civil war era

In 1642, the political climate in England took a dramatic turn for the worse when repeated political stand-offs between king and parliament culminated in the first of the English civil wars. During the civil war era, ordinary people were compelled to take sides, and the standard subject matter of modern political philosophy – such as the limits of political authority, and the extent of the individual's obligation to obey the king – became popular topics of discussion. In the literature of the time, we find questions about what legitimates political authority, about the political obligations of subjects and sovereigns, the connection between church and state, the best way to uphold the liberty of subjects, and theories of civil disobedience and resistance to authority. In this chapter (and in subsequent chapters), we show that the writings of early modern women reflect the changing language and content of political thought of this period.

We have seen that in early modern Venice, the political rhetoric of liberty and slavery was applied to the situation of women within marriage. The Venetian women did not offer any detailed or concrete feminist proposals for reform. But they did criticise male usurpation of women's property, and they suggested that women retain their liberty, and avoid a life of slavery, by remaining unmarried. Prior to the civil war era, it is difficult to find the rhetoric of male tyranny and female slavery in English women's writings. It is not present in *Jane Anger her Protection for women* (1589),[1] nor can it be found in the Swetnam controversy works of 1615–17.[2] The authors of these earlier texts use arguments that are reminiscent

---

[1] 'Jane Anger', *Jane Anger her Protection for women* (London: Richard Jones and Thomas Orwin, 1589). Some scholars doubt that 'Jane Anger' was in fact a woman.

[2] 'Constantia Munda', *The Worming of a mad Dogge: Or, a Soppe for Cerberus the Jaylor of Hell* (London: Laurence Hayes, 1617); 'Ester Sowernam', *Ester Hath Hang'd Haman: Or An Answere to a lewd Pamphlet, entituled, The Arraignement of Women* (London: Nicholas Bourne, 1617); Rachel Speght, *A Mouzell for Melastomus: The Cynicall Bayter of, and Foule Mouthed Barker against Evahs*

of Christine de Pizan and the *querelle des femmes* of the fifteenth century. They appeal to biblical, ancient, and historical precedents of 'female worthies', and they defend female virtue against misogynist critics; but they do not construct reason-based arguments about the injustice of women's lack of liberty compared to men. In the mid to late seventeenth century, however, English women writers start to appropriate the popular terminology of political debates of their time – the language of 'tyranny', 'slavery', 'passive obedience', and 'liberty'. Like the Venetian women, many English female authors draw parallels between the situation of women and that of slaves. Some complain about the 'Violations of the *Liberties of Freeborn English Women*',[3] and of women submitting 'their Necks to the slavish Yoke' of men;[4] while others observe that the tyranny of men over women 'extends farther than the most absolute Monarchs in the World'.[5]

On first reading, these women sound like feminists or proto-feminists, supporters of toleration and freedom of conscience, and heralds of egalitarianism, democracy, revolution, and divorce. But the political language of early modern English women can be deceptive: the rhetoric of revolution does not always amount to argument for resistance. When it comes to the civil war women, in particular, we are reminded that they wrote in an age in which religion and politics were often inseparable. Like the earlier women we have discussed, these writers appeal to biblical authority in their arguments for political ends; many of them still believe that magistrates are divinely appointed to protect the welfare of the community (they do not openly support contractual or conventional theories of political authority); and key political concepts such as liberty and tyranny still have

Sex (London: Nicholas Okes, 1617). These texts are republished in Simon Shepherd (ed.), *The Women's Sharp Revenge: Five Women's Pamphlets from the Renaissance* (London: Fourth Estate, 1985). For details, see Melinda J. Gough, 'Women's Popular Culture? Teaching the Swetnam Controversy', in Malcolmson and Suzuki (eds.), *Debating Gender*, pp. 79–100; Katherine Usher Henderson and Barbara F. McManus (eds.), *Half Humankind. Contexts and Texts of the Controversy about Women in England, 1540–1640* (Urbana and Chicago: University of Illinois Press, 1985); Diane Purkiss, 'Material Girls: The Seventeenth-Century Woman Debate', in *Women, Texts and Histories 1575–1760*, ed. Clare Brant and Diane Purkiss (London and New York: Routledge, 1992), pp. 69–101; and Lisa J. Schnell, 'Muzzling the Competition: Rachel Speght and the Economics of Print', in *Debating Gender in Early Modern England 1500–1700*, ed. Christina Malcolmson and Mihoko Suzuki (New York: Palgrave Macmillan, 2002), pp. 57–77.
[3] Elizabeth Johnson, 'Preface to the Reader', in [Elizabeth Singer Rowe], *Poems On Several Occasions. Written by Philomela* (London: John Dunton, 1696), sig. A3r.
[4] [Judith Drake], *An Essay In Defence of the Female Sex* (London: Printed for A. Roper, E. Wilkinson, and R. Clavel, 1696), p. 21.
[5] 'Eugenia', *The Female Advocate; Or, A Plea for the just Liberty of the Tender Sex, and particularly of Married Women* (London: Andrew Bell, 1700), p. 28.

strong religious connotations. For these reasons, even the political views of radical Protestant women of the time – and especially their views about male–female power relations – can be surprisingly conservative.

In the civil war era in England, public petitions addressed to parliament were not only an accepted way of expressing political opinions, but also a means of drawing the common people into political action.[6] These petitions usually consisted of two or three pages of printed text, and were typically presented to parliament by a large (and sometimes clamorous) group. Women were among the many petitioners of the civil war era. Though they would often present petitions for personal reasons – to secure their estates or to defend their persecuted husbands[7] – some were also motivated to air their political grievances as a social group. These women wrote and supported petitions not only because their personal circumstances had grown intolerable, but because they claimed their rights and liberties as subjects had been neglected.[8] They were strongly influenced by the radical ideas of the Leveller movement, a group that has been described as 'the first democratic political movement in modern history'.[9] In a number of petitions from 1642 to 1653, Leveller-inspired women defend the spiritual and political interests of subjects, the toleration of non-conformist religion, and – above all – the individual's freedom of conscience.[10] A handful of women also published pamphlets

---

[6] The discussion in this chapter draws on material in an earlier article: Jacqueline Broad, 'Liberty and the Right of Resistance: Women's Political Writings of the English Civil War Era', in Broad and Green (eds.), *Virtue, Liberty, and Toleration*, pp. 77–94. The material is used here by kind permission of Springer Science and Business Media.

[7] See, for example, [Anonymous], *To the Supreme Authority of this Common-wealth, The Parliament of England. The humble Petition of Severall of the Wives and Children of such Delinquents, whose Estates are propounded to be sold, as the Petitioners are informed* ([London: n.p., August 1650]).

[8] There is some debate about whether or not women themselves actually wrote these petitions; see, for example, *Puritanism and Liberty: Being the Army Debates (1647–9) from the Clarke Manuscripts with Supplementary Documents*, ed. and introduced A. S. P. Woodhouse, with a foreword by A. D. Lindsay (London: J. M. Dent and Sons, 1951), p. 367. Given the lack of conclusive evidence on either side, we do not propose to enter into this debate. We examine instead the concepts of liberty, religious toleration, and so on, as they are presented in relation to women or from a woman's point of view.

[9] G. E. Aylmer, 'Introduction', in *The Levellers in the English Revolution*, ed. G. E. Aylmer (London: Thames and Hudson, 1987), p. 9. On the history of the Leveller movement, see H. N. Brailsford, *The Levellers and the English Revolution*, ed. Christopher Hill (London: Cresset Press, 1961); Ian Gentles, 'London Levellers and the English Revolution: The Chidleys and Their Circle', *Journal of Ecclesiastical History* 29 (1978), 281–309; Christopher Hill, *The World Turned Upside Down: Radical Ideas during the English Revolution* (London: Temple Smith, 1972); and David Wootton, 'Leveller Democracy and the Puritan Revolution', in *The Cambridge History of Political Thought 1450–1700*, ed. J. H. Burns, with Mark Goldie (Cambridge University Press, 1991), pp. 412–42.

[10] On the wider activities of the women petitioners, see Patricia Higgins, 'The Reactions of Women, with Special Reference to Women Petitioners', in *Politics, Religion, and the English Civil War*, ed.

of a political nature under their own names: among them Katherine Chidley (*fl.* 1616–53), the mother of Samuel Chidley (a treasurer of the Leveller party), who published three justifications for the toleration of separatist religion in England;[11] and Elizabeth Poole (*fl.* 1649), a visionary or 'prophetess', who wrote three works of advice to the General Council of the New Model Army concerning the trial and execution of Charles I.[12]

Some scholars see these women as natural predecessors to revolutionary feminists such as Mary Wollstonecraft (1759–97). One historian of the Leveller movement, H. N. Brailsford, suggests that the female petitioners 'may be reckoned in their modest anonymity among the forerunners of Mary Wollstonecraft'.[13] More recently, Katharine Gillespie has suggested that, like later liberal feminists, some of the early non-conformist women make a significant connection between the subject's right to resist a tyrannical ruler, on the one hand, and a woman's right to resist a tyrannical husband, on the other.[14] Gillespie asserts that the arguments of the civil war women ought to lead us to rethink our assumptions about early modern feminism and its almost exclusive association with conservative Anglican and royalist politics. In the writings of early women radicals, such as Chidley and Poole, we see the first steps toward extending the norms governing the social contract in the public sphere to those governing the marriage contract in private. Consequently, it is argued, their 'texts rightfully deserve to be included in "genealogies" of liberal political theory'.[15]

In this chapter, we examine the key political themes in women's writings of the civil war era, with particular emphasis on the transition in their arguments from the spiritual liberty of souls to the political liberty of subjects, and their apparent justifications of the right to resist unjust authority at both the family and state level. But we believe that care needs

Brian Manning (London: Edward Arnold, 1973), pp. 177–222; Keith Thomas, 'Women and the Civil War Sects', in *Crisis in Europe 1560–1660*, ed. Trevor Aston (London: Routledge and Kegan Paul, 1965), pp. 317–40, reprinted from *Past and Present* 13 (1958), 42–62.

[11] Katherine Chidley, *The Justification of the Independant Churches of Christ* (London: William Larner, 1641); *A New-Yeares-Gift, or A Brief Exhortation to Mr. Thomas Edwards* ([London: n.p.], 1645 [i.e. 1644]); and *Good Counsell, to the Petitioners for Presbyterian Government* ([London: n.p., 1645]).

[12] Elizabeth Poole, *A Vision: Wherein is manifested the disease and cure of the Kingdome* (London: n.p., 1648 [i.e. 9 January 1649]); *An Alarum of War, Given to the Army* (London: n.p., [17 May] 1649); *An [other] Alarum of War, Given to the Army* ([London: n.p.], 1649).

[13] Brailsford, *The Levellers*, p. 317.

[14] Katharine Gillespie, *Domesticity and Dissent in the Seventeenth Century: English Women's Writing and the Public Sphere* (Cambridge University Press, 2004).

[15] Ibid., p. 13.

to be taken in arguing for the significance of these women's writings for the history of feminism, in particular, and liberal political theory, in general. On the one hand, the women petitioners undoubtedly deserve recognition for their astute observations about the political status of women in their time; and, with their emphasis on liberty and the right of resistance, there is some sense in which the civil war women anticipate some strands of thought in modern liberalism and feminism. But liberalism and feminism are both complex doctrines that come in different varieties. There are important features of the dominant modern versions of these doctrines missing from the thought of these petitioners.

I

The English civil war period saw a marked increase in female participation in public controversies. During the civil war decade, women published 112 pamphlets of a political nature, despite their lack of training in classical political rhetoric. In the preceding four decades, a mere forty-two works – on a range of subjects – were by women.[16] Following the demise of the Star Chamber and relaxation of censorship laws, it seems that there were greater opportunities for women to express their political ideas. Despite the common view that women had no role in public affairs, many English women – from both the elite and non-elite sectors of society – considered their political engagement to be unproblematic. Like Elizabeth I and her Renaissance predecessors, the civil war women look to traditional and biblical examples, arguments, and stereotypes, in their justifications of female political activity.[17] They appeal to female role models from Scripture – such as the woman of Tekoa, Esther, Deborah, and Jael – as honourable precedents for women offering advice and passing judgement on political matters.[18] More generally, again like

---

[16] Lois G. Schwoerer, 'Women's Public Political Voice in England: 1640–1740', in Smith (ed.), *Women Writers and the Early Modern British Political Tradition*, p. 61. See also Patricia Crawford, 'Women's Published Writings 1600–1700', in *Women in English Society: 1500–1800*, edited by Mary Prior (London: Methuen, 1985), pp. 211–31.

[17] On their appeals to 'Female Worthies', see Ann Marie McEntee, '"The [Un]Civill-Sisterhood of Oranges and Lemons": Female Petitioners and Demonstrators, 1642–53', *Prose Studies* 14 (1991), 92–111; and on Elizabeth and the civil war women, see 92, 98, and 109. On the Leveller presentation of women more generally, see Ann Hughes, 'Gender and Politics in Leveller Literature', in *Political Culture and Cultural Politics in Early Modern England: Essays Presented to David Underdown*, ed. Susan D. Amussen and Mark A. Kishlansky (Manchester and New York: Manchester University Press, 1995), pp. 162–88.

[18] See Chidley, *Justification*, title page; and Anonymous, *A True Copie of the Petition of the Gentle-women, and Tradesmens-wives, in and about the City of London* (London: R. O. & G. D. for John

Elizabeth I, the civil war women claim authority for their political advice by presenting themselves as instruments of God. In the Bible, as many women point out, it is common for God to use 'weak vessels' to enact his will.[19]

The civil war women justify their incursions into religious politics with reference to the view that an individual's spiritual insights can have worth and integrity, despite that individual's poor social and educational background. In the previous chapter, we saw that some continental women embraced the individualist implications of the Protestant religion: they argued in favour of each individual's own spiritual authority against the authority of the Pope, and they emphasised the importance of searching Scripture for themselves. In England during the civil war era, many women pamphleteers were associated with radical Protestant sects, such as the Independents, Anabaptists, Fifth Monarchists, and Quakers (the subject of our next chapter). Like their continental counterparts, these sects were opposed to the Catholic emphasis upon ceremony and ritual, and they rejected the need for an intermediary between themselves and God. They were especially critical of the monopolisation of religious studies by a privileged, educated elite. Like Marguerite de Navarre, they insisted that Christ's message was available to simple souls. And – in principle, at least – they accorded respect to the individual's religious experiences and spiritual insights, regardless of their learning, social status, or gender. In this context, women were able to take an active role in the government of congregations: some were permitted to act as preachers and religious advisers, and some were permitted to vote in church elections.[20] As a natural consequence, women were also empowered to write works commenting on the political and religious conflicts of the day.

Bull, 1641 [i.e. 1642]), pp. [4]–7. This work is hereafter referred to as *A True Copie*. See also, Anonymous, *To the Supream authority of this Nation, the Commons assembled in Parliament: The humble Petition of divers wel-affected Women* (London: n.p., [24 April] 1649), pp. 4–5. This petition was first circulated on 22 April 1649, and published two days later. The work is hereafter referred to as *Humble Petition I*.

[19] See, for example, Anonymous, *To the Supream Authority of England The Commons Assembled in Parliament. The humble Petition of diverse wel-affected WEOMEN* (London: n.p., [5 May] 1649), p. 1. This work is hereafter referred to as *Humble Petition II*.

[20] See Hill, *World Turned Upside Down*, p. 250; Dorothy P. Ludlow, 'Shaking Patriarchy's Foundations: Sectarian Women in England, 1641–1700', in *Triumph over Silence: Women in Protestant History*, ed. Richard L. Greaves (London and Westport: Greenwood Press, 1985), p. 107; Patricia Crawford, 'The Challenges to Patriarchalism: How Did the Revolution Affect Women?', in *Revolution and Restoration: England in the 1650s*, ed. John Morrill (London: Collins and Brown, 1992), p. 127; Patricia Crawford, ' "The Poorest She": Women and Citizenship in Early Modern England', in *The Putney Debates of 1647: The Army, The Levellers, and the English State*, ed. Michael Mendle (Cambridge University Press, 2001), pp. 197–218.

Not surprisingly, the primary political content of women's civil war writings derived from their religious views. In particular, many women petitioners followed the lead of the Leveller men, John Lilburne and Richard Overton. These men also translated a religious point of view into a political programme: much of the Leveller political outlook was born of universalism, or the view that all human beings are capable of attaining salvation through their own efforts.[21] According to the Levellers, all Christian subjects have a duty to attain their own salvation, and, for this reason, they must share an interest in the government of the church. If the state church is unjust, or requires something that sins against the conscience of the individual, then that individual is entitled to separate from or resist the state church, rather than betray his or her conscience. All souls are free in the sense that they owe their primary allegiance to God alone; their consciences are not, strictly speaking, bound by any civil or earthly authority.[22]

A similar concept of religious liberty can be found in the works of the civil war women associated with the Leveller group. Women first appeal to their liberty of conscience in the early petitions of 1642. In *A True Copie of the Petition of the Gentlewomen, and Tradesmens-wives, in and about the City of London*, of 4 February 1642, the petitioners claim that they consider themselves 'to have an interest in the common priviledges with [their husbands]'.[23] These privileges, it is implied, consist in the 'liberty of our conscience and the freedome of the Gospell, and the sincere profession and practice thereof'.[24] They express a fear 'that unlesse the blood-thirsty faction of the Papists and Prelates be hindred in their designes' they will be exposed to 'the thraldome of our soules and consciences in matters concerning GOD, which of all things are most deare unto us'.[25] Freedom of conscience, for them, is the freedom to believe and worship as they see fit, without fear of persecution, external compulsion, or threat. In a long justification of their right to petition, these women spell out the reasons for their defence of freedom of conscience. They say that

It may be thought strange, and unbeseeming our sex to shew our selves by way of Petition to this Honourable Assembly: but the matter being rightly considered, of the right and interest we have in the common and publique cause of the

---

[21] Brailsford, *The Levellers*, pp. 33, 64.
[22] Sharon Arnoult refers to this as the 'sovereignty of the soul'; see Sharon L. Arnoult, 'The Sovereignties of Body and Soul: Women's Political and Religious Actions in the English Civil War', in Fradenburg (ed.), *Women and Sovereignty*, pp. 228–49.
[23] Anonymous, *A True Copie*, pp. 2–[3].   [24] Ibid., p. 5.   [25] Ibid., p. [4].

Church, it will, as we conceive (under correction) be found a duty commanded
and required.[26]

According to these women, they have an interest in the government of
the church because they have a duty of obedience to Christ, who died for
female as well as male sins; their happiness, as well as that of men, consists
in living in a land where Christ's religion is permitted to flourish; con-
versely, women also partake in the misery that accompanies the oppression of church and state. They end their petition with the words:

On which grounds we are imboldned to present our humble Petition unto this
Honourable Assembly, not weighing the reproaches which may and are by many
cast upon us, who (not well weighing the premisses) scoff and deride our good
intent. We doe it not out of any selfe conceit, or pride of heart, as seeking to
equall our selves with Men, either in Authority or wisdome: But according to our
places to discharge that duty we owe to God, and the cause of the Church, as
farre as lyeth in us.[27]

These women explicitly shun any assertion of their political equality
'either in Authority or wisdome' with men. Their point is simply that, like
men, they have a duty to fulfil their obligations to God and the church,
and therefore an equal interest in freedom from religious oppression.
Needless to say, this is a coherent position: having a duty may mean that
you owe something to yourself or to others, or that others have the right
to expect a particular kind of treatment from you – but it does not
amount to you having the same right in return. Likewise, having an equal
interest as men does not equate to having the same political rights as men.
Children's interests, for example, are sometimes equal to those of adults,
but this fact does not justify giving children the political status of adults.
The women petitioners are therefore consistent when they assert that
while they have an equal interest in freedom from religious persecution,
this does not (in itself) amount to them calling for equal political standing
with men.

But what of their view that women possess an equal spiritual liberty to
that of men: does this have feminist implications? For the petitioners,
spiritual liberty consists in freedom of the mind or soul: if women are
spiritually free, they cannot be forced to believe a religious doctrine that,
in good conscience, they cannot support. In the civil sphere, this translates into women having an equal interest in resisting a state of religious

---

[26] Ibid., pp. 6–[7].   [27] Ibid.

'thraldome' or a state in which prelates are given an unlimited authority over their consciences. But this does not automatically translate into an equal civil or bodily liberty for women as a social group; nor does it amount to a call for their freedom from the arbitrary oppression of men as a social group. In so far as recognition of women's spiritual liberty translates into recognition of some civil liberties, the women petition only for freedom from tyranny over their religious beliefs and practices. 'Liberty for women' is thus confined to a narrow sphere of choice; religious liberty does not, in itself, entail a challenge to those civil hierarchical structures in which women always occupy a subordinate position to men.

II

With these sentiments, then, the early petitioners do not develop a full-blooded feminist concept of political equality. Do the later women offer anything more? According to Katharine Gillespie, they do: in the late 1640s, claims about the equal spiritual liberty of men and women develop into a 'feminist concept of political equality' or 'an early theory of women's rights'.[28] Gillespie points to the works of Katherine Chidley and the later women petitioners, in particular.

Chidley upholds a slightly more complex concept of religious liberty than that of the early women petitioners. A London seamstress or 'stocking-seller', she was closely associated with the Leveller organisation of women's petitions from 1649 to 1653.[29] Some scholars maintain that Chidley herself is the most likely author of the 1649 women's petitions: there are many stylistic and thematic similarities between Chidley's works and the *Humble Petitions* of April and May.[30] As a member of a persecuted religious sect, she was a fierce supporter of toleration for separatist congregations.[31] Her first work, the *Justification*, was written against the Presbyterian minister, Thomas Edwards, the author of *Reasons against the*

[28] Katharine Gillespie, 'A Hammer in her Hand: The Separation of Church from State and the Early Feminist Writings of Katherine Chidley', *Tulsa Studies in Women's Literature* 17 (1998), 213, 223; Gillespie, *Domesticity and Dissent*, pp. 85, 91. Sharon Achinstein also asserts that the women petitioners 'followed a logic of gender equality, asking for the same fundamental rights as the Leveller men': 'Women on Top in the Pamphlet Literature of the English Revolution', *Women's Studies* 24 (1994), 131–63.
[29] On one occasion in 1653, Chidley organised a group of 6,000 women to sign a petition for the release of the Leveller leader, John Lilburne.
[30] Brailsford, *The Levellers*, p. 318 (n. 8); Gentles, 'London Levellers', 292; Gillespie, 'A Hammer in her Hand', 223.
[31] Unusual for her time, Chidley was also a supporter of toleration for Jews; see Chidley, *Justification*, p. 44.

Independant Government of Particular Congregations (1641).[32] In this short tract, Edwards argues in favour of centralised church government. He maintains that a show of goodwill toward non-conforming sects 'will make great disturbance in the Church, both to the outward peace, and to the faith and conscience of the people of the Kingdome'.[33] Edwards sees the central role of government as the maintenance of civil peace and harmony; and for him, state control of religion is essential to fulfilling that role.

Against Edwards, Chidley calls on parliament to permit separatist congregations to operate independent of the state church. She maintains that 'liberty, power, and rule, should be in the whole and not in one man or few';[34] church government must rest with the entire body of Christian worshippers, and not just one or two officers of the state church. Freedom or liberty is contrasted with tyrannical church government:

> The way of the Gospell, as hath beene plainely proved, is not to live without Gods Ordinances, nor to live at liberty (as you say) except you meane the liberty wherein Christ hath set them, and commanded them to stand fast, because he hath made them free, *Gal.* 5.1. By this you may see the Saints are called into liberty; but not a liberty to sinne (as you would insinuate) but to be freed from the yoake of bondage, which is the tyranny, or tyrannical government of the Canon, Lawes, either of *Rome* or *England*.[35]

In Galatians 5.1, Paul urges the Galatians to 'maintain their Christian liberty': 'Stand fast . . . in the liberty wherewith Christ hath made us free, and be not entangled again with the yoke of bondage'. Christian liberty is the freedom to live according to the spirit of Christ, and to believe and worship independent of constraint or coercion. According to Chidley, individuals ought to be permitted the freedom to search Scripture for themselves, rather than adopt an implicit faith and simply take for granted whatever religion the state dictates.[36] But this spiritual liberty also amounts to a kind of civil liberty: for Chidley, true freedom of worship means being free from the arbitrary tyranny or discretionary power of others. In a significant passage of his *Reasons*, Edwards suggests that the separatists may live in England and enjoy their liberties. They may do so, he says, if they make an outward show of attending state church

---

[32] Thomas Edwards, *Reasons against the Independant* [sic] *Government of Particular Congregations* (London: Richard Cotes for Jo Bellamie and Ralph Smith, 1641). For an analysis of the Chidley–Edwards exchange, see Marcus Nevitt, *Women and the Pamphlet Culture of Revolutionary England, 1640–1660* (Aldershot: Ashgate, 2006), Chapter 1.

[33] Quoted in Chidley, *Justification*, p. 21.   [34] Ibid., pp. 24–5.   [35] Ibid., p. 38.   [36] Ibid., p. 45.

services: '[they may be tolerated] so long as they keepe communion with the Church, and submit to the Discipline and orders, and be peaceable, and not speake against what is established by common consent nor practise to the scandall and contempt of the Magistrate and Church'.[37] For Chidley, this kind of toleration does not promote true liberty: under this 'toleration' the separatists are still liable to pay their dues to the state church, and to face penalties if they are caught in their private conventicles. In her second work against Edwards, *A New-Yeares-Gift* (1644), Chidley points out that 'the thing we plead for, is a peaceable enjoyment of our liberty to worship God, publikely, according to his revealed word ... without feare of the execution of such *unjust Lawes* which former Parliaments have made'.[38] True liberty is impossible so long as the church governors have the power to persecute separatists for their beliefs – even if those governors never exercise that power. True religious freedom does not depend on the mere goodwill of governors or their willingness to turn a blind eye to separatist beliefs. According to Chidley, 'We plead for one intire *governement* established upon *sound principles*, unalterable. And not a *government* which may looke with *severall faces*, in *severall times*, upon *severall occasions*, according to *mens fancies*.'[39]

In these passages, Chidley's sentiments are certainly consistent with a modern liberal position on the limits of political authority. Like later liberal philosophers, Chidley holds the view that the magistrate is not entitled to interfere in the religious lives of subjects. But she also expresses some sympathy for what recent theorists call a 'republican' or 'neo-roman theory' of liberty.[40] This pre-liberal concept of liberty, which was prevalent in the English civil war era, has its origins in the classical ideal of the *civitas libera* or free state. While modern liberal theorists, such as John Stuart Mill, argue for strict limits on the right of the state to interfere with individual freedom, neo-romans characterise freedom according to non-domination, or the absence of arbitrary sway.[41] For the

---

[37] Quoted ibid., p. 73.   [38] Chidley, *A New-Yeares-Gift*, pp. 16–17.   [39] Ibid., p. 20.

[40] See Philip Pettit, *Republicanism: A Theory of Freedom and Government* (Oxford: Clarendon Press, 1997); Quentin Skinner, *Liberty Before Liberalism* (Cambridge University Press, 1998). One might argue, as Steve Pincus does, that republicanism was not as strong in this period as some scholars maintain. See Steve Pincus, 'Neither Machiavellian Moment nor Possessive Individualism: Commercial Society and the Defenders of the English Commonwealth', *The American Historical Review* 103 (1998), 705–36. For our purposes here, however, it is enough that the so-called republican concept of liberty which can be found in political literature of the period is distinct from the modern liberal concept.

[41] An act is arbitrary if 'it is subject just to the *arbitrium*, the decision or judgement, of the agent; the agent was in a position to choose it or not choose it, at their pleasure' (Pettit, *Republicanism*, p. 55).

liberal theorist, you are unfree when you are threatened or forced to act contrary to your will; for the neo-roman, you are unfree if your will is simply subject to, or dependent upon, the arbitrary power of another. While the liberal contrasts freedom with state interference, the neo-roman contrasts freedom with a condition of arbitrary and non-law-governed dependence or domination, as exemplified by slavery. As Philip Pettit says, the neo-romans acknowledge that 'Domination can occur without interference, because it requires only that someone have the capacity to interfere arbitrarily in your affairs; no one need actually interfere.'[42] The neo-romans thus do not posit a conflict between the freedom of individuals and the powers of the state. In their view, individuals are not free if they are subject to the arbitrary sway or jurisdiction of another. For individual liberty to flourish, the rights of individuals must be explicitly guaranteed by the power of the state, and their freedoms must be enshrined in law. The individual's liberty cannot be upheld under an absolute monarch, for example, if that monarch has the power to interfere with the individual's 'life, liberties, and estate' on an arbitrary basis – even if the monarch never uses that power.

Chidley appeals to a similar notion of liberty when she says that true freedom of conscience requires that separatists are permitted to worship openly and publicly, with some degree of security, and without fear of persecution from the powers that be. For Chidley, it is possible to be unfree without actual interference: that is, when a government governs 'according to *mens fancies*', and not on the basis of sound, unalterable principles. Edwards's proposed toleration of separatists (or, we might say, his policy of non-interference), on the proviso that they make an outward show of conformity, does not therefore guarantee true liberty.

Similar sentiments are echoed in a May 1649 petition, titled *To the Supream Authority of England The Commons Assembled in Parliament. The humble Petition of diverse wel-affected WEOMEN* – a petition that may have been the work of Chidley herself. These women assert their equal interest (as women compared to men) in the protection of civil liberties. The petitioners ask 'must we keep at home in our houses, as if we, our lives and liberties all, were not concerned?'[43]

Have we not an equal interest with the men of this Nation, in those liberties and securities contained in the Petition of Right, and other good Lawes of the Land?

For the classic statement of the limits to the state's right to interfere with individual liberty, see John Stuart Mill, *On Liberty*, ed. C. L. Ten (New York: Oxford University Press, 1980).
[42] Pettit, *Republicanism*, p. 23.   [43] Anonymous, *Humble Petition II*, p. [1].

are any of our lives, limbs, liberties, or goods to be taken from us more then from Men, but by due processe of Law, and conviction of twelve sworn men of the Neighbourhood?

And can you imagine us to be sottish or stupid, as not to perceive, or not to be sencible when daily those strong defences of our Peace and wellfare are broken down, and trod under-foot by force and arbitrary power?[44]

These women claim an equal interest in securing their civil liberties against arbitrary power in the state. Their appeal to the Petition of Right (1628) is significant: this document spells out the civil rights and liberties of English subjects under the crown. The Petition, first drafted by Sir Edward Coke, insists (among other things) that subjects ought to be granted freedom from arbitrary arrest and imprisonment. For the women petitioners, this statute applies to female as well as male subjects: women's 'lives, limbs, liberties, or goods' are also protected by law. No free woman may be taken or imprisoned, or dispossessed of her goods and liberties, but by the lawful judgement of her peers. They will not rest, the women argue, till 'We, our husbands, Friends, and Servants, may not be liable to be abused, violated and butchered at mens Wills and pleasures.'[45]

A similar point is made in an earlier *Humble Petition* of April 1649. In this work, the women complain that their governors are simply repeating the tyrannies of former rulers instead of delivering their 'promises of freedom and prosperity to the Nation'.[46] The foundations of true freedom require that there be no 'exercise of arbitrary Power, or continuance of Authoritie Civil or Military, beyond the time limited by Trust or Commission, or the perverting of either to unjust, bloudy, or ambitious ends'.[47] Like Chidley, these women articulate a concept of civil liberty as freedom from arbitrary sway and domination. They see this liberty as compatible with the 'due process of the law', despite the law being a form of interference in the lives of subjects.[48] In other words, their call for liberty is not a call for non-interference (the modern liberal ideal), but rather for an institutionalised guarantee of personal safety and security (the ideal of non-domination). Their notion of liberty is conceptually distinct from at least one influential strand of the modern liberal notion.

According to Katharine Gillespie, these women's writings ought to prompt us to rethink our assumptions about the history of liberal feminism. The prevailing scholarly view is that early modern feminist ideals are primarily derived from conservative royalist or Tory political

---

[44] Ibid.   [45] Ibid.   [46] Anonymous, *Humble Petition I*, p. 5.   [47] Ibid., p. 7.
[48] On freedom as non-domination and the law, see Pettit, *Republicanism*, pp. 35–41.

origins.[49] It is not until the eighteenth century – or so the story goes – that we see the liberal conception of the individual in the public domain being extended to women in the domestic sphere. Contrary to this view, Gillespie argues that radical political movements of the seventeenth century made a significant contribution toward early liberal feminist thinking. In particular, she says, we might think that Chidley and the women petitioners translated a 'concept of spiritual equality into the earliest notion of female political equality grounded in contract and consent'.[50] Gillespie argues that sectarian women's voices ought to be assimilated into the history of liberalism.[51]

We do not deny that Chidley and the women petitioners anticipated some elements of the historical liberal tradition, but we think it anachronistic to read back into them either liberty as non-interference or the full-blown doctrine of political obligation grounded in consent. Chidley and the petitioners certainly called for liberty or freedom against their oppressors. But these women regarded this oppression or domination as affecting a particular aspect of their lives – their freedom of conscience; they did not characterise their oppression as one that entered into every aspect of their lives. It is therefore difficult to see this as a straightforward feminist call for women's equality with men. First, there is no overt recognition that women are oppressed as a social group compared to men. According to their arguments, it is simply the case that both male and female separatists suffer the same fear of persecution as a result of their religious affiliations; both men and women are therefore entitled to call for liberty. In the 1649 petitions, the authors point out that women, as well as men, suffer the terrible consequences of arbitrary arrest and imprisonment; and so they too have an interest in seeing the due process of law respected. Nothing about this challenge to state control necessarily implies a feminist challenge to men's domination of women in the public and private spheres. It simply amounts to a claim that women are entitled to call for change, because they too are oppressed by their dependence upon arbitrary power.

In addition, it is not clear that Chidley and the women petitioners uphold a straightforward liberal conception of liberty as freedom from

---

[49] See, for example, Joan K. Kinnaird, 'Mary Astell and the Conservative Contribution to English Feminism', *The Journal of British Studies* 19 (1979), 53–75; Catherine Gallagher, 'Embracing the Absolute: The Politics of the Female Subject in Seventeenth-Century England', *Genders* 1 (1988), 24–39.
[50] Gillespie, 'A Hammer in her Hand', 214; Gillespie, *Domesticity and Dissent*, p. 76.
[51] Gillespie, *Domesticity and Dissent*, p. 14.

interference. On the one hand, these women would certainly agree with the liberal position on freedom from state interference in one's religious practices. But on the other, in calling for liberty against their oppressors, they express a desire to live without anxiety and fear of random persecution on the basis of their beliefs. The condition of liberty is contrasted, not with interference, but rather the slave-like state or 'vassalage' of being subject to the discretionary power of others. In their view, the interference of the law need not entail a loss of liberty, provided that it is extended to separatists and non-separatists alike on a just and non-arbitrary basis.

III

To establish whether or not these women offer a truly feminist theory of equality, we must determine not only the extent to which they grant both male and female subjects the liberty to challenge authority in the state, but also the extent to which they grant women as a social group the freedom to challenge the tyranny of men as a social group. So we now turn to the textual evidence concerning Katherine Chidley's and Elizabeth Poole's theories of resistance to the authority of husbands in the home.

In her *Justification*, Chidley challenges the notion that married women are always required to obey their husbands. This challenge is a natural extension of her view that the people are entitled to separate themselves from those magistrates who do not practise true worship. As we have seen, Chidley opposes the view that the only legitimate religion is one sanctioned by the king or parliament. Against this, she maintains that the only thing that confers true authority on a preacher is that they have been trained in the school of Christ. This training simply consists in being obedient to Christ and keeping God's commandments.[52] As Chidley repeatedly insists, the primary role of the magistrate is to give praise to those who do well, and to punish evil doers.[53] If the separatists show a due obedience to God, then the magistrate has no right to arrest or imprison them for their beliefs. On the flip side, if the magistrate does not practise true obedience to God, or compels his subjects to practise an anti-Christian religion, then those subjects have a religious duty to separate themselves from their ruler. It is the Christian's duty 'to put it [God's true worship] into practise, not onely in a Land where they have Toleration, but also where they are forbidden to preach'.[54] Christians will therefore sometimes be compelled to defy the laws of the land, and to separate

---

[52] Chidley, *Justification*, p. 7.   [53] Ibid., p. 38.   [54] Ibid., sig. *2r.

themselves from the state religion, in order to do what is right and engage in the proper worship of God. Magistrates, on this view, have a power over the 'bodies, estates, and lives' of their subjects, but they cannot be 'Lords over their consciences'.[55] In civil matters, our bodies and lives are those of the sovereign in whose land we dwell; but in the realm of spiritual worship, we belong to God alone.[56] Her attitude anticipates Locke's position in his *Letter Concerning Toleration*.[57] Matters of conscience are special and the magistrate should not attempt to force conscience. This does not, however, imply restrictions on the magistrate's authority in temporal matters.

Chidley's justification of separatism is entailed by her notion of liberty. Her theory about the subject's right to separate from the state church is based upon her assertions about every subject's freedom to live according to the spirit of Christ, and to believe and worship without oppression. In her *Justification*, she points out that many people refuse to conform to the Church of England because its government is perceived to be 'vaine and Popish'.[58] Such non-conformity is justified – and ought to be tolerated – because all Christians have a religious duty to follow the true worship. Against this view, Thomas Edwards claims that the toleration of separatists 'will breed divisions, and Schismes, disturbing the peace and quiet of Churches, and Townes'; and it will also 'breed divisions in families betweene husband and wife, brother, and brother'.[59] If we grant the right to resist the government in religious matters, then this will ultimately undermine patriarchal authority in other spheres. If subjects can dissent from the views of their rulers, then wives might dissent from their husbands, servants from their masters, children from their parents, and so on.

By contrast, Chidley denies that this toleration will unduly disrupt the patriarchal authority of fathers over their families and of husbands over their wives:

Next you say O! how this will take away that power & authority which God hath given to Husbands, Fathers, and Masters, over wives, children, and servants.

To which I answer, O! that you would consider the text in I Cor. 7. which plainely declares that the wife may be a beleever, & the husband an unbeleever, but if you have considered this text, I pray you tell me, what authority this unbeleeving husband hath over the conscience of his beleeving wife; It is true he

---

[55] Ibid., p. 29.   [56] Ibid., p. 32.

[57] John Locke, *A Letter Concerning Toleration*, ed. James Tully (Indianapolis: Hackett Publishing, 1983).

[58] Chidley, *Justification*, p. 23.   [59] Quoted ibid., p. 25.

hath authority over her in bodily and civill respects, but not to be a Lord over her conscience; and the like may be said of fathers and masters, and it is the very same authority which the Soveraigne hath over all his subjects, & therfore it must needes reach to families: for it is granted that the King hath power (according to the Law) over the bodies, goods and lives of all his subjects; yet it is Christ the King of Kings that reigneth over their consciences: and thus you may see it taketh away no authority which God hath given to them.[60]

If subjects have a duty to pursue the true worship of God, then wives are entitled to defy the religious beliefs of their husbands whenever those beliefs contravene true worship. But does this amount to an argument for a woman's right to resist unjust authority in the home? This interpretation is not borne out by the text.[61] Chidley affirms that the husband has authority over the wife 'in bodily and civill respects'. She also refers to I Corinthians 7, in which it is said that 'the woman which hath an husband that believeth not . . . let her not leave him'. On Chidley's view, it is acceptable for wives to adhere to a different religion from that of their husbands, but it does not follow that wives might consider themselves to be free from their spousal obligations. A woman's right to 'separate' from her husband is limited to the sphere of religious worship alone. Chidley applies something like the separation of church and state to the private sphere, and argues for a wife's spiritual freedom without extending it to include full civil liberty. Her argument in this key passage is not in favour of divorce; it amounts to an argument for female spiritual freedom or 'Christian liberty' alone. This position is consistent with women practising an outward conformity to their husband's beliefs, while at the same time privately adhering to their own; it is not about challenging the authority of the husband in the home. We might think that to be truly consistent, Chidley ought to have extended her challenge to patriarchal authority in the state to patriarchal authority in the home; but she stops short of doing so – as did so many other republicans of the time. Chidley does not, strictly speaking, extend the notion of civil liberty to women in the private domestic sphere; she does not develop a full-fledged theory of female political liberty.

[60] Ibid., p. 26.
[61] Marcus Nevitt points out that in I Corinthians 7 the wife is also granted power over her husband's body: 'The wife hath not power of her own body, but the husband: and likewise also the husband hath not power of his own body, but the wife.' Nevitt claims that Chidley may have been subtly pointing us to the 'more daring reading' (*Women and the Pamphlet Culture*, p. 45). But it still remains that Chidley's explicit point is that the granting of liberty of conscience will not challenge the husband's civil and bodily authority over his wife.

The Baptist prophet Elizabeth Poole takes a similar position on marriage to that of Katherine Chidley.[62] A member of a Baptist separatist congregation, Poole was known in political circles as 'a woman of great wisedom and gravity'.[63] On 29 December 1648, and then again on 4 January 1649, Poole visited Whitehall in order to offer advice to the General Council of the New Model Army about the trial of Charles I. At the time, the army was reluctant to negotiate, and few members of parliament were inclined to protect the king. In her advice to the council, which was later published as *A Vision: Wherein is manifested the disease and cure of the Kingdome* (1649), Poole claims to be interpreting a vision from God by the 'gift of faith'. In this vision, the kingdom is represented as a 'woman, crooked, sick, weak & imperfect in body',[64] and the army is appointed as her physician. According to Gillespie, Poole uses this metaphor to advise the council that 'the sick body politic must exercise its right to break contract with the monarch . . . "she" should divorce him as fast as a sectarian wife would an unregenerate husband'.[65] Poole boldly advises the army to take away Charles's kingly powers, but she warns against his execution.

Poole begins by drawing a literal connection between kings, fathers, and husbands. Her argument draws on the parental and conjugal paradigms, or the identification of kings with fathers and husbands, and subjects with children and wives.[66] She advises the army that 'the King is your Father and husband, which you were and are to obey in the Lord, & no other way'.[67] It is true, she says, that

when he forgot his Subordination to divine Faith hood and headship, thinking he had begotten you a generation to his own pleasure, and taking you a wife for his own lusts, thereby is the yoake taken from your neck (I meane the neck of the spirit and Law, which is the bond of your union, that the holy life in it might not be prophaned; it being free and cannot be bound: *For the law of the Spirit of life in Christ Jesus, hath freed us from the law of sinne and of death* . . .[68]

When the husband/king forgets his religious duty to his wife/subject, then the subordinate parties are entitled to consider themselves 'freed from the bonds of their union', according to 'the law of the Spirit of life

---

[62] On Poole as a regicide disputant, see ibid., pp. 69–84.
[63] Anonymous, *The Manner of the Deposition of Charles Stewart* ([London: n.p.], 1649), p. 6, quoted in Gillespie, *Domesticity and Dissent*, p. 139.
[64] Poole, *A Vision*, p. 1.   [65] Gillespie, *Domesticity and Dissent*, p. 116.
[66] For a discussion of the significance of Elizabeth I's appropriation of these paradigms, see Chapter 4.
[67] Poole, *A Vision*, p. 6.   [68] Ibid.

in Christ Jesus'. But although they may consider their spiritual covenant to be dissolved, subordinates are still required to honour their superiors: 'although he would not be your Father and husband, Subordinate, but absolute, yet know that you are for the Lords sake to honour his person. For he is the Father and husband of your bodies, as unto men, and therefore your right cannot be without him, as unto men.'[69] Their earthly or civil contract, in other words, is not dissolved. Although the husband/king may have refused to be subordinate to God, 'You never heard that a wife might put away her husband, as he is the head of her body.'[70] Although the husband/king has no authority over his wife/subject's conscience, by law he still possesses authority over her bodily self. The wife/subject must therefore endure her husband/king's tyranny in the flesh – to be insensible to her earthly 'interests, lives, liberties, freedoms',[71] while being assured that she is 'free in the spirit of the Lord'.

To support this point, Poole appeals to the story of Abigail in I Samuel. This story demonstrates that although the husband/king may be unjust or irreligious, his ultimate punishment will come from God alone. Abigail, 'a woman of good understanding, and of a beautiful countenance', is married to Nabal, a 'churlish and evil man' (I Samuel 25.3). When David comes to kill Nabal, Abigail pleads on her husband's behalf, and persuades David not to take Nabal's life with his own hands. A few days later, 'the Lord smote Nabal' and he died (I Samuel 25.38). By analogy, according to Poole, the army should not kill the king:

> For as the Lord revenged his owne cause on him [Abigail's husband], he shall doe on yours [the king]; . . . Stretch not forth the hand against him: For know this, the Conquest was not without divine displeasure, whereby Kings came to reigne, though through lust they tyranized: which God excuseth not, but judgeth; and his judgements are fallen heavy, as you see, upon *Charles* your Lord.[72]

A wife/subject may act in self-defence by holding the hands of her husband/king, but she must not proceed to take his life.[73] In the end, therefore, Poole advises the army to bring Charles to trial so 'that he may be convicted in his conscience, but touch not his person'.[74] The army, in other words, represents the wife/subject who may 'hold the hands' of her husband/king, but must wait for God to inflict the ultimate punishment (in this case, death). Poole does not support the Leveller position on 'sovereignty for the people'; the wife/subject is not entitled to usurp her husband/king's authority for herself.

[69] Ibid.   [70] Ibid., p. 5.   [71] Ibid., p. 2.   [72] Ibid., p. 5.   [73] Ibid., p. 6 [7].   [74] Ibid., p. 6.

According to Gillespie, 'Poole's call for a trial ... bespeaks a con-tractual interest in a limited rather than an absolutist monarchy, one that preserves the King's life while also managing to infuse his "wife" with new powers.'[75] Poole implicitly challenges the traditional view that wives must always obey their husbands. Instead, wives have the right 'to appropriate a measure of "sovereign" self-rule for themselves',[76] and they are 'entitled to invoke the right of exit' or 'the right to withdraw' from the marriage contract.[77] In this sense, according to Gillespie, Poole presents a radical challenge to patriarchal authority: she 'raises new questions about the parameters of patriarchal authority, both at state level as well as within the home'.[78] Poole implies that it is 'the wife's right to consent that forms the original grant of a contract theory',[79] and she may very well 'withdraw consent in the face of tyranny'.[80] Once the husband/king has violated the trust of the wife/subject, the latter is relieved of her obligation to obey – the wife/subject has grounds, in other words, for divorce.

But it is not clear that Poole thinks that it is permissible for the wife/subject to divorce her husband/king. The textual evidence does not unequivocally support this interpretation. According to most patriarchal theories, although the consent of both parties may be necessary to initiate the marital union, once the vows have been taken, a woman is unable to dissolve the contract. When a woman marries, as Mary Astell astutely observed in 1700, she 'Elects a Monarch for Life' and gives him 'an Authority she cannot recall however he misapply it'.[81] Although marriage is a contract, the husband has a 'sacred and inalienable' authority over the wife.[82] According to Robert Filmer, for example, God alone invested this authority in the first patriarch, Adam, and in his successors; the wife does not have the power to give or take away such authority by her consent or dissent.[83] Poole's advice to the council is entirely consistent with this patriarchal outlook: a wife must endure her husband's physical abuse, Poole says, because by law he possesses authority over her bodily self. His punishment – and her reward – will come from God alone. The spiritual equality of men and women, on this view, does not translate easily into a right to resist unjust authority. The only 'divorce' a woman can obtain from an unregenerate spouse is a spiritual one – she need not adhere to

---

[75] Gillespie, *Domesticity and Dissent*, p. 142.   [76] Ibid., p. 143.   [77] Ibid., pp. 147, 149.
[78] Ibid., p. 149.   [79] Ibid., p. 150.   [80] Ibid., p. 151.
[81] Mary Astell, *Reflections upon Marriage*, in *Astell: Political Writings*, p. 48.
[82] Ibid., p. 17.
[83] Robert Filmer, *Patriarcha and Other Political Works of Sir Robert Filmer*, ed. Peter Laslett (Oxford: Basil Blackwell, 1949).

her husband's religious beliefs, but she cannot physically withdraw from their union.[84]

This interpretation of Poole's text is confirmed in her later works. Needless to say, her prophetic advice was ignored. Shortly after the beheading of Charles I on 30 January 1649, Poole published *An Alarum of War, Given to the Army*, foretelling 'the judgements of God ready to fall upon them for disobeying the word of the Lord, in taking away the life of the King' (title-page). At about the same time, another work titled *Alarum of War* also appeared (here referred to as *Another Alarum of War*). The text includes material that does not appear in the first *Alarum*. Poole reminds the Army that

I told you, that the King was your Father and Husband, which you were to obey in the Lord, and none otherwaies; for when he forgot his subordination to Divine fatherhood and headship, thereby was the Yoak of the spirit, and Law, taken off from your necks, for though ye were bound in the bodie, yet are ye free in the spirit to the Lord, but were to suffer his [the King's] terrour to your flesh for the Lords sake; according to another sentence in that paper, *True liberty is not bound to any thing, nor from any thing.*[85]

In this passage, Poole expands her original statement by providing a definition of what it means to be 'free in the spirit to the Lord'. Her concept of liberty is similar to Chidley's notion of Christian liberty. Poole tells the army that 'you are men that have professed your selves hot pursuers after libertie',[86] but true liberty consists in being free in a spiritual sense, and regarding all earthly interests as subordinate to the divine will.

Katherine Chidley and Elizabeth Poole may be, as Brailsford observes, 'pioneers of women's emancipation' in some sense.[87] In her *Vindication of the Rights of Woman* (1792), Mary Wollstonecraft says that in an enlightened age it is to be hoped that 'The *divine right* of husbands, like the divine right of kings, may ... be contested without danger.'[88] Wollstonecraft takes the ideals of female spiritual and political liberty to a liberal conclusion: a call for the recognition of equal political rights for

[84] For an alternative interpretation of Poole's text, see Brian Patton, 'Revolution, Regicide, and Divorce: Elizabeth Poole's Advice to the Army', in *Place and Displacement in the Renaissance*, ed. Alvin Vos (Binghamton, NY: Medieval & Renaissance Texts & Studies, 1995), pp. 133–45. Patton points to a tension in Poole's *Vision*. According to his analysis, Poole figuratively represents the army *both* as the ruling husband/king and the subordinate wife/subject. On our reading, Poole avoids explicitly characterising the army as the husband/king of the people; this metaphor is reserved for the disgraced king alone.
[85] Poole, *Another Alarum of War*, p. 7.   [86] Ibid.   [87] Brailsford, *The Levellers*, p. 38.
[88] Wollstonecraft, *A Vindication of the Rights of Man and a Vindication of the Rights of Woman*, p. 112.

men and women. In the civil war era, there was certainly the potential for women to exploit the upheavals in state government in order to disrupt the political power of men within the home. The civil war women petitioners were radical for their time: they extended the concept of liberty of conscience to women as subjects, and they affirmed that while women might not be independent or full-blooded citizens, they nevertheless shared an interest in the political management of the country. But in their critiques of the marriage/social contract analogue, Chidley and Poole do not anticipate the universal challenge to divine right in Wollstonecraft and her liberal successors. While Chidley and Poole may support a wife's spiritual freedom within marriage, they nevertheless advocate wifely obedience in a bodily and civil respect. They wrote at a time when the power of the magistrate to interfere with conscience was being contested, but they did not in general challenge hierarchical authority based on divine edict. Although these women were radicals, they respected the Bible as God's word on the subject of male–female power relations, and thus they still upheld the husband's temporal authority in the home.

CHAPTER 7

Quaker women

During the period of the interregnum in England, some members of non-conformist religious groups gradually discovered that the new political regime was little better than the old. In the 1650s, English society was still very much a society in which religious persecution and intolerance were the norms. Throughout this decade, members of the Quaker movement (or the Society of Friends, as it is now known) were particularly vocal in their calls for social justice. In his *Collection of the Sufferings Of the People called Quakers* (1753), Joseph Besse reports on a religious debate between two Quaker women and a group of scholars at Sidney Sussex College, Cambridge, in 1653. The women, named Elizabeth Williams and Mary Fisher, reprove the scholars for their ignorance of 'the *true God and his Worship*',

Whereupon the Scholars began to mock and deride them: The Women, observing the Froth and Levity of their Behaviour, told them *they were Antichrists*, and that *their College was a Cage of unclean Birds, and the Synagogue of Satan* . . . Complaint was forthwith made to *William Pickering*, then Mayor, that two Women were preaching: He sent a Constable for them, and examined them . . . He demanded their Husbands Names: They told him, *they had no Husband but* Jesus Christ, *and he sent them*. Upon this the Mayor grew angry, called them Whores, and issued his Warrant to the Constable *to Whip them at the Market-Cross till the Blood ran down their Bodies*; and ordered three of his Serjeants to see that Sentence, equally cruel and lawless, severely executed.[1]

This incident – in which the women were publicly stripped and then whipped till 'their Flesh was miserably cut and torn'[2] – aptly demonstrates the lengths that women were prepared to go in their efforts to promote the Quaker cause.

---

[1] Joseph Besse, *A Collection of the Sufferings Of the People called Quakers, For The Testimony of a Good Conscience*, 2 vols. (London: Luke Hinde, 1753), vol. 1, pp. 84–5.
[2] Ibid., p. 85.

The Quaker movement originated in England in the decade or so following the civil wars. At the start of the 1650s, the movement was composed of only a small band of Protestant separatists, brought together under the guidance of one or two charismatic leaders. By the end of the decade, there were reportedly 40,000 to 60,000 Quakers spread throughout England, a large number of whom were women.[3] Women were active pioneers in the early establishment of Quakerism in England: they preached both at home and abroad, they disrupted state church services, they travelled throughout Europe and North America, they wrote letters of news and support to Friends, and they were persecuted and imprisoned for their activities.[4] In the seventeenth century alone, female authors were responsible for more than 200 published Quaker works in England;[5] some Quaker women were also publishers in their own right.[6] The bulk of their writings are in popular religious genres, such as memorials for the dead, spiritual autobiographies, conversion narratives, works of prophecy, and records of prison sufferings.[7]

In some cases, Quaker women wrote petitions and pamphlets that are remarkably similar in political content to those of the Leveller-inspired women. Some Quaker women express opinions about what legitimates political authority, about the roles and responsibilities of government, and they offer arguments for resistance to authority, for religious toleration, and for the separation of church and state. They also appeal to the

---

[3] Barry Reay, *The Quakers and the English Revolution*, with a foreword by Christopher Hill (London: Temple Smith, 1985), p. 26.

[4] On Quaker women, see Mabel Richmond Brailsford, *Quaker Women 1650–1690* (London: Duckworth, 1915); Christine Trevett, *Women and Quakerism in the Seventeenth Century* (York: Sessions Book Trust, The Ebor Press, 1991); Phyllis Mack, *Visionary Women: Ecstatic Prophecy in Seventeenth-Century England* (Berkeley, CA: University of California Press, 1992); and Catie Gill, *Women in the Seventeenth-Century Quaker Community: A Literary Study of Political Identities, 1650–1700* (Aldershot: Ashgate, 2005).

[5] Patricia Crawford says that Quaker women's writings 'amounted to about 20 per cent of women's output for the whole century, a disproportionate share given their numbers in society'; see Crawford, 'Women's Published Writings 1600–1700', p. 213. This disproportion might be attributed to the fact that, compared to other sects, the early Friends were careful to preserve their publications and so their women's writings have had a higher rate of survival.

[6] Maureen Bell, 'Mary Westwood – Quaker Publisher', *Publishing History* 23 (1988), 5–66; Paula McDowell, *The Women of Grub Street: Press, Politics, and Gender in the London Literary Marketplace, 1678–1730* (Oxford: Clarendon Press, 1998), Chapter 1 (on Tace Sowle).

[7] For Quaker women's writings in these genres, see Mary Garman, Judith Applegate, Margaret Benefiel, and Dortha Meredith (eds.), *Hidden in Plain Sight: Quaker Women's Writing 1650–1700*, with a foreword by Rosemary Radford Ruether (Wallingford, PA: Pendle Hill Publications, 1996); David Booy (ed.), *Autobiographical Writings by Early Quaker Women* (Aldershot: Ashgate, 2004). See also Rosemary Foxton, *Hear the Word of the Lord: A Critical and Bibliographical Study of Quaker Women's Writing, 1650–1700* (Melbourne: The Bibliographical Society of Australia and New Zealand, 1994).

modern political themes of social justice and egalitarianism, broadly conceived. In this chapter, we focus on the political writings of Quaker women in the decades following the English civil wars, with particular emphasis on the concept of equality that emerges in their writings. We examine the significance of their claims about spiritual equality for their judgements about the moral permissibility or impermissibility of social inequalities; and we discuss the extent to which the Quaker arguments for egalitarianism are consistently applied to women.

I

The Quakers maintain that the Light of Christ is in every individual, regardless of gender, social status, race, or nationality. All human beings are capable of achieving redemption, provided that they recognise the presence of this Light within the self – a light that both reveals one's sinfulness, and yet enables one to overcome sin and to attain inner strength and peace. Such beliefs had implications for early Quaker practice. The Quakers took a collaborative rather than a hierarchical approach to prayer meetings: there would be no head preacher, but after a reading from the Bible, members would sit in silence till someone felt the Light stir within and offer an interpretation of the text. The Quakers were suspicious of university-educated preachers, believing that the Light made everyone capable of interpreting Scripture for themselves, without the need for an education in Hebrew, Greek, or Latin. In fact, some Quakers shunned appeals to the Bible altogether, believing that if someone were 'in the Light', then they already had direct understanding of the Word of God. The Quakers held that all human beings were equal in the eyes of Christ, and that God was 'no respecter of persons' (Acts 10.34). In their everyday dealings with social superiors, Quaker men would refuse to doff their hats, and Quaker women would not curtsey. They refused to take oaths (such as the Oaths of Allegiance and Supremacy), they dressed plainly and without ornamentation, and they did not use deferential titles, preferring to use 'thee' and 'thou' instead.

In the first period of Quakerism, the movement was closely associated with a strong political stance against the payment of tithes. In early modern England, tithes were a kind of compulsory tax that went toward the maintenance of the local church minister.[8] They were typically one-tenth

---

[8] In some cases, tithes were also paid to 'impropriators' or laymen who had purchased blocks of tithes from the government. On the subject of Quakers and tithes, see Margaret James, 'The

of the parishioners' produce and livestock, or one-tenth of the money earned from their labour. If an individual refused to pay tithes, then a minister could appeal to a Justice of the Peace, who had the power to fine or imprison the offender. Early Quakers in England were strongly opposed to compulsory tithe payments to national church ministers. Their refusal to pay tithes was primarily a matter of conscience: it was morally unconscionable for Quakers to pay others to spread 'false religion' as the 'truth', or to pay ministers who provided no spiritual service for them.[9] But it was also a question of politics.[10] Many Quakers resented the coercive interference of the magistrate, and maintained that tithes should be paid on a voluntary basis alone, to a minister of choice. They also resented the fact that tithes were taken from the poor in order to keep privileged persons (such as younger sons of the gentry) in wealth and idleness. They would point out that, according to the Bible, the tithe system was originally intended to assist the poor – people such as widows and orphans. In the eyes of their enemies, the Quakers (like the Levellers before them) were seen as a threat to the structure of society and as destroyers of the right to property. In his *Looking Glasse for the Quakers* (1657), Thomas Collier claims that the Quakers seek nothing less than the 'Levelling all conditions, witnessed likewise: Magistrate, People, Husband, Wife, Parents, Children, Master, Servant, all alike, no difference in the Quakers Religion'.[11] Bonnelyn Young Kunze observes that the Quakers (and other socially conscious sectarians) 'introduced a new unsettling egalitarian-style ideology that challenged "the existence of hierarchy"'.[12]

Like their menfolk,[13] some Quaker women took issue with the compulsory payment of tithes. Their special concern stemmed partly from the

---

Political Importance of the Tithes Controversy in the English Revolution 1640–60', *History* 26 (1941), 1–18; Barry Reay, 'Quaker Opposition to Tithes 1652–1700', *Past and Present* 86 (1980), 98–120; and Nevitt, *Women and the Pamphlet Culture of Revolutionary England*, pp. 145–78.

[9] One group of Quaker women wrote that 'it is an unrighteous thing to force people to maintain a Minister that they know in their consciences they are contrary to God; & then again it is an unrighteous thing that they should not have their liberty to question and try their doctrine without imprisonment'; see Mary Forster [and 7000 others], *These several Papers Was sent to the Parliament, The twentieth day of the fifth Moneth, 1659* (London: Mary Westwood, 1659), pp. 51–2.

[10] On the political dimension of Quaker opposition to tithes, see James, 'The Political Importance of the Tithes Controversy'; Reay, 'Quaker Opposition', 106; and Reay, *Quakers and the English Revolution*, p. 37.

[11] Thomas Collier, *A Looking Glasse for the Quakers, Wherein They may behold themselves* (London: Thomas Brewster, 1657), p. 12.

[12] Bonnelyn Young Kunze, 'Religious Authority and Social Status in Seventeenth-Century England: The Friendship of Margaret Fell, George Fox, and William Penn', *Church History* 57 (1988), 171.

[13] In June 1659, a group of Quaker men presented an anti-tithe petition with 15,000 signatures to the Rump Parliament. The text of this petition (published without the signatures) is titled *The Copie*

fact that many widows were taxable citizens, but also because wives contributed their labour toward the payment of tithes.[14] The most famous anti-tithe tract by Quaker women, *These Several Papers* (1659), is signed by more than 7000 'Hand-maids and Daughters of the Lord'. Catie Gill describes it as 'one of the most powerful demonstrations of women's public action in all seventeenth-century writing'.[15] This work – addressed to '*the Parliament of* England, *who are set in place to do justice, to take off oppression, and to stop the oppressors*' – begins like a Leveller women's petition:

Friends,
   It may seem strange to some that women should appear in so publick a manner, in a matter of so great concernment as this of *Tithes*, and that we also should bring in our testimony even as our brethren against that Anti-christian law and oppression of *Tithes*, by which many of the Servants of the Lord have suffered in filthy holes and dungeons until death; But let such know, that this is the work of the Lord at this day, even by weak means to bring to pass his mighty work in the earth, that all flesh may be silent.[16]

   This opening address is followed by several short pieces of text signed by Quaker women from different regions of England. In some pieces, the women draw their arguments from biblical sources, but many women present the abolition of tithes as a social justice issue. One group of women recommends to parliament that 'You should have sold all the Gleab-lands, and sold all the Bells, saving one only in a Town, and Colledges and their Lands, and given them to all the poor of the Nation; that there need not have been this lamentable cry for bread and cloathes among the poor.'[17] They also ask parliament to 'give over setting up of images, in your steeple-houses, and daubing them over with gold . . . let the money that you bestow on such vain things be given to buy the poor

---

Of A Paper Presented to the Parliament: And read the 27th of the fourth Moneth, 1659 (London: A.W. for Giles Calvert, 1659).

[14] In an epistle sent to women's meetings (c. 1675–80), one woman (who may have been Sarah Fell) writes that 'Since the priests claimes, and challenges a tithe, which belongs to women to pay, as well as the men, not only for widdows, but them that have husbands, as piggs, geese, henns and eggs, hemp and flax, wooll and lamb: all which women may have a hand in: Soe it concerns the womens meetings, to looke strictly to every particular meeting, that every woman bring in their testimony against tithes.' For a transcription of this manuscript, see Milton D. Speizman and Jane C. Kronick, 'A Seventeenth-Century Quaker Women's Declaration', *Signs* 1 (1975), 242–3.

[15] Gill, *Women in the Seventeenth-Century Quaker Community*, p. 110.

[16] Forster *et al.*, *These Several Papers*, 'To The Reader', no pagination; italics reversed.

[17] Ibid., p. 65.

cloathes and bread, and that wholsome places may be provided for them, as Nurseries, that none may be starved or perish for hunger'.[18]

In such passages, the writers appeal to a simple distributive egalitarianism, or the idea that justice requires the equal distribution of goods among members of society. In this view, the political authorities are not justified in arbitrarily privileging the interests of one social group, such as members of the state religion, at the expense of another, such as poor non-conformists – especially when the state ministers perform no service for them. In their view, the glebe-lands (portions of land given to the clergy), and other church property, might be put to better use: they might benefit all persons in society, regardless of their religious affiliation. Along similar lines, the women of 'Glocester-shire' petition parliament

To do *equity*, to take off this *unequal* maintenance of the Teachers, which do take of people whom they do no work for, who swallowes down the needy for a thing of nought; and the Judges of their Courts have been like ravening Wolves, prisoning such *unequally* on the Priests behalfe, whom they do no work for, and will not give them maintenance; Therefore if you *equally* do weigh and consider things to bring the Nation into peace, it must be *in equity*, for if you do but consider these Priests, which are the bringers of the Nations into troubles, setting them one against another (which was not the way of the Ministers of Christ, whose) throates are as open Sepulchres, who drinks up iniquity, and who swollowes down all; (mark) the fatherlesse part, the widdowes part, and the strangers part, and so are worse then the Jews.[19]

These women enlist a principle of equality or 'equity' in favour of the impartial treatment of different religious groups. This principle goes hand-in-hand with their conception of the role of a just political authority: for them, it is the magistrate's duty to oversee the equal distribution of goods, and to maintain peace between different social groups.

Similar themes arise in Priscilla Cotton's anti-tithe tract, *A Briefe Description by Way of Supposition*, also published in 1659. Not much is known about Cotton (née Martyn), but we do know that she lived in Plymouth, and that she was imprisoned in Exeter gaol from 1655 to 1656 for disruptive behaviour in her home town.[20] She was the author of at

---

[18] Ibid., p. 66.   [19] Ibid., p. 51; our italics.
[20] For biographical details, see the short entry on Priscilla Cotton in Maureen Bell, George Parfitt, and Simon Shepherd, *A Biographical Dictionary of English Women Writers 1580–1720* (Hemel Hempstead: Harvester Wheatsheaf, 1990), p. 56. Catie Gill reports that Cotton and her fellow Quaker, Mary Cole, were imprisoned for interrupting a minister named George Hughes (*Women in the Seventeenth-Century Quaker Community*, p. 51). Joseph Besse simply observes that, in 1655, 'Priscilla Cotton and Margaret Cole [sic] were imprisoned at *Exeter*, for speaking to the People in

least four published works: the *Briefe Description, A Visitation of Love Unto all People* (1661), *A Testimony of Truth to all Friends* (no date), and, as co-author with Mary Cole, *To the Priests and People of England* (1655).[21] Cotton wrote a manuscript account of her trial, titled 'Concerning the Passages of her Trial [at Exeter]', most likely dated 1656;[22] and she and her merchant husband, Arthur Cotton (whom she married in 1646), corresponded with Margaret Fell and George Fox in the 1650s.[23] Of all these writings, the four-page pamphlet *A Briefe Description* is Cotton's most overtly political, and a fine example of an early utopia – or, perhaps, a dystopia – by a woman. Yet there are no analyses of Cotton's political vision by modern commentators. Hilda Smith and Susan Cardinale describe it as a 'rare example of original political theory by a woman',[24] but they do not elaborate on where the originality lies.

Generally speaking, the political content of Cotton's work might be seen as rather typical of anti-tithe tracts of the period. Cotton's proposals are not dissimilar to those of another sectarian woman, the Fifth Monarchist Mary Rande (also known as Mary Cary, fl. 1647–53). In her *Twelve Humble Proposals* (1653), Rande proposes that magistrates ought to rule according to the principles of justice and equity; that in their role as leaders of the people, they must be indifferent to their own interests and advantage; and that they must 'resolve with all possible speed to repeal the Law of Tithes, which is a great oppression not onely to the estates, but to the consciences of many good people'.[25] Rande also proposes a reformation of the universities. She suggests that 'godly scholars' of poor

the publick Place of Worship, after the Priest had done' (Besse, *A Collection of the Sufferings*, vol. 1, p. 149).
[21] Priscilla Cotton, *A Briefe Description by way of supposition holding forth to the Parliament and such as have but common reason, wherein a true Common-wealth consisteth* (London: n.p., 1659); *A Visitation of Love Unto all People* (London: Thomas Simmons, 1661); *A Testimony of Truth to all Friends* (n.p.: Printed for M.W. [Mary Westwood], no date), this item is not in Wing; and Priscilla Cotton and Mary Cole, *To the Priests and People of England, we discharge our consciences, and give them warning* (London: Giles Calvert, 1655), hand-dated by Thomason as 16 October 1655.
[22] Priscilla Cotton, 'Concerning the Passages of her Trial [at Exeter]' (1656?), in *Original Records of Sufferings*, 8 vols. Manuscript in Friends House Library, London, vol. 111 (items 251–375), item 310.
[23] See Bell, 'Mary Westwood', 17–18. There is a 1660 letter from Cotton to Margaret Fell in Lucy Violet Hodgkin, *A Quaker Saint of Cornwall: Loveday Hambly and Her Guests* (London: Longmans, Green and Co, 1927).
[24] Hilda L. Smith and Susan Cardinale, *Women and the Literature of the Seventeenth Century: An Annotated Bibliography based on Wing's 'Short-title Catalogue'* (Westport: Greenwood Press, 1985), p. 33.
[25] [Mary (Cary) Rande], *Twelve Humble Proposals To the Supreme Governours of the three Nations now assembled at* Westminster (London: Henry Hills, for R. C. and Giles Calvert, 1653), pp. 3, 5.

means ought to be subsidised by the state, because it is an injustice that 'many Scholars that are mens sons of vast estates, must have fellow-ships ... and those that are mean (though their children are godly) cannot have any thing toward their maintenance'.[26] In short, she suggests to parliament that 'you seriously and in good earnest lay to heart the condition of the poor, and make it your care to provide for the supply of their wants'.[27] These social justice issues are also the subject of Cotton's *Briefe Description* – as well as numerous other sectarian works of the period, by both men and women alike.

But Cotton's work is original and innovative in terms of its use of rhetorical strategy. *A Briefe Description* begins with a supposition or a hypothetical state of affairs:

Suppose that ten or twelve sorts of people (being of severall opinions) are all together willing to inhabit a fruitfull Island, yet before they resolve to plant or build, they judge it necessary to have one of the wisest of them to be their Magistrate or chiefe overseer, with so many servants as the time requires, not only to keep the people in order, but also to be in a posture of defence, against all enemies whatsoever, maintaining the same (for their service to the Common-wealth) out of the Common stocke.[28]

Given this supposition, what principles would 'common reason' tell us that our magistrate should act upon? Suppose, for example, that 'all persons that are of one and the same opinion' gather themselves together into 'ten or twelve different Congregations, every one providing main-tenance for his own Ministers'.[29] Let us also suppose that it is the magistrate's role to 'stand unmoveable (as a centre) between them all, to keep the ballance in the Government, that one sect may not domineer over another'.[30] What would then be permissible? In a 'true and perfect Common-wealth',[31] would it be just for the magistrate to favour one congregation over another? And if the magistrate were to become a member of a particular congregation, would he be at liberty to use the army or the treasury in order to honour that congregation?

With her opening hypothesis, Cotton is not proposing a typical state of nature or an account of the historical origins of the social contract. Cotton's island community is not a primitive, pre-political society of the

---

[26] Ibid., p. 7.   [27] Ibid., p. 8.   [28] Cotton, *Briefe Description*, p. 1.   [29] Ibid.
[30] Ibid. Cotton seems to regard this supposition as a natural consequence of her view that the magistrate's role is to 'keep the people in order' and to provide a defence against 'all enemies whatsoever'.
[31] Ibid.

Hobbesian kind, and her inhabitants immediately accept a particular system of government. Cotton instead uses her supposition to draw her readers into implicit agreement with her about the principles of justice that must govern a 'true and perfect Common-wealth'. Cotton's strategy thus bears some resemblance to that of the modern political theorist John Rawls. At the start of his *Theory of Justice* (1972), Rawls adopts an imaginative rhetorical strategy in order to articulate his theory of a just society: he asks his readers 'to imagine that those who engage in social cooperation choose together, in one joint act, the principles which are to assign basic rights and duties and to determine the division of social benefits'.[32] This joint act takes place in the 'original position', a fictional situation in which participants strive together to characterise a certain conception of justice:

Among the essential features of this situation is that no one knows his place in society, his class position, or social status, nor does any one know his fortune in the distribution of natural assets and abilities, his intelligence, strength, and the like. I shall even assume that the parties do not know their conceptions of the good or their special psychological propensities. The principles of justice are chosen behind a veil of ignorance. This ensures that no one is advantaged or disadvantaged in the choice of principles by the outcome of natural chance or the contingency of social circumstance.[33]

Cotton's argument implicitly relies upon a 'veil of ignorance' of her own. In her supposition, the reader does not know which religious congregation the magistrate has favoured, whether it be the national church, the Quakers, the Fifth Monarchists, the Baptists, or some other sect. All we know is that there are at least ten groups on the island with different religious opinions, and that the magistrate has decided to join one of them. Without knowing the religious beliefs of that group, readers are able to abstract themselves from their own circumstances and preferences, and thus consider impartially the question of whether or not it is just for the king to use his political authority to privilege that group. Cotton apparently speaks for common reason when she says that

If he (to wit the Magistrate) joyne himself (as a member) to one particular Congregation he hath his liberty to honour the same, with his presence, with his tongue, with his pen, and with his own money: but not with the sword or money of the Common-wealth, for he is in regard of his Office to be considered not as a particular but as a generall person standing for the good of all: just as it is with a

---

[32] John Rawls, *A Theory of Justice* (Oxford: Clarendon Press, 1972), p. 11.   [33] Ibid.

Treasurer, who is intrusted with a summe of money to imploy the same not for his own, or any ones private advantage in particular, but for the benefit of all those that have intrusted him.[34]

Cotton's analogy between magistrate and treasurer is significant: the magistrate's relationship to the people is likened to a contractual relationship based on trust. When a society appoints a treasurer, they trust that that person will use the money for the benefit of the society as a whole, and not for his or her own personal ends. Similarly, on this imaginary island, the people have trusted the magistrate to maintain social and political order, and to defend the inhabitants against their enemies. The people trust, moreover, that the magistrate will provide 'peace and safety' to all *equally*, without favour or prejudice.[35] If the magistrate betrays this trust, then he has acted in an unjust manner – and considerably undermined public confidence in him as 'a generall person standing for the good of all'. This undermining of confidence can have disastrous implications for political stability. Cotton's island community thus descends into a dystopia when the magistrate favours the interests of one congregation over another with his political power and the public purse. In Cotton's view, the magistrate's actions license the persecution of other religious sects, and their branding as 'hereticks and blasphemers' and holders of 'dangerous principles'.[36]

Needless to say, Cotton's supposition is designed to highlight the injustice of the tithes system in seventeenth-century England. Toward the middle of her pamphlet, she lifts the veil of ignorance from her readers by drawing attention to the abuses perpetrated against non-conformists 'here in England'.[37] Up to that point, she has appealed to the reason of parliament and the common people to spell out the principles of justice in a 'true and perfect Common-wealth'. All would agree, she suggests, that such a commonwealth has a magistrate who acts impartially for the public benefit, and not for private interests. All would agree that a magistrate who favours one congregation over another with the public power and purse is acting in an unjust manner. And yet this is precisely the way in which the magistrate acts *in England*, by persecuting those of the reformed Protestant religion, by favouring the national church, and by forcing separatists to pay tithes. Regardless of which congregation her readers belong to, Cotton's supposition has shown them that such practices are 'unreasonable', and that 'equity requires, that, that law (whereby the

---

[34] Cotton, *Briefe Description*, p. 1.   [35] Ibid., p. 4.   [36] Ibid., pp. 3, 2.   [37] Ibid., p. 3.

people are forced to pay tythes to Ministers) ought without delay to be abolished'.[38] *A Briefe Description* is, in other words, a call for the principles of justice and equity to be applied without partiality in her home land.

Cotton's proposal for an egalitarian society does not begin and end with the abolition of tithes. She also wants our intuitions to provide a moral basis for the reform of other social institutions, such as the health and education systems. On the first page of her pamphlet, Cotton suggests that 'Hospitalls for the poor' would be part of a 'true and perfect Common-wealth', and that the poor would be provided with opportunities to work and earn their keep. On the last page, she proposes that the commonwealth 'Erect Schools of learning in all Cityes and market Towns or other convenient places, throughout these nations; to instruct every one as wel poor as rich that have a desire to learn Arts and Sciences to answer the ends of nature for the Common good'.[39] In sum, like the Quaker women petitioners of *These Several Papers*, Cotton implies that a just society ought to be regulated according to the egalitarian principles of distributive justice. In such a society, the magistrate will strive to distribute goods equitably among members of society, such that some social groups are not unfairly disadvantaged compared to others.

II

We have seen, then, that some Quaker women call for legal and social reforms designed to bring about an end to certain social inequalities. Given their concern for the impartial treatment of some social groups, one might think that it would be logical to extend these egalitarian principles to women as a social group. But does any Quaker woman offer a feminist theory of political equality between men and women? Based upon the available textual evidence, the answer appears to be 'no'. Contemporary critics claimed that the Quakers aimed to level all conditions, including the hierarchical relationship between husband and wife. But in their writings devoted to the subject of women, both male and female Quakers fall disappointingly short of such a levelling philosophy. For some scholars, the failure to adopt a feminist standpoint amounts to an 'ideological inconsistency' in their writings.[40] Other commentators point to a discrepancy between Quaker egalitarian theology and Quaker practice.[41] But on closer inspection, Quaker egalitarianism in itself

---

[38] Ibid.   [39] Ibid., p. 4.   [40] Gill, *Women in the Seventeenth-Century Quaker Community*, p. 42.
[41] Kunze, 'Religious Authority and Social Status', 185.

does not necessarily imply that women should be treated as the social or political equals of men. This point can be demonstrated through a brief examination of Quaker women's arguments in defence of female preaching. In these works, the most common theory of male and female equality does not provide the basis for an unqualified gender egalitarianism in the political sphere.

One of the earliest Quaker defences of women's speaking in church is Priscilla Cotton and Mary Cole's *To the Priests and People of England* (1655).[42] In this work, written during their period of imprisonment in Exeter gaol, Cotton and Cole address some of the most common arguments against women's speaking in church. In doing so, they apply the methods of the *querelle des femmes*. In keeping with tradition, they challenge the notion of women's innate inferiority with reference to biblical sources. The offending passages include 1 Corinthians 14:34, 'Let your women keep silence in the churches: for it is not permitted unto them to speak', and 1 Timothy 2:11–12, 'Let the woman learn in silence with all subjection. But I suffer not a woman to teach, nor to usurp authority over the man, but to be in silence.'[43] Cotton and Cole suggest alternative interpretations of such remarks to make them consistent with other biblical passages that imply that it is permissible for women to speak in church. They say:

thou tellest the people, Women must not speak in the Church, whereas it is not spoke onely of a Female, for we are all one both male and female in Christ Jesus, but it's weakness that is the woman by the Scriptures forbidden, for else thou puttest the Scriptures at a difference in themselves ... for the Scriptures do say, that all the Church may prophesie one by one, and that women were in the Church, as well as men, do thou judge; and the Scripture saith, that a woman may not prophesie with her head uncovered, lest she dishonour her head.[44]

In Galatians 3:28, 'there is neither male nor female: for ye are all one in Christ Jesus', we are told that women and men are spiritually equal; and in 1 Corinthians 14:31, 'For ye may all prophesy one by one, that all may

---

[42] For an in-depth reading of this work, see Chapter 7 and Appendix C of Hilary Hinds, *God's Englishwomen: Seventeenth-Century Radical Sectarian Writing and Feminist Criticism* (Manchester University Press, 1996), pp. 180–208, 222–6. The appendix is a reprint of the Cotton–Cole text in its entirety.

[43] To this list, we might also add Ephesians 5:22–4 ('Wives, submit yourselves unto your own husbands, as unto the Lord. For the husband is the head of the wife, even as Christ is the head of the church: and he is the saviour of the body. Therefore as the church is subject unto Christ, so *let* the wives *be* to their own husbands in everything').

[44] Cotton and Cole, *To the Priests and People*, pp. 6–7.

learn, and all may be comforted', it is implied that women as well as men are permitted to prophesy. In such cases, the Bible endorses a woman's capacity for equal spiritual authority and her entitlement to speak in church. A different meaning must therefore be given to those apparent injunctions that women must not speak. If we do not look for an alternative meaning, then we are faced with contradictory propositions – but the Word of an infinitely wise God could never be contradictory.[45] Instead we must interpret 'woman' to mean 'weakness', and accept that womanliness can be a property of both males and females. Consider 1 Corinthians 11:4–5, the warning that 'Every man praying or prophesying, having *his* head covered, dishonoureth his head. But every woman that prayeth or prophesieth with *her* head uncovered, dishonoureth her head.' This passage can be reinterpreted in a favourable light. Cotton and Cole say:

> now thou wouldst know the meaning of that Head, let the Scripture answer, *I Cor. 11.3. The head of every man is Christ.* Man in his best estate is altogether vanity, weakness, a lye. If therefore any speak in the Church, whether man or woman, and nothing appear in it but the wisdom of man, and Christ, who is the true head, be not uncovered, do not fully appear, Christ the head is then dishonoured. Now the woman or weakness, that is man, which in his best estate or greatest wisdom is altogether vanity, that must be covered with the covering of the Spirit, a garment of righteousness, that its nakedness may not appear, and dishonour thereby come. Here mayst thou see from the Scriptures, that the woman or weakness, whether male or female, is forbidden to speak in the Church.[46]

Both males and females may speak in church, but if they speak then they 'must be covered with the covering of the Spirit' – they must be in the Light, as it were. If they are not in the Light, then they speak as 'women' regardless of their actual gender: they speak, that is, with a lack of authority or with 'weakness' rather than strength. Thus Cotton and Cole taunt the priests who visit them in prison, by saying that 'you your selves are the women, that are forbidden to speak in the Church'.[47]

Margaret Fell (1614–1702) also reinterprets key biblical passages in her 1666 defence of women's preaching, *Womens Speaking Justified, Proved and Allowed of by the Scriptures*.[48] Together with George Fox and William

---

[45] On this point, see Hinds, *God's Englishwomen*, p. 183.
[46] Cotton and Cole, *To the Priests and People*, pp. 6–7.   [47] Ibid., pp. 7–8.
[48] Margaret Fell, *Womens Speaking Justified, Proved and Allowed of by the Scriptures* (London: n.p., 1667 [i.e. 1666]).

Penn, Fell (née Askew, and later Margaret Fox) is regarded as one of the founding figures of the Quaker movement: she corresponded with almost every major Quaker of the period, she wrote at least forty-five pamphlets of a religious and political nature, and she held some of the earliest meetings in her home.[49] Despite her social status as a gentry woman and the wife of a judge, she was imprisoned three times for activities on behalf of the Quaker cause.

In *Womens Speaking Justified*, written during a period of imprisonment in Lancaster Castle, Fell appeals to the notion that men and women are spiritually equal. She repeatedly says that 'God joyns them [male and female] together in his own Image, and makes no such distinctions and differences as men do',[50] that 'God hath put no such difference between Male and Female as men would make',[51] that when God made 'man' in his own Image 'he made them *male* and *female*',[52] and that 'God the Father made no such difference between the Male and the Female, but always out of his Mercy and loving kindness, had regard unto the weak.'[53] Like Cotton and Cole, she also points out that 'Christ in the Male and in the Female is one.'[54] This theory of equality – or the view that men and woman have equal spiritual standing in the eyes of God – grounds Fell's arguments in favour of women's speaking. She says that

Those that speak against the Power of the Lord, and the Spirit of the Lord speaking in a woman, simply, by reason of her Sex, or because she is a Woman, not regarding the Seed, and Spirit, and Power that speaks in her; such speak

[49] On Margaret Fell's life and works, see Isabel Ross, *Margaret Fell: Mother of Quakerism* (3rd edn, York: The Ebor Press, 1996); Bonnelyn Young Kunze, *Margaret Fell and the Rise of Quakerism* (New York: Macmillan, 1994); Terry S. Wallace (ed.), *A Sincere and Constant Love: An Introduction to the Work of Margaret Fell* (Richmond, IN: Friends United Press, 1992); Elsa F. Glines (ed.), *Undaunted Zeal: The Letters of Margaret Fell* (Richmond, IN: Friends United Press, 2003); Judith Kegan Gardiner, 'Margaret Fell Fox and Feminist Literary History: "A Mother in Israel" Calls to the Jews', *Prose Studies* 17 (1994), 42–56; Achsah Guibbery, 'Conversation, Conversion, Messianic Redemption: Margaret Fell, Menessah ben Israel, and the Jews', in *Literary Circles and Cultural Communities in Renaissance England*, ed. Claude J. Summers and Ted-Larry Pebworth (Columbia and London: University of Missouri Press, 2000), pp. 210–34; Kunze, 'Religious Authority and Social Status'; and Marilyn Serraino Leucke, '"God Hath Made No Difference Such as Men Would": Margaret Fell and the Politics of Women's Speech', *Bunyan Studies* 7 (1997), 73–95.
[50] Fell, *Womens Speaking*, p. 3.   [51] Ibid.   [52] Ibid., p. 12.   [53] Ibid., p. 5.
[54] Ibid., p. 13; and Cotton and Cole, *To the Priests and People*, p. 6. Fell, Cotton, and Cole are not the only authors to make this point; it is a common refrain in Quaker writings. Along similar lines, in an epistle sent to Quaker women's meetings (c. 1675–80), the author (who may have been Margaret's daughter, Sarah Fell) writes that 'we are all the children of God by faith in Christ Jesus, where there is neither male nor female' and that God 'made them male and female in the beginning: and in this his own Image God blessed them both' (Speizman and Kronick, 'A Seventeenth-Century Quaker Women's Declaration', 235 and 236).

against Christ, and his Church, and are of the Seed of the Serpent, wherein lodgeth enmity.[55]

So long as a woman speaks in the Light, then her words ought to be granted spiritual authority. For this reason, we must reinterpret, or recontextualise, those common injunctions against women's speaking, such as 1 Corinthians 14:34, 'Let your women keep silence in the churches.' In a passage preceding this statement, according to Fell, 'the Man is commanded to keep silence as well as the woman, when they are in confusion and out of order'.[56] She thus suggests that 'here you ought to make a distinction what sort of Women are forbidden to speak':[57] the reader ought to distinguish between those women who are mere '*busie-bodies, and tatlers*'[58] and those women who have the Spirit of the Lord. The following passage, moreover, warns that if women have any inquiries, then they should wait and ask their husbands at home rather than speak in church (1 Corinthians 14:35). But this injunction obviously cannot apply to widows and virgins – women who have no husbands to instruct them.[59] If it did, then the four virgin daughters of Philip in the Bible (Acts 21:9) would be despised as prophets, and yet they are not. We might also consider the idea that a woman's 'husband' in this passage is in fact Christ himself, and that if a woman learns from this Husband, then she ought to be permitted to speak.[60]

In such texts, we find arguments in which women are granted some equality with men: they are accorded equal spiritual worth or equal spiritual authority in the religious sphere, provided that they are in the Light. To the extent that the early modern church was a political domain, this granting of spiritual equality to women has some notable political implications. Margaret James highlights the political significance of religious meetings in the seventeenth century. She points out that 'The parish was the unit of much social and economic organisation, and in the days of illiteracy and scanty newsprint the pulpit was the great disseminator of news and opinion.'[61] If one controlled the pulpit, then one controlled an early equivalent of the present-day mass media. It was partly for this reason that tithes were such a pressing political issue: 'Obviously, it was of the highest importance how such a body was financed, in particular whether its means of support were collected authoritatively and by right, or whether . . . they were collected voluntarily and by the

[55] Fell, *Womens Speaking*, p. 5.   [56] Ibid., p. 8.   [57] Ibid., p. 13.   [58] Ibid.   [59] Ibid.
[60] Ibid., p. 17.   [61] James, 'Political Importance of the Tithes Controversy', 5.

goodwill of congregations.'[62] If one accepts this view, then in their calls for a woman's right to speak in church, the Quakers were calling for a tremendous amount of political authority for women. As one Quaker critic, Joshuah Miller, points out, the 'monstrous Doctrine' of women preachers allows some women to 'be rulers over, and directors of men's consciences' – certainly no small matter, as John Knox had argued a century before.[63]

Cotton, Cole, and Fell all argue that some women ought to be permitted to occupy an authoritative position in a highly influential political domain, regardless of their gender. But we must remember that their egalitarian approach to church preaching is built upon a theory of spiritual equality and a religious conception of what makes all human beings equal. Fell emphasises that 'God hath put no such difference between Male and Female as men would make',[64] and Cotton and Cole likewise advocate that male and female are 'all one' in Jesus Christ, and that God is 'no respecter of persons'.[65] This spiritual equality does not necessarily translate into political equality for women in a more general sense. To see this, we need only consider Fell's response to 1 Timothy 2:11–12, 'I suffer not a woman to teach, nor to usurp authority over the man, but to be in silence.' Fell points out that

Here the Apostle speaks particularly to a Woman in Relation to her Husband, to be in subjection to him, and not to teach, nor usurp authority over him, and therefore he mentions *Adam* and *Eve*: But let it be strained to the utmost, as the opposers of Womens Speaking would have it, that is, That they should not preach nor speak in the Church, of which there is nothing here.[66]

Fell implicitly accepts the husband's authority over the wife within marriage – her stand on women's preaching is not meant to challenge hierarchical relations within this institution, it challenges only women's subordinate position in the church.

At this point, then, we may reconsider those allegations of inconsistency in the Quaker philosophy. In the writings of Cotton and the Quaker women petitioners, a just society is one that is organised according to the principles of distributive egalitarianism, and a just magistrate is duty

[62] Ibid.
[63] Joshuah Miller, *Antichrist in Man The Quakers Idol. Or a faithfull discovery of their ways and opinions by an eye and ear-witness thereof* (London: J. Macock for L. Lloyd, 1655), p. 27. For Knox's arguments against women rulers, see our Chapter 4.
[64] Fell, *Womens Speaking*, p. 3. [65] Cotton and Cole, *To the Priests and People*, pp. 7–8.
[66] Fell, *Womens Speaking*, p. 9.

bound to distribute goods equally amongst all social groups, regardless of their religious affiliation. We might think that women's equal education, or recognition of women's equal political standing, are natural consequences of such egalitarian principles. It is not the case, however, that a theory of distributive egalitarianism must be unqualified or unlimited in terms of its sphere of application. The Quaker women we have discussed embrace the view that all human beings, regardless of their social status or gender, have the Light within them, and hence that all human beings may have the authority to preach the word of God. Without risk of inconsistency, this theory of equality – a purely religious conception of what makes human beings equal – may place constraints on Quaker egalitarianism in the political domain. The Quaker women petitioners suggest that it is unjust to expect Quakers to pay tithes because human beings require no intermediary between themselves and Christ: all human beings have a minister in their own breast, capable of leading them toward salvation. Similarly, because a classical education is not required in order to preach the Gospel, they believe that the universities should not be devoted exclusively to the propagation of the state religion. And finally, the Quakers hold that women, as well as men, can have the spiritual authority to speak about religious matters, provided that they are 'covered in the Spirit'. In all these cases, the principle of equality underlying the Quakers' stance is a religious and not a secular one. The spiritual equality of all human beings places some limitations on what the government may do to its citizens: it cannot justifiably exact tithes, it cannot use state resources to privilege the rich at the expense of the poor, it cannot monopolise the universities, and it cannot punish women for speaking in church. But this theory still permits certain social inequalities between men and women.

There is, then, no necessary inference from the Quaker theory of spiritual equality to the view that women as well as men ought to have equal access to social goods, such as education. Their theory does not logically lead to equal education for women, since women do not require an education in order to attain salvation or to be 'in the spirit of the Lord'; in this respect, women are already on a par with men. This theory does not logically lead to equal employment opportunities for women, and it does not logically require women's full political participation either, since it is only necessary that women be active and employed in a spiritual sense or in religious matters. Without inconsistency, the egalitarian theology of the Quaker women discussed here need not amount to an untempered political egalitarianism or a full-fledged feminist theory of equality.

In mid seventeenth-century England, the practical implications of social and gender inequalities were alarmingly real. Women preachers of the Quaker faith were not just derided, they were beaten and whipped '*till the Blood ran down their Bodies*'.[67] But when Quaker women call for equality in their writings, they do not call for female political equality, or the equal political standing of men and women – they simply call for the equal standing of all religious groups in the eyes of the magistrate. Like the Leveller women of the previous chapter, Quaker women stop short of explicitly demanding equality with men in the political sphere. This is because the Quaker arguments against tithes, and other social injustices, are ultimately based on a spiritual principle, or the view that all human beings possess the light of God, and that all human beings are therefore on the same spiritual footing. This religious notion limits the sphere of application of their particular brand of distributive egalitarianism.

Nevertheless, in the writings of these early Quaker women, we find once again that the political concerns of women are brought to the fore. In their opposition to the compulsory payment of tithes, Mary Forster and 7,000 other 'Handmaids and Daughters of the Lord' highlight the fact that women hold a legitimate interest in such political matters. To the extent that some widows were taxable citizens, and to the extent that women contributed their labour to production, the political debate over tithes had relevance for the lives of women as well as men. More importantly, Quaker women's arguments in favour of female preaching also had strong political implications, in so far as the church pulpit was an influential political domain during this period. Women preachers of the Quaker faith had the power to interpret biblical injunctions, and to make those interpretations public. As Joshuah Miller points out, the granting of female spiritual authority permitted women to be directors or rulers over men's consciences. In previous chapters, we saw that the conscience figured prominently in Jeanne d'Albret's justifications for following God rather than her earthly superiors. In coming chapters, we will see that the individual's conscience is also a strong feature of seventeenth-century arguments for religious toleration and, in some cases, resistance to political authority.

---

[67] Besse, *A Collection of the Sufferings*, p. 85.

CHAPTER 8

The Fronde and Madeleine de Scudéry

During the seventeenth century in France, women began to exercise more influence in a wider range of political and literary movements than had been the case in any previous century. Arguably, they were more influential during this period than they were to be during the two following centuries.[1] This was the period of the rise of salon culture, and an explosion in women's writing, particularly poetry, portraits, novels, and moral maxims. It also embraced the political disturbances called the 'Fronde', which involved a number of central female actors.[2] Literature and politics were closely entwined, for during this period in particular women used literature 'to assert their influence on the century's political and social structures'.[3]

Various reasons may be proposed for women's literary and political emergence in France at this time. It may well have had something to do

---

[1] See Ian Maclean, *Woman Triumphant: Feminism in French Literature, 1610–1652* (Oxford: Clarendon Press, 1977). For evidence that women were particularly influential in the seventeenth century, see Faith E. Beasley, *Salons, History and the Creation of Seventeenth-Century France: Mastering Memory* (Aldershot: Ashgate, 2006), esp. pp. 199–204; and Joan DeJean, 'Amazones et femmes de lettres: pouvoirs politiques et littéraires à l'âge classique', in *Femmes et pouvoirs sous l'Ancien Régime*, ed. Danielle Hasse-Dubosc and Elaine Viennot (Paris: Rivages/Histoire, 1991), p. 153. Beasley discusses earlier authors who acknowledged women's significant influence on seventeenth-century thought, such as Stéphanie Félicité de Genlis's *De l'influence des femmes sur la littérature française, comme protectrices des lettres et comme auteurs (ou Précis de l'histoire des femmes françaises les plus célèbres)* (Paris: Maradan, 1811), as well as later accounts which underplayed its importance. For DeJean's account of the processes which led to the eclipse of women's literary influence, see her *Tender Geographies: The Politics of Female Authorship under the Late Ancien Régime* (New York: Columbia University Press, 1991); *Ancients Against Moderns: Culture Wars and the Making of a Fin de Siècle* (Chicago and London: Chicago University Press, 1997). For a discussion of salon culture which examines women's ethical thought rather than their literary influence, see John J. Conley, *The Suspicion of Virtue: Women Philosophers in Neoclassical France* (Ithaca: Cornell University Press, 2002).

[2] For a brief overview of the Fronde which discusses the many interpretations of this complex event and offers a comprehensive bibliography, see R. J. Knecht, *The Fronde* (London: The Historical Association, 1986).

[3] Beasley, *Salons, History*, p. 317.

with their political prominence at court. During the first half of the seventeenth century, the advent of two regencies, those of Marie de Medici and Anne of Austria, demonstrates that women's prudence and capacity to rule was widely accepted, though still contested.[4] These regencies were associated with the emergence of new forms of literature discussing the virtues of women under the rubrics *honnête femme* and *femme forte*. This literature is different from the earlier *querelle des femmes* in that it assumes that women are capable of virtue and outlines the character of the honourable, heroic, and strong woman. Such texts were usually male-authored and often dedicated to queens or princesses, continuing the pattern observed in the fifteenth century.[5]

The appropriateness of women expressing themselves by means of publication was still contested by men.[6] But women who came to writing during the seventeenth century could look back to the already considerable achievements of sixteenth-century women. Madeleine de Scudéry (1607–1701), for example, did not fail to include women in her history of French poetry up to Henri IV, which she published in 1684. In her account she mentions Marie de France and Marguerite de Navarre, as well as Madeleine and Catherine des Roches. She also praises Catherine de Medici for having employed Amyot (who had translated Plutarch into French), an event which also allows her to mention the sixteenth-century translator Mme de Neufvic.[7] Her short account of the history of French poetry demonstrates that Renaissance authors, who were deeply influenced by the Neoplatonic theory of love, had not been forgotten in the seventeenth century, and the literature written by women during this period builds on the discussion of love and sexual politics in the previous century. While travelling to Marseille with her brother, Madeleine de Scudéry visited the tomb of Petrarch's Laura in Avignon – evidence of her respect for this even earlier theorist of love, and of her self-conscious participation in a tradition of literary and philosophical discourse on the place of love in society.[8]

Other seventeenth-century works also attest to Marguerite de Navarre's continuing influence. Jean Renault de Segrais wrote *Les Nouvelles*

---

[4] Evidence for the contesting of this power is found in Joan DeJean's claim that Richelieu's *Testament politique* represents women and the feminine novel as the origin of revolution and destruction of the state: *Tender Geographies*, pp. 164 and 69. She does not give a precise reference.

[5] See Maclean, *Woman Triumphant*, pp. 27–35 and 76–7.

[6] On this topic, see Timmermans, *L'accès des femmes à la culture*.

[7] Madeleine de Scudéry, *'De l'air galant' et autres conversations. Pour une étude de l'archive galante*, ed. Delphine Denis (Paris: Champion, 1998), pp. 255–63.

[8] Nicole Aronson, *Mlle de Scudéry* (New York: Twayne, 1978), p. 31.

Françaises ou les divertissements de la princesse Aurélie, a collection of tales based on stories told at Saint-Fargeau during the exile of one of the colourful women involved in the Fronde, the daughter of Louis XIV's uncle Gaston d'Orléans, Anne-Marie Louise d'Orléans Montpensier, or La Grande Mademoiselle (1627–93). This collection was explicitly constructed in imitation of that of Marguerite de Navarre – La Grande Mademoiselle's 'grandmother' – and returns to its 'naturalism' at least in so far as the stories, no matter how improbable, are given contemporary settings.[9] Self-conscious participation by these women in an acknowledged tradition is also evident in the most famous women's novel of the seventeenth century, *The Princess of Cleves*, written by Marie Madeleine Pioche de la Vergne, Comtesse de La Fayette (1634–93), which is set in the court of Henri II. The plot of this novel could be a reprise of one of the dramas involving courtly love found in the *Heptameron*. Although the description of interior psychological states is innovative, the plot, and the conclusion of the novel – the princess's decision not to marry and her partial retreat to a convent, which makes little psychological sense for the modern reader – are comprehensible when read in the light of Marguerite's doctrine of the superiority of women's love. Thus, by the seventeenth century, women writers could build on a tradition of women's courtly writing, and they can be read as extending and elaborating the political questions it had broached.

Madeleine de Scudéry, in particular, used her novels to comment on political events and to develop a new model of male–female relations in polite society, as well as to mount what is, in effect, a critique of ambition and of the desire to wield coercive power over others. There is considerable dispute in the secondary literature over the exact character of Scudéry's political message. Scudéry's book *Artamène, ou Le Grand Cyrus* came out in instalments at the height of the Fronde (1648–53), and each volume was dedicated to the Duchess of Longueville, Anne Geneviève de Bourbon, who had married Henri, Duke of Longueville, in 1624. Anne was the sister of Armand de Bourbon, Prince of Conti, and her husband and younger brother were involved in the Fronde from its inception. When the Prince of Conti and the Duke of Longueville decided to support the parliament against Anne of Austria, who was regent on behalf

---

[9] Jean Renault de Segrais, *Les Nouvelles Françaises ou les divertissements de la princesse Aurélie*, ed. Roger Guichemerre (Paris: Société des Textes Français Modernes, 1990), pp. 22–4. In fact La Grande Mademoiselle was the great-great-grand-daughter of Marguerite de Navarre. Though attributed to Segrais, the work was a collaborative compilation; see DeJean, *Tender Geographies*, p. 72.

of the young Louis XIV, the Duchess of Longueville and Mme de Bouillon offered themselves as hostages to the Parisians, to show their husbands' good faith, and set up court in the Hôtel de Ville.[10] During this first stage of the civil war, the parliamentary Fronde (1648–9), the duchess's older brother, Le Grand Condé, Louis II de Bourbon, sided with the royal court against the parliament. In the second stage, the princely Fronde (1650–2), initiated by Condé's imprisonment, he was to take up arms against Mazarin and the court. France was then embroiled in civil war and Anne de Longueville, after a dramatic flight from the threat of imprisonment, oversaw the government of Bordeaux for the Fronde party.

Following a seventeenth-century 'key' discovered by Victor Cousin, the principal figures of the novel *Artamène*, Cyrus and Mandane, are taken to be modelled on Condé and his sister.[11] Because of this, and because Georges de Scudéry, under whose name the novel was published, ultimately had to leave Paris as a result of his support for those involved in the Fronde, some commentators represent Madeleine de Scudéry as having had radical sympathies.[12] Others, with more justice, claim that she was always a faithful monarchist.[13] To yet others her later support for Louis XIV, combined with her apparent sympathy for the rebels of the Fronde, has seemed paradoxical.[14] The paradox is partly dissolved if one looks more closely at the politics of the Duchess of Longueville, which were not democratic but were based on a certain understanding of the tradition of regency in France, and particularly the role of the princes of the blood in preventing a monarch from becoming a tyrant.[15] We will maintain, moreover, that Madeleine and her brother Georges came to diverge in their attitudes, both in relation to the Fronde and in relation to the kind of glory to which women should aspire.

Marie le Jars de Gournay praises the French custom of regency in her 'Equality of Men and Women', saying, 'The French have served

---

[10] Vita Sackville-West, *Daughter of France. The Life of Anne Marie Louise d'Orléans Duchesse de Montpensier* (London: Michael Joseph, 1959), p. 95.

[11] Victor Cousin, *La Société française au XVIIe siècle d'après Le Grand Cyrus de Mlle de Scudéry*, 2 vols. (Paris: Didier, 1858), vol. II, pp. 21, 31, 72; DeJean, 'Amazones et femmes de lettres', p. 158.

[12] DeJean, for example, says of *Artamène*: 'The bond forged thereby between prose fiction and political subversion marks the origin of the modern French novel' (*Tender Geographies*, pp. 45–6). She thereby implies a radical commitment to the subversion of the crown, although she recognises that this is not justified by the evolution of the text.

[13] For those on the monarchist side, see Aronson, *Mlle de Scudéry*, pp. 35–6; Cousin, *La Société française*, vol. I, pp. 38, 63.

[14] DeJean, *Tender Geographies*, p. 46.   [15] Knecht, *The Fronde*, p. 26.

themselves well, however, in discovering the invention of regents as equivalent to kings during minorities: for without it how often would their state have been brought low?'[16] Yet the actual regencies of Marie de Medici and Anne of Austria exposed tensions in regency government, and in particular pitted those who expected a regency to be a period during which power would be shared between the regent, parliament, and princes of the blood against Richelieu and then Mazarin, who each attempted to coalesce ultimate power in the king, exercised through the agency of his prime minister.

During the Fronde, the earlier period of the regency of Marie de Medici would come to be represented, with hindsight, as a time during which the traditional claims of the princes of the blood, and other established loci of power, were respected. And, indeed, it was during Anne's regency, in 1614, that the last meeting of the Estates General prior to that called on the eve of the French Revolution took place. Once Louis XIII came of age, and fell under the influence of Cardinal Richelieu, all sources of power other than those controlled by the monarch and his personal minister would be increasingly suppressed. In 1617, Carlo Concini, the Marshal Ancre, who was Marie de Medici's chief minister, was assassinated. This assassination, arranged by Charles d'Albret, Duke of Luynes, was followed by Marie de Medici's exile, as well as that of her second son, Gaston d'Orléans, who would later be involved in the princely Fronde. Subsequently Louis XIII's government increasingly came to be dominated by Cardinal Richelieu, whose doctrine, as expressed in his *Testament politique* addressed to the king, was 'to ruin the Huguenot faction, to tame the pride of the nobility, reduce all his subjects to their duty and to lift his name in other countries to the position it ought to hold'.[17] Richelieu monopolised power in the name of the king, stirring up considerable resentment as a consequence.

When Anne of Austria was first made regent, the court looked forward to a new kind of government and the restitution of power to the leaders of factions who had been exiled from the court by Richelieu. In her *Mémoires pour servir à l'histoire d'Anne d'Autriche*, Françoise Bertaut de Motteville (c. 1621–89) describes how, at the beginning of the regency, Anne of Austria had been received with considerable sympathy, owing to

---

[16] Gournay, *Oeuvres complètes*, vol. 1, p. 977.
[17] Françoise Hildersheimer (ed.), *Testament politique de Richelieu* (Paris: Société de l'Histoire de France, 1995), p. 43; Alan James, *The Origins of French Absolutism, 1598–1661* (Harlow: Pearson Education, 2006), p. 114.

the bad treatment meted out to her by her husband and Cardinal Richelieu. Yet Motteville's comments bring out the extent to which, although well established, the institution of regency was frail. Anne, unloved and distrusted by her husband, partly because of her Spanish blood, which made her allegiance to France suspect, had never previously been given any place in the government. Motteville suggests that, emerging from a life of idleness and being naturally lazy, she soon realised that she was incapable of governing the French state without help. That help was available in the person of Cardinal Mazarin, whose advice increasingly dominated her actions.[18] Thus, the factions were disappointed and the princes soon came to resent the power of the foreign Mazarin, who dominated the queen's policy. La Grande Mademoiselle similarly comments in her *Mémoires*:

One would still not believe, if it were not now evident, that she, who had had such an unhappy experience of the dangers of leaving all the authority of government to a single minister, even one who was talented, would have been capable of abandoning it absolutely, as she has done, to the least talented and most unworthy man in the world.[19]

Motteville was, for most of her life, a close companion and friend to Anne of Austria, while La Grande Mademoiselle was deeply involved in the second act of the Fronde. La Grande Mademoiselle played the role of Joan of Arc in securing the city of Orléans for her father, and at one stage during the siege of Paris, she ordered the cannons of the Bastille to be turned and fired on the king's troops. Yet despite appearing to have belonged to different factions, Motteville and La Grande Mademoiselle agree that the issues that divided the court had more to do with how, and by whom, power should be exercised within the monarchy, rather than with the legitimacy of monarchy itself. And this observation needs to be kept in mind in reading Madeleine de Scudéry's works. Like earlier women whose political thought we have examined, Scudéry was not opposed to monarchy, but only to tyranny. From the point of view of the women studied here, the two opposing sides in the Fronde should not be seen as pitting monarchy against democracy (though it was in the interests of Mazarin and the court to represent it that way), but rather as supporting two different conceptions of the operation of a just monarchy.[20]

---

[18] Motteville, *Mémoires pour servir*, p. 55.

[19] Anne-Marie Louise d'Orléans Montpensier, *Mémoires*, 2 vols. (Paris: Fontaine, 1985), p. 57.

[20] It may well be that further research would reveal women with more radical views whose writing was published among the many *Mazarinades* which appeared during the Fronde. A number of

While Marie le Jars de Gournay had written to Marie de Medici in 1610, advising her on the principles of good government and insisting on the obligation of the monarch to care for the people, she was less than explicit in spelling out what justice required. Gournay's critique of tyranny, following La Boëtie, suggests that the influence of favourites, courtiers, and hangers-on, whose actions were dominated by their private interests, could corrupt the crown and encourage tyranny, putting the needs of particular clients of the government above those of the people. This suggests that she would not necessarily have objected to the absolutism that was beginning to dominate French royal politics, so long as the monarch defended the people. Indeed, late in life she received a pension from Richelieu, whose doctrines were associated with the absolutist tendency already implicit in Henri IV's consolidation of monarchical power.[21] Like Richelieu, Gournay was opposed to duelling, which the former opposed as an abrogation by a private individual of the right to condemn to death, which even the king did not have unless a subject had committed a crime.[22]

Similarly, the ideas expressed during the Fronde were not necessarily anti-monarchical, or even anti-absolutist, and they sometimes echoed La Boëtie's and Gournay's distrust of courtly favourites.[23] Just as in the previous century, in France, when female Protestant rebels had represented themselves as loyal to a crown that had been hijacked, so too the supporters of the Fronde represented themselves as faithful to the king, but bitterly opposed to Cardinal Mazarin, who they argued was a client of the state who had usurped royal power, turning the monarchy into a tyranny. Mazarin may have represented the rebels as comparable to Cromwell and Fairfax, yet the aim of the princes was never to abolish the monarchy.[24] This explains why, following Mazarin's death, when the king resolved to govern without a prime minister, those who had been

women printers were active publishers of this political pamphlet material; see Roméo Arbour, *Les Femmes et les métiers du livre* (Chicago and Paris: Garamond Press & Didier Erudition, 1997), pp. 70–8. By contrast with the English women pamphleteers, French women's participation in these pamphlet wars has been little documented.

[21] Alan James, *The Origins of French Absolutism*, p. 10.
[22] Cardinal Richelieu, *Testament politique*, ed. Louis André (Paris: Laffont, 1947), p. 104.
[23] See, for example, the poem 'La France ruinée par les favoris' in Hubert Carrier, *La Fronde. Contestation démocratique et misère paysanne, 52 Mazarinades*, 2 vols. (Paris: Editions d'histoire sociale, 1982), vol. 1, p. 13.
[24] La Grande Mademoiselle refers to Mazarin's discourse on Cromwell and Fairfax in Montpensier, *Mémoires*, vol. 1, p. 150; see also Knecht, *The Fronde*, p. 28.

involved in the Fronde were happy to return to the court and receive the king's favour.[25]

The *Apologie pour Messieurs les Princes* and *Manifeste de Mme la duchesse de Longueville* were written for Anne Geneviève de Bourbon, Duchess of Longueville by her secretary, Jean-François Sarasin, in 1650, after the arrest of her brothers and husband, and can be presumed to represent the political issues at stake during the Fronde as she saw them.[26] In the *Apologie* she responds to the accusations made in a letter, published in the name of the king, in which Condé is accused of treacherously aiming to take over the government of France.[27] Her counter-accusation is that it is Cardinal Mazarin, a foreigner, who is attempting to usurp royal authority. She has no objection in principle to absolute royal power, but argues that in a situation of regency, government should include the princes of the blood and parliament:

For, despite the fact that the power of our kings is entirely independent, that they recognise none other than God above them, and that they need only account to him for their actions, nevertheless, these same kings, who established the foundations of our empire and established the absolute rights of the monarchy, have since judged that it is necessary for its conservation, during the minority of their successors and the weakness of their youth, that the realm should be governed by the council of the princes of the blood, and that, in matters of greatest importance, those who have been invested with the regency ought to consult the Estates of the realm in resolving and executing them.[28]

Even in the *Manifeste*, where the duchess declares that she has allied her troops with those of the king of Spain, then at war with France, she insists that her actions are intended to bring about peace, which will be delivered once the princes are liberated. Although she calls the people and parliament of Paris the source and most solid foundation of the monarchy, her rhetoric is not intended to oppose the king's power; rather she calls on the people and parliament to help maintain the king's state, by liberating the princes who are his traditional support.[29]

So, despite the existence of pamphlets published during the Fronde which tend in the direction of democracy and which argue for constitutional limits to monarchical power, these are not theses to which the

[25] The Duchess of Longueville, in a letter to Mme de Sablé, written on 15 September 1667, expressed her gratitude for the king's civility towards her; see Victor Cousin, *Madame de Sablé* (Paris: Didier, Libraire-Editeur, 1854), p. 387.

[26] *Oeuvres de J.-Fr. Sarasin*, ed. Paul Festugière, 2 vols. (Paris: Champion, 1926), vol. 11, pp. 244–88, 309–441.

[27] Sarasin, *Oeuvres*, vol. 11, p. 295.   [28] Ibid., p. 313–14.   [29] Ibid., vol. 11.

Duchess of Longueville was committed.[30] Nor should we assume, therefore, that the fact that the Scudérys dedicated their work to her implied democratic tendencies, or even an opposition to absolutism. Indeed, by the Fronde's end it was not clear that Madeleine de Scudéry approved even of the limited ambitions of the Frondeurs. *Clélie*, which appeared between 1654 and 1657, and is more thoroughly attested as completely the work of Madeleine than is *Le Grand Cyrus*, is dedicated to the Duchess of Longueville's step-daughter, Marie d'Orléans-Longueville (1625–1707), who would become the Duchess of Nemours, and who had ceased to support the Fronde before the final act in 1652, which saw Mazarin and the king return to Paris, and Gaston d'Orléans and La Grande Mademoiselle exiled. In her *Mémoires*, Marie represents most of the actors in the rebellion as motivated by private interests rather than concern for the public good.[31]

Scudéry's similar reservations concerning the motives for rebellion emerge in the second book of *Clélie*. The story of the novel is constructed around the tyranny of Tarquin, who usurped the throne of Rome by violently murdering his father-in-law, the king. Nevertheless, one of its most admirable characters, Herminius, raises doubts as to whether rebellion is justified, even in such a case.[32] He suggests that there is a danger that those who propose to foment an uprising can be accused of preferring private revenge to public peace. When the hero Brutus finally leads a successful rebellion against the tyrant, he is represented as incapable of controlling the unleashed passions of the crowd, and has to acquiesce to the execution of his own sons, who have been manipulated into supporting a counter-coup.[33] In general this work questions the politics of power and ambition and proposes instead a retreat to a private realm of sociable and tender friendship. Indeed, in Scudéry's novels one can see the emergence of the notion of a feminine private realm governed by principles of affection and love, which was to come to prominence in altered form during the eighteenth century.[34]

---

[30] Some of the more radical and democratic pamphlets are published in the second volume of Carrier, *La Fronde*, and discussed in the introduction: see vol. 1, pp. 8–12.

[31] *Mémoires de Marie d'Orléans, duchesse de Nemours. Suivis de Lettres inédites de Marguerite de Lorraine, duchesse d'Orléans*, ed. Micheline Cuénin (Paris: Mercure de France, 1990).

[32] Madeleine de Scudéry, *Clélie. Histoire romaine. Seconde partie* (*1655*), ed. Chantal Morlet-Chantalat (Paris: Champion, 2002), pp. 64–5.

[33] *Clélie. Histoire romaine. Troisième partie* (1657), ed. Chantal Morlet-Chantalat (Paris: Champion, 2003), pp. 44–5 and 217–37.

[34] See Jean Bethke Elshtain, *Public Man, Private Woman* (Princeton University Press, 1981).

It is generally accepted that the Fronde marks a turning point, when images of heroic and even violent women, popular in the first half of the century, were replaced by a new more 'feminine' model of female excellence, and that Madeleine de Scudéry was enormously influential in developing a form of feminism that became so acceptable as to cease to be recognised as feminist.[35] Indeed, it is arguable that Rousseau's romantic conception of the place of love in society, and his representation of feminine difference, were influenced by Scudéry, whose novels he read with his father at a very young age.[36] These novels provided him with notions of human existence which he later condemned as 'bizarres et romanesques' but of which, he says, experience and reflection were never able to cure him. In place of an image of female excellence, which represented women as taking on the heroic characteristics of men, Scudéry developed an ideal of feminine sociability, governed by friendship and love.

The Fronde thus marks a turning point in the representation of legitimate modes of female political influence. The year before its outbreak saw the publication of Pierre Le Moyne's *La Gallerie des femmes fortes* (1647), which celebrated the famous heroines of the past – Judith, Jael, Deborah, and so on. Some twenty years earlier, the bicentenary of Joan of Arc's victories had been the occasion for the appearance of works commemorating her earlier intervention in France's political history, to which Gournay had contributed. That Joan remained a popular precursor for women who saw women's political interventions as having a military and heroic character is suggested by the fact that the Longuevilles (who were descendants of Joan's companion Dunois, Louis of Orléans's illegitimate son) commissioned Jean Chapelain to compose the heroic poem *La Pucelle* during the 1640s.[37] It seems fair to say that prior to and during the Fronde, women's political intervention was imagined in heroic and Amazonian terms, modelled on the same heroic women to whom Joan had been compared: Judith, Deborah, and Penthesilia. Female heroism, epitomised in the actions of contemporary women such as the taking of Orléans by La Grande Mademoiselle, the defence of her lands

[35] Noemi Hepp, 'La notion d'héroïne', in *Onze études sur l'image de la femme dans la littérature française du XVIIe siècle* (Paris: J.-M Place, 1978), pp. 9–27; Maclean, *Woman Triumphant*; Timmermans, *L'accès des femmes à la culture*, p. 320.

[36] Jean-Jacques Rousseau, *Oeuvres complètes*, 5 vols. (Paris: Gallimard, 1959), vol. 1, p. 8. For a discussion of how some of Rousseau's ideas about the difference between the sexes anticipate late twentieth-century feminisms of difference, see Karen Green, *The Woman of Reason* (Cambridge: Polity, 1995).

[37] Jean Chapelain, *La Pucelle, ou la France délivrée* (1656; reprint, Paris: Marpon & Flammarion, 1891); Cousin, *La Société française*, p. 58.

by Barbe d'Ernecourt, Countess of Saint-Baselmont, the androgynous behaviour of Queen Christina who modelled herself on Alexander the Great, the escape of Mme de Chevreuse, and the military leadership assumed by the Duchess of Longueville, often implied extreme courage, the donning of masculine forms of dress, and the undertaking of military exploits.[38] Glory and heroism were thus imagined as masculine traits acquired by exceptional women. During the second half of the century a new model of feminine glory and masculine sensibility began to be articulated, particularly in Scudéry's novels.

Even in her letters concerning Joan of Arc, which she wrote to defend Joan's chastity, Scudéry questions the Amazonian model: 'The Clorindas, Marphisas and Bradamants do not seem to me to be likeable in Tasso and in Ariosto, any more than [they do] to Balzac, and however gallant Amazons may appear in paintings, they do not appeal to me.'[39] In *Le Grand Cyrus*, the violent Amazonian princess Thomaris is represented as both brutal and tragic, while the female-dominated land of the Sauromates is civilised and tender, and shares little, other than the possibility of freedom from marriage, with earlier representations of Amazonian culture.

In one of her earliest works, *Les Femmes illustres* (1642), written with her brother, Madeleine de Scudéry was beginning to introduce a more feminine model of women's political and intellectual participation. She continued to develop these ideas in *Le Grand Cyrus*, the novel *Clélie*, and in later works which were to have an enormous influence. Prefiguring the twentieth-century turn from feminisms of equality to feminisms of difference, Scudéry turned against heroic and pedantic women who attempt to play the roles of men, and developed an ideal of feminine sociability or civility which is learned without seeming so, and for which utopia is figured as either freedom from marriage, or marriage based on free and

---

[38] For a recent discussion of strong or violent women in the seventeenth century, see Joan DeJean, 'Violent Women and Violence Against Women: Representing the "Strong" Woman in Early Modern France', *Signs* 29 (2003), 117–47. DeJean suggests a male backlash against these images, yet in Scudéry we find a female rejection of violence as an ideal for women. For Saint-Baselmont, see DeJean, *Tender Geographies*, pp. 24–8, and Jean-Marie de Vernon, *L'Amazone chrestienne; ou, les avantures de Madame Saint-Balmon* (Paris: Gaspar Méturas, 1678). Recent studies of Queen Christina which represent her androgyny and desire to be a man include Veronica Biermann, 'The Virtue of a King and the Desire of a Woman? Mythological Representations in the Collection of Queen Christina', *Art History* 24 (2001), 213–30.

[39] Edouard Barthélemy and René Kerviler (eds.), *Un Tournoi de trois pucelles en l'honneur de Jeanne d'Arc. Lettres inédites de Conrart, de Mlle de Scudéry et de Mlle du Moulin* (Paris: Alphonse Picard, 1878), pp. 23–4.

equal inclination.[40] Writing at the dawn of modernity, Scudéry also expresses a certain suspicion of speculative philosophy that presages some themes in late twentieth-century feminisms of difference.

In the harangue that concludes *Les Femmes illustres*, delivered by Sappho to Erinna, the poet urges her younger friend to write and to use her judgement, which she assures her is just as good as a man's; but she does not encourage her friend to pursue 'thornie Sciences' and 'such studies as make the complexion yellow, the eyes hollow, the countenance ghastlie'.[41] Women, she believes, should be educated and cultivated, while at the same time being sociable, polite, and modest. Later, by reconfiguring feminine glory as conquest through love, Scudéry solved the conflict between female education, the pursuit of glory, and feminine modesty, that (as we have seen) troubled women as early as Laura Cereta.

Vanity and ambition are passions which too often lead to murder and impiety. In *Les Femmes illustres*, Mariam calls ambition 'the error of great spirits' which, while being the mark of those born to great things, was also responsible for Herod's murderous usurpation of the throne.[42] Sophonisba, insisting that she prefers liberty to life, says of Rome, 'vanity is the soul of that Nation' and leads it to conquer lands beyond its own continent, usurp kingdoms, and desolate the world.[43] Tullie, the monstrous anti-heroine of *Clélie* who becomes the wife of Tarquin, is governed by a passionate ambition, which results in her becoming a murderer and callously driving her chariot over the body of her freshly murdered father.

Like early seventeenth-century Italian women writers, Scudéry's female characters often voice a suspicion of marriage. In *Le Grand Cyrus*, Sappho, who is taken to be modelled on Scudéry, considers marriage to be an unending slavery and avers that all men are inclined to become tyrants once they become husbands.[44] In this story it is only by resisting her lover's desire for marriage that Sappho is able to enjoy his undying ardent love. At the same time, some reasons for rejecting marriage are painted in a very negative light by Scudéry. In *Clélie*, the ambitious Tullie revolts against the feminine condition. Extending Sappho's critique of marriage,

[40] Nicole Aronson, 'Amour et mariage dans les œuvres de Mlle de Scudéry', *L'Esprit Créateur* 19 (1979), 26–39; DeJean, 'Amazones et femmes de lettres'.
[41] Madeleine de Scudéry, *Les Femmes Illustres: or Twenty Heroick Haranges of the most Illustrious Women of Antiquity* (London: Dorman Newman, 1693), p. 232.
[42] Scudéry, *Les Femmes Illustres*, p. 12.   [43] Ibid., p. 49.
[44] Madeleine de Scudéry, *The Story of Sappho*, trans. Karen Newman (Chicago and London: University of Chicago Press, 2003), p. 19; *Artamène, ou le grand Cyrus*, 10 vols. (Geneva: Slatkine Reprints, 1972), vol. X, p. 343.

Tullie represents the general situation of women as one of slavery. Rejecting, equally, the situation of married submission, and the life of a vestal virgin, she says: 'rather than wishing to consign myself to new laws and a new submission, I would willingly free myself from all those to which nature and custom have subjected all women'.[45] She expresses a preference for being a poor soldier rather than the most revered vestal, since women have no liberty, whereas a man is free to come and go as he chooses. Tullie's ambition leads to murder, to impiety, and to partici-pation in her husband Tarquin's tyranny. For Scudéry, clearly, the rejection of slavery for oneself is valueless if what one desires instead is the slavery of others. In this story, it is Tullie's sister, a princess cruelly murdered by her husband Tarquin, who is represented as admirable. Thus, it would seem that although Scudéry sees freedom from marriage as a potential good, she rejects the absolute freedom desired by those whose ambition is to wield self-interested power.

According to Tullie's sister, the virtuous princess, women are lucky to find themselves in a social position in which not too much is demanded of them. A woman requires no more than 'a little agreeableness, a modest wit, and plenty of modesty, to be an honourable woman; while, by contrast, to be a truly honourable man a thousand natural and acquired good qualities are required'.[46] Women are blessed because they are allowed to be mediocre and also because they 'enjoy eternal peace, since we are not required to go to war'.[47] Later she expresses herself happy with the situation of constraint and obedience in which she finds herself:

I find it even more glorious to rule without force than to rule with violence, and that it is so easy to submit one's spirit to decorum that there is nothing simpler. It is true that the passion of ambition is not appropriate to women, but it is such a tumultuous passion that I find it an advantage to be devoid of it.[48]

The princess is an ineffectual heroine who is quickly despatched by her husband; but she expresses, in her desire to rule without force, one of the guiding principles of Scudéry's imagined kingdom of tenderness.

This country, mapped in the famous 'Carte de Tendre', is governed by gratitude, mutual recognition, inclination, and esteem. Part fantasy, part idealised evocation of the operation of Scudéry's famous Saturday salon, the Carte de Tendre maps the possible paths that can lead to a tender

---

[45] Madeleine de Scudéry, *Clélie. Histoire romaine. Première partie* (*1654*), ed. Chantal Morlet-Chantalat (Paris: Champion, 2001), p. 322.
[46] *Clélie, première partie*, p. 323.   [47] Ibid.   [48] Ibid., p. 325.

friendship between people, whether of the same or opposite sexes.[49] Like
Moderata Fonte's garden, Tendre is a utopia free from slavery and tyranny, but unlike Fonte's private paradise, it is a country where men are
welcome, so long as they are prepared to live by Scudéry's laws. There are
also echoes of Montaigne's idealised friendship in Scudéry's descriptions,
but unlike Montaigne, Scudéry leaves us in no doubt as to women's
capacity for friendship, and indeed, Clélie is represented as understanding
friendship and the realm of Tendre better than any other. The governing
emotion of this country is tenderness, defined in the following terms:

it is a kind of sensibility of the heart, which is hardly ever found dominant,
except in those with noble souls, virtuous inclinations, a well-turned wit, and
who are such that when they have a friendship are sincere and ardent, and feel so
strongly all the pains and joys of those they love that they forget their own.[50]

Such tender friendships are possible only with a select few and are
characterised by a self-less love, which feels for lover or friend. In a letter
to Madeleine de Scudéry, Mlle Descartes (René's niece) wrote:

> Your beautiful books have acquainted me
> With a generous love, pure and disinterested,
> And those who have seen what it ought to be
> Cannot put up with it as it is.[51]

Tender friendship should be mutual, as should be the more passionate
tender love. In *Le Grand Cyrus*, Sappho declares that 'there is nothing
sweeter than to be loved by the person you love ... Women who take
pleasure in being loved without loving satisfy only their own vanity.'[52]
And this is a doctrine repeated throughout *Clélie*, which holds up as an
ideal for women a single, faithful, mutual love relationship in which the
woman loves as much as she is loved.[53]

---

[49] There are numerous discussions of the origins of the 'Carte de Tendre' in the literary
entertainments of Scudéry's salon and its status as a declaration of the nature of close friendships
within that salon. See, for example, DeJean, *Tender Geographies*, pp. 71–93; Myriam Maître,
'Sapho, *reine de Tendre*: entre monarchie absolue et royauté littéraire', in *Madeleine de Scudéry:
Une femme de lettres au XVIIe siècle*, ed. Delphine Denis and Anne-Elizabeth Spica (Arras: Artois
Presses Université, 2002), pp. 179–93; James S. Munro, *Mademoiselle de Scudéry and the Carte de
Tendre* (Durham: Durham Modern Language Series, 1986).

[50] Scudéry, *Clélie, première partie*, p. 118. See also Munro, *Mademoiselle de Scudéry*, p. 56.

[51] Quoted ibid., p. 68.   [52] Scudéry, *The Story of Sappho*, p. 50.

[53] This is the pattern of all the noble if tragic loves in the novel – those which bind Aronce and
Clélie, Brutus and Lucrece, and Artémidore and Bérélise – and it is a view that Plotine attempts to
teach to Cesonie; Scudéry, *Clélie, seconde partie*, pp. 416–17.

As she aged, Scudéry turned away from writing novels towards explicitly didactic collections of conversations in which her commitment to the strong and stable monarchy of Louis XIV is made manifest in many dedications and eulogies.[54] In 1687, she was invited to St Cyr by Madame de Maintenon, who had secretly married Louis XIV in 1683, and in her *Nouvelles Conversations de morale* (1688) she includes a description of St Cyr.[55] This suggests that in turning to explicitly didactic conversations such as the 'Histoire de la morale' she has in mind an educative purpose. These essays also demonstrate why she has no objections to monarchy, and show that, while her sexual politics has moved in the direction of modern notions of an ideal freedom to follow one's inclination in love, her conception of good government echoes the monarchism of earlier women. Scudéry adopts the view that there is a natural morality, grounded in a sense of justice, which is common to all human beings and was put 'in the heart of the first man by the creator of the universe'.[56] This leads her to reject the conventionalism of 'un grand homme' (perhaps Hobbes or Montaigne?) who supposes that there was no vice or virtue prior to the establishment of law.

Natural morality consists in a prohibition against killing oneself or others and in not doing to others what one would not wish to be done to oneself. It can be understood through the use of reason, and is perfected in good laws.[57] Natural morality is, however, insufficient by itself: it requires revealed religion, and in particular Christianity, for its perfection. The bulk of Scudéry's history consists in a criticism of the ethical doctrines of the Stoics, Epicureans, Pyrrhonists, and Cynics, to which is contrasted Christian morality as practised by Jesus, which perfects natural morality. In particular, by introducing the virtue of humility, Christianity perfects morality:

Pagan morality, rather than combatting pride, permitted it up to a point, and having only an imperfect understanding of pardoning enemies, was inclined to injustice and cruelty. But Christian morality banishes pride, self-interest, and vanity and substitutes for them charity and humility, and true justice is its rule. Love of one's country was well known to the Greeks and Romans, but a universal charity towards all friends and enemies has only been taught by Jesus Christ.[58]

[54] Madeleine de Scudéry, *Conversations sur divers sujets* (Paris: Claude Barbin, 1680); *Entretiens de morale dediez au Roy* (Paris: Chez Jean Anisson, 1692); *Nouvelles Conversations de morale dédiées au Roy* (Paris: Chez la Veuve de Sebastien Marbre-Cramoisy, 1688).
[55] Scudéry, 'De l'air galant', p. 39; *Nouvelles Conversations*, pp. 247–79.   [56] Ibid., p. 63.
[57] Ibid., pp. 65–71.   [58] Ibid., pp. 227–8.

This doctrine can be seen to underpin Scudéry's critique of ambition, based on pride and vanity, which, in her novels, leads to social upheaval and civil war. She implies that there is greater peace and fewer conspiracies in a monarchy where subjects cannot become kings and must simply obey.[59]

Quoting Confucius, whose sayings she interpolates into her history of morality, Scudéry asserts that 'The prince should have shown the concern of a father and the tenderness of a mother for his people.'[60] And, having called Confucius the Chinese Socrates, she attributes to him an account of human perfection which appears close to her own: 'The true fortitude of a perfect man and his true grandeur consists in self-conquest, commanding with equity, or obeying without murmur when he must, avoiding pride and all baseness, and persevering in virtue until death.'[61] This kind of moral self-perfection can be attained as well within a monarchy as in any other political system, and there is reason to think that Scudéry also finds monarchy superior, in so far as it fosters the development of polite society grounded in manners and civility.

In her 'De la politesse', which first appeared in 1684 in *Conversations nouvelles sur divers sujets*, the question is raised why it is that although all people are born equal, 'politesse' is only rarely found far away from the court. In the discussion that follows it is suggested that its development is encouraged in monarchies:

The source of civility being the desire to please for some motive, whether ambition or love, this desire must be stronger in a monarchy than in a republic, because since favours depend on a single person, the desire to please him makes it possible to please all. The prince attracting and assembling in his court the large number of people of quality who surround him, one could say that they make use of one another to acquire civility. Those who are born at court have the advantage of having seen it from birth. Those who come from outside conform to these, and become like the others, especially if the prince himself practises civility, and there are women of the court who know how to ensure that they are given the respect that they are owed: who know, I say, how to praise those that have it, distinguish true civility, and practise it themselves. This advantage, Cléonte added, is not equally available in modern republics, where conversation with women is not as free as in France: they see and are seen but are hardly ever spoken to; public entertainments, operas, balls, concerts make up almost all the

---

[59] Scudéry, *Conversations sur divers sujets*, p. 263. [60] Scudéry, *Nouvelles Conversations*, p. 198.
[61] Ibid., p. 198.

interaction between the sexes, which makes me think that true civility is found more often in the court of a great king than in a republic.[62]

Thus, according to Scudéry, within a monarchy the power of the king, and the practices of the court, ensure a standard of civilised behaviour whereby women are treated with respect. People, whatever their sex, can practise the art of civilised conversation, and develop the arts and sciences without troubling themselves with the direction of government:

In a monarchy the prince principally aspires to establish good morals and civility among his subjects, and he should be in the state that a pilot is in a ship, on whom the whole company relies, sleeping in confidence, without meddling in the observation of the stars or holding onto the rudder.[63]

There is sufficient honour and glory to be had conquering the heart of an honourable man for a woman to be content to rule her private social sphere through tenderness and without violence.

In his book *Woman Triumphant: Feminism in French Literature, 1610–1652*, Ian Maclean represents the end of the Fronde as a point in time when women's political engagement declined. Against this, Joan DeJean has argued that, while women had fewer opportunities for political engagement after the coming of age of Louis XIV, it is possible to read the literature of the second half of the seventeenth century as continuing the tradition of female political engagement characteristic of the first half.[64] We agree with DeJean's claim that Scudéry is as political at the end of the century as in the middle, but disagree with DeJean's implication that this political engagement should be thought of as radical or democratic, in any contemporary understanding of the word. In her book on the battle between the ancients and the moderns, DeJean argues that thinkers like Habermas are wrong to locate the origins of the 'public sphere' – a broad critical audience of readers whom writers consciously attempt to influence – in late seventeenth-century England, whence it moved to France. Her book attempts to establish that the idea of the 'public' developed in late seventeenth-century France, during the 'battle between the ancients and the moderns'. As well as criticising Habermas's chronology, DeJean criticises his political understanding: 'When the birth

---

[62] Scudéry, *'De l'air galant'*, p. 137. The translation of *politesse* poses some problems. The most obvious choice, 'politeness', sounds too constrained in English. 'Civility' has the advantage of having a similar etymology in *cive* as the *polis* from which *politesse* was originally derived, while retaining in English more of an association with civic virtue than has 'politeness'.

[63] Ibid., p. 138.   [64] DeJean, 'Amazones et femmes de lettres', p. 154.

of the phenomenon is situated in late-seventeenth-century France, it becomes evident that the sexual politics that surrounded its creation were just as complex as the class politics. In particular, women played an active, at times the most active, role in the democratisation of culture.'[65] But while DeJean provides ample evidence of the emergence of a literary public during the reign of Louis XIV, it is questionable whether 'democratisation' is the correct term to apply to this phenomenon. The public that engaged in the literary disputes concerning appropriate behaviour, how a husband and wife should communicate, the nature of politeness and civility, and other issues that stirred early educated society was a public that could operate quite happily subjected to the absolute power of a monarch. If there are origins of later democratic ideas to be found in Scudéry these are to be located in her construction of a realm of private sociable relations governed by tenderness and love, later co-opted by Rousseau. The sociable 'public' whose manners and intrigues she describes in her novels has much in common with the feminine 'private' realm which is domesticated and divorced from the masculine public realm in Rousseau's republicanism. Scudéry imagines a feminised public who do not meddle in political affairs but leave the government of the country to those to whom it has been entrusted.[66] Rousseau extracts the men, who are to be sovereign, from Scudéry's feminised polite society, putting them in the place of the sovereign, and leaving women uncontested power to govern the hearts and passions of men that must be confined in what becomes the private sphere.[67]

Seventeenth-century women theorists have posed something of a conundrum for modern female historians who have grown up with democratic sentiments. Time and again one finds women who are at the forefront of the critique of marriage and of the lack of educational opportunities for women, who are also fervent defenders of monarchical rule. Madeleine de Scudéry's writing enables us to understand this position as developing out of a critique of arbitrary power. We have seen how, in the fifteenth century, women needed to overcome the Aristotelian ideology which denied them the prudence, fortitude, and strength to rule. One way to overcome this ideology was to insist on the existence of exceptional women who were manly, and, although we have seen that this

---

[65] DeJean, *Ancients Against Moderns*, p. 38.
[66] See in particular 'Contre ceux qui décrient le gouvernement, quel qu'il soit', in Scudéry, *Conversations sur divers sujets*, pp. 251–70.
[67] On this topic, see Karen Green, 'Madeleine de Scudéry on Love and the Emergence of the "Private Sphere"' (unpublished paper).

strategy went hand in hand with another which attempted to promote a more maternal or parental conception of power, power itself remained a masculine quality. Thus women who found themselves in positions of power were forced to imagine themselves as male. There is no more evident example of this tendency than that of Queen Christina of Sweden, whose ideas we examine in a later chapter. Against the dead end of the heroic woman who struggles against her insufficiency as a man, epitomised by Christina, Scudéry imagined a political subject who patiently accepted subjection to a sovereign, but who also operated as a tender friend and loving equal in his or her relationships with other virtuous subjects. If illegitimate masculine power is based on force, vanity, ambition, and arbitrary subjection, it cannot be sufficient for women simply to acquire such power. Even legitimate male glory, grounded in courage in battle, is not really available to women. Scudéry offers an alternative feminine glory based on inclination, the desire to be loved by the virtuous other, and a freely accepted servitude to the virtuous beloved. Power becomes sentimental and egalitarian, and 'there is nothing sweeter than to be loved by someone one loves'. This feminised and egalitarian conception of legitimate power stands as an implicit critique of the pursuit of masculine prowess, represented in her novels by the vile Tullie.

CHAPTER 9

Margaret Cavendish, Duchess of Newcastle

During the civil war era in England, Leveller women were not the only female group to voice their political concerns: a few royalist women also addressed petitions to parliament. In 1642, on the eve of the first civil war, a group of 'Gentle-women, Citizens Wives, [and] Tradesmens Wives' published a petition addressed 'To the Queens most Excellent Maiestie'.[1] In this one-page text, the women do not assert their spiritual liberty or equality with men, they do not call for the right to separate from the national church, nor do they spell out their 'equal interest' in the commonwealth. Instead their humble petition is a call for Queen Henrietta Maria to show 'tender Compassion', and not to forsake her loyal subjects by moving abroad.[2] A few years later, a woman named Mary Pope (d. 1653?) published three works in defence of the divine authority of kingship: *A Treatise of Magistracy* (1647), *Behold, Here is a Word* (1648), and *Heare, heare, heare, heare, A Word or Message from Heaven* (1648).[3] In these works, Pope demonstrates a remarkable knowledge of biblical passages in support of 'the absolute Impunity of Kings' and of the absolutist claim that 'they are not accountable to any on earth'.[4] She argues in favour of both active and passive obedience to kings, because 'God hath shewed unto you, that you are not to meddle with the King, no not although he hath acted and done contrary to the command of God and his own laws.'[5] Pope beseeches parliament to 'thinke it noe dishonour to heare the counsell of a woman, being nothing but what is

---

[1] Anonymous, *To the Queens most Excellent Majestie. The Humble Petition of divers Gentle-women, Citizens Wives, Tradesmens Wives, and other Inhabitants in the Cities of London and Westminster, and the Suburbs thereof* (London: n.p., 1642).

[2] In February 1642, Queen Henrietta Maria left England for the Netherlands, where she spent a year at The Hague rousing support for her husband, Charles I.

[3] Mary Pope, *A Treatise of Magistracy* (London: n.p., 1647); *Behold, Here Is A Word Or, An Answer To The Late Remonstrance of the Army* (London: n.p., 1648); *Heare, heare, heare, heare, A Word or Message from Heaven* (London: n.p., 1648).

[4] Pope, *Behold, Here Is a Word*, p. 2.   [5] Ibid., p. 7.

according to the Word'.[6] When she attempted to deliver her work to parliament in 1647, however, her messenger was arrested: religious or not, Pope's views were not welcome.[7]

In this chapter, we examine the ideas of another supporter of monarchy: Margaret Cavendish, Duchess of Newcastle (1623–73). We find that Cavendish's royalism is of a very different stamp to that of Mary Pope. Cavendish developed her political outlook in the aftermath of the Fronde and the English civil wars: she wrote during the interregnum, and following the restoration of Charles II in 1660. Like that of many writers of her time, Cavendish's political thought is a critical response to the horrors of civil war, and her central problem is how to secure the obedience of subjects and maintain peace and order in civil society. Her royalism is thus based upon pragmatic concerns and not biblical arguments concerning the foundations of political authority.

Born in 1623, Margaret was the youngest daughter of the royalist Lucas family of Colchester. As a young woman of twenty, she joined the royal court in Oxford as a maid of honour to Henrietta Maria, and later followed the Catholic queen into exile in 1644.[8] While in France, Margaret met the former royalist military commander, William Cavendish (then the Marquess of Newcastle), and after a short period of courtship they were married in 1645. In 1651, it was decided that Margaret would travel to England to petition for her one-fifth share of William's estate (a wife's entitlement by law). Her appeal to the parliamentary Committee on Compounding was unsuccessful: 'I found their hearts as hard as my fortunes,' she says, 'and their Natures as cruell as my miseries, for they sold all my Lords Estate ... and gave me not any part thereof.'[9] After eighteen months in England, Margaret returned empty-handed, and the couple remained in exile in Europe till the restoration of the monarchy. Upon her departure from England in 1653, however, Margaret Cavendish made a bold political stand by refusing to declare allegiance to the new

---

[6] Pope, *A Treatise of Magistracy*, p. 123.

[7] See Catie Gill, 'Pope, Mary (*d.* 1653?) ', in *The Oxford Dictionary of National Biography* (Oxford University Press, 2004), http://www.oxforddnb.com/view/article/69153, accessed 6 August 2007. On Pope, see also Nevitt, *Women and the Pamphlet Culture of Revolutionary England*, pp. 64–9.

[8] Later, in praise of the queen, Cavendish says that she 'shewed as much Courage as ever any person could do; for Her undaunted and Generous spirit was like her Royal Birth'; see Margaret Cavendish, *The Life of the Thrice Noble, High and Puissant Prince William Cavendishe* (London: A. Maxwell, 1667), p. 23.

[9] Margaret Cavendish, 'A True Relation of My Birth, Breeding and Life', in *Paper Bodies: A Margaret Cavendish Reader*, ed. Sylvia Bowerbank and Sara Mendelson (Ontario: Broadview Press, 2000), p. 51.

government. When she first arrived, Cavendish did not expect to take the Oath of Engagement: the parliamentarians did not require women to declare their political allegiance, or, for that matter, to take part in any public affairs.[10] But when Cavendish applied to the Council of State to return to the continent, she was asked – like all emigrants from England – to swear loyalty to parliament. She refused to do so, and with this act, we gain the first glimpse of Cavendish's position on the limits of political obligation.[11]

Cavendish's theoretical views on political obligation can be found in her later works of philosophy, oration, and prose. Not surprisingly, in these writings, Cavendish expresses disapproval of the Leveller programme and their methods of negotiation with parliament. In a mock speech in Cavendish's *Orations of Divers Sorts* (1662), one speaker warns his ruler that

These petitioners that petition for reformations of government, and complain for the breach of their privileges, and exclaim against their magistrates and your Majesty's ministers of state, are to be considered as dangerous persons, for their petitioners are forerunners of civil wars if not timely prevented; for though they cloak their treacherous designs under fair and humble words at the first, yet no doubt but they will persist and go on in a rough and rude manner; for what they call in their petition their humble complaints are factious and seditious murmurings, and what they name their humble desires of redress are presumptuous demands, and the number of the petitioners are a rebellious insurrection, for which they ought to be severely punished.[12]

Although the orator adopts a rhetorical stance, these sentiments accord with Cavendish's more explicit remarks. In her autobiographical piece 'A True Relation of My Birth, Breeding and Life' (1656), Cavendish openly criticises women petitioners who run about 'with their severall Causes, complaining of their severall grievances, exclaiming against their severall enemies'.[13] This comment and the 1662 oration express a conviction that civil war must be avoided at all costs, that citizens owe an absolute obedience to the government, and that governors ought not to tolerate

[10] See Katie Whitaker, *Mad Madge: The Extraordinary Life of Margaret Cavendish, Duchess of Newcastle, the First Woman to Live by Her Pen* (New York: Basic Books, 2002), p. 133.

[11] Whitaker observes that Cavendish was nevertheless permitted to leave the country, 'for women's political compliance was of little importance compared to men's' (ibid., p. 159).

[12] Margaret Cavendish, 'A Privy Councillors Speech to his Majesty at the Council Board', in *Orations of Divers Sorts, Accommodated to Divers Places* (1662), in *Political Writings*, ed. Susan James, Cambridge Texts in the History of Political Thought (Cambridge University Press, 2003), p. 192.

[13] Cavendish, 'A True Relation', p. 52.

dissent or faction of any kind. In the first part of this chapter, we examine the theoretical foundations for these views. For Cavendish, what is the basis of legitimate government in the state? On what grounds should citizens pledge their allegiance to the powers that be? And what exactly constitutes the 'liberties' and 'privileges' of subjects?

Some scholars warn that there may be no precise or definite answers to these questions. One problem is that Cavendish's political ideas are dispersed throughout her numerous works: she never published a classic political treatise as such, with a unified viewpoint or a central argument. On political subjects, Cavendish often makes 'Declamations' in which she considers the pros and cons of a position, but she rarely takes a positive stance of her own.[14] It is thus extremely difficult to differentiate between Cavendish's genuinely held views and those that she defends simply for the sake of rhetorical effect. More recently, scholars have highlighted the number of non-royalist sentiments in Cavendish's writings.[15] In some orations, Hilda Smith suggests, Cavendish may simply be mouthing the conservative views of her husband, William.[16] Yet, in other orations, she seemingly challenges his views by supporting religious toleration and freedom of conscience: 'Strongly royalist ... Cavendish nevertheless did not feel obligated to follow the royalist position on a wide range of social, religious, and political issues.'[17] Mihoko Suzuki likewise suggests that Cavendish espouses an 'ambiguous royalism', because she often voices opposition to the dominant royalist discourse of the day.[18]

In this analysis, we are not concerned with whether or not Cavendish herself was a devout royalist, but rather the way in which she characterises the royalist viewpoint. There are several recurring statements and arguments in Cavendish's works that together constitute a defence of monarchy as the best form of government. We argue that this royalist outlook is not necessarily incompatible with Cavendish's views on religious toleration and liberty of conscience. In what follows, we concentrate primarily on her overt political statements in the *Blazing World*, the *Orations*, and

---

[14] Margaret Cavendish, *CCXI. Sociable Letters, Written By The Thrice Noble, Illustrious, and Excellent Princess, the Lady Marchioness of Newcastle* (London: William Wilson, 1664), 'The Preface', sig. c1ʳ.
[15] On this topic, see Hilda L. Smith, '"A General War Amongst the Men . . . But None Amongst the Women": Political Differences Between Margaret and William Cavendish', in *Politics and the Political Imagination in Later Stuart Britain: Essays Presented to Lois Green Schwoerer*, ed. Howard Nenner (Rochester, NY: University of Rochester Press, 1997), pp. 143–60; Mihoko Suzuki, *Subordinate Subjects: Gender, the Political Nation, and Literary Form in England, 1588–1688* (Aldershot: Ashgate, 2003), pp. 182–202.
[16] Smith, 'A General War Amongst the Men', p. 151.   [17] Ibid., p. 153.
[18] Suzuki, *Subordinate Subjects*, pp. 182–202.

various individual pieces. Cavendish's fictional tale, *The Description of a New World, Called The Blazing World* (first published in 1666),[19] provides us with substantial insight into Cavendish's views on the role of government in the maintenance of peace. This work might be seen as a political utopia in the tradition of Thomas More's classic *Utopia* (1516) or Francis Bacon's *New Atlantis* (1627): it offers a blueprint for an ideal political system, in which the rights and obligations of citizens and sovereigns are delineated. Some recent scholars also identify embedded political commentaries in Cavendish's philosophical works, the *Philosophical Letters* (1664), her *Observations upon Experimental Philosophy* (1666), and the *Grounds of Natural Philosophy* (1668).[20] And various short pieces – in *The World's Olio* (1655) and the *Sociable Letters* (1664) – also enable us to form a complete picture of Cavendish's conception of royalism.

In the final part of the chapter, we examine Cavendish's views about women's relationship to political authority. In her *Sociable Letter* no. 16, Cavendish makes the now-famous remark that women 'are not tied, nor bound to State or Crown; we are free, not Sworn to Allegiance, nor do we take the Oath of Supremacy; we are not made Citizens of the Commonwealth . . . and if we be not Citizens in the Commonwealth, I know no reason we should be Subjects to the Commonwealth'.[21] We shall discuss the implications of this view about female non-citizenship for the liberty of women in general.

I

Like her contemporary, Thomas Hobbes, Cavendish takes a distinctly secular approach to the topic of the foundations of political authority. In Elizabeth I's time, as we have seen, the prevailing view was that the sovereign's authority is ultimately founded in God, and that active disobedience to the sovereign constitutes unlawful rebellion against divine authority. This view is supported by Romans 13.1, the biblical injunction to 'Let every soul be subject unto higher powers.' In her royalist works of

---

[19] Margaret Cavendish, *The Description of a New World, Called The Blazing World. Written by the Thrice Noble, Illustrious, and Excellent Princess, the Duchess of Newcastle*, in *Political Writings*, pp. 1–109.
[20] Neil Ankers, 'Paradigm and Politics: Hobbes and Cavendish Compared', in *A Princely Brave Woman: Essays on Margaret Cavendish, Duchess of Newcastle*, ed. Stephen Clucas (Aldershot: Ashgate, 2003), pp. 242–54; John Rogers, *The Matter of Revolution: Science, Poetry and Politics in the Age of Milton* (Ithaca and London: Cornell University Press, 1996), pp. 177–211.
[21] Cavendish, *Sociable Letters*, pp. 26–7.

the civil war era, Mary Pope repeatedly cites this biblical passage in favour of unquestioning submission to the crown.[22] In the aftermath of the English civil wars, however, the precept came under political pressure. How far did the injunction 'to obey higher powers' extend to *de facto* governments? Did royalist resistance to the new parliamentary regime constitute rebellion against divine authority? And were royalists duty bound to swear the Oath of Engagement in favour of the new government?[23] In response to such pressing questions, some writers, such as the Presbyterian Francis Rous, reinterpreted the Romans precept as a command 'to obey *whatever* powers are in a position to demand our obedience'.[24] But Quentin Skinner observes that this providentialist style of argument was still vulnerable to attack: the biblical passage could be easily reinterpreted to suit royalist as well as parliamentary purposes.[25] As a result, in the late 1640s and early 1650s, a number of secular arguments arose, spelling out practical reasons for submission to the new regime. In this historical-political context – in works such as *De Corpore Politico* (1650), *De Cive* (1642; translated into English as *Philosophicall Rudiments Concerning Government and Society* in 1651), and *Leviathan* (1651) – Hobbes develops the doctrine that we are obliged to submit to any government that can secure our peace and protection. Hobbes wrote these political works amidst the upheavals of the Fronde in France and the Thirty Years' War in Germany, and during the civil war period in England. Accordingly, his emphasis is upon the maintaining of peace and the quelling of dissent. His theory of political obligation does not appeal to whether or not the regime is ordained by God, but whether or not that regime can provide for the basic security needs of civil society.

Thomas Hobbes was a close associate of William Cavendish, and a frequent visitor to the Cavendish household in Paris.[26] According to her own testimony, it seems that Margaret Cavendish had little interaction with Hobbes. In *Philosophical and Physical Opinions* (1655), she reports that as 'for Master *Hobbes*, it is true I have had the like good fortune to

---

[22] See, for example, Pope, *Behold, Here Is a Word*, p. 2.

[23] On this topic, see Quentin Skinner, 'Conquest and Consent: Hobbes and the Engagement Controversy', in *Visions of Politics*, Volume 3: *Hobbes and Civil Science* (Cambridge University Press, 2002), pp. 287–307.

[24] Ibid., p. 292. Rous presents this argument in his *The Lawfulness of Obeying the Present Government* (1649).

[25] Skinner, 'Conquest and Consent', p. 293.

[26] For an overview of Hobbes's relationship with the Cavendish family, see Anna Battigelli, 'Political Thought/Political Action: Margaret Cavendish's Hobbesian Dilemma', in Smith (ed.), *Women Writers*, pp. 41–3.

see him, and that very often with my Lord at dinner . . . yet I never heard Master *Hobbes* to my best remembrance treat, or discourse of Philosophy, nor I never spoke to Master *Hobbes* twenty words in my life'.[27] Nevertheless, Cavendish confesses that she has read 'a little book called *De Cive*';[28] and despite her protestations, she seems to have been present when Hobbes discussed the writing of *Leviathan* with her husband.[29] Cavendish also engages with Hobbes's philosophy in her written works.[30] In her *Philosophical Letters*, she critically addresses the materialist philosophy of the first six chapters of *Leviathan*; in *The Blazing World*, she satirises his mechanistic theory of causation.[31] In the *Philosophical Letters*, Cavendish has little to say about Hobbes's political views, apparently on the grounds, 'First, That a Woman is not imployed in State Affairs, unless an absolute Queen. Next, That to study the Politicks, is but loss of Time, unless a man were sure to be a Favourite to an absolute Prince. Thirdly, That it is but a deceiving Profession, and requires more Craft then Wisdom.'[32] In her one explicit comment on Hobbesian politics, she says that

If men do not naturally agree, Art cannot make unity amongst them, or associate them into one Politick Body and so rule them . . . [I]t is not the artificial form

---

[27] Margaret Cavendish, 'An Epiloge [*sic*] to my Philosophical Opinions', in *The Philosophical and Physical Opinions, Written by her Excellency, the Lady Marchionesse of Newcastle* (London: J. Martin and J. Allestrye, 1655), sig. B 3v. In response to Cavendish's comments, we should keep in mind Sarah Hutton's remark that 'at the time when she published, to admit mere acquaintance with Hobbes, "the Beast of Malmesbury", never mind affinity for his thinking, was hardly likely to endear her to the thinking public'; see Sarah Hutton, 'In Dialogue with Thomas Hobbes: Margaret Cavendish's Natural Philosophy', *Women's Writing* 4, no. 3 (1997), 426. In 1662, Hobbes wrote a letter to Margaret expressing his thanks for a gift that may have been one of her own works; see Thomas Hobbes to Margaret Cavendish, 9 February 1661 [i.e. 1662], in Margaret Cavendish, *A Collection of Letters And Poems: Written by several Persons of Honour and Learning, Upon divers Important subjects, to the Late Duke and Dutchess of Newcastle* (London: Langly Curtis, 1678), pp. 67–8.

[28] Cavendish, *Philosophical and Physical Opinions*, sig. B 4r.

[29] Cavendish, *Life of William Cavendishe*, pp. 143–5.

[30] On Cavendish and Hobbes, see Ankers, 'Paradigm and Politics', pp. 242–54; Battigelli, 'Political Thought/Political Action', pp. 40–55; Broad, *Women Philosophers of the Seventeenth Century*, pp. 46–50; Hutton, 'In Dialogue with Thomas Hobbes', 421–32; Susan James, 'The Philosophical Innovations of Margaret Cavendish', *British Journal for the History of Philosophy* 7 (1999), 219–44; Rogers, *Matter of Revolution*, pp. 177–211; and Lisa T. Sarasohn, '*Leviathan* and the Lady: Cavendish's Critique of Hobbes in the *Philosophical Letters*', in *Authorial Conquests: Essays on Genre in the Writings of Margaret Cavendish*, ed. Line Cottegnies and Nancy Weitz (London: Associated University Presses, 2003), pp. 40–58.

[31] Margaret Cavendish, *Philosophical Letters: Or, Modest Reflections Upon some Opinions in Natural Philosophy, Maintained By several Famous and Learned Authors of this Age* (London: privately published, 1664), pp. 18–48; *Blazing World*, pp. 74–5.

[32] Cavendish, *Philosophical Letters*, p. 47.

that governs men in a Politick Government, but a natural power, for though natural motion can make artificial things, yet artificial things cannot make natural power, as to say man is ruled by the art and invention of men. The truth is, Man rules an artificial Government, and not the Government Man, just like as a Watch-maker rules his Watch, and not the Watch the Watch-Maker.[33]

On this view, Hobbes's 'Artificial animal' (the commonwealth) and its 'Artificiall Soul' (the sovereign) provide no guarantee of peace and stability:[34] if men are naturally inclined to disagree, then nature will prevail.[35] Later in the same work, Cavendish says that 'it is easier to make disorders then to rectifie them: as for example, in a Common-wealth, the ruines of War are not so suddenly repaired, as made' and that 'a war or rebellion in Nature cannot be avoided'.[36] These suggestions about the natural unsociability of mankind and the human tendency toward war are developed in other works. Two years later, in *The Blazing World*, a character called the 'Duchess of Newcastle' becomes the favourite of an absolute sovereign, the Empress of the Blazing World. In this work, we learn about Cavendish's reception of Hobbes's ideas from the discussions and pronouncements of these characters – two female characters who, by Cavendish's own lights, have a legitimate say in political affairs.

In *The Blazing World*, Cavendish recounts the adventures of a young woman who is kidnapped by a lustful foreign merchant. When the merchant's ship is caught in a tempest and carried to an alien world beyond the North Pole, everyone on board freezes to death except the young woman. The strange inhabitants of this world rescue the lady and then present her to their emperor. Upon meeting her, the emperor makes her his wife and gives her an absolute power to rule and govern the world. The Blazing World, as it is known, is presented as a kind of paradise: the new empress can hardly make any alterations to the Blazing World 'by reason it was so well ordered that it could not be mended; for it was

---

[33] Ibid., pp. 47–8.
[34] Thomas Hobbes, *Leviathan*, ed. Richard Tuck, Cambridge Texts in the History of Political Thought, revised student edition (Cambridge University Press, 1996), p. 9.
[35] There is an alternative interpretation of Cavendish's comments: she may be implying that true political authority is natural rather than conventional (or contracted) in the Hobbesian sense. This natural theory is consistent with Cavendish's panpsychist metaphysics of matter and motion, according to which every part of nature has intelligence and is therefore capable of governing itself. Following this line of thought, it might be possible to read more political commentary into the *Philosophical Letters* than scholars have done hitherto. In this chapter, however, we aim simply to show that Cavendish's explicit royalist statements on political authority are consistent with her statements about liberty of conscience.
[36] Cavendish, *Philosophical Letters*, pp. 408–9.

governed without secret and deceiving policy; neither was there any ambition, factions, malicious detractions, civil dissensions, or home-bred quarrels, divisions in religion, foreign wars, etc. but all the people lived in a peaceful society, united tranquillity, and religious conformity'.[37] Cavendish does not allow us to forget, however, that this state of peace can be easily destroyed. When the empress visits the Duchess of Newcastle's world (earth), she is struck by the chaos and disorder. The empress wonders

that for all there were so many several nations, governments, laws, religions, opinions, etc. they should all yet so generally agree in being ambitious, proud, self-conceited, vain, prodigal, deceitful, envious, malicious, unjust, revengeful, irreligious, factious, etc. She did also admire, that not any particular state, kingdom, or commonwealth, was contented with their own shares, but endeavoured to encroach upon their neighbours, and that their greatest glory was in plunder and slaughter.[38]

This same view is presented in an earlier work, Cavendish's *Orations of Divers Sorts*. For Cavendish, this collection of speeches is principally an exercise in rhetoric. Her stated aim is to persuade and inspire her audience with a natural eloquence: 'I have endeavoured in this book to express perfect orators that speak perfect orations, as to cause their auditors to act or believe according to the orator's opinion, judgement, design, or desire.'[39] But the views and opinions in certain speeches echo Cavendish's pronouncements in the *Philosophical Letters* and *The Blazing World*. In one oration, she warns that 'it is as difficult and hard to keep a commonwealth in peace and order as it is easy to cause wars and ruin'.[40] This difficulty stems from the inherently anti-social nature of human beings: even ties of friendship and family are no reliable safeguard against occasional outbursts of anger and conflict.[41] Most of 'Mankind', in Cavendish's view, is naturally inclined 'to be ungrateful, malicious, revengeful and inhumane'.[42] As a consequence, nature has made 'more enemies than friends, and so more pains than pleasures';[43] and the bulk of mankind is 'more apt to make war than to keep peace'.[44]

---

[37] Cavendish, *Blazing World*, p. 76.   [38] Ibid.
[39] Cavendish, 'To the Readers of My Works', in *Orations*, p. 118.
[40] 'An Oration to those Soldiers that are against an Agreement with the Citizens', in *Orations*, p. 161.
[41] 'An Oration against the Breaking of Peace with their Neighbour-Nation', in *Orations*, p. 134.
[42] 'An Oration to those Soldiers that are against an Agreement with the Citizens', in *Orations*, p. 144.
[43] 'An Oration for Men to Please themselves', in *Orations*, p. 244.
[44] 'To the Readers of My Works', in *Orations*, p. 119.

In such passages, Cavendish echoes Hobbes's profoundly pessimistic view of human nature.[45] In *Leviathan*, in a key chapter on the 'Naturall Condition of Mankind', Hobbes says that nature has given each man an 'equality of ability' or power, such that most men have an 'equality of hope' in the attainment of their ends.[46] If any two men desire the same object, and they cannot both possess that object, then this equality of hope inevitably leads to conflict: the two men 'become enemies; and in the way to their End . . . endeavour to destroy, or subdue one an other'.[47] Thus, for Hobbes, the natural state of man is a state of war. 'Hereby it is manifest, that during the time men live without a common Power to keep them all in awe, they are in that condition which is called Warre; and such a warre, as is of every man, against every man.'[48] In such a state, the social life of man is accompanied by an enormous amount of misery and grief. Because every man has a right to every thing necessary to secure his preservation – including another man's body[49] – the pre-political state of man is characterised by continual fear of an untimely and violent death.[50]

In the *Orations*, many of Cavendish's speakers embrace these Hobbesian sentiments. One orator declares that

there is no law in Nature, for Nature is lawless, and hath made all her creatures so, as to be wild and ravenous, to be insatiable and injurious, to be unjust, cruel, destructive, and so disorderous that, if it were not for civil government ordained from a higher power, as from the creator of nature herself, all her works would be in a confusion, and sow their own destruction.[51]

Another asks:

Can any man be happy when injustice reigns and force rules? . . . Or can any man think to advance himself, when as every particular desires and endeavours to

[45] While we do not wish to suggest that Cavendish was a Hobbesian, it is fair to affirm that Hobbes had a notable influence on her political outlook. Anna Battigelli points out that Cavendish was introduced to Hobbes's ideas in a favourable light: she would most likely have learned about Hobbesian politics on the continent, and not in the context of the hostile reception of *Leviathan* in England (Battigelli, 'Political Thought/Political Action', p. 42). On Hobbes's reception in England, see Samuel I. Mintz, *The Hunting of Leviathan: Seventeenth Century Reactions to the Materialism and Moral Philosophy of Thomas Hobbes* (Cambridge University Press, 1970); and Quentin Skinner, 'Thomas Hobbes and his Disciples in France and England', *Comparative Studies in Society and History* 8 (1965), 153–67.
[46] For reasons that should become obvious, we follow Hobbes in his use of the terms 'man' and 'mankind', rather than 'human beings' or 'humankind'.
[47] Hobbes, *Leviathan*, p. 87.   [48] Ibid., pp. 88–9.   [49] Ibid., p. 91.
[50] In his famous summary of the natural state of man, Hobbes says that 'In such condition, there is . . . no Society; and which is worst of all, continuall feare, and danger of violent death; And the life of man, solitary, poore, nasty, brutish, and short' (ibid., p. 89).
[51] Cavendish, 'A Cause pleaded at the Bar before Judges Concerning Theft', in *Orations*, p. 177.

be superior? For though authority may be pulled down, yet where no single authority is suffered by the power of many, no particular person can be advanced, they must all continue equal or be all destroyed to one man, and that man will only be superior in his single person and life, but not have authority or power over other men; for if there be none to be governed, it cannot be said he governs, and where there is none to obey there is none to command.[52]

The speakers support Hobbes's view that there is no law of nature in the natural condition of man, only a right of nature – the right to self-preservation. By contrast, in *The Blazing World*, Cavendish does not adopt an explicit position on pre-political human beings or the state of nature. In this work, the empress learns that 'Although there be numerous, nay, infinite worlds . . . yet none is without government'; that is to say, that there are no societies without some ruling political authority or other.[53] But while Cavendish does not develop a theory about the state of nature, she does warn that human society might easily fall into a state of war. Typically, for Cavendish, the condition of war is not the original condition of human beings prior to the formation of the commonwealth, but rather a state of chaos that the commonwealth might descend into, and for which obedience to a sovereign is the only preventative. In this sense, Cavendish's political outlook is very much shaped by her experience of the civil wars. As Anna Battigelli observes, Cavendish focuses obsessively on 'the great problem that emerged in the wake of the English Civil Wars: the problem of maintaining political order'.[54] Cavendish's views thus markedly differ from those of earlier royalist women, such as Mary Pope, who base their arguments on religious grounds.

Like Hobbes, Cavendish maintains that obedience to a common power is a practical necessity. In *Leviathan*, Hobbes claims that out of a desire for peace – prompted by fear of untimely death, a desire for personal security, and the hope of attaining that security – each man can be drawn to agreement. For the sake of 'some *Good to himselfe*',[55] each man may voluntarily lay aside his right to all things by simply renouncing it or transferring it to another.[56] Hobbes calls this mutual transference of rights the forming of a contract or a covenant.[57] A covenant can be successfully enforced only by an authority with sufficient coercive power. In *The Blazing World*, Cavendish likewise emphasises the importance of an

---

[52] Cavendish, 'An Oration against Civil War', in *Orations*, p. 268.
[53] Cavendish, *Blazing World*, p. 71; see also Susan James's annotation (n. 144) on this page.
[54] Battigelli, 'Political Thought/Political Action', p. 41.   [55] Hobbes, *Leviathan*, p. 93.
[56] Ibid., p. 92.   [57] Ibid., p. 94.

over-awing authority to keep the masses from civil war; in a particularly cynical speech in the *Orations*, she writes that 'when they fear their sovereign, they are obedient; for it is impossible to work upon their good nature as to make them obey through love and good will, because they have no good natures to work on; wherefore, there is none other way but force, to make them loyal and keep them to their allegiance'.[58] A common power is required to over-awe the people because they are not naturally inclined to keep peace among themselves. A state of absolute liberty, without some political authority or other, is a state of misery and confusion:

if every one hath liberty to do what he list, not any man will have power to do what he would; for liberty will be lost if every man will take upon him to rule, and confusion will take the place of government. Thus, striving for liberty you will thrust yourselves into slavery, and out of ambition to rule you will lose all government, and out of covetousness to be rich you'll make yourselves miserably poor; for if there be no government there can be no order, if there be no order there can be no justice, and if no justice there can be no safety, if no safety no peace, if no peace no trade, and if no trade there will be no riches.[59]

So what type of government, we might ask, can best secure this state of peace? Both Hobbes and Cavendish consider the merits of three types of rule: monarchy, democracy, and aristocracy.[60] They agree that these governments differ in terms of their 'Aptitude to produce the Peace, and Security of the People'.[61] A democracy, for Cavendish, offers less security than a monarchy because it encourages diversity of opinion. In the *Orations*, she emphasises that unity cannot be achieved in a democracy, because 'many politicians will be apter to dissolve than agree to make good laws, and will sooner cause a destruction than govern a common-wealth; for every several politician would have a several policy'.[62] 'As for democracy,' says one speaker, 'I like that the worst, for the common people is not only insolent when they have power, commanding imperi-ously, condemning unjustly, advancing unworthily, but they are so inconstant there is no assurance in them.'[63] According to these orators, there is no adequate assurance of order and peace in a democratic regime,

---

[58] Cavendish, 'A Privy Councillors Speech to his Majesty at the Council Board', in *Orations*, p. 193.
[59] Cavendish, 'A Kings Speech to his Rebellious Rout', in *Orations*, p. 196.
[60] Hobbes, *Leviathan*, p. 129; Cavendish, *Orations*, pp. 275–81.
[61] Hobbes, *Leviathan*, p. 131.
[62] Cavendish, 'An Oration Concurring with the Former', in *Orations*, p. 164. See also Cavendish's comments on democracy in *Sociable Letters*, p. lxv.
[63] Cavendish, 'A Soldiers Oration concerning the Form of Government', in *Orations*, p. 276.

and similar problems are likely to arise in an aristocracy. Monarchy is
therefore the only trustworthy form of government – largely due to its
simplicity. In *The Blazing World*, the empress asks her advisers

> why they preferred the monarchical form of government before any other? They
> answered that, as it was natural for one body to have but one head, so it was also
> natural for a politic body to have but one governor; and that a commonwealth,
> which had many governors was like a monster with many heads: besides, said
> they, a monarchy is a divine form of government, and agrees most with our
> religion; for as there is but one God, whom we all unanimously worship and
> adore with one faith, so we are resolved to have but one Emperor, to whom we
> all submit with one obedience.[64]

Though she claims that monarchy is 'a divine form of government',
Cavendish does not base her argument for political authority solely on
religious principles. Instead she draws an analogy between the harmony
that results from worshipping one God and the peace that is assured by
submission to a single ruler. With this analogy, Cavendish appeals to
practical reasons for supporting one rather than many. In *The Worlds
Olio*, she likewise asserts that an ideal commonwealth is 'governed by one
Head or Government, as a King, for one Head is sufficient for one Body:
for several Heads breed several Opinions, and several Opinions breed
Disputations, and Disputations Factions, and Factions breed Wars, and
Wars bring Ruin and Desolation; for it is more safe to be governed,
though by a Foolish Head, than a Factious Heart'.[65] There is a similar
appeal to practical necessity in *The Blazing World*, when the empress fears
that the changes she has made to government will lead her people to
rebellion. The Duchess of Newcastle advises the empress 'to introduce the
same form of government again, which had been before; that is, to have
but one sovereign, one religion, one law, and one language, so all the
world might be as one united family, without divisions; nay, like God,
and his blessed saints and angels'.[66] Again, Cavendish's appeal to God is
not an appeal to a religious justification for monarchical rule; it is an
appeal to the pragmatic ideals of simplicity and unity in government.

For Hobbes, simplicity or unity of rule is a necessary condition for
reaching consensus about what might be considered just and unjust, right
and wrong, good and evil. In the condition of nature, there is no objective

---

[64] Cavendish, *Blazing World*, pp. 18–19.
[65] Margaret Cavendish, *The Worlds Olio. Written By the Right Honorable, the Lady Margaret Newcastle* (London: J. Martin and J. Allestrye, 1655), pp. 205–6.
[66] Cavendish, *Blazing World*, pp. 87–8.

or common moral standard: 'To this warre of every man against every man, this also is consequent; that nothing can be Unjust. The notions of Right and Wrong, Justice and Injustice have there no place. Where there is no common Power, there is no Law: where no Law, no Injustice.'[67] For Hobbes, as Richard Tuck observes, the true war of every man against every man is essentially a conflict of belief: conflict arises because each man is his own judge about the most desirable means to his self-preservation.[68] To resolve this conflict, men consent to set up a common power and thereby establish an ultimate arbitrator of good and evil.[69] In her *Orations*, Cavendish supports this view. She says that a government without rules restricting the liberty of citizens is no true government: 'for if there be no rules there can be no laws, and if there be no laws there can be no justice, and if no justice no safety, and if no safety no propriety, neither of goods, wives, children nor lives'.[70] For Cavendish, as for Hobbes, it is crucial that the sovereign's power be simple and undivided. This is the only way in which human beings might gain some unanimity in their opinions about right and wrong: that is, by subordinating their judgement to the judgement of one individual. Thus, in Cavendish's utopia, there is 'but one sovereign, one religion, one law, and one language, so that all the world might be as one united family'.[71]

II

Such views form the basis of Cavendish's secular theory of political obligation, and provide an answer to the question 'On what grounds should citizens pledge their allegiance to the powers that be?' The ultimate basis of allegiance to our rulers is not divine authority, but the pursuit of good for ourselves. Cavendish argues that disobedience to rulers is highly irrational or contrary to our sense and reason. We submit to a governing authority so that its judgements about right and wrong may henceforth become our own. The good of the sovereign simply *is* the good of the citizen: to undermine the authority of the sovereign is to undermine ourselves. In one speech from a collection of 'Orations in a Disordered and Unsettled State or Government', Cavendish writes that

---

[67] Hobbes, *Leviathan*, p. 90.   [68] Tuck, introduction to Hobbes, *Leviathan*, p. xxvii.
[69] Hobbes, *Leviathan*, p. 39.
[70] Cavendish, 'An Oration against Liberty of Conscience', in *Orations*, p. 167.
[71] *Blazing World*, p. 87.

if you take a sovereign power from the commonwealth, it dies, dissolves and consumes with disorder, war, and ruin, and if your sense and reason perceive a commonwealth must of necessity have a supreme power, your sense and reason will show you that you must trust that supreme power, which power is to command, order, and dispose of all as it shall think fit, or as it pleases, without giving any account.[72]

For Cavendish, a severe ruler is – paradoxically – the protector of human liberties: only by voluntarily giving up their absolute liberty to a coercive power can human beings have the peace and security they desire.[73] In *The Worlds Olio*, Cavendish writes that 'factious persons . . . are not onely the cause of the taking away our goods . . . and our lives, but our religion, our frends, our laws, *our liberties*, and peace; For a factious man makes a commotion, which commotion raises civil wars . . . a factious man is a humane Devil.'[74] In the *Orations*, we are reminded that 'the readiest and surest means to lose your privileges was to rebel against your sovereign . . . by this rebellious stir you have not only lost your privileges, but you are forced to pay more than your privileges are worth'.[75]

For these reasons, we should all be opposed to 'faction' or the toleration of dissenting political groups within a commonwealth. In *Leviathan*, Hobbes emphasises that all factions are unjust because they are inimical to the safety of the people.[76] He says that 'there happeneth in no Common-wealth any great Inconvenience, but what proceeds from the Subjects disobedience, and breach of those Covenants, from which the Common-wealth hath its being'.[77] Cavendish likewise warns that a good ruler must be intolerant of dissent or faction; even the worst tyrant is better for the country than the disharmony and disorder that follows from faction. 'Though a king may err in his government, yet a people errs more in their rebellion, for the greatest tyrant that ever was was never so destroying or cruel as a rebellion or civil war, for this makes a dissolution, whereas the other makes but some interruptions.'[78] These sentiments are directly opposed to the philosophy of the Leveller movement: in Cavendish's view, subjects never have the right to resist their rulers, even those rulers who turn out to be tyrannical or irreligious.

---

[72] 'An Oration Contrary to the Former', in *Orations*, p. 263.
[73] Cavendish, 'A Kings Speech to Discontented Subjects', in *Orations*, p. 197.
[74] *Worlds Olio*, p. 42; our italics.
[75] 'An Oration to Mutinous yet Fearful Citizens', in *Orations*, p. 271.
[76] Hobbes, *Leviathan*, p. 164.   [77] Ibid., p. 145.
[78] Cavendish, 'A Kings Oration or Speech to his Subjects', in *Orations*, p. 282.

One solution to faction is to curtail freedom of speech and freedom of the press. In *The Blazing World*, the empress keeps a close eye on intellectual disagreements and disputes among her councillors. She warns her subjects to 'confine your disputations to your schools, lest besides the commonwealth of learning, they disturb also divinity and policy, religion and laws, and by that means draw an utter ruin and destruction upon church and state'.[79] In *Leviathan*, Hobbes warns that 'in the wel governing of Opinions, consisteth the well governing of men's Actions, in order to their Peace'.[80] Likewise, for Cavendish, true conflict is a conflict of opinion. The maintenance of peace relies on keeping the dissemination of opinions to a minimum. 'None should write of state-affairs,' Cavendish says in the *Orations*, 'but those the state allows or authorises.'[81] Seditious authors should be silenced, and the common people should remain uneducated and ignorant: this is the best way to uphold unity and peace.

Cavendish's claims that 'the pen doth more mischief than the sword'[82] are strongly reminiscent of William Cavendish's own statements about the subversive power of the press. In his *Advice to Charles II* (first written c. 1658), William Cavendish advises the prince that disputations must be confined to the schools, and 'no bookes of controversey, writt butt in Latin, for Else the People would bee over heated with itt, for controversey is a Civill warr with the Pen, which Pulls out the sorde soone afterwards'.[83] In this work, William Cavendish is strongly influenced by Niccolò Machiavelli's advice to Lorenzo de' Medici in *The Prince* (1532). William Cavendish's experiences of civil war had further taught him that religious and intellectual differences were the key threats to princely power.[84] A prince must therefore take a tough stance on freedom of conscience and diversity of opinion. The head of state must be the supreme ecclesiastical authority, and 'all Bookes whatsoever Is written Eyther by Devines, or

---

[79] Cavendish, *Blazing World*, pp. 48–9.   [80] Hobbes, *Leviathan*, p. 124.

[81] Cavendish, 'An Oration against some Historians or Writers of State Affairs or Policy', in *Orations*, p. 163.

[82] Ibid.

[83] William Cavendish, *Ideology and Politics on the Eve of the Restoration: Newcastle's Advice to Charles II*, transcribed with an introduction by Thomas P. Slaughter (Independence Square, Philadelphia: The American Philosophical Society, 1984), p. 21. Margaret Cavendish paraphrases this remark in her *Life of William Cavendishe*, p. 167. Conal Condren notes that about thirty of the eighty-five sayings in Book 4 of Margaret Cavendish's *Life* are drawn from William Cavendish's *Advice*: 'Casuistry to Newcastle: "The Prince" in the World of the Book', in *Political Discourse in Early Modern Britain*, ed. Nicholas Phillipson and Quentin Skinner (Cambridge University Press, 1993), p. 165, n. 5.

[84] Condren, 'Casuistry to Newcastle', p. 176.

Philosophers, or any that Make the Leaste rente In Church, or state, presently to bee Condemnd, & burnte by the hands of the Hangman, & the Authtors severly punisht'.[85] In general, Margaret Cavendish seems to support her husband's hardline approach. She frequently emphasises that human beings might avoid war, and secure peace, by submitting to one ruler, one law, one religion, and so on. This simplicity of rule is best achieved through a policy of intolerance: the sovereign possesses an absolute rule, and subjects are never justified in deposing their rulers. On first reading, protection of the liberties of subjects, and toleration of religious differences, seem to be antithetical to Cavendish's political outlook.

One recent scholar, however, challenges the strength of Cavendish's commitment to the 'Machiavellian conservatism' of William Cavendish. Hilda Smith points out that while many of Margaret Cavendish's statements in the *Orations* reflect those of her husband, there are a number of speeches 'diametrically opposed' to his viewpoint. In particular, Margaret Cavendish 'does not display the immediate loyalty to the Crown that her husband does or identify with policies that would protect the king's authority'.[86] Smith points to her statements 'on behalf of social equality or freedom of conscience', claiming that they are 'inconsistent' with those statements that echo William Cavendish's viewpoint.[87] In the *Orations*, there are three speeches explicitly dealing with liberty of conscience: one in favour, one against, and one proposing a middle way between the two.[88] In the first oration, Margaret Cavendish's speaker asserts that

if all the people of this nation is so foolish or wilfil or factious or irreligious as not to agree in one opinion and to unite in one religion, but will be of divers opinions, if not of divers religions, the governors must yield, or they will consume the civil government with the fire of their zeal; indeed they will consume themselves at last in their own confusion. Wherefore the best remedy to prevent their own ruin, with the ruin of the commonwealth, is to let them have liberty of conscience, conditionally that they do not meddle with civil government or governors.[89]

Some statements in this speech clearly reflect the Leveller viewpoint. The speaker proposes a law, for example, that will protect 'our just rights', 'our civil and common laws', and our 'ancient customs', all for the sake of 'peace and quiet in the kingdom'.[90] In the second speech, the orator

---

[85] Cavendish, *Advice*, p. 21.   [86] Smith, 'A General War Amongst the Men', p. 151.   [87] Ibid.
[88] Cavendish, 'An Oration for Liberty of Conscience', 'An Oration against Liberty of Conscience', and 'An Oration proposing a Mean betwixt the Two Former Opinions', in *Orations*, pp. 166–8.
[89] Cavendish, 'An Oration for Liberty of Conscience', in *Orations*, pp. 166–7.   [90] Ibid., p. 167.

urges, much like William Cavendish, that liberty in the church will inevitably lead to liberty in the state, and thus chaos and confusion for the commonwealth. But in the final speech, according to Smith, Cavendish's speaker 'leans decisively toward the one favouring freedom of conscience'.[91] The speaker says that subjects should neither be forced to believe against their will, nor granted an absolute liberty. But 'if those sects or separatists disturb not the canon, common or civil laws, not to disturb their bodies, minds, or estates ... if they disturb not the public weal, why should you disturb their private devotions?'[92] The people, in this view, can believe whatever they like and ought to have 'leave to follow their several opinions in their particular families'.[93]

To be sure, Cavendish's husband does not openly endorse this moderate position on liberty of conscience. In his *Advice*, religious dissent is strongly associated with the political upheavals that led to the civil wars and the downfall of Charles I. But it is difficult to see how Margaret Cavendish's views – especially those in her final speech – are inconsistent with those policies that 'protect the king's authority'. Cavendish's remarks on liberty of conscience are compatible with her general characterisation of the ideal type of government. This is because her royalist viewpoint does not rule out the toleration of religious differences and liberty of conscience under certain conditions. In her *Grounds of Natural Philosophy*, she says that the human conscience 'cannot be altered by force, without a Free-will: so that several Societies, or Communicants, commit an Error, if not a Sin, to endeavour to compel their Brethren to any particular Opinion'.[94] For Cavendish, it is unwise to force individuals into believing something: they simply cannot choose to believe an opinion in the same way that they can choose to act in a particular manner.[95] Governors thus risk resentment and rebellion by compelling subjects to betray their conscience: 'the more earnest the *Compellers* are, the more do the *Compelled* resist'.[96] 'Wherefore, *Liberty of Conscience* may

[91] Smith, 'A General War Amongst the Men', p. 152.
[92] Cavendish, 'An Oration proposing a Mean betwixt the Two Former Opinions', in *Orations*, pp. 167–8.
[93] Ibid., p. 168.
[94] Margaret Cavendish, *Grounds of Natural Philosophy: Divided into Thirteen Parts: With an Appendix containing Five Parts*, with an introduction by Colette V. Michael, facsimile reprint of 1668 edition (West Cornwall, CT: Locust Hill Press, 1996), Appendix, p. 249.
[95] Many years later, John Locke made a similar point in his *Letter Concerning Toleration* (1689). On the topic of Locke and toleration, see our Chapter 10.
[96] Cavendish, *Grounds of Natural Philosophy*, Appendix, p. 249. Similar sentiments are expressed in *The Blazing World*. The empress shuns the use of violence when converting subjects to her

be allowed, conditionally, [if] it be no ways a prejudice to the Peaceable Government of the State or Kingdom.'[97] In the *Orations*, Cavendish's emphasis is also on conditionality: 'let them have liberty of conscience, conditionally that they do not meddle with civil government or governors'.[98] This granting of conditional liberty is consistent with her view that the sovereign's office is to secure peace and protection for citizens. If granting liberty of conscience is the best way to maintain political order, and subjects still practise an outward obedience to their rulers' judgements, then it is an acceptable policy. Cavendish's views about liberty of conscience are not, therefore, at odds with her royalist sentiments.

Mihoko Suzuki provides different grounds for the view that Cavendish adopts an 'ambiguous royalism'. Suzuki points to evidence that 'in analyzing the factors in Charles I's rule that led to the Revolution, Cavendish articulates the claims made by Charles's opponents in the Long Parliament of 1642'.[99] In her 'Oration concerning Disorders, Rebellion, and Change of Governments', the speaker says that the kingdom

was at first monarchical, where in a long peace flattery, vanity, and prodigality got into the monarchical court, all which caused poverty, and so injustice . . . which caused the selling of all offices and places of judicature, for those that buy dear sell dear, and this caused exactions and extortions, besides bribes given and bribes taken, insomuch that no justice was done for justice's sake, but for bribes' sake.[100]

In the same speech, Cavendish criticises those 'monopolizers' who raised the price of commodities, and 'hindered the general trade and traffic'; and she laments the 'great taxes laid upon the people and the kingdom'. According to Suzuki, Cavendish thus 'forcefully presents a surprisingly critical view of Charles I's responsibility in triggering his own overthrow'.[101]

But there is little reason to think that Cavendish's criticisms of Charles I call into question her 'credentials as a loyalist'.[102] In his *Advice to Charles II*, William Cavendish presents an equally unflattering account of Charles I's responsibility for his downfall. Conal Condren observes that 'the final sub-theme of the *Advice*, the loss of political power, effectively casts Charles I

---

religion, because belief is 'not a thing to be forced or pressed upon the people' (*Blazing World*, p. 51).
[97] *Grounds of Natural Philosophy*, Appendix, p. 249.
[98] 'An Oration for Liberty of Conscience', in *Orations*, p. 167.
[99] Suzuki, *Subordinate Subjects*, p. 185.
[100] Cavendish, 'Oration concerning Disorders, Rebellion, and Change of Governments', in *Orations*, p. 279.
[101] Suzuki, *Subordinate Subjects*, p. 185.   [102] Ibid.

in the role of failed prince'.[103] William Cavendish provides a long list of 'The Errors Off State', among them a lack of money, illegal taxes, and the selling of titles.[104] He advises Charles II that monopolies must be abolished because they are 'the moste Distructive Thinge to the Comon wealth, in the world'.[105] Elsewhere, William Cavendish warns against employing those who 'by reason of their poverty' will be inclined to take bribes.[106] The upshot of William's remarks is not to express a disloyalty to the crown, but rather, as Conal Condren notes, to uphold Elizabeth I's government as an ideal regime.[107] Margaret Cavendish also mythologises the reign of Elizabeth I. Some scholars claim that many of Cavendish's heroines, including the Empress of the Blazing World, are modelled on Elizabeth.[108] Margaret Cavendish's criticisms of Charles I need not, therefore, be an expression of an 'ambiguous royalism'. Rather, they conform to the well-established genre of advice to monarchs, and they indicate her views on how sovereigns can guard against the loss of political control in future.

III

In this final section, we turn to Cavendish's views about women and their power status in the public and private spheres. Some scholars suggest that Cavendish departs from the conventional royalist position with her conception of women's relationship to political authority.[109] In her *Sociable Letter* no. 16 – a piece that Hilda Smith describes as 'one of the more remarkable political statements penned by a woman in the seventeenth century'[110] – Cavendish outlines the nature of women's relationship to the crown. She addresses an imaginary female correspondent, saying that 'I Hope I have given the Lady *D.A.* no cause to believe I am not her Friend ... though she hath been of Ps. and I of Ks. Side'.[111] Though in the recent civil wars Cavendish may have supported the king and her friend the parliament, this should 'make us Enemies, no more than cases of Conscience in Religion, for one may be my very good Friend, and yet not of my opinion, every one's Conscience in Religion is betwixt God and themselves, and it belongs to none other'.[112] This

---

[103] Condren, 'Casuistry to Newcastle', p. 181.   [104] Cavendish, *Advice*, p. 49.   [105] Ibid., p. 37.
[106] Cavendish, *Life of William Cavendishe*, p. 171.   [107] Condren, 'Casuistry to Newcastle', p. 183.
[108] See Claire Jowitt, 'Imperial Dreams? Margaret Cavendish and the Cult of Elizabeth', *Women's Writing* 4 (1997), 383–99.
[109] Smith, 'A General War Amongst the Men', p. 154.   [110] Ibid.
[111] Cavendish, *Sociable Letters*, p. 26.   [112] Ibid.

position is consistent with Cavendish's other statements about liberty of conscience. Once again, she affirms that peace and harmony are best maintained by keeping differences of opinion to ourselves. Cavendish goes on to say that

> as for the matter of Governments, we Women understand them not; yet if we did, we are excluded from intermedling therewith, and almost from being subject thereto; we are not tied, nor bound to State or Crown; we are free, not Sworn to Allegiance, nor do we take the Oath of Supremacy; we are not made Citizens of the Commonwealth, we hold no Offices, nor bear we any Authority therein; we are accounted neither Useful in Peace, nor Serviceable in War; and if we be not Citizens in the Commonwealth, I know no reason we should be Subjects to the Commonwealth: And the truth is, we are no Subjects, unless it be to our Husbands, and not always to them, for sometimes we usurp their Authority, or else by flattery we get their good wills to govern.[113]

By insinuating themselves into men's affections, Cavendish says, women 'oftener inslave men, than men inslave' women.[114] This passage is considered to be remarkable for several reasons. First, Cavendish presents a view of women as free from political obligations to the crown. Hilda Smith observes that 'While seeming to separate women from governments (because "we Women understand them not" and are not "bound to State or Crown" through either oaths of loyalty or allegiance), she ends by coming close to treason: "if we be not Citizens in the Commonwealth, I know no reason we should be Subjects to the Commonwealth".'[115] This would appear to grant women a certain natural liberty compared to men. Secondly, Cavendish suggests that while men seem to have dominion over their wives, women really govern the world, in that they govern men by an insensible power in the private sphere. This is quite a strong position on women's political influence.

It is not obvious, however, that in this letter Cavendish 'breaks with royalist orthodoxy' about women's subjection to the crown.[116] At the time, it was a common view that a wife's immediate duty was to her husband. But a wife was also subject to the crown in so far as her husband was subject and *she* was subject to *him*. This is one possible reading of Cavendish's statement that 'I know no reason we should be Subjects to the Commonwealth: And the truth is, we are no Subjects, unless it be to our Husbands.' Women are not immediately subject to the commonwealth,

---

[113] Ibid., pp. 26–7.   [114] Ibid., p. 27.   [115] Smith, 'A General War Amongst the Men', p. 154.
[116] Ibid.

but they are subject to their husbands – individuals who owe a duty of allegiance to the crown.

As for Cavendish's second point – about women's enslavement of men – it is true that she puts a positive spin on women's power in these statements. This is consistent with another remark in her 'Female Orations', that out of desire men 'deliver to our disposals their power, persons, and lives, enslaving themselves to our will and pleasures'.[117] But it is difficult to decide whether or not Cavendish is being serious in these statements about women's power over men. In other writings, she has an entirely negative view of male–female power relations. In 'The Preface to the Reader' in the *Worlds Olio*, Cavendish says

True it is, our Sex make great complaints, that men from their first Creation usurped a Supremacy to themselves, although we were made equal by Nature, which Tyrannical Government they have kept ever since, so that we could never come to be free, but rather more and more enslaved, using us either like Children, Fools, or Subjects, that is, to flatter or threaten us, to allure or force us to obey, and will not let us divide the World equally with them, as to Govern and Command, to direct and Dispose as they do.[118]

Women are not free because they are, quite simply, coerced, threatened, or forced into obedience. In this way, men keep women in the subordinate position of children and fools – human beings without the full use of their reason.

Cavendish develops the theme of female slavery in various orations. In 'A Child-bed Womans Funeral Oration', the speaker says that

The truth is nature hath made her male creatures, especially mankind, only for pleasure, and her female creatures for misery; men are made for liberty and women for slavery, and not only slaves to sickness, pains, and troubles in breeding, bearing, and bringing up their children, but they are slaves to men's humours, nay, to their vices and wickedness, so that they are more enslaved than any other female creatures, for other female creatures are not so enslaved as they; wherefore those women are most happy that never marry, or die whilst they be

---

[117] Cavendish, 'Female Orations', in *Orations*, p. 251.
[118] Cavendish, 'The Preface to the Reader', *Worlds Olio*, sig. A4r. Though Cavendish does not explicitly endorse Hobbes's concept of the state of nature, in this passage she shares his view about the original equality of men and women. On this topic in Hobbes, see Karen Green, 'Christine de Pisan and Thomas Hobbes', in *Hypatia's Daughters: Fifteen Hundred Years of Women Philosophers*, ed. Linda Lopez McAlister (Bloomington and Indianapolis: Indiana University Press, 1996), pp. 48–67; Gabriella Slomp, 'Hobbes and the Equality of Women', *Political Studies* 42 (1994), 441–52; and Joanne H. Wright, 'Going Against the Grain: Hobbes's Case for Original Maternal Dominion', *Journal of Women's History* 14 (2002), 123–55.

young, so that this young woman that died in childbed is happy in that she lives not to endure more pain or slavery.[119]

In this oration, married women are unfree because a physical impediment (their reproductive capacity) deprives them of the power to determine the course of their own lives. They are not at liberty to avoid 'breeding, bearing, and bringing up' children, if they so desire, because they are compelled to obey their husbands. Women do not have liberty, in other words, in the sense of the power to do, or to forbear from doing, what they will with their own bodies.[120] Similarly, in her 'Female Orations', Cavendish's first speaker complains that

Men are so unconscionable and cruel against us, as they endeavour to bar us of all kinds of liberty, as not to suffer us freely to associate among our own sex, but would fain bury us in their houses or beds, as in a grave; the truth is, we live like bats and owls, labour like beasts, and die like worms.[121]

In her famous address 'To the Two Universities', at the start of her Philosophical and Physical Opinions, Cavendish likewise laments that women 'are kept like birds in cages to hop up and down in our houses, not sufferd to fly abroad to see the several changes of fortune'.[122] Women are, moreover, 'shut out of all power, and Authority by reason we are never imployed either in civil nor marshall affaires, our counsels are despised, and laught at, the best of our actions are troden down with scorn, by the over-weaning conceit men have of themselves and through a dispisement of us'.[123] The second 'Female Oration' repeats this view about women's powerlessness: the speaker says that 'men, that are not only our tyrants but our devils, keep us in the hell of subjection, from whence I cannot see any redemption or getting out ... our power is so inconsiderable as men laugh at our weakness'.[124] In all these cases, lack of freedom consists in the confinement of women to the domestic sphere – and the marital bed – as well as the inability to associate with whomever they please.

So it would appear that the freedom that women experience because they do not take oaths of allegiance is a rather hollow kind of freedom.

[119] Cavendish, 'A Child-bed Womans Funeral Oration', in Orations, p. 226.
[120] On this concept of freedom in Hobbes, see Quentin Skinner, 'Hobbes on the Proper Signification of Liberty', in Visions of Politics, pp. 209–37.
[121] 'Female Orations', in Orations, p. 248.
[122] 'To the Two Universities', in Philosophical and Physical Opinions, sig. B2v.   [123] Ibid.
[124] 'Female Orations', in Orations, p. 248.

In her writings, Cavendish distinguishes between, first, the liberty that individuals enjoy when they are free from obligations to political authority; and, secondly, the power of individuals to do what they will, without physical impediment, constraint, or compulsion. In letter 16, Cavendish implies that political obligations place constraints upon the first kind of liberty: in civil society, subjects become 'tied' or 'bound' to live in accordance with the law. Because women are 'not Sworn to Allegiance', and are not regarded as fully independent political and social beings, they remain free in this sense. But while all women might be free in the first sense, most women are not free in the second. Generally speaking, Cavendish maintains that women's subjection to men deprives women of their liberty in the sense of the power to do what they will.

Finally, there is little evidence that Cavendish was committed to ending female slavery. To be sure, she often laments that women are intellectually deficient because they are prevented from improving their natural reasoning abilities.[125] But some of her other remarks suggest that women's state of subjection to men is just and fair. 'To speak the truth, Men have great Reason not to let us in to their Government', she says, because women's minds and bodies are in fact inferior to those of men.[126] Similar points are made in the 'Female Orations', where Cavendish seems to rehearse the for and against arguments of the *querelle des femmes*.[127] In Cavendish's writings, we do not find any unambiguous calls for female emancipation: she does not argue unequivocally for a woman's right to divorce her tyrannical husband, nor does she maintain that women ought to have equal political rights to men. In this respect, her views on women reflect a conservatism that is typical of the times.

In 1653, Cavendish refused to take the oath of allegiance to the new commonwealth. Though we can only speculate about her motives, this act seems to be representative of her position on the limitations of political obligation. In many statements, she suggests that only a monarchical form of government can adequately ensure our protection. To resolve conflict, human beings require a single arbitrator of right and wrong, and a sole monarch can best fulfil this criterion of simplicity. Democracies and aristocracies are unstable because they encourage a diversity of opinion, for 'several Heads breed several Opinions, and several Opinions breed Disputations, and Disputations Factions, and Factions breed Wars,

---

[125] On this topic, see Broad, *Women Philosophers*, p. 41.
[126] Cavendish, 'The Preface to the Reader', *Worlds Olio*, sig. A 4r.
[127] See Susan James's footnote in Cavendish, *Orations*, p. 248.

and Wars bring Ruin and Desolation'.[128] Thus, Cavendish may have refused to swear the Oath of Allegiance on the grounds that the new regime had no legitimacy because it had usurped the powers of a monarch; or because, as a non-monarchical regime, the government could not adequately ensure the protection of its citizens from 'Ruin and Desolation'.

It is difficult to determine with any certainty that these are in fact Cavendish's views, and it is especially difficult to establish her political position on the basis of a few selective comments from the *Orations*. After all, in the *Orations*, a work devoted to spelling out the pros and cons of various positions, Cavendish may be echoing Hobbes and her husband merely for the sake of rhetorical effect. Nevertheless, we have found that, even if Cavendish herself did not endorse the Hobbesian standpoint, the royalist outlook that she presents in the *Orations* (and elsewhere) is not inconsistent with other views that some scholars have labelled as 'non-royalist'. Cavendish's statements on liberty of conscience, religious toleration, and the reign of Charles I are entirely compatible with a post-civil-war conception of the role of government: to provide peace and protection in the state.

Finally, there is one further reason why Cavendish might not have pledged allegiance to the new regime: because she believed that women were not directly subject to the commonwealth. In letter 16 of her *Sociable Letters*, Cavendish points out that women do not have to pledge allegiance, or swear oaths of supremacy, to the public authorities. In this sense, she says, women are free. It stands to reason, then, that Cavendish should have refused to swear an oath that no other woman in her age was bound to take. Nevertheless, while women are not 'tied' or 'bound' to the commonwealth, in Cavendish's view it does not follow that they are at liberty to do what they will. In allowing that women are still subject to their husbands (and are therefore 'the subjects of subjects'), Cavendish's views are conventional for her time. We might give some weight to Cavendish's conviction that *some* women can rule or govern their husbands as they please. In her view, some lucky and attractive women enjoy the liberty to do what they will and thus escape utter powerlessness within marriage. But we should bear in mind that, for every statement about women's power over men, Cavendish makes numerous counter-statements about women's lack of personal liberty and their enslavement to their husbands. These statements do not amount to a feminist programme of

---

[128] *Worlds Olio*, p. 206.

reform in her writings. While her political theory grants her an insight into the so-called liberty of subjects, this is not an insight that logically leads to calls for emancipation for the subjects of subjects in the private sphere.

It should not surprise us, however, to learn that Cavendish may have had access to a copy of Christine de Pizan's *City of Ladies*. In 1414, Christine prepared a collection of her works for Isabeau de Bavière. Now kept in the British Library, London, this manuscript collection (known as Harley MS 4431) is inscribed with the signature 'Henry, Duke of New-castle, 1676' – the signature of Cavendish's stepson. In a recent paper, Cristina Malcolmson suggests that William Cavendish may have brought back a copy of Christine's *City of Ladies* (among other works) from Europe.[129] This hypothesis appears impossible to substantiate.[130] But whether Margaret Cavendish knew Christine's works or not, she seems to have been familiar with the arguments of the *querelle des femmes*, and, like her late-medieval predecessor, she is keenly attuned to women's political concerns. Recent scholars point to the fact that seventeenth-century male theorists, such as Thomas Hobbes, maintain an odd silence about women's political standing in the commonwealth.[131] While Cavendish fails to call explicitly for the emancipation of women, the same criticism cannot be levelled at her work. For all her feminist ambiguity, Cavendish is one of the few writers of her time to make detailed pronouncements on women's lack of direct political obligation to the crown, the constraints of their reproductive capacity, their lack of freedom to do as they will (their 'slavery' under male 'tyranny'), and the 'hell of subjection' awaiting women in marriage.

---

[129] See Malcolmson, 'Christine de Pizan's *City of Ladies* in Early Modern England'.

[130] The last known owner of Harley MS 4431 was Louis of Bruges, who may have acquired it during his stay in England in 1472–3. His Flemish library was acquired by Louis XII of France and was housed at Blois by 1518, but Harley MS 4431 was not then included among his books. On this topic, see Curnow, 'The *Livre de la cité des dames* of Christine de Pisan: A Critical Edition', pp. 377 and 431–2. It is therefore possible that the manuscript was never taken out of England, and there is no reason to assume that it was in Flanders during the Cavendishes' exile, as Malcolmson proposes.

[131] See, for example, Pateman, *The Sexual Contract*.

CHAPTER 10

Women of the Glorious Revolution

In a 1646 letter to René Descartes (1596–1650), Princess Elisabeth of Bohemia (1618–80) defends a ruler's use of extreme violence on pragmatic grounds. When the people are negatively disposed toward political authority, she says, then

large violences are less evil than small ones, because the small do damage as well as the large, and give a subject for a long war; but the large take away the courage for this, as well as the means by which the great will be able to undertake such a war. In the same way, when violences come promptly and all at once, they annoy less than they astonish, and they are also more supportable by the people than is the long series of miseries that civil wars bring.[1]

In this letter, Elisabeth defends the maxims of Niccolò Machiavelli (1469–1527), 'not as being good in themselves' but because they 'all tend to the maintenance of things' – at least, where the ruler is a usurper.[2] Perhaps these political views are not surprising, coming as they do from the grand-daughter of James I of England.[3] Though his reign was an era of relative peace and religious tolerance, James I himself was an absolutist: he maintained that political rulers are accountable to God alone, and that subjects are never justified in resisting authority. According to this viewpoint, rulers may sometimes be justified in using great severity in order to quash rebellion and maintain the public peace. Elisabeth writes in a historical-political context in which the use of violence by the

---

[1] Elisabeth to Descartes, 10 October 1646, in *Descartes: His Moral Philosophy and Psychology*, translated with an introduction by John J. Blom (New York: New York University Press, 1978), p. 193. For the letter in its original language, see *Oeuvres de Descartes*, ed. Charles Adam and Paul Tannery, new edition, 11 vols. (Paris: Librairie Philosophique J. Vrin, 1996), vol. IV, p. 519.
[2] Elisabeth to Descartes, 10 October 1646, in *Descartes: His Moral Philosophy and Psychology*, p. 193.
[3] Elisabeth was the eldest daughter of Elisabeth Stuart (James's daughter) and Frederick V the Elector Palatine, the exiled 'Winter King' of Bohemia.

authorities – especially in the form of religious persecution[4] – was not uncommon.

But one wonders if Elisabeth would have still supported the Machiavellian approach thirty years later. In 1676, she was engaged in a correspondence with the Scottish Quaker Robert Barclay (1648–90);[5] and in her letters to Barclay, Elisabeth shows support for Quakers in exile and in prison, and expresses great sympathy for the plight of the persecuted religious movement. In the 1670s, as abbess of the Protestant Herford Abbey, Elisabeth offered asylum to both Quakers and Labadists. Shortly thereafter, from the reign of James II (1685–8) till that of his daughter Anne (1702-14), religious toleration – or the legal granting of freedom of worship to non-orthodox religious groups – became one of the most controversial political issues in England. The controversy reached its peak immediately following the Glorious Revolution,[6] an event that resulted in the overthrow of James II in 1688, and the coronation of William III and Mary II in his place in 1689. In the years roughly before and after the revolution, women were active contributors to both sides of the toleration debate.[7] In this chapter, we focus on the writings of the London printer and author Elinor James (c. 1645–1719), the former Quaker and 'prophetess' Joan Whitrowe (*fl.* 1665–97), the Quaker pamphleteer Anne Docwra (c. 1624–1710), and the philosopher Damaris Cudworth Masham (1659–1708).[8]

---

[4] On the justifications for such persecution, see Mark Goldie, 'The Theory of Religious Intolerance in Restoration England', in *From Persecution to Toleration: The Glorious Revolution and Religion in England*, ed. Ole Peter Grell, Jonathan Israel, and Nicholas Tyacke (Oxford: Clarendon Press, 1991), pp. 331–68.

[5] For Elisabeth's letters to Barclay, see *Reliquiae Barclaianae: Correspondence of Colonel D. Barclay and Robert Barclay of Urie and his son Robert, including Letters from Princess Elisabeth of the Rhine, the Earl of Perth, the Countess of Sutherland, William Penn, George Fox and others* (London: Winter & Bailey, 1870).

[6] In *Women of Grub Street*, Paula McDowell avoids the term 'Glorious' because many early modern women take a critical attitude toward the overthrow of James II and the coronation of William and Mary in the post-revolution era: *The Women of Grub Street*, p. 1. But some women are also strongly supportive of the revolution – among them Damaris Masham, who refers to it as the 'Happy Revolution': see the letter from Damaris Masham to Jean Le Clerc, 12 January 1705, in the Amsterdam University Library (UVA), MS J.57.a. Here we retain the phrase 'Glorious Revolution' because it has become common usage.

[7] For a general overview of women's participation in the revolution, see Lois G. Schwoerer, 'Women and the Glorious Revolution', *Albion: A Quarterly Journal Concerned with British Studies* 18 (1986), 195–218.

[8] Englishwomen were also engaged in the toleration debate before and after the period in question: among them, Katherine Chidley, Anne Conway, Margaret Cavendish, Mary Astell, and Delarivier Manley. On Conway and toleration, see Sarah Hutton, 'Philosophy and Toleration: A Discussion of Anne Conway's *Principia Philosophiae*', in *La formazione storica della alterità*, ed. Antonio

Like Princess Elisabeth, some of these women support the use of force
and coercion for pragmatic reasons, while others reject the idea that
coercive religious uniformity promotes peace and social unity (a view that
Margaret Cavendish sometimes expressed). Like their male contemporaries, women writers almost never advocate an absolute or limitless toleration: even some of the strongest pro-tolerationists draw the line at
atheism. Religious toleration, moreover, usually amounts to a negative
legal concept: the freedom to pursue religious worship in peace, without
fear of punishment by the law. In the first two sections of this chapter, we
focus on women's justifications for either extending or contracting the
legal bounds of toleration in relation to Catholics and Protestant dissenters in England. Their writings shed an interesting light on the pre-
Enlightenment history of toleration as a concept. For a modern reader
well versed in the liberal history of toleration, the results may be surprising. Susan Mendus claims that in the liberal tradition, toleration
typically occupies a special, exalted position: it is upheld as a chief liberal
characteristic, and it is seen as morally valuable in itself, and 'not a mere
pragmatic device or prudential expedient'.[9] The modern reader might
also expect there to be a natural connection between toleration and
scepticism, and that religious toleration will commonly be grounded on
doubts about the possibility of knowing religious truth (as was implicit in
Marie le Jars de Gournay). But English women's writings reveal that the
differences between early modern tolerationists and anti-tolerationists do
not always stem from scepticism or radical philosophical differences. In
their justifications, both sides appeal to the king's spiritual duty to promote religious truth in the community. And both sides seek to promote
the pragmatic ideals of peace and social unity: toleration is treated as a
device that might achieve or prevent certain practical outcomes, and not
as intrinsically desirable or undesirable in itself. In the third and final
section of this chapter, we focus on one female tolerationist's discussion
of the implications of liberty of conscience for women's education.

I

Elinor James (née Banckes) enjoyed an extraordinarily prolific writing
career that spanned the lives of six English monarchs, from Charles II to

Rotondo (Florence: Leo. S. Olschki Editore, 2001), pp. 541–58. See also Sarah Hutton, *Anne
Conway: A Woman Philosopher* (Cambridge University Press, 2004).
[9] Susan Mendus, *Toleration and the Limits of Liberalism* (Basingstoke: Macmillan, 1989), p. 3.

George I.[10] The wife of a printer, Thomas James (c. 1640–1710), and the mother of at least four children, Elinor James nevertheless found the time to write and publish more than ninety works, many of them broadsides. In her texts – variously addressed to monarchs, parliamentarians, aldermen, and other political figures – James comments on some of the most pressing political issues of her time. Modern scholars might hesitate to call the self-educated James a political theorist in the strictest sense. Ruth Perry claims that, unlike Mary Astell, James 'was not an intellectual and did not reach for historical precedent or philosophical rationale to justify her attitudes'.[11] Paula McDowell points out that it is likely that many of James's works were composed with type at the printing press: 'The "endings" of James's papers are not pre-planned conclusions to carefully developed arguments but rather simply a matter of coming to the end of the sheet.'[12] It is also likely that her works were put together with oral presentation in mind.

As a result of her oral activism on the streets of London, James's views about the Exclusion Crisis of 1678–81, the Monmouth Rebellion of 1685, and the Glorious Revolution of 1688–9 seem to have reached (and possibly influenced) both a literate and illiterate audience.[13] For the frequent public airing of her views, James was seen as a political nuisance: in 1689, she was arrested and sent to Newgate for 'dispersing scandalous and reflecting papers' in condemnation of William III.[14] (Several of James's works are openly critical of the Revolution.) Like Cavendish before her, James was also dismissed as a 'Mad Woman'.[15] But despite this perception – or perhaps because of it – she seems to have been well known and widely read. The oral context of James's writings should also alert us to the fact that her writings were *meant* to be digressive and lacking

[10] For further details on Elinor James, see McDowell, *The Women of Grub Street*, pp. 128–45; Paula McDowell, 'James, Elinor (1644/5-1719)', in *The Oxford Dictionary of National Biography* (Oxford University Press, 2004), www.oxforddnb.com/view/article/14600, accessed 15 February 2007; introductory note to *Elinor James*, selected and introduced by Paula McDowell, in *The Early Modern Englishwoman: A Facsimile Library of Essential Works. Series II. Printed Writings, 1641–1700: Part 3, vol. 11* (Aldershot: Ashgate, 2005), pp. xvii–xxviii; and Schwoerer, 'Women and the Glorious Revolution', pp. 204–8.

[11] Ruth Perry, *The Celebrated Mary Astell: An Early English Feminist* (Chicago and London: Chicago University Press, 1986), p. 183.

[12] McDowell, *The Women of Grub Street*, p. 134.

[13] On the oral context of James's writings, see ibid., pp. 128–45.

[14] Narcissus Luttrell, *A Brief Historical Relation of State Affairs from September 1678 to April 1714*, 6 vols. (Oxford University Press, 1857), vol. 1, p. 617; quoted in McDowell, introductory note to *Elinor James*, p. xvii.

[15] One of James's works is inscribed with the words 'a Mad Woman who used to attend at the Doors of the House of Lds & Commons'; see McDowell, introductory note to *Elinor James*, p. xxiii.

in theoretical content, for the sake of entertaining the common crowd.[16] If we look closely, however, we can see that James's anti-tolerationist arguments have discernible premises and conclusions – premises that, in some cases, even a sophisticated tolerationist such as John Locke would have been compelled to accept. Despite the seemingly artless tone of her work, James's writings do provide some insight into the philosophical rationale behind anti-tolerationist attitudes of the period.

To understand James's position, it is necessary to begin with her conception of political authority more generally. A staunch royalist, James maintains that we ought passively to submit to the king's authority, even if the king commands something that sins against our conscience.[17] This obligation stems from the fact that the king is 'Christ's Vice-gerent', and subjects must 'own none (for our Governour on Earth) but He'.[18] When James II was overthrown, Elinor James wrote to William, Prince of Orange, to remind him that James was 'Gods Anointed'.[19] Nobody can blame William for protecting 'the *Right* of his *Wife*', Mary, but it is highly condemnable for him 'to receive, the *Right* of the *King*; and you must not think to go unpunished'.[20] She tells William that 'the whole Nation rejoyced at Your Coming, as a Reconciler, but not half the Nation thought You would have accepted of the Crown, as long as the King your Father [i.e. father-in-law] was alive'.[21] Like Elizabeth I, whom she admired,[22] James maintains that it is not for mere mortals to judge their rulers: kings are accountable to God alone, 'and who knows but that it was the Will of God, to suffer His Majesty [James II] to incline towards *Rome*, that he might be as an Angel to try our Sincerity, and that the Errors of *Rome* might have a Total Overthrow'.[23] If the king turns out to be an irreligious person or a tyrant, this does not annul our political

---

[16] McDowell, *The Women of Grub Street*, p. 140.

[17] See, for example, the opening paragraph of Elinor James, *A New Answer To A Speech* (1681), in *Elinor James*, p. 1. This work was written in the aftermath of the Exclusion Crisis. During this time, the two parties later known as the 'Whigs' and 'Tories' debated a bill proposing that the Catholic James II, then Duke of York, ought to be excluded from the throne.

[18] Elinor James, *Mrs. James's Vindication of the Church of England, In An Answer To A Pamphlet Entituled, A New Test Of The Church of England's Loyalty* (London: Printed for Elinor James, 1687), in *Elinor James*, p. 44.

[19] *May it please your Royal Highness, To Grant me Grace and Favour in Your Sight* (1688 or early 1689), in *Elinor James*, p. 63.

[20] *My Lords, You can't but be sensible of the great Zeal I have had for King and Kingdom* (possibly February 1689), in *Elinor James*, p. 67.

[21] *This being Your Majesty's Birth-Day* (1689), in *Elinor James*, p. 79.

[22] *November the 17th, 1714. This Day ought never to be forgotten, being the Proclamation Day for Elizabeth I* (1714), in *Elinor James*, pp. 209–10.

[23] *Mrs. James's Advice to the Citizens of London* (early 1689), in *Elinor James*, p. 69.

obligations as subjects: Scripture tells us that we still owe a passive obedience: 'The Apostle Exhorteth likewise the Christians to be Obedient to Unbelieving Kings, and to submit to all Power and Authority, not only for Wraths sake but for the Lords sake.'[24]

In turn, James maintains, the king has an obligation to protect the community – in both a civil and spiritual sense. In the time of Charles II, James said that 'I am certain the King will do nothing but what is for his own safety and your good: And how contrary is it to reason, that a King should betray himself; and what advantage would it bring him? Is not his safety the Peoples safety, and the Peoples safety his safety?'[25] Of James II, she said 'it is His Whole Care to keep His Kingdom in Peace, and to have His People Flourish, and will not disturb the Peace thereof upon any Condition whatsoever'.[26] In a piece urging obedience to the Catholic king, she wrote that a king not only takes care 'of the Welfare of your Bodies,' but also 'your Souls'.[27] Elsewhere she repeats Charles I's sentiment that 'The true Glory of Princes consists in advancing Gods Glory, in the maintenance of True Religion, and practising the same for the Churches Good: Also in the Dispensation of Civil Power, with Justice and Honour to the Publick Peace.'[28]

James's justification of religious intolerance stems from her conception of political authority, and especially the king's obligation to uphold civil peace and political stability. In April 1687, James II issued the first of his two Declarations of Indulgence. This declaration 'to all his loving subjects for liberty of conscience' resulted in the suspension of penal laws in matters ecclesiastical. In principle, the declaration was supposed to encourage the free exercise of religion in England. Protestant dissenters, Catholics, and persons of other religious persuasions were no longer required to attend Church of England services, and could now hold their own religious services without fear of penalties. In addition, subjects were no longer required to swear oaths of allegiance in order to obtain civil or military positions. In April 1688, James II issued a second declaration of liberty of conscience, stating that his intentions in the first were unchanged. Elinor James offers her cautious support for the king's declarations, but

[24] *Sir, I Hope this Day will never be forgotten, nor the Afflictions of that Pious Prince* (1685), in *Elinor James*, p. 19.
[25] *A New Answer*, in *Elinor James*, p. 2.
[26] *Mrs. James's Vindication of the Church of England*, in *Elinor James*, p. 38.
[27] *Sir, I Hope since God has been so infinite Gracious to this Nation* (after 6 February 1685), in *Elinor James*, p. 21.
[28] *Sir, I Hope this Day will never be forgotten*, in *Elinor James*, p. 19.

her general stance is one of intolerance toward Catholics and Protestant dissenters.

In James's opinion, neither the dissenters nor the Catholics ought to be tolerated because they cannot pledge unconditional, passive obedience to the king. The dissenters owe their primary allegiance to conscience, and the Catholics owe theirs to a spiritual authority, the Pope. In a 1685 work, James says of the Catholics that 'they cannot serve two Masters, neither can any man be a friend to the King that espouses any Interest contrary to the Kings Interest; and whosoever doth in his own thoughts love and prefer any Man above the King, he is a Spiritual Enemy and no Friend to the Government'.[29] In a later work, she likewise says that 'whoever is for the Interest of another [Prince], cannot be a True Subject to their own'.[30] To tolerate Catholics in England is to encourage the very rebellion and dissent that magistrates must strive to avoid in the pursuit of peace and social unity. 'Therefore,' James says, 'I humbly intreat you Roman Catholicks, who have made it your business to pervert the Kings Subjects from their Liege Duty, that they owe to God and their King, that you would repent of that evil and do it no more.'[31]

A similar justification of intolerance toward Catholics can be found in the work of some tolerationists of the period, such as John Locke. In his *Letter Concerning Toleration* (1689), Locke says that magistrates have the authority to repress those religious practices that are prejudicial to the safety and security of civil society. Magistrates are therefore justified in not tolerating those subjects who yield up a blind obedience to another authority, such as the '*Mufti* of *Constantinople*': otherwise, 'by this means the Magistrate would give way to the settling of a forreign Jurisdiction in his own Country, and suffer his own People to be listed, as it were, for Souldiers against his own Government'.[32] In a recent study, Jeremy Waldron points out that by the lights of his own philosophy, Locke could consistently extend toleration to Catholics, but only on the condition that they do not pledge their political allegiance to a foreign power.[33]

Elinor James also expresses anti-tolerationist sentiments against Protestant dissenters. In one of her best-known works, *Mrs. James's Vindication of the Church of England* (1687), she responds to a dissenter's argument that

[29] Ibid.   [30] *Mrs. James's Vindication of the Church of England*, in *Elinor James*, p. 40.
[31] *Sir, I Hope this Day will never be forgotten*, in *Elinor James*, p. 19.
[32] Locke, *A Letter Concerning Toleration*, p. 50. Tully's modern edition is based on William Popple's 1689 English translation of Locke's *Epistola de Tolerantia*.
[33] Jeremy Waldron, *God, Locke, and Equality: Christian Foundations of Locke's Political Thought* (Cambridge University Press, 2002), pp. 218–23.

the Test Act and Penal laws ought to be abolished or repealed (by par-
liamentary statute), rather than simply suspended (by royal indulgence).[34]
James says, '*You think you should be Happy if the Test and Penal Laws were
Taken Away*, but I hope the *King will not satisfie your Desires*; for though
his Majesty doth not make use of them, *They may stand as Rods doth upon
Mantle-Trees, to keep Rebellious Children in Subjection.*'[35] James would
have had no sympathy for the arguments of Katherine Chidley and the
Leveller women petitioners in favour of freedom from arbitrary power in
the state. In James's view, the penal laws against dissenters are necessary in
order to guarantee political stability in the community – even if the king
never uses them. The danger is that following one's conscience may lead
to civil disobedience; in certain circumstances, the dissenter's allegiance to
her inner spiritual authority could override her obligations to secular
authority: 'As for Conscience, I do not count it a sufficient Guide,
because it is not so Infallible, but it is subject to Err, and therefore it
ought to be Guided by the Word of God; for I find those that will not be
Guided by that, doth not yield Civil Obedience to Temporal Magistrates,
and how can they to God.'[36] James opposes liberty of conscience but gives
her qualified support to King James's declaration: 'since it is the Kings
Pleasure, I rest satisfied; for if they misimploy it, is not Gods Hand long
enough to reach them?'[37] Again, it is not for her to pass judgement on
the king's decision; if he has made the wrong move, then God will put
things right.

In another work of 1687, her *Defence of the Church of England*, James
says of the dissenters 'that nothing but a Throne will Content you; so that
it is not *Liberty of Conscience* will satisfie you'.[38] In his *Good Advice to
the Church of England, Roman Catholick, and Protestant Dissenter* (1687),
the Quaker tolerationist William Penn (1644–1718) writes against coercive
churches on the grounds that faith cannot be forced, and calls for the

---

[34] James is responding to an anonymous dissenting work titled *A New Test of the Church of England's
Loyalty* (1687). For a facsimile reprint of this text, see *Elinor James*, pp. 267–74. In turn, James's
Vindication sparked a response by a woman, *Elizabeth Rone's Short Answer to Ellinor James's Long
Preamble* (1687), a broadsheet of verse. For a facsimile reprint of this text, see *Elinor James*,
pp. 280–2.

[35] *Mrs. James's Vindication of the Church of England*, in *Elinor James*, pp. 44–5.   [36] Ibid., p. 36.

[37] Ibid.

[38] *Mrs. James's Defence of the Church of England, In A Short Answer To The Canting Address, &c.
With a Word or Two Concerning a Quakers Good Advice To the Church of England, Roman
Catholick, and Protestant Dissenter* ([London:] Printed for Elinor James, 1687), in *Elinor James*,
p. 52.

abolition of the Test Act and Penal Laws against Protestant dissenters.[39] In response to Penn, James says:

And since *Liberty of Conscience* cannot content you without taking away the *Test* and *Penal Laws*, it makes me to think that you have some Design under-hand more than the World knows of: Therefore I count you a Person not fit to be Trusted; for the King hath been so Gracious, that He hath given *Liberty of Conscience* Freely: But you say, *The Penal Laws hinder you from coming into Action*: Therefore the *Laws* must be taken away to humour you! Yes: For what Cause? That the King should lessen Himself for you: And if you will not Trust His Majesty with the *Laws*, why should the King trust you Without them? If you do well, there is no Law can hurt you, but if you do Ill, why should not the King and the Church have Power to Help themselves? For They are not to be Divided, no more than a Man should be from his Wife: For the King is to defend the Church, and to keep all in Peace.[40]

In James's view, Penn is suggesting that true toleration requires more than just an indulgence or a 'leaving alone': it requires that magistrates should have no legal power to interfere with the worship of dissenting subjects. By contrast, James argues that there are justifiable limits to religious toleration, and that those limits involve magistrates retaining the legal power to punish subjects with penalties if the practical circumstances so dictate. The king must uphold a policy of intolerance toward dissenters – at least, to the extent of not repealing the laws against them – in order to ensure civil peace and political stability.

In sum, James appeals to her conception of political authority, and the subject's obligation to give absolute obedience, to justify her defence of intolerance. Subjects ought to follow the word of God and offer up obedience to all earthly authority, allowing that God (and not men) will punish unjust rulers. The problem with Catholics is that they owe their primary allegiance to a foreign spiritual power, and this may potentially lead to social disturbance. The problem with dissenters is that if their primary obligation is to their conscience, then they cannot yield unquestioning obedience to the magistrate: they allow that it is sometimes permissible to resist one's rulers. If a king is to avoid political disturbances and uphold peace, then he must be intolerant of such religions.

This position was likely held by other female royalists of the period, such as the Tory playwright, poet, and novelist Aphra Behn (1640–89).

[39] William Penn, *Good Advice to the Church of England, Roman Catholick, and Protestant Dissenter* (London: Andrew Sowle, 1687).
[40] *Mrs. James's Defence of the Church of England*, in *Elinor James*, p. 56.

In *Love Letters* (1684), Behn's protagonist Sylvia (Henrietta) reminds Philander (Grey) that the king 'holds his crown by right of nature, by right of law, and by right of heaven itself'.[41] In Behn's play *The City Heiress* (1682), one Anglican character remarks, 'I love good wholesome Doctrine, that teaches obedience to the King and Superiors, without railing at Government, and quoting Scripture for Sedition, Mutiny, and Rebellion.'[42] A strong supporter of James II, Behn was also apparently critical of the Glorious Revolution: her last known work was a justification of her refusal to write a celebratory poem upon the coronation of William and Mary.[43] The 'prophetess' and former Quaker Joan Whitrowe (*fl.* 1665–97), was also openly critical of William and Mary.[44] The author of at least eight works published between 1677 and 1697, Whitrowe considers herself 'one that is of no Sect or gathered People whatsoever'.[45] On the one hand, she claims that it is not outward services that please God, but rather 'it's Truth in the inward Parts that God requires'.[46] On the other, she maintains that the king ought to impose 'Proclamations, and Penalties' against sinners.[47] The king and queen 'standest in the place of GOD to the People, to bring their Causes unto GOD, and to reveal the Will of GOD to them, and to shew them the Way

[41] Quoted in Melinda Zook, 'Contextualizing Aphra Behn: Plays, Politics, and Party, 1679–1689', in Smith (ed.), *Women Writers*, p. 88.

[42] Quoted ibid., p. 86.

[43] Aphra Behn, *A Pindaric Poem To The Reverend Doctor Burnet, On The Honour he did me of Enquiring after me and my Muse* (1689). On Behn and politics, see Zook, 'Contextualizing Aphra Behn', pp. 75–93. See also McDowell, *The Women of Grub Street*, pp. 1–4.

[44] For further details on Whitrowe, see Phyllis Mack, 'Whitrowe, Joan (*fl.* 1665–1697)', in *The Oxford Dictionary of National Biography*, http://oxforddnb.com/view/article/45833, accessed 15 February 2007; Mack, *Visionary Women*, pp. 386–7; McDowell, *The Women of Grub Street*, pp. 156–67; and Schwoerer, 'Women of the Glorious Revolution', pp. 204–7.

[45] Joan Whitrowe, *The Humble Address Of The Widow Whitrowe To King William: With a Faithful Warning To the Inhabitants of England* ([London: n.p.,] 1689), p. 13.

[46] Joan Whitrowe, *Faithful Warnings, Expostulations and Exhortations, To The several Professors of Christianity in England, as well those of the Highest as the Lowest Quality* (London: E. Whitlock, 1697), p. 47. At 192 pages, *Faithful Warnings* is Whitrowe's longest work and dedicated 'To the KING, and Both Houses of PARLIAMENT', whom she addresses as God's 'Vicegerents on Earth ... the great Instruments in GOD's Hand, who can Cure the Nation of its Malady' (*Faithful Warnings*, sig. A2r).

[47] *To Queen Mary: The Humble Salutation, And Faithful Greeting of the Widow Whitrowe. With A Warning To The Rulers of the Earth Before The Day of the LORD* breaks forth, that shall burn as an Oven, all the Wicked, and all the Ungodly shall be as Stubble: The Mouth of the LORD hath spoken it ([London: n.p.,] 1690), p. 19. In this work, Whitrowe draws Mary II's attention to a '*Brewers*-Tax [that] falls heavily upon the poor', 'scant Measures, with ... false Weights (which Robs the Poor of their Right)', a fashion for 'monstrous *Babylonish* Dress of the Head', 'those cursed Play-houses', and other debaucheries (p. 18). She says that the king and queen may clear their consciences by 'using all means possible to rectify these things; First, in their own Examples, then by Proclamation, and Penalties' (p. 19).

wherein they must walk, and the Work they must do'.[48] To fulfil their spiritual duty, the king and queen will sometimes be required to adopt a policy of intolerance. In a passage addressed to bishops (but equally a warning to monarchs), Whitrowe says that 'Toleration proclaim'd upon the House-top, for the Door to be open that lets in all manner of Ungodliness' is 'the very thing that destroys Nations and Kingdoms; for what need we fear all the Enemies in the World, if it were not for our Sins? It's the Sins of a People that draws down the Wrath and Vengeance of GOD upon Nations and Kingdoms.'[49] Above all, the nation's leaders ought to be vigilant lest toleration lead to the 'Spirit of Atheism'.[50]

II

We turn now to the views of a female tolerationist, Anne Docwra (née Waldegrave).[51] Docwra was the daughter of a justice of the peace, William Waldegrave, a man who actively encouraged her interest in the law (he argued that 'it was as proper for a Woman as a Man to understand the Laws, because they must live under them as well as Men').[52] Although the details of her education are unknown, Docwra shows a strong familiarity with both law and philosophy: she regularly quotes from the statutes, and more than once refers to Nicolas Malebranche's *Search after Truth* (1674–5).[53] In her early years, Docwra appears to have been a royalist and a supporter of the Church of England;[54] later, sometime after her marriage to a landed gentleman, James Docwra (1617–72), she converted to Quakerism.[55] Following her husband's death, she

---

[48] *The Humble Salutation And Faithful Greeting of the Widow Whitrowe To King William* ([London: n.p.,] 1690), p. 14.

[49] *Faithful Warnings*, p. 119.   [50] Ibid., p. 108.

[51] For further details on Docwra, see Michael Mullett, 'Docwra, Anne (*c.* 1624–1710)', in *The Oxford Dictionary of National Biography* http://oxforddnb.com/view/article/45813, accessed 15 February 2007; Mack, *Visionary Women*, pp. 315–18; McDowell, *The Women of Grub Street*, pp. 145–56; and Schwoerer, 'Women of the Glorious Revolution', pp. 204–8.

[52] See Anne Docwra, *An Apostate-Conscience Exposed, And The Miserable Consequences thereof Disclosed, For Information and Caution. By an Ancient Woman, and Lover of Truth, and the sincere Friends thereof, A.D.* (London: T. Sowle, 1699), pp. 24–5.

[53] For her references to Malebranche, see Docwra, *An Apostate-Conscience Exposed*, p. 50, and *The Second Part of An Apostate-Conscience Exposed: Being an Answer to a Scurrilous Pamphlet* (London: T. Sowle, 1700), p. 46.

[54] Docwra says that 'I and my Husband, and my Father also, were of the old Royallists, and suffered much in the time of the civil Wars in *England*, in the days of King *Charles* the first, upon the Account of Loyalty' (*An Apostate-Conscience Exposed*, p. 63).

[55] On Docwra as a Quaker, see Mack, *Visionary Women*, pp. 315–18; David Booy, 'Anne Docwra', in *Autobiographical Writings by Early Quaker Women*, pp. 161–2; Laurel Phillipson, 'Quakerism in Cambridge before the Act of Toleration (1653–1689)', *Proceedings of the Cambridge Antiquarian*

lived in Cambridge, and, from 1682 to 1699, wrote at least seven works on religious and political topics, many of them promoting Quaker ideas. Her two longest pamphlets, *An Apostate-Conscience Exposed* (1699) and *The Second Part of an Apostate-Conscience Exposed* (1700), are part of an acrimonious personal dispute with a former Quaker and possible kinsman, Francis Bugg (1640–1727). But generally speaking, Docwra's writings are devoted to justifications for the religious toleration of Protestant dissenters in England.

In her first extant work, *A Looking-Glass for the Recorder and Justices of the Peace* (1682), Docwra discusses the power of 'the civil Magistrate to enquire into matters touching the Service of God, and establishing of true Religion in this Nation'.[56] She agrees that 'the civil Magistrate ought to correct the vicious Lives and Manners of such as live in their own Sensuality, either without the knowledge or due fear of God; and to do it according to Truth'.[57] The magistrate has a spiritual duty to ensure that his subjects are set on the right path to truth and salvation. But she believes that to bring subjects to the true religion, a magistrate must adopt a Christian approach:

when men do undertake either to Inform or Correct others in matters of Religion, it ought to be done in Truth and Righteousness, from that inward Principle of the divine Life, whereby good men govern their Actions, and where that Principle rules, the Gospel of Jesus Christ is manifest in them, which is *Peace on Earth, Good Will towards men*; there is no other way for our Magistrates to perform any Duty towards God in order to establish true Religion in this Nation.[58]

Docwra maintains that, in the case of religious worship, the ends do not justify the means: 'Men must not play the Devil for Gods sake, to polute the Church by forcing Conformity upon such a Generation of Vipers as those of these late times.'[59] In short, a Christian king must exemplify the Christian virtues of peaceableness and goodwill in dealing with his subjects.

Many of Docwra's contemporaries would have found such an *ad hominem* argument persuasive. A similar argument is put forward in the

   Society 76 (1987), 1–25 and 'Quakerism in Cambridge from the Act of Toleration to the End of the Nineteenth Century', *Proceedings of the Cambridge Antiquarian Society* 77 (1988), 1–33.
[56] Anne Docwra, *A Looking-Glass for the Recorder and Justices of the Peace, and Grand Juries for the Town and County of Cambridge* ([London: n.p.,] 1682), p. 2.
[57] Ibid., p. 3.   [58] Ibid., p. 7.   [59] Ibid., p. 4.

opening paragraph of Locke's *Letter Concerning Toleration.*[60] Locke warns that if a man is 'destitute of Charity, Meekness, and Good-Will in general towards all Mankind, even those that are not Christians, he is certainly yet short of being a true Christian himself'.[61] This topic preoccupies a great deal of Locke's subsequent defences of toleration in response to Jonas Proast.[62] But the argument would not have convinced someone like Elinor James who maintains that magistrates do not unfairly persecute dissenters and Catholics so much as justly punish them.

Like James, however, Docwra also addresses the topic of the subject's duty of obedience to magistrates, and the best way to ensure political stability in the community. In a 1687 work titled *Spiritual Community, vindicated amongst people of different perswasions in some things,* Docwra inquires into the idea of the 'bond of the community'. In what, she asks, does such a bond or unity consist? Some place the bond of the community 'in Church Tradition, and the severe Opinions or Expositions of the Fathers', and 'others in the Penal Statutes and Ecclesiastical Laws made against Dissenters, for the upholding their Church Liturgy'.[63] But there is a crucial problem with forced conformity as the basis of social unity: it creates *hypocrites*, or people who profess beliefs that they do not inwardly hold. In the *Looking-Glass*, Docwra says that as 'for forcing Conformity upon any, there can be no service to God in that; for Force makes Hypocrites'.[64] In her *Spiritual Community*, she repeats the sentiment, noting that 'No Nation or People can be really Happy when an intire Liberty is not granted to all peaceable people; forcing mens Consciences makes Hypocrites.'[65] Coercive uniformity, moreover, rewards those subjects who willingly become hypocrites, and punishes those who do not; and this, in turn, creates resentment and dissent – recipes for political disaster.[66] The bond of the community and public peace cannot therefore be adequately promoted by penal statutes against non-conformists.

In April 1687, Docwra congratulated James II for his first Declaration of Indulgence, claiming that it would be 'a certain way to root out

---

[60] For a brief evaluation of this argument, see Jeremy Waldron, 'Locke: Toleration and the Rationality of Persecution', in *Justifying Toleration: Conceptual and Historical Perspectives*, ed. Susan Mendus (Cambridge University Press, 1988), pp. 61–86.

[61] Locke, *Letter Concerning Toleration*, p. 23.

[62] John Locke, *A Second Letter Concerning Toleration* (1690), *A Third Letter for Toleration* (1692), and *A Fourth Letter for Toleration* (written c. 1704, published posthumously).

[63] Anne Docwra, *Spiritual Community, vindicated amongst people of different perswasions in some things* (London: [n.p.,] 1687), p. 1.

[64] Docwra, *A Looking-Glass for the Recorder*, p. 3. [65] Docwra, *Spiritual Community*, p. 2.

[66] Ibid., p. 3.

Hypocrisie and self ended worldly profession out of the Kingdom'.[67] Many years later, in her *Apostate-Conscience Exposed*, she repeated the view that liberty in the exercise of religion is 'a great means to root *Hypocrisie* out of this Nation, for forced Conformity makes *Hypocrites*, but never makes good *Christians*, or Subjects to any Prince'.[68] Far from encouraging resistance to the government, a policy of toleration will in fact quell dissent. This is because 'Now Liberty is granted, there can be no pretence of quarelling with the Government that is kind to them.'[69]

A policy of toleration will also help to create social unity by promoting Christian virtues in the community: 'It is Divine Love and Charity that brings a Nation or People into such Unity as to love God above all, and their Neighbours as themselves.'[70] In an earlier work, *An Epistle of Love and Good Advice* (1683), Docwra expands on the same theme. She says that it is her ambition

to awaken those that are asleep in their mistaken Judgment, and led away by the dreaming Conceits of Imagination: These are they that have taken up a Religion upon Trust, upon the Credit and Relation of the Sons of Tradition, whose *Faith*, *Doctrine* and *Discipline* are the *Commandments of Men*, making a Money-Trade of Religion, and Persecuting such as do not conform to it.[71]

Here again Docwra anticipates a Lockean sentiment – the view that an individual's religion should not simply be a matter of that 'which either Ignorance, Ambition, or Superstition had chanced to establish in the Countries where they were born'.[72] True Christians must not take their religion upon trust, but from reflection on their own inner light. For Docwra, this is why a policy of toleration is the best way to create a Christian community: in a tolerant nation, men might freely take notice of 'the Universal Light, or Spirit of Grace, which is an inward principle of the Divine Life, whereby all good people governs [*sic*] their Actions'.[73] And 'this Divine Principle is sufficient to preserve a Nation, or People in Peace, if men would regard it'.[74]

Therefore let all cease from imposing Faith and Worship towards God upon his People, and let God alone to be King and Law-giver in mens Consciences, in matters of *Faith* and *Worship* towards him, unto whom alone it belongeth . . .;

---

[67] Ibid., p. 2.   [68] Docwra, *An Apostate-Conscience Exposed*, p. 4.   [69] Ibid.
[70] Docwra, *Spiritual Community*, p. 2.
[71] Anne Docwra, *An Epistle of Love And Good Advice, To my Old Friends & Fellow-Sufferers in the Late Times, The Old Royalists And their Posterity, And to all others that have any sincere Desires towards God* (London: Andrew Sowle, 1683), p. 7.
[72] Locke, *Letter Concerning Toleration*, p. 28.   [73] Docwra, *Spiritual Community*, p. 1.   [74] Ibid.

they that do otherways, do but lead men out from God, into Man's Contrivances, from that inward Principle of the divine Life, that God hath put in their Hearts and Consciences, to be the Guide of all Mankind, and is the only Infallible Way for them to trust to.[75]

Docwra's support for toleration stems from a conviction that the path to religious truth cannot be found by blindly following the religion of one's country, but rather by following one's own inner spiritual guide. Religious toleration, in turn, will promote the development of a loving, peaceable Christian community.

There are obvious differences between the early modern debate and the modern liberal discussion on toleration. Docwra's writings show that, in this pre-liberal period, the tolerationists' arguments did not always differ so dramatically from those of anti-tolerationists such as Elinor James. First, like Margaret Cavendish, both Docwra and James are eager to avoid the sort of social and political upheaval that resulted from the English civil wars: both writers assume that the political authorities must adopt the course of action that best upholds peace and unity in the kingdom. The main difference between the two amounts to a disagreement about empirical or causal facts – about which policy *is* going to foster peace and unity most effectively in the community. James believes that social unity can be maintained by following a policy of intolerance toward Protestant dissenters and Catholics – two religious groups that cannot promise unconditional obedience to rulers. Docwra, by contrast, believes that forced conformity cannot make subjects happy, and that a policy of toleration will quell rather than foster social dissent. Toleration, moreover, will lead to greater freedom to examine the 'inner light' of Christ and therefore promote a 'spiritual community' in the nation. In short, one writer asserts that a policy of religious intolerance is the best course of action for the sake of promoting peace and unity in society; the other claims that a policy of toleration is better. Neither writer exalts toleration as morally valuable in itself, or as a value that ought to be upheld regardless of the outcomes for civil society.

Docwra comes close to advocating toleration as intrinsically valuable when she suggests that magistrates ought to exercise the Christian virtues of goodwill and love of peace. But goodwill and peaceableness alone do not amount to toleration. As recent scholars have pointed out, the concept of toleration necessarily implies that the tolerator takes a negative

---

[75] Docwra, *An Epistle of Love*, p. 8.

attitude toward the object of toleration. We cannot tolerate something that we morally approve of, nor can we tolerate something that inspires indifference – we must take a negative stance toward it.[76] Goodwill and the love of peace do not capture this negative aspect of toleration.

Second, James and Docwra appeal to the notion that there is a knowable religious truth; both writers support a non-sceptical position. In the modern liberal tradition, toleration and scepticism are thought to have a natural affinity. Richard Tuck observes that 'It is natural to suppose that there is – at the very least – a certain emotional kinship between a belief in the desirability of toleration and a sceptical attitude towards religious and ethical beliefs.'[77] There are many early modern political thinkers – Jean Bodin among them – who build their tolerationist thought upon sceptical foundations.[78] But we do not find such scepticism in the arguments of Anne Docwra; quite the opposite. Both James and Docwra maintain that the magistrate has a spiritual duty to assist his subjects toward finding religious truth, but they differ in terms of the best way to bring this about. James supports the view that coercive uniformity will bring subjects to the true religion, while Docwra maintains that religious truth must be found by the individual alone.

In these women's writings, then, we do not see a straightforward conflict between an old world view and a modern, secular political vision. In some respects, the toleration debate in this era was a natural development of the earlier views about good government and peace that we saw in the writings of Christine de Pizan, Elizabeth I, and others. Like their forebears, James and Docwra subscribe to the view that political leaders have a duty of pastoral care to the nation: they are obliged to protect its spiritual welfare as well as its civil interests. They must promote peace, social unity, and political stability; but they must also assist subjects along the path to truth and salvation. In addition, the magistrate is expected to have the attributes not only of a good Christian, but also of a good parent: Elinor James calls on James II to make peace, urging that he 'has the Nature of an Indulgent Father, who values the Lives and

---

[76] Susan Mendus notes that this concept of toleration gives rise to the 'paradox of toleration' or, roughly, the assertion that it is permissible not to prevent that which is impermissible. On this topic, see Mendus, *Toleration and the Limits of Liberalism*, Chapter 1.

[77] Richard Tuck, 'Scepticism and Toleration in the Seventeenth Century', in Mendus (ed.), *Justifying Toleration*, p. 21.

[78] See Quentin Skinner, *The Foundations of Modern Political Thought*, 2 vols. (Cambridge University Press, 1978), vol. 11, pp. 247–9.

Interest of his Children before the Gain of the World';[79] and in a reference to Isaiah 49:23, Joan Whitrowe says of William and Mary that 'here the KING shall be a Nursing-Father and QUEEN a Nursing Mother'.[80]

III

In their lifetime, both James and Docwra faced critics who drew attention to their gender in the assessment of their political ideas.[81] In response, James wryly points out that her critics make an issue of her sex only when it suits them: 'I know you will say *I am a Woman, and why should I trouble my self? Why was I not always so*, when I pleaded with the Parliament about the *Right of Succession*, and with *Shaftsbury*, and *Monmouth*, and at *Guild-Hall*, and elsewhere?'[82] But generally speaking, James is dismissive rather than defensive of her status as a woman writing on political matters; it is simply not an issue.[83] Whitrowe and Docwra, however, both offer defences of women's spiritual authority along the lines of those put forward by earlier Quaker women.[84] In one work, Whitrowe urges William III to consider her advice, 'though from a Woman', for 'the LORD is no respecter of Persons'.[85] In another work, she asks: 'And why should it be thought incredible for a Woman to write truth, any more than a Man? Is the Spirit of the LORD straightned, that it cannot operate in a Woman as well as in a Man? ... Dare you presume to limmit the Maker of all things, to any thing that had a beginning?'[86] In the spirit of the earlier *querelle des femmes*, Whitrowe also cites a list of biblical

[79] Elinor James, *Dear Sovereign, May it please your Majesty, to accept my thanks for your gracious Act in restoring the Charter* (1688), in *Elinor James*, p. 61.

[80] Joan Whitrowe, *To King William And Queen Mary, Grace and Peace. The Widow Whitrow's Humble Thanksgiving to the LORD of Hosts, the King of Eternal Glory, the GOD of all our Mercies, unto whom be Glory, Glory, and Praise for the King's safe Return to England* (London: [n.p.,] 1692), pp. 8–9.

[81] On this topic, see McDowell, *The Women of Grub Street*, pp. 181–214.

[82] *Mrs. James's Vindication of the Church of England*, in *Elinor James*, p. 37.

[83] One work addressed to James II begins with the observation that 'I have had many Children, and have Nurs'd them all my self, and I have had Three and Four Children Young and no Maid, and none to help me neither in Sickness or Health and yet I have found Opportunity to come to White-hall' (*May it please Your Most Sacred Majesty, Seriously to Consider my great Zeal and Love*, in *Elinor James*, p. 23).

[84] For a discussion of the arguments of Priscilla Cotton, Mary Cole, and Margaret Fell Fox, see our Chapter 7.

[85] Whitrowe, *The Humble Salutation And Faithful Greeting of the Widow Whitrowe To King William*, p. 14.

[86] *The Widow Whiterows Humble Thanksgiving For The Kings Safe Return* (London: D. Edwards, 1694), p. 38.

exempla: Mary Magdalene, 'the other *Mary*', Lidia, Deborah, Jael, Huldah the prophetess, and others. She says that 'Hear [*sic*] you may see the LORD made use of Women, as well as Men, and will make use of them yet more'.[87] In *An Epistle of Love*, Docwra also points to biblical passages that allow that both men and women are capable of receiving the 'Light, Power and Spirit of the Lord God'.[88] She argues that women might receive 'Power from God to Pray, Prophecy or declare the Glad-tidings of the Light of the Glorious Gospel of Christ Jesus'.[89]

Both Docwra and Whitrowe allow that women, as well as men, are capable of finding and spreading the truth, and ought to be permitted to do so. Neither writer, however, expands on the implications of a tolerationist ethic for women's education. We turn now to Damaris Cudworth Masham, a writer who does consider the significance of the political campaign for liberty of conscience with regard to the education of women. The daughter of a Cambridge theologian, Ralph Cudworth (1617–88), and the close friend of the philosopher John Locke, Masham was the author of two short works: *A Discourse Concerning the Love of God* (published anonymously in 1696) and the *Occasional Thoughts in Reference to a Vertuous or Christian Life* (also anonymous, 1705).[90] Though they are not overtly political works, these tracts reflect the controversial political climate of William III's final years and the early days of Queen Anne's reign.[91] *Occasional Thoughts* was published in 1705, but Masham says that the manuscript '*was written some years since*' and had lain by '*for above two Years unread, and almost forgotten*'.[92] This places the writing of the work sometime between 1702 and 1705, a period of renewed controversy in England about the practice of occasional conformity and the toleration of non-conformist religious sects. In this work, Masham does not explicitly refer to the toleration debate or to Locke's *Letter Concerning Toleration*, but she does build her arguments upon common tolerationist principles of the time.[93]

[87] Ibid., p. 38.   [88] Docwra, *An Epistle of Love*, pp. 3–4.   [89] Ibid., p. 4.
[90] Damaris Masham, *A Discourse Concerning the Love of God* (London: Awnsham and John Churchil, 1696); *Occasional Thoughts in Reference to a Vertuous or Christian Life* (London: A. and J. Churchil, 1705). For a facsimile reprint of these works, see *The Philosophical Works of Damaris, Lady Masham*, introduced by James G. Buickerood (Bristol: Thoemmes Continuum, 2004).
[91] On the general political content of Masham's works, see Regan Penaluna, 'The Social and Political Thought of Damaris Cudworth Masham', in Broad and Green (eds.), *Virtue, Liberty, and Toleration*, pp. 111–22.
[92] Masham, *Occasional Thoughts*, sig. A2r.
[93] For a more in-depth study of this topic, see Jacqueline Broad, 'Damaris Cudworth Masham on Women and Liberty of Conscience', in *A Feminist History of Philosophy*, ed. Eileen O'Neill and Marcy Lascano (Dordrecht: Springer, forthcoming).

First, Masham subscribes to Locke's view that the authorities should not use coercion and penalties as ways of imposing religious beliefs on others. According to Locke, she says, 'true and saving Religion consists only in the inward perswasion of the Mind, without which nothing can be acceptable to God. And such is the nature of the Understanding that it cannot be compell'd to the belief of anything by outward force.'[94] Masham does not make Locke's epistemological point that belief cannot be forced, but she does emphasise that it *should* not be forced because of the negative social consequences of such coercion. Masham tells the story of 'a good Lady of the Church of *Rome*' who instructs her child in religion. When the girl tells her mother than she cannot believe in transubstantiation, her mother replies '*What? do you not believe in Transubstantiation? You are a naughty Girl, and must be whip'd.*'[95] Masham opposes such punitive practices because, after a short time, children hesitate to question their religious teachers, and simply profess 'that they *do Believe* whatever their Teacher tells them they must Believe, whilst in Truth they remain in an ignorant unbelief'.[96] The results are harmful both for the individual and for society: in the first case, the individual leaves herself exposed to 'the most pitiful Arguments of the Atheistical' and thus places her salvation in jeopardy;[97] in the second, the country is exposed to all the chaos that necessarily follows from atheism and scepticism. If people are not taught the foundations of their religious beliefs, then they might come to believe that 'All Religions are, alike, the Inventions and Artifices of cunning Men to govern the World by; unworthy of imposing upon such as have their good Sense.'[98] This unbelief can have disastrous implications for the virtue, 'prosperity',[99] and 'flourishing'[100] of the commonwealth. 'A general Contempt of Religion towards God,' Masham says, was always a forerunner of 'approaching Ruine to the best and most flourishing Governments which have been in the World'.[101]

In his argument for toleration, Locke also makes the religious point that no one can obtain salvation by blindly leaving the matter of his faith up to someone else's choice and prescription. If we outwardly profess but do not inwardly believe, then this cannot be pleasing to God; it simply makes us guilty of hypocrisy (an issue that concerned Anne Docwra). An individual's acceptance before God depends upon inward sincerity. God requires human beings to attain salvation through their own efforts, and not by blindly following the dictates of the state-established religion.

[94] Masham, *Occasional Thoughts*, p. 27. [95] Ibid., p. 39. [96] Ibid., pp. 39–40. [97] Ibid., p. 39.
[98] Ibid., p. 209. [99] Ibid., pp. 2 and 232. [100] Ibid., pp. 95 and 96. [101] Ibid., p. 232.

In similar terms, Masham says that a truly virtuous and religious man cannot be someone 'whose Interest it has been to keep up the Credit and Authority of vain Traditions and superstitious Practices'.[102] It is important that Christians have the liberty to reflect critically upon their religious beliefs, with reason as their guide. 'Civil and Religious Liberties' are necessary for virtue to abound in society,[103] otherwise Christians can give no more reason for their beliefs and practices than 'a *Mahumetan*' – that is, that 'their God fathers and God mothers ingag'd for them that they should believe so'.[104]

For Masham, educational reform is the key to bringing about a truly Christian commonwealth. In their education, children should never be rebuked for having doubts about their religious instruction: they must be given the freedom to examine the grounds of their beliefs for themselves, according to the light of reason.[105] Freedom of conscience, however, brings with it difficulties of its own. Masham observes that in our early years, before we master the use of our reason, 'an evil indulgence of our Inclinations has commonly establish'd Habits in us too strong to be over-rul'd by the Force of Arguments'.[106] There is a common human tendency to act in opposition to what our reason tells us is the morally best thing to do. In such cases, the freedom to question our beliefs, and to subject them to the light of our reason, is not enough to make us virtuous agents because we may already be disposed to moral weakness. The right instruction regarding virtue thus requires joining together '*good Principles with early Habits*'.[107]

The main thrust of Masham's book is that if *women* are educated to become wise and virtuous, then this will assist in the flourishing of the nation. Women in their capacity as mothers have a profoundly significant role to play in society, in so far as they have a 'strong and unalterable influence upon their [children's] future Inclinations and Passions'.[108] From a young age, children must be taught to use their reason in order to overcome the temptations of 'present pleasure'. The assistance of mothers in early education is thus 'necessary to the right forming of the Minds of their Children of both Sexes'.[109] If a woman herself has some under-standing of languages, 'the useful Sciences',[110] and her religion, and she is closely involved in her child's tuition for the first ten years or so, then this is bound to have a positive impact on the child's intellectual development.

---

[102] Ibid., p. 97.   [103] Ibid., p. 4.   [104] Ibid., p. 47.   [105] Ibid., p. 41.   [106] Ibid., p. 53.
[107] Ibid., sig. A 3r.   [108] Ibid., p. 8.   [109] Ibid.   [110] Ibid., p. 192.

But a woman's education has intrinsic as well as instrumental worth. Religion is 'the Duty of all Persons to understand, of whatever Sex, Condition, or Calling they are of';[111] and to fulfil this duty, women must improve their understandings. Most women could not inform 'a rational Heathen' about the grounds of their Christian faith.[112] Typically speaking, a woman is required only 'to believe and practice what she is taught at Church, or in such Books of Piety as shall be recommended to her by her Parents, or some Spiritual Director'.[113] She thus has no more reason for going to an Anglican church than she should 'have had to go to Mass, or even to the Synagogue', had she been brought up a Catholic or a Jew.[114] As a result, women are easy prey to those men who wish to convert them to a different religion or to persuade them out of their religious beliefs altogether. For the sake of their spiritual welfare, women need to know what the Christian religion consists in and why they believe it. Keeping them in ignorance is in fact an 'injustice' to women,[115] 'For if Christianity be a Religion from God, and Women have Souls to be sav'd as well as Men; to know what this Religion consists in, and to understand the grounds on which it is to be receiv'd, can be no more than necessary Knowledge to a Woman, as well as to a Man.'[116] Women require the freedom of conscience or freedom of worship that is the birthright of all human beings. Christian women need to be taught that 'what they have learn'd to be their Duty is not grounded upon the uncertain and variable Opinion of Men'.[117]

In sum, Masham's point is that every human being has a duty to search the Scriptures for herself, to determine exactly what God expects from her. This spiritual duty has priority over any duty that women might have to their terrestrial superiors, including men as a social group. Women should not be encouraged to have 'such a Notion of Honour as if the Praise of Men ought to be the Supreme Object of their Desires, and the great Motive with them to Vertue'.[118] Women should be granted the freedom to think for themselves, and to interpret the Scriptures according to their own reason. Only in this way will women be protected from the specious arguments of sceptics, atheists, and non-Christians.

We have seen that the history of women's political thought is not always progressive or liberal in character; and a so-called 'feminine' devotion to peace, harmony, and love does not always imply that a writer has tolerationist attitudes. We have found that some English women,

---

[111] Ibid., p. 159.   [112] Ibid., p. 161.   [113] Ibid., p. 207.   [114] Ibid., p. 208.   [115] Ibid., p. 191.
[116] Ibid., p. 166.   [117] Ibid., p. 17.   [118] Ibid., p. 21.

such as Elinor James and (to a lesser extent) Joan Whitrowe, provide reasoned justifications for an anti-tolerationist stance. James's writings, in particular, reveal that some pragmatic reasons for accepting toleration might also be the very grounds for rejecting it: in some circumstances, a policy of religious intolerance might be the best course of action for the sake of peace and harmony in civil society. In a later chapter, we will see that one of the most respected female political thinkers of this time, the conservative Tory Mary Astell, also writes in opposition to religious toleration. Like James, Astell bases her arguments upon a religious theory of the foundations of political authority, and a justification of passive obedience to one's rulers.

Nevertheless, there is also a long tradition of women thinkers who have written in defence of toleration as a political ideal. In early modern France, tolerationist ideas were present (at least implicitly) in the writings of Marguerite de Navarre and another royalist woman, Marie le Jars de Gournay. In the civil war era in England, Katherine Chidley and the Leveller women petitioners, and then the Quaker women writers of the 1650s, all argued in defence of liberty of conscience and the political conditions to make it possible. Even a royalist thinker such as Margaret Cavendish allowed that sometimes the best way to avoid national ruin is to let rebellious subjects have their liberty of conscience. Cavendish was highly critical of the activities of the civil war women petitioners; but provided that non-conformists did not disturb the public peace, she allowed that such subjects might be left alone or tolerated by the authorities. In the work of Anne Docwra, we again see an inclination toward the toleration of non-conformity, in the spirit of promoting love and peace in society. And finally, in the early eighteenth century, Damaris Masham maintained that liberty of conscience requires that women be properly educated so that they do not have to base their faith upon trust. Her political vision is distinctive in that, unlike even the most radical male thinkers of her time, she considers the implications of common tolerationist principles for 'the other half' of the human race.

CHAPTER II

Women of late seventeenth-century France

In late seventeenth-century Europe, women wrote in numbers never previously encountered. Whereas in England a significant proportion of the women who engaged with political ideas were from the middle class, in France authors of the works that we have access to were from the aristocracy or associated with aristocratic circles. Their works emerged out of the salons and mixed polite society established in the middle of the seventeenth century, and the maxim form was particularly popular. Madeleine de Souvré, Marquise de Sablé (1598–1678), Marguerite Hessein, Madame de la Sablière (1640–93), Françoise d'Aubigné, Madame de Maintenon (1653–1711), and Queen Christina of Sweden (1626–89) all left collections of moral maxims.[1] These works attempt to pithily characterise human vice and virtue. Yet they only rarely have an explicit political bearing and their form is not conducive to the development of a systematic philosophy. Increasingly women also published novels, stories, plays, poetry, and memoirs. Even their letters, though not necessarily intended for publication, were offered to the public, the most famous and abundant example being those of Madame de Sévigné (Marie de Rabutin-Chantal).[2]

Women such as Marie Madeleine Pioche de la Vergne, Comtesse de La Fayette (1634–93),[3] Marie-Catherine Le Jumel de Barneville, Comtesse

---

[1] Madame la Marquise de Sablé, *Maximes* (Paris: Sebastien Marbre-Cramoisy, 1678), edited as 'Maximes de Madame de Sablé' in John J. Conley, *Suspicion of Virtue: Women Philosophers in Neoclassical France* (Ithaca: Cornell University Press, 2002), pp. 167–74; Madame de la Sablière, 'Maximes chrétiennes de Madame de la Sablière', edited in Conley, *Suspicion of Virtue*, pp. 181–7; Christina, Queen of Sweden, *Mémoires concernant Christine, reine de Suède*, ed. Johan Arckenholtz, 4 vols. (Amsterdam: Pierre Mortier, 1751), vol. IV, pp. 1–52.

[2] *The Letters of Madame de Sévigné* (London: W. T. Morrell and Co., 1928); and Madame de Sévigné, *Correspondance*, ed. Roger Duchêne (Paris: Gallimard, 1972).

[3] Marie Madeleine Pioche de la Vergne, Comtesse de La Fayette, *The Princesse of Cleves*, trans. Mary Mitford (Harmondsworth: Penguin, 1950); Marie Madeleine Pioche de la Vergne, Comtesse de La Fayette, *La Princesse de Clèves* (Geneva: Droz, 1950), *Mémoires de la cour de France pendant les années 1688–1689* (Amsterdam: Chez Jean-Frédéric Bernard, 1731), *Histoire de Madame Henriette*

d'Aulnoy (1650–1705),[4] Marie-Catherine-Hortense Desjardins, Madame de Villedieu (1640–83)[5] and Antoinette du Ligier de la Garde, Madame Deshoulières (1638–94)[6] wrote to entertain and met with considerable critical and financial success. Their works reflect the political intrigues of the time, and sometimes highlight the problematic character of arranged marriage; they implicitly criticise the enforced confinement of women, or religious intolerance, and are often philosophically informed. They continue the trend, begun by Madeleine de Scudéry, of using the past as a mirror for the present, and of introducing women into history by embellishing the recorded achievements of men with accounts of their loves and female friends.[7] Yet, although these works do reflect political issues, this is often implicit rather than explicit. The clearer didactic purpose of a Marguerite de Navarre or Madeleine de Scudéry is subsumed beneath a more immediate goal of entertainment and emotional engagement, or possibly more heavily masked in order to avoid Louis XIV's censorship.[8] And while a more extended treatment than we are able to offer could mine these fictions for their implicit political commentary, we leave the continuation of that project to future scholars.

Many members of this generation of French women, who began to write after Madeleine de Scudéry, appear to have taken to heart her model

d'Angleterre (Paris: Chavaray Frères, 1882), *Histoire de la princesse de Montpensier*, ed. Micheline Cuénin (Geneva: Droz, 1979), and *Oeuvres de Madame de Lafayette* (Paris: Chardon, 1786).
[4] Her works include *Relation du voyage d'Espagne* (Paris: Claude Barbin, 1691); *Nouvelles espagnolles* (Paris: Claude Barbin, 1692); *Nouvelles ou Mémoires historiques* (Paris: Claude Barbin, 1693); *Les Mémoires de la cour d'Angleterre* (Paris: Claude Barbin, 1695); Marie-Catherine baronne d'Aulnoy, *Mémoires secrets de Mr L. D. D. O., ou Les avantures comiques de plusieurs grands princes de la cour de France* (Paris: J. Bredou, 1696); Marie-Catherine baronne d'Aulnoy, *Les Illustres Fées, contes galans* (Paris: M.-M. Brunet, 1698); *Le Comte de Warwick* (Amsterdam: Desbordes, 1704); *L'Histoire d'Hypolite comte de Duglas*, ed. Shirley Day Jones (Somerset: Castle Cary Press, 1994); Marie-Catherine baronne d'Aulnoy, *Contes I*, ed. Philippe Hourcade (Paris: Société des Textes Français Modernes, 1997); and *Contes II*, ed. Philippe Hourcade (Paris: Société des Textes Français Modernes, 1998). For a discussion of the political aspects of d'Aulnoy's fiction, see Anne E. Duggan, *Salonnières, Furies and Fairies: The Politics of Gender and Cultural Change in Absolutist France* (Newark: University of Delaware Press, 2005), pp. 165–200.
[5] Micheline Cuénin, *Madame de Villedieu: Marie-Catherine Desjardins 1640–1683* (Paris: Champion, 1979); Marie-Catherine-Hortense de (Mlle Desjardins) Villedieu, *Œuvres complètes* (Geneva: Slatkine Reprints, 1971), *Memoirs of the Life of Henriette-Sylvie de Molière*, trans. Donna Kuizenga (Chicago and London: Chicago University Press, 2004), and *Selected Writings of Madame de Villedieu*, ed. Nancy Deighton Klein (New York: Peter Lang, 1995).
[6] For an account of Mme Deshoulières's philosophical poetry, see Conley, *Suspicion of Virtue*, pp. 45–74.
[7] This is particularly true of Madame de Villedieu: see Faith E. Beasley, *Revising Memory: Women's Fiction and Memoirs in Seventeenth-Century France* (New Brunswick: Rutgers University Press, 1990), pp. 162–89.
[8] Duggan, *Salonnières, Furies and Fairies*, p. 167.

of engagement in polite society. She had made Sappho pronounce an ideal of an educated but sociable woman, whose learning facilitated polite and engaging conversation and tender friendship, but who kept away from political intrigue, leaving the direction of the state to the monarch and his agents. This was an attitude that also suited the political reality that existed in France. Madame de Sablé, for example, is described in the introduction to her *Maxims*, published in the year of her death, as having, 'discovered so well how to perfectly combine all the virtues of civil society with the Christian virtues that she was equally respected by recluses and socialites'.[9] She had brought politeness to its highest possible point of perfection and her *Maxims* are 'admirable advice as to how to behave in society'.[10] These *Maxims* show an acute awareness of human foibles, and offer good advice on how to accommodate oneself to social circumstances. It is evident, when she gives advice such as the following, that she understands the personal politics of managing people:

When important people wish to make one believe that they have some good quality which they lack, it is dangerous to make it clear that one doubts them. For, by removing the hope that they might trick the eyes of the world, one removes, as well, their desire to act in conformity with the good qualities that they pretend to possess.

However, Madame de Sablé does not comment on political principles, structures or theories.

It is hardly surprising that Madame de Maintenon, born as Françoise d'Aubigné and famous for her secret marriage to Louis XIV, said nothing politically contentious. Nevertheless she was an important educational innovator, who subscribed to the view that education is necessary for the development of the virtues, established the college of St Cyr for poor aristocratic girls, and emphasised the need to teach through conversation and dialogue. She espouses a kind of practical Christianity that values duty and hard work, believing that women from different classes should be given an appropriate education for the social function they were to perform.[11]

---

[9] Sablé, *Maximes*, p. 6. [10] Ibid., pp. 6, 8.
[11] Françoise d'Aubigné, Marquise de Maintenon, *Lettres sur l'éducation des filles*, ed. Théophile Lavallée (Paris: Charpentier, 1854); *Entretiens sur l'éducation des filles*, ed. Théophile Lavallée (Paris: Charpentier, 1854); *Lettres historiques et édifiantes*, ed. Théophile Lavallée, 2 vols. (Paris: 1856); *Conseils aux demoiselles pour leur conduite dans le monde*, ed. Théophile Lavallée (Paris: Charpentier, 1857); *Madame de Maintenon, extraits de ses lettres, avis*, ed. Octave Gréard (Paris: Hachette, 1884); *Comment la sagesse vient aux filles*, ed. Pierre-E. Leroy and Marcel Loyau (Paris: Bartillat, 1998); and *Dialogues and Addresses*, trans. John J. Conley (Chicago and London: Chicago University Press, 2004).

The education she offered was designed to form virtuous women who were not arrogant or vain and who practised the cardinal virtues, in particular temperance. Although she has been unfairly accused of encouraging Louis XIV's decision to revoke the Edict of Nantes in 1685, one searches her letters in vain for any discussion either for or against religious toleration.[12]

Among the moral maxims and letters published by women, one might expect that at least those published by the ex-queen Christina of Sweden would contain some political reflections.[13] And, up to a point, one is not disappointed. In a letter written in 1686, she expresses her pity for the Huguenots who were being persecuted in France: 'I regret that these unhappy creatures are born into error, but it seems to me that they are more worthy of our pity than hatred.'[14] She goes on to offer pragmatic reasons for not persecuting them, for those who harbour hidden heresies are likely to be a dangerous source of future trouble. Yet, though Christina also supports tolerating the Jews, and does reflect on the position and virtues of a prince, she does not advance any distinctively new political ideas.

From our point of view, one of the more interesting, though disheartening, features of Christina's *L'Ouvrage du loisir*, the longer of her two collections of maxims, is the way in which they reveal her equivocal attitude to her own status as a female ruler. Despite having been brought up to govern, and having been amply informed concerning the history of Elizabeth I, who confirmed Justus Lipsius' claim that women could be possessed of the virtues required of a prince, Christina abdicated from her throne in 1654, officially converted from Lutheranism to Catholicism in 1656, and ended her life a rather isolated figure, surrounded by paintings and manuscripts, but without great power, in a palazzo in Rome.[15]

---

[12] See Jean-Christian Petitfils, *Louis XIV* (Paris: Perrin, 1997), p. 478.
[13] Christina called her collections of maxims *Les Sentiments* and *L'Ouvrage du loisir*. They are reprinted in Christina, Queen of Sweden, *Apologies*, ed. Jean-François de Raymond (Paris: Editions du Cerf, 1994). The second was originally published in her *Mémoires*, and translated into English as *The Works of Christina Queen of Sweden. Containing Maxims and Sentences, In Twelve Centuries; and Reflections on the Life and Actions of Alexander the Great* (London: Wilson and Durham, 1753).
[14] *Mémoires concernant Christine, reine de Suède*, ed. Johan Arckenholtz, 4 vols. (Amsterdam: Pierre Mortier, 1751), vol. IV, p. 231.
[15] For Christina's education, which included William Camden's history of Elizabeth, see M. L. Clarke, 'The Making of a Queen: The Education of Christina of Sweden', *History Today* 28 (1978), 228–35; and Susanna Åkerman, 'Kristina Wasa, Queen of Sweden', in *A History of Women Philosophers*, ed. Mary Ellen Waithe (Dordrecht: Kluwer Academic Publishers, 1991), pp. 21–40. For the view that some women have the virtues of a ruler, see Justus Lipsius, *Six Bookes of Politickes or Civil Doctrine. Done into English by William Iones [London 1594]* (Amsterdam: Da Capo Press, 1970), II.17–20.

Various interpretations of her motives for giving up her throne have been offered, perhaps none of them entirely satisfactory, but we shall largely limit our discussion to her own self-representation through her collections of maxims and letters.[16]

Christina composed her maxims relatively late in her life, that is to say between 1666 and 1680 when she reached the age of fifty-four. *L'Ouvrage du loisir* was published in 1751 by Arckenholtz and translated into English two years later.[17] Her maxims are difficult to interpret, since sometimes opposing ideas are displayed sequentially. Nevertheless, they provide some evidence that, by late in life, Christina believed that women were not capable of ruling. Moreover, her biography shows that she thought of herself as unfeminine and ascribed what capacity to rule she possessed to her 'masculinity'.[18]

L'Ouvrage du loisir was divided by Arckenholtz into twelve sections, called 'Centuries', each containing one hundred short observations. The seventh 'century' begins with some comments on peace or tranquillity. The first is 'Tranquillity is a good, which consoles us for everything.'[19] The third sentence suggests that political calm is included in the tranquillity intended, for it tells us that 'Severe punishment of leaders, and a general pardon of the rest, are the proper remedies for rebellions.'[20] Next, a few reflections on the giving and receiving of presents are followed by remarks which appear to be a reflection on Anne of Austria and the Fronde: "'Tis a false politick in princes to approve of everything their ministers do, whether good or bad, and the effect of their weakness and idleness; or rather it proceeds from a false principle of looking upon themselves as infallible in their choice."[21] This is followed by a few more reflections on ministers, lying, beauty, and marital infidelity, and then a series of comments which are quite depressing for anyone who might hope to find progress in women's political attitudes as one advances through the centuries. Christina asserts in quick succession:

---

[16] For a sense of the diversity of the interpretations of Christina's motives in abdicating, see Susanna Åkerman, *Queen Christina of Sweden and Her Circle: The Transformation of a Seventeenth-Century Philosophical Libertine* (Leiden: E. J. Brill, 1991), pp. 4–13.

[17] Christina, *Mémoires*, vol. IV. For a discussion of the theme of dissimulation, see Monica Setterwall, 'Queen Christina and Role Playing in Maxim Form', *Scandinavian Studies* 57 (1985), 162–73.

[18] Christina, *Apologies*, pp. 121–2; Veronica Buckley, *Christina, Queen of Sweden* (London: Harper Perennial, 2005), p. 74.

[19] *Works of Christina*, p. 61; *Mémoires*, vol. IV, p. 25.

[20] *Works of Christina*, p. 61; *Mémoires*, vol. IV, p. 26.

[21] *Works of Christina*, p. 62; *Mémoires*, vol. IV, p. 26.

25. The Salick law, which excludes women from the throne, is just.
26. The female sex is a great obstacle to reigning well.
27. If there has been in former times queens that have reign'd gloriously, as Semiramis, Nitocris, Zenobia and others, these instances are so rare, that we ought not to reckon upon such prodigies.
28. It is true that the soul is of no sex.
29. The weaknesses of the female sex do not always interest the soul.
30. Temperament and education make all the difference that is observ'd between the sexes.
31. From the birth to the death of princes people labour only to spoil them.[22]

So, while Christina does seem to admit that women and men have in common a soul that has no sex, she also accepts that the female sex is an impediment to government. It is a disadvantage of the maxim form that it does not offer any clear explanations or arguments, and so one is forced to attempt to reconstruct Christina's reasons for these views on the basis of thoughts that she expresses elsewhere. Her autobiography is a little more forthcoming. She makes it a mark of her father's good sense that he denied the regency to her mother, and claims that none of the women whose reigns she experienced was any more capable of governing well than her mother had been.[23] These are, we argue, mature views, which do not correspond to the ideas that she earlier expressed in her letters, and they appear to constitute a critique of her former self and justification of her abdication and retreat from politics.

One can read Christina's maxims overall as an attempt at self-justification, as is implied by Jean-François de Raymond's decision to publish them with the title *Apologies*. She begins the longer collection thus:

1. We ought to forget what is past; bear or enjoy the present; and resign ourselves to what is to come.
2. We ought to harbour nothing in the heart, that may prove shameful to it.
3. Merit is of greater worth than thrones and fortune.
4. Thrones are not worthy of being purchased at the price of crimes.[24]

Since in the tenth 'century' Christina asserts the validity of the Catholic faith, one is led to conclude that she was forced to abdicate in order to avoid continuing in her crime of Protestantism. Her short account of her own life backs up this interpretation, for she writes to thank God for

---

[22] *Works of Christina*, pp. 63–4; *Mémoires*, vol. IV, p. 26. A slightly different version is provided in *Apologies*, pp. 229–32. It is no more complimentary to women.
[23] *Apologies*, pp. 135–6.   [24] *Works of Christina*, p. 1; *Mémoires*, vol. IV, p. 1.

having made her strong enough to overcome her passions and ambition in order to love and serve Him.[25] Added to this self-justification is the consolation that as a woman she was not properly equipped for the role of a prince, and she hints, moreover, that the role itself is not as desirable as it seems: 'If people knew the duty of princes, they would less desire to be such.'[26] Perhaps this is all sour grapes. Or perhaps it was easier for Christina to blame her own failings on her sex than her individual mistakes. Whatever the cause, Christina seems to have ended her life in a spirit of resignation which questions the worth of glory. In the twelfth 'century' of her collection she asserts that self-knowledge brings misery:

41. The famous maxim, Know thy self, which some would make the source of all human wisdom, is only the source of human misery.
42. That irrevocable decree imposed upon mankind the hard necessity of knowing their own worthlessness, and of not being able to disguise themselves to themselves.[27]

And Christina concludes with the remark: 'This is the work of one, who desires nothing of, fears nothing from, and imposes nothing on, any mortal.'[28] One is left with a sense of a person who, having lost power, is attempting to make a virtue out of her lack of power, by questioning whether it is power to which one ought to aspire. Indeed, Christina comments elsewhere, referring to her abdication and making a virtue of her capacity to renounce power, 'Glory was hers because she put under her feet what other monarchs place on their heads.'[29] However, if this was Christina's mature attitude, it was not apparently the attitude of her younger self but was perhaps born out of the disappointment of grandiose dreams.

Almost thirty years earlier Christina had appeared to be the embodiment of the *femme forte*, and there is some evidence that she had dreamed of exercising an imperial power greater than any previous woman.[30] When she visited France soon after her abdication, she wore short 'masculine' skirts and sensible boots, and bemused the ladies of the French court with her strange rough ways. She was then representing herself as the epitome of the strong, ambitious, and masculine woman that Madeleine de Scudéry

---

[25] *Apologies*, pp. 126–7.   [26] *Works of Christina*, p. 4; *Mémoires*, vol. iv, p. 2.
[27] *Works of Christina*, p. 125; *Mémoires*, vol. iv, p. 50.
[28] *Works of Christina*, p. 129; *Mémoires*, vol. iv, p. 52.
[29] Quoted by Setterwall, 'Queen Christina', 163.
[30] The idea that Christina imagined herself as fulfilling some version of the imperial prophecies is proposed in Åkerman, *Queen Christina of Sweden*.

opposed. Georges de Scudéry, by contrast, wrote a long heroic poem which he dedicated to Christina, and here we find considerable divergence between Madeleine's views and her brother's.

After the Fronde, Madeleine and Georges de Scudéry parted ways, as did their literary productions. Georges was forced to leave Paris, terminating the siblings' collaboration. The year of Christina of Sweden's abdication, 1654, was both the year that the first volume of *Clélie* appeared and the year that Georges's heroic poem, *Alaric, ou Rome vaincue*, dedicated to Christina, was published.[31] It is tempting, given the historical circumstances, to read Madeleine's Tullie, the ambitious princess who rode heartlessly over her father's dead body, as a figure of Christina, and it is also quite clear that Georges intends the Gothic king Alaric to be read as a representation of the Swedish queen. Georges invites the reader to interpret his poem allegorically, reading Alaric as man's soul, while his wife Amalasonthe (who opposes his quest to conquer Rome) as the temptations of the flesh. Alaric, by his victory over Rome, signifies the victory of reason over the senses.[32] Thus, Georges structures his allegory in accordance with the well-worn association of masculine spirit and feminine flesh. In inviting Christina to identify herself with his hero, Alaric, Georges invites this 'belle Reine Amazone' to interpret her own history according to this structure. She should follow her rational and masculine side in order to conquer Rome as her 'ancestor' had done. And there is some evidence that she in fact did leave Sweden with the intention of conquering a greater prize.[33] Susanna Åkerman has suggested that Christina abdicated because she hoped to fulfil the old prophecies of a universal Christian emperor who would unite Christendom.[34] And in Georges de Scudéry's poem we find this promise voiced by the sibyl.

Could Christina really have thought that she, like Alaric, would conquer Rome and become a new emperor, a new all-conquering Alexander? She certainly took on Alexander's name and took him as her hero.[35] And in *L'Ouvrage du loisir* she comments (IX.15): 'When I reflect upon the present state of our part of Europe, I cannot comprehend upon what foundation those beautiful hopes were built, which some have entertain'd of the total destruction of the Ottoman empire.'[36] A sentiment which

---

[31] Georges de Scudéry, *Alaric ou Rome vaincue*, ed. Cristina Bernazzoli (Fasano: Schena-Didier Erudition, 1998).

[32] Ibid., p. 100.   [33] Ibid., pp. 89 and 123.

[34] Åkerman, *Queen Christina of Sweden*, pp. 196–224.

[35] She wrote a laudatory and completely uncritical biography of Alexander which is included in Christina, *Mémoires*.   [36] *Apologies*, p. 258.

suggests that she was, at least in the past, party to these 'beautiful hopes,' which she now finds incomprehensible.

Whatever the reality of Christina's aspirations and whatever the much-disputed truth behind her abdication, at the end of her life she chose a life more in accordance with the ideals that Madeleine de Scudéry had put into Sappho's mouth than with those attributed to her by Georges. Like Sappho, Christina expressed a dislike of marriage and sex, and echoed the conclusion of the story of Sappho, that they are incompatible with love.[37] She thanked God for having preserved her from marriage by having made her love Him more than any pleasure she might have found in marriage.[38] The academies which she set up to discuss philosophical questions had something of the character of a salon. Her life conforms to Madeleine de Scudéry's rejection of political ambition in women, also implicit in the works of other women from this period. One apparent exception, how-ever, is found in the work of the little-known writer Gabrielle Suchon (1631–1703), who argues at some length that queens have governed just as well as kings. Suchon's aspirations are not limited to queens, for her examples can be read as proposing political authority for ordinary women, through access to both ecclesiastical and secular power.[39] Suchon would nevertheless have approved of Christina's choice not to marry, since she believed that it is virtually impossible for women who are not single to attain complete liberty.

While the Renaissance women whom we have studied organised their political ideas around notions of virtue, and while virtue was still important in the seventeenth century, in Suchon's writing it cedes first place to liberty, its nature, and how it ought to be realised by women. Virtue, the central concept of an earlier Aristotelian or Stoic way of thinking, gives way to freedom, though the sources for Suchon's dis-cussion of liberty hardly differ from those which ground the virtues tradition. Her transformation of the reading of these texts is mediated by the fact that liberty comes to be recognised as a precondition for virtue. The qualities which the ancients ascribed to virtue are attributed by Suchon to liberty, which she deems the origin of virtue.[40] In the remainder of this chapter we will examine the way in which these themes are developed in her two published works, the *Traité de la Morale & de la Politique*

---

[37] Ibid., p. 203. See Madeleine de Scudéry, *Artamène, ou le grand Cyrus*, vol. X, p. 607.
[38] Christina, *Apologies*, pp. 126–7.
[39] Gabrielle Suchon, *Traité de la Morale & de la Politique, divisé en trois parties*, 3 vols. (Lyon: B. Vignien, 1693), vol. III, pp. 35–67.
[40] Ibid., vol. I, p. 176.

(On Morality and Politics) (1693) and *Traité du Célibat volontaire* (On Voluntary Single Life) (1700).[41]

Until quite recently Suchon's works were almost entirely forgotten, and this is not really surprising, since her style is laborious, scholastic, and excessively long-winded.[42] Her works are philosophical treatises, carefully constructed to defend her conclusions, using the best established authorities and methods. Yet she reads these authorities differently, so that from sources almost identical to those cited by Christine de Pizan three hundred years earlier she hints at surprisingly modern conclusions. While Suchon works hard to demonstrate her Catholic orthodoxy, she uses an orthodox starting point to draw clear conclusions concerning women's right to an education and right to exercise political and religious authority. Nevertheless even she does not completely challenge the appropriateness of women's subjection in marriage. Tellingly, the third part of her 'On Morality and Politics' is subtitled 'Of Authority'. 'Women can participate in it without leaving behind the submission that they owe to those of the first sex.' Suchon does, however, interpret the Bible as implying that men have obligations to their wives, which, if they are not fulfilled, can justify divorce, and she asserts, in particular, that both sexes should have a right to divorce in the case of adultery.[43] Yet as we will see, though she offers many arguments for the injustice of women's submission, she cannot bring herself, whether from fear of censorship, or genuine Christian humility, to advocate the justice of rebellion.

Gabrielle Suchon came from a well-to-do family and was born in Burgundy. Like Arcangela Tarabotti, she entered a convent, but became disaffected with convent life. Unlike Tarabotti, she left no biography, so we cannot be sure whether she was originally forced into a convent by her family, though this is quite possible. It is equally possible that she chose her vocation while young and later regretted it, for she condemns the

[41] *Traité de la Morale*; and Gabrielle Suchon, *Traité du Célibat volontaire, ou la Vie sans engagement*, 2 vols. (Paris: J. and Mich. Guinard, 1700).
[42] Her recent rediscovery is largely due to Sonia Bertolini, 'Gabrielle Suchon: une vie sans engagement?', *Australian Journal of French Studies* 37 (2000), 289–308. Bertolini acknowledges the earlier work of Pierre Ronzeaud, 'La femme au pouvoir ou le monde à l'envers', *Dix-Septième Siècle* 108 (1975), 9–33, and others. See also Michèle Le Dœuff, *Le Sexe du savoir* (Paris: Aubier, 1998), which is available in English as *The Sex of Knowing*, trans. Kathryn Hamer and Lorraine Code (New York and London: Routledge, 2003), pp. 34–42, 'Gabrielle Suchon', in *The Routledge Encyclopedia of Philosophy*, ed. Edward Craig, 10 vols. (London and New York: Routledge, 1998), vol. 9, pp. 211–13; 'Feminism is Back in France, or Is It?', *Hypatia* 15 (2000), 243–55; and Wallace Kirsop, 'Gabrielle Suchon et ses librairies: une note complémentaire', *Australian Journal of French Studies* 37 (2000), 309–11.
[43] Suchon, *Traité de la Morale*, vol. 1, pp. 26–7.

practice of allowing the immature to commit themselves.[44] She attempted to get the Pope to release her from her vows and had some success, yet she was legally required to return to her monastery, an order which she appears to have disobeyed.[45] It is therefore not surprising that her political works praise liberty as the quality that makes us distinctively human, and argue for women's right to live a 'vie sans engagement' (an uncommitted life) which she equates with voluntary celibacy.

Like Tarabotti, Suchon bases her arguments on the orthodox Catholic view that it is free will which makes us human, and she bases her demand for the right to lead a life free from constraint on our nature as free, rational beings. Her condemnation of the practice of enforced claustration is highly reminiscent of Tarabotti's, for she laments 'the hardheartedness of those cruel parents who often uselessly sacrifice their children, and through a misguided or malicious zeal condemn them to things which are beyond their capacity and which will cause their perdition'.[46] Basing her argument on St Paul, Suchon insists that 'in man, liberty is a natural right'.[47] And she infers the consequence that we should be free to choose a profession to which our capacities and dispositions suit us. She adds to this the observation that, in order to be genuinely free, the choice of a vocation, or the choice of a marriage partner, ought not to be made until one is sufficiently mature.[48] It is easy to overlook how radical her assertions are on these matters, for we have forgotten that until the eighteenth century, parents' right to determine whom, and whether, their offspring should marry was seldom challenged. Although consent was officially upheld by the church, as Suchon reminds her reader, it was generally understood to be simply consent to one's parents' choices, and in the light of the obedience one owed them, it was not necessarily voluntary, as Marguerite de Navarre's attitude to her daughter's marriage made clear.

The first volume of Suchon's treatise concerns liberty, with which she deals at length, and it is clear from the definitions that she provides that for her, liberty is what we would now call 'rational autonomy'. In order to have absolute freedom one requires well-educated reason, freedom from external constraint, and a certain strength, or at least lack of timidity.[49] But few individuals are absolutely free, and many social conditions involve servitude. Because human nature is to be free, servitude is the greatest ill.[50] Yet one does not lose one's natural freedom even in a state of

[44] Ibid., pp. 22–32.   [45] Bertolini, 'Gabrielle Suchon', 292.
[46] Suchon, *Traité de la Morale*, vol. 1, p. 129.   [47] Ibid., p. 23.   [48] Ibid., pp. 22–32.
[49] Ibid., pp. 12–13.   [50] Ibid., p. 17.

servitude, nor does one lose the desire for liberty.[51] There are many kinds of servitude, according to Suchon, including, most commonly, poverty, and the reader catches the voice of experience in a passage in which she calls poverty the greatest misery, a domestic captivity accompanied by disdain, abandonment, and insecurity.[52]

Suchon's discussion of liberty vacillates between the external conditions necessary for liberty and its internal character. She spends two chapters arguing that in order fully to exercise one's liberty one needs freedom of movement, that is, freedom to travel and to enlarge the mind.[53] But she then turns to what she calls 'liberté d'esprit' (freedom of the soul or spirit) by which she means disengagement from material things.[54] She insists that the truly free spirit can raise itself above petty fortune, yet her praise of Diogenes the Cynic seems somewhat inconsistent with her earlier condemnation of poverty.[55] Like the much later existentialists, Suchon takes liberty to be both a metaphysical state essential to every human being – a free capacity to choose between good and evil – and a social condition which is valuable because it allows the exercise of our fundamental essence. Since we cannot be deprived of our essence, one might wonder why we need certain social conditions to express it, but following a logic that was to become well entrenched after her death, Suchon's critique of servitude implies that since we are metaphysically free, we ought to be socially free to exercise that freedom. Unlike the existentialists, however, she has no doubt that there is an objective moral truth that can be known, and that the perfection of our freedom resides in the free choice of the moral good. Social freedom is not necessary in order to enable us to choose, but in order to enable us to live a life that offers us the opportunity of judging correctly, on the basis of our own reason, what is good, and of freely and autonomously acting on that judgement. Nevertheless, Suchon in fact spends far more time discussing the inner preconditions of freedom – 'liberté d'esprit' (freedom of the soul), 'liberté du cœur' (freedom of the heart), and 'liberté de conscience' (freedom of conscience [from sin]) – than the outer conditions.

Freedom of the heart, as Suchon conceives it, is freedom from the love of all creatures, which is replaced by a total love of the Creator. Thus, like her freedom of spirit, it is a form of detachment from passion and worldly

---

[51] Ibid., pp. 19, 123.   [52] Ibid., p. 21.
[53] Ibid., pp. 32–46.   [54] Ibid., pp. 46–64. Suchon uses 'l'esprit' and 'l'âme' interchangeably.
[55] Ibid., p. 53.

desire.[56] Freedom of conscience is freedom from sin. No one with a bad conscience can be free, for such a person will be full of self-hate and remorse.[57] Clearly, a good conscience is an inner state. However, Suchon explains that a person who is not suited to a certain social role may be tempted by that role into sin; thus the freedom to choose a life that suits one's capacities is an important precondition for avoiding sin.[58] Tranquillity and joy are the reward of the complete inner freedom of the spirit, heart, and conscience that Suchon sets out as the ideal liberty, which she finds in Christianity and Stoicism alike.[59] Yet, unlike the Stoics, and unlike Mary Astell, whose views we examine in the next chapter, Suchon does not think that external constraint is compatible with inner freedom. Rather she sees external constraint as an evil which prevents us from exercising our liberty to its full extent.

Suchon's reasoning seems to be that our love of liberty causes us to be angered and upset by constraint, and so constraint gets in the way of the attainment of full moral freedom and the tranquillity and happiness that are its reward:

Among all the sentiments natural to man, none is more pertinent than the love of liberty; and also none is more troubling than fear of constraint: and one cannot deny that there is no more legitimate passion than this, which makes us hate everything which could deprive us of the first and threaten us with the other.[60]

Suchon understands by a state of constraint a state which is not freely chosen. Thus the cloister is a state of constraint for anyone who does not have a true vocation.[61] And marriage is a state of constraint if one enters it for reasons of ambition, greed, or sexual desire, rather than out of a desire to please God, who has destined some people for this state.[62] Suchon also makes it clear that marriage is a state which she believes few rational women would choose voluntarily. While young they would judge themselves too immature to make such a demanding choice; once old, too feeble to take on its physical challenges.[63] But here her orthodox Christianity does lead her to equivocate. Marriage is a blessed institution of the church, and she does not want to persuade all women against marrying.[64] However, she wants women to have the same opportunities to realise their liberty as are offered to men.

[56] Ibid., pp. 65–79.   [57] Ibid., pp. 82–3.   [58] Ibid., p. 94.   [59] Ibid., pp. 110–17.
[60] Ibid., p. 123.   [61] Ibid., p. 127.   [62] Ibid., p. 141.   [63] Ibid., p. 144.
[64] Ibid., pp. 140, 145.

Because of its inner and outer aspects, the liberty that Suchon espouses is not the unrestricted freedom of modern liberalism, though it is no doubt one of its precursors. She explicitly distinguishes liberty from libertinage: 'liberty is a fertile mother who gives birth to all the virtues, while libertinage is the deadly father who produces vice and voluptuousness'.[65]

Liberty is rational autonomy, constraint is opposed to autonomy, but libertinage is opposed to rationality: 'reason is a natural light given to man by God to lead him along all his ways; the freedom which always follows the direction of this wise governess finds its perfection and merit in the just rules that she inspires'.[66] Thus, perhaps more consistently than a liberal like John Stuart Mill, who also argued that social liberty is a good because it allows us to discover what is genuinely good, Suchon can claim that freedom from constraint will lead us to virtue, because our God-given reason will enable us to discover the moral truth and willingly follow it.[67]

Suchon punctuates her discussion of freedom in general with passages, usually at the conclusion of a chapter, which assert that women are as capable as men of achieving all the forms of liberty, knowledge, and authority that she outlines in the three volumes of 'On Morality and Politics'. Her argument is usually by example, and the exemplars from the old *querelle des femmes* re-emerge as cases of women who have exercised their freedom, achieved wisdom, and exercised authority. The Queen of Sheba and Jerome's disciple, Pauline, are examples of women who have travelled, while others show that women have freedom of spirit and the heart. Saint Catherine is introduced to show how knowledge in women is persecuted. The sibyls demonstrate that women can achieve wisdom, and the Amazons that they are capable of government.[68] Since women are capable of exercising true liberty, the constraints on their lives which prevent them from achieving it are inimical to their well-being.

The second volume turns to wisdom, arguing that women's want of education and knowledge is equally harmful, and causes their vanity, self-love, greed, and worldliness.[69] Since universities and colleges are closed to women, and since Suchon suspects that mingling with male students would corrupt women's morals, she advocates private study in the home; thus she places the onus for obtaining an education on women, whom she calls on to improve themselves, and her demands are not very radical.

---

[65] Ibid., p. 176.   [66] Ibid.   [67] Mill, *On Liberty.*
[68] Suchon, *Traité de la Morale*, vol. I, pp. 59, 78, 118–19; vol. II, pp. 25, 41–3; vol. III, pp. 42, 55–6.
[69] Ibid., vol. II, pp. 24, 195–225.

It is in her third book, where she discusses authority, that she can be read as proposing a model of justice between the sexes which would have had radical consequences, had it been taken up.

According to Suchon, temporal power derives from God: 'worldly monarchies and sovereignties are the works of divine institution'.[70] Moreover the rise and fall of temporal powers is due to Him, as the history of Nebuchadnezzar shows. And as Jesus said, we should obey the temporal powers. However, from these altogether traditional precepts, Suchon derives quite unusual consequences concerning women's right to authority:

> But if one comes to consider that God is the author of both the ecclesiastic and secular hierarchies which make up government, one would not have the slightest doubt that authority is both an honour and a good, nor that those who possess it are more evidently images of the divine power than the rest of men. Which is why women and maidens who are deprived of it cannot but take this privation as disadvantageous to their sex.[71]

This is the first time we have encountered an explicit attempt to ground a claim that it would be just for women to participate in political authority, given that they are created in the image of God. For Suchon, women are deprived of their right to demonstrate their participation in God's power by being excluded from temporal and ecclesiastical authority. She goes on to insist that God gave dominion over the animals, fishes, and birds to both men and women, and commanded both Adam and Eve to go forth and populate and subdue the earth. In the *Two Treatises of Government*, Locke argues as a kind of *reductio* against Robert Filmer that if political authority was invested in Adam as the first parent, it ought to be ascribed to mothers as well as fathers, as the parents of families.[72] Suchon, like Filmer, accepts that political authority derives from God, but reads Genesis as investing both men and women, since equally made in God's image, with authority over the things of the earth. Therefore men have usurped women's legitimate authority, and, she asserts, they deprive them of freedom and knowledge in order to prevent them from exercising the authority which is their due. Women are perfectly capable of governing, since they are equal to men with regard to the capacity for reason and good sense, which are necessary for good government.[73] She emphasises

[70] Ibid., vol. III, pp. 1–2.   [71] Ibid., p. 7.
[72] Locke, *Two Treatises of Government*, pp. 287–8. See also Green, *The Woman of Reason*, pp. 61–2.
[73] Suchon, *Traité de la Morale*, vol. III, pp. 11–12, 61, 86, 136.

the importance of the maintenance of peace, and cites as a virtue of women as governors that women are naturally peace-loving and merciful.[74] In this context, she shows that she knows François Poullain de la Barre's arguments for the equality of the sexes, and she takes from him the thought that we often mistake custom for nature, so that if it were customary to see women occupying the offices only open to men, no one would find it surprising.[75]

Suchon claims that in order for human beings to live together under a single law there must be some sovereign power to conserve their unity. However, she does not take this to rule out republics as sound governments, and some of the things she says suggest that she imagines the possibility of an egalitarian republic in which men and women are bound by civic friendship. This would for her be just one form of good government, for she explicitly disagrees with the universalist cosmopolitanism of the Stoics, arguing that different kinds of government suit different nations, and there is beauty in diversity.[76] Nevertheless, she claims that 'concord, conversation and friendship are the only marks of a true society'.[77] And, she says, one can hardly deny that women contribute to peaceable sociability, agreeable conversation, and tender friendship.[78] She argues against those who say women are incapable of perfect friendship, suggesting that any failings in women's friendship and conversation come simply from their lack of education. And while she does not explicitly argue for a republican constitution, in which women vote, she quotes St Augustine as claiming that in ancient times, women cast their votes at Athenian public consultations, obviously approving of this lost practice.[79] She also shows herself generally committed to egalitarianism: 'Who does not know that friendship wishes equality in the distribution of worldly commodities, not being able to bear that its neighbours should suffer from scarcity?'[80] By implication, if men were women's friends, they would not suffer women to live in poverty.

On the question of ecclesiastical authority, Suchon's orthodoxy forces her to equivocate. Although she spends a long time arguing that women's dependence on men for spiritual guidance and confession is fraught with dangers and drawbacks, she does not fail to call Luther a scandalous heretic, in the same breath as she mentions that he thought women capable

---

[74] Ibid., p. 42.
[75] Ibid., p. 67; François Poullain de la Barre, *De l'égalité des deux sexes* (Paris: Jean du Puis, 1676).
[76] Suchon, *Traité de la Morale*, vol. III, p. 46.   [77] Ibid., p. 43.   [78] Ibid., p. 49.
[79] Ibid., p. 61.   [80] Ibid., p. 48.

of hearing confession and absolving sins.[81] So although she concludes her chapter on spiritual dependence with the assertion that 'women are not as devoid of the qualities necessary for the direction of souls as is claimed',[82] one is left somewhat unsure whether she is really intending to propose the ministry of women as allowed by Luther. Despite this equivocation, her general conclusion is that in regard to women 'one is obliged to agree that they suffer no failing which prevents them from reigning, governing, commanding, and leading other than that which is imposed on them by custom, the laws, and the absolute power of men.'[83] And this does seem to imply that women are unjustly excluded from being spiritual guides as well as temporal leaders.

In her later work, 'On Voluntary Single Life', Suchon appears to limit her aspirations. She confines herself to arguing that along with the cloister and marriage, a third kind of life, one of voluntary celibacy and lack of commitment, should be recognised as equally worthy of pursuit. Because of her orthodoxy, Suchon is unable to deny that within marriage women were justly dependent on men. And although she argues that men usurp far greater power over their wives than they are entitled to, her Christianity prevents her from completely rejecting the dominion of husbands over wives. Indeed, in one place she seems to make it a sign of women's virtue that they do not rebel against their husbands.[84] Under these circumstances it is only when single, and free from the constraints of the cloister, that women can exercise a fully independent rational autonomy, and so the single life comes to be defended as the only realistic path for women intent on fully developing their nature as free human beings. This aspiration – that women should at least have the option to remain single – is common to many of the seventeenth-century women whose works we have studied, from Moderata Fonte to Mary Astell. While Suchon argues at length that women are unjustly deprived of political, ecclesiastic, and domestic authority, she explicitly abjures any intention of encouraging women to aspire to acquire them, citing the ubiquitous passage from Peter 2.13 which teaches us to submit to any man who has power over us.[85] If we take her to be here genuinely advocating acceptance of even an unjust servitude, rather than dissimulating for the sake of the censors, this passage brings her political philosophy very much in line with that of her English contemporary, Mary Astell. Nevertheless, in

---

[81] Ibid., p. 82.   [82] Ibid., p. 85.   [83] Ibid., p. 136.   [84] Ibid., p. 116.
[85] Suchon, Foreword to *Traité de la Morale*, vol. III.

ending her Foreword with a passage from the Psalms, and glorifying God's capacity to bring about miracles, Suchon, at the very least, calls on God to overthrow the unjust exclusion of women from their rightful heritage. For He 'can raise the poor man from the earth and place him at the level of the princes of his people, giving him the throne of glory and making him participate in his heritage'.

CHAPTER 12

Mary Astell

In 1700, the same year in which Gabrielle Suchon's *Du Célibat volontaire* ('On Voluntary Single Life') appeared on the continent, an English woman known only as 'Eugenia' issued 'A Plea for the just Liberty of the Tender Sex, and particularly of Married Women'.[1] In *The Female Advocate* (1700), Eugenia responds to the claim that a wife should not desire anything 'but what her husband approves of', asserting that

This is a Tyranny, I think, that extends farther than the most absolute Monarchs in the World; for if they can but fill their Gallies with slaves, and chain them fast to the Oar, they [i.e. the absolute Monarchs] seldom have so large a Conscience to expect they should take any great pleasure in their present Condition, and that the very *Desires of their Hearts* should strike an Harmony with the clattering Music of their Fetters.[2]

Like Suchon, Eugenia claims that if women cannot have freedom in their thoughts, and enjoy 'the Liberty of Rational Creatures', then they are certainly 'very Slaves'.[3] In her Preface, she urges English women to fill their minds with true knowledge and to follow the example of 'French *Ladies*', as well as a lady known only as '*Mr* Norris's *Correspondent*'.[4] The English woman to whom Eugenia refers is Mary Astell (1666–1731),[5] now one of the better-known female figures in the history of political thought. In 1694, Astell established a feminist reputation with her *Serious Proposal to the Ladies*, a call for an academic institute for unmarried women; in 1700 she wrote a scathing attack on marriage titled *Some Reflections upon Marriage*. In this chapter, we discuss Astell's political arguments in relation to the thought of her famous contemporary, John Locke (1632–1704).

---

[1] 'Eugenia', *The Female Advocate*.   [2] Ibid., p. 28.   [3] Ibid., pp. 49 and 41.   [4] Ibid., p. vii.
[5] For the Astell–Norris correspondence, see [Mary Astell and] John Norris, *Letters Concerning the Love of God, Between the Author of the Proposal to the Ladies and Mr. John Norris* (London: J. Norris, 1695).

In the past decade or so, Patricia Springborg has revived Astell's status as a political commentator of note.[6] Among those who knew her, Astell enjoyed a reputation as a Tory pamphleteer, but in recent decades she has become better known as an early feminist[7] or a Cartesian philosopher.[8] To re-emphasise Astell's significance as a political writer, Springborg hails Astell as 'among the first systematic critics of Locke' and the author of 'one of the most important early critiques of his entire corpus'.[9] Among Astell scholars, Springborg's claims are somewhat contentious.[10] For one thing, it is unclear precisely in what sense Astell's critique is systematic: her explicit comments on Locke's ideas are relatively brief, and they are scattered throughout her works. There is no sustained treatment of Locke from the start to finish of a work, nor does Astell criticise all of his writings.[11] In terms of explicit political commentary, Astell has as much (if not more) to say about Niccolò Machiavelli, John Milton, and Thomas Hobbes.

To be fair to Springborg, Astell is a systematic critic of Locke to the extent that, when she does consider the political ideas of the *Two Treatises of Government* (1689), she regards his political, religious, and philosophical thought as a continuous whole. But while Springborg highlights the fact that Astell's opposition to Locke is motivated by distaste for Whig politics,[12] we propose to highlight the 'philosophy' rather than the 'politics' in Astell's political philosophy. We examine Astell's criticisms of

---

[6] Patricia Springborg, *Mary Astell* (Cambridge University Press, 2005); 'Republicanism, Freedom from Domination, and the Cambridge Contextual Historians', *Political Studies* 49 (2001), 851–76; 'Mary Astell, Critic of the Marriage Contract/Social Contract Analogue', in *A Companion to Early Modern Women's Writing*, ed. Anita Pacheco (London: Blackwell, 2002), pp. 216–28; 'Astell, Masham, and Locke: Religion and Politics', in Smith (ed.), *Women Writers*, pp. 105–25; 'Mary Astell and John Locke', in *The Cambridge Companion to English Literature, 1650 to 1750*, ed. Steven Zwicker (Cambridge University Press, 1998), pp. 276–306; and Patricia Springborg, 'Mary Astell (1666–1731), Critic of Locke', *American Political Science Review* 89 (1995), 621–33. See also Springborg's introduction to *Astell: Political Writings*, pp. xi–xxix.

[7] See e.g. Perry, *The Celebrated Mary Astell*.

[8] See Broad, *Women Philosophers of the Seventeenth Century*, pp. 90–113, and Jacqueline Broad, 'Astell, Cartesian Ethics, and the Critique of Custom', in *Mary Astell: Reason, Gender and Faith*, ed. William Kolbrener and Michal Michelson (Aldershot: Ashgate, 2007), pp. 165–79.

[9] Springborg, 'Mary Astell (1666–1731)', 621, and Springborg, *Mary Astell*, p. 3.

[10] See, for example, Mark Goldie, 'Mary Astell and John Locke', in Kolbrener and Michelson (eds.), *Mary Astell: Reason, Gender and Faith*, pp. 65–85; and Springborg's 'Reply to My Critics', *Mary Astell*, pp. 1–7.

[11] Astell explicitly addresses Locke's *Essay Concerning Human Understanding*, his *Reasonableness of Christianity*, the *Vindication of the Reasonableness of Christianity*, his *Third Reply* to Stillingfleet, and his *Two Treatises of Government*. Mark Goldie argues that Astell also knew Locke's *Paraphrase and Notes on the Epistles of St. Paul* ('Mary Astell and John Locke'). But Astell does not criticise Locke's *Letter Concerning Toleration* or his *Thoughts Concerning Education*.

[12] Springborg, 'Mary Astell (1666–1731)', 621–33.

Locke not in terms of their party political content, but in terms of a philosophical disagreement about what constitutes the self. This disagreement leads Astell to an alternative interpretation of Locke's 'fundamental law of nature', the proposition that the law of reason places upon all human beings an obligation to preserve 'God's Workmanship'. To demonstrate this, we shall situate Astell's critique of Locke in the context of her general political thought: in the context, that is, of her views about the foundations of political authority, and the concepts of the state of nature, political obedience, and the liberty of subjects.[13] In the second half of the chapter, we examine the implications of Astell's interpretation of Locke's 'fundamental law of nature' for her views about women and liberty; and we show that Astell's criticisms of male tyranny within marriage, like those of Suchon and Eugenia, are not as far-reaching as they might seem.

At first glance, then, Mary Astell would not appear to be an appropriate 'Enlightenment' figure with which to end our study of the history of women's political thought. As we will see, she is critical of religious toleration as a political ideal; she grounds her royalist arguments about political authority on biblical sources and religious principles; she promotes the idea of spiritual rather than political liberty; and she is fiercely opposed to popular sovereignty and the right of resistance – even in those cases in which one's ruler is an irreligious tyrant. Astell is certainly not representative of a steady progression toward modern political ideals, or toward liberalism and democracy in particular.

---

[13] For articles on Astell's politics (other than those of Springborg mentioned above), see Carol Barash, '"The Native Liberty . . . of the Subject": Configurations of Gender and Authority in the Works of Mary Chudleigh, Sarah Fyge Egerton, and Mary Astell', in *Women, Writing, History 1640–1740*, ed. Isobel Grundy and Susan Wiseman (London: Batsford, 1992), pp. 55–69; Gallagher, 'Embracing the Absolute'; Goldie, 'Mary Astell and John Locke', pp. 65–85; Van C. Hartmann, 'Tory Feminism in Mary Astell's *Bart'lemy Fair*', *The Journal of Narrative Technique* 28 (1998), 243–65; Kinnaird, 'Mary Astell and the Conservative Contribution to English Feminism'; William Kolbrener, ' "Forc'd into an Interest": High Church Politics and Feminine Agency in the Works of Mary Astell', *1650–1850: Ideas, Aesthetics, and Inquiries in the Early Modern Era* 10 (2004), 3–31; John McCrystal, 'Revolting Women: The Use of Revolutionary Discourse in Mary Astell and Mary Wollstonecraft Compared', *History of Political Thought* 14 (1993), 189–203; Ruth Perry, 'Mary Astell and the Feminist Critique of Possessive Individualism', *Eighteenth-Century Studies* 23 (1990), 444–57; Hilda L. Smith, '"Cry up Liberty": The Political Context of Mary Astell's Feminism', in Kolbrener and Michelson (eds.), *Mary Astell: Reason, Gender and Faith*, pp. 193–204; Kirstin Waters, 'Sources of Political Authority: John Locke and Mary Astell', in Waters (ed.), *Women and Men Political Theorists*, pp. 5–19; Rachel Weil, 'Mary Astell: The Marriage of Toryism and Feminism', in *Political Passions: Gender, the Family, and Political Argument in England, 1680–1714* (Manchester: Manchester University Press, 1999), pp. 142–59; Penny A. Weiss, 'Mary Astell: Including Women's Voices in Political Theory', *Hypatia* 19 (2004), 63–84; and Melinda Zook, 'Religious Nonconformity and the Problem of Dissent in the Works of Aphra Behn and Mary Astell', in Kolbrener and Michelson (eds.), *Mary Astell: Reason, Gender and Faith*, pp. 99–113.

Nevertheless, in previous chapters we have highlighted the ambiguous nature of women's discussions on political authority and political obedience in the seventeenth century. Unlike their medieval and Renaissance forebears, early modern women appear to use modern political concepts, such as liberty, equality, and the right of resistance – concepts that might provide the basis for a critique of the political subordination of women. When Eugenia observes that male tyranny 'extends farther than the most absolute Monarchs in the World', it is natural for the modern reader to suppose that she supports a woman's right to divorce or resist her husband's authority. But on closer inspection, these early modern concepts are not completely divorced from their religious meanings. While they might be the ancestors of our secular political concepts, they are not identical; and, in many cases, they have a greater affinity with ancient rather than modern ideas about government, especially with regard to the subject of virtue. In her writings on the subject of political obedience, Astell exploits these equivocations to their full potential, with the aim of destroying the Whig argument for resistance. When it comes to her position on women, she applies the same religio-political concepts with remarkable philosophical consistency. Astell is thus representative of the women we study to the extent that she considers the implications of her political views for the situation of women in the home – even when those implications turn out to be negative ones in terms of women's social and political status.

I

In 1704, Astell published three anonymous political pamphlets: *Moderation truly Stated*, *A Fair Way with the Dissenters*, and *An Impartial Enquiry Into The Causes of Rebellion and Civil War*. The first two pamphlets deal with contemporary political issues arising from the occasional conformity debates in early eighteenth-century England;[14] the third is a reflection on events leading up to the death of Charles I in 1649, as a lesson about the toleration of dissenters in Astell's own time. Though Astell denies that she writes from the point of view of a political party, her attitudes are recognisably those of a committed Tory. In the early eighteenth century, Tory supporters typically stood for High-Church Anglicanism and passive obedience to the crown. By contrast, the Whigs placed a high value

---

[14] 'Occasional conformity' was the practice of those Protestant dissenters who would take occasional communion in the Church of England for the purpose of retaining a government position.

on 'English liberties' (such as liberty of conscience) and advocated the right to resist unjust princely authority. Though the Whig–Tory alignment was a fluid one, it also typically marked the divide between advocates of religious toleration and their opponents. Today Astell's pamphlets are difficult to read without some knowledge of the seventeenth-century Whig–Tory division and a familiarity with the key players in the occasional conformity debate – men such as James Owen, Charles Davenant, Henry Sacheverell, Daniel Defoe, and Charles Leslie. Many of the allusions and insinuations in Astell's texts are lost on the modern reader; and for a political philosopher, it can be difficult to see anything of philosophical interest in the party political wrangling of these pamphlets. In what follows, however, we draw out the key features of Astell's political philosophy with the aid of these three pamphlets, as well as her *magnum opus*, *The Christian Religion as Profess'd by a Daughter of the Church of England* (1705), and the famous third edition of her *Reflections upon Marriage* (1706).

On first reading, Astell's views on political authority seem to accord with those of sixteenth and seventeenth-century supporters of the divine authority of kingship. Like Elizabeth I in her speeches, and Mary Pope and Elinor James in their pamphlets, Astell repeatedly appeals to the Romans 13 injunction to obey the powers that be. 'We have been taught indeed that *there is no Power but of God*, and that the *Powers that be* (that is the Lawful Powers, for St. *Paul* was no Friend to Robbery and Usurpation) *are ordain'd of* GOD.'[15] Among God's commands, 'the being Subject to, and the not Resisting the Lawful Power that God has set over us (*Rom.* 13), is none of the least'.[16] According to this precept, whoever resists the powers that be is subject to punishment by eternal damnation.

But there is one key difference between the early absolutists and Astell: while Elizabeth, Pope, and James all maintain that the sovereign has an absolute, unlimited power and is accountable to God alone, Astell is a supporter (in principle, at least) of constitutional monarchy. For Astell,

---

[15] Prefatory discourse to *Moderation truly Stated*, p. xxx. In her political pamphlets, Astell often expresses admiration of Elizabeth I's style of government: see *Moderation truly Stated*, pp. xxiii, xxiv, xxviii, 29–30, 78, 82–3, and 118; and *An Impartial Enquiry Into The Causes Of Rebellion and Civil War In This Kingdom: In an Examination of Dr. Kennett's Sermon, Jan. 31, 1703/4. And Vindication of the Royal Martyr* (London: E. P. for Richard Wilkin, 1704), republished in *Astell: Political Writings*, pp. 172, 186, and 195.

[16] *The Christian Religion, As Profess'd by a Daughter Of The Church of England. In a Letter to the Right Honourable, T.L. C. I.* (London: R. Wilkin, 1705), p. 331.

princely power is justifiably limited and constrained by a government and a constitution that ensure that the rights and liberties of subjects are protected by law. On this view, the monarch does not enjoy sole discretionary power over the lives, liberties, and estates of his or her subjects. Astell says that

the truth is, Arbitrary Power how much soever Corrupt Nature may hanker after it, is no fine thing, 'tis a Burden no Wise and Good Prince would wish for, much less endeavour after, where Customs and Laws do not allow it. 'Tis the taking upon himself an Intolerable Burden, a heavy account for the next World, and Distracting Cares in this, of which the Laws do very much ease the Prince in a well regulated Monarchy.[17]

Astell offers conservative reasons for supporting constitutional monarchy: her opinion of arbitrary power is qualified by the remark that it is to be avoided 'where Customs and Laws do not allow it', and her main argument against arbitrary rule is merely the moral and religious burden that this places upon the prince. There is no liberal concern for the rights and liberties of political subjects. She simply concedes that the legislative power lies not solely with the prince, but with the prince and parliament together: 'Since our Constitution lodges the Legislative Power in the Prince and the Three Estates assembled in Parliament; as it is not in the Power of the Prince and one of the Houses, to Make or Abrogate any Law, without the concurrence of the other House, so neither can it be Lawfully done by the Prince alone, or by the two Houses without the Prince.'[18]

While Astell may be a constitutional monarchist, she is no supporter of the view that the prince gains his authority from the consent of the people. She rejects the idea that political society originates in a voluntary agreement between human beings. In her view, there is no such thing as a state of nature or an original condition that human beings choose to leave in exchange for the securities of political society.[19] In *Moderation truly Stated*, Astell addresses the idea of a state of nature put forward by the political economist Charles Davenant (1656–1714), author of the *Essays upon Peace at Home and War Abroad* (1704). In his *Essays*, Davenant muses on the recalcitrant nature of human beings and their tendency to

[17] Prefatory discourse to *Moderation truly Stated*, p. xxxvi.   [18] *An Impartial Enquiry*, pp. 170–1.
[19] For an alternative female view on the state of nature, see [Judith Drake], *An Essay In Defence of the Female Sex*. Drake observes that in the 'Infancy of the World', women were the equals of men, but over time men made use of 'Force (the Origine of Power) to compel us to a Subjection, Nature never meant' (p. 21).

find fault with political authority. One of the causes, he suggests, is that human beings can somehow recall the equality that they enjoyed in the free state of nature.[20] Using Lockean language, Davenant says that 'Man, having first subjected himself to Government, for Ease, Plenty, and Protection; if he is neither Happy, nor Safe, through their Fault who Rule, begins to believe that the Contract is broken, into which he enterd for the Benefit of Society.'[21] In response, Astell mockingly says:

Sir, I am to thank you for a Discovery, alas! I have hitherto thought, that according to *Moses*, we were all of *Adam's* Race, and that a State of Nature was a meer figment of *Hobbs's* Brain, or borrow'd at least from the Fable of *Cadmus*, or *Aeacus* his Myrmidons, till you were pleas'd to inform me *"of that Equality wherein the Race of Men were plac'd in the free State of Nature["]*. How I lament my Stars that it was not my good Fortune to live in those Happy Days when Men sprung up like so many Mushrooms or *Terrae Filii*, without Father or Mother or any sort of dependency!²²

Astell's ridicule highlights the obvious empirical fact that human beings are not born into independence, but rather into dependence upon their parents.[23] For her, the state of nature *is* a mere figment of Hobbes's imagination.

It does not follow, however, that Astell believes that human beings are born without rights or liberties. To see this, we must consider her direct

---

[20] Davenant, *Essays upon Peace at Home, and War Abroad*, p. 352.
[21] Ibid., p. 355. Locke refers to the 'Safety, Ease, and Plenty' provided by civil society in Locke, *Two Treatises of Government*, 11.101.
[22] Prefatory discourse to *Moderation truly Stated*, pp. xxxv–xxxvi. Astell refers to the English translation of Thomas Hobbes's *De Cive*, known as *The Philosophicall Rudiments concerning Government and Society*: 'Let us return again to the state of nature, and consider men as if but even now sprung out of the earth, and suddainly (*like* mushromes) come to full maturity without all kind of engagement to each other' (Thomas Hobbes, *The Philosophicall Rudiments concerning Government and Society*, London: J.G. for R. Royston, 1651, p. 127). Astell may also be referring to the Tory John Nalson's *The Common Interest of King and People* (London: Jonathan Edwin, 1677). Nalson opposes the Hobbesian view that in the state of nature all men have a desire to do mischief to one another. Nalson says that this 'Assertion is false to every Reason; unless he will revive the old Fable of *Cadmus* in *Ovid*, and slurr it upon us for an Historical Truth; and suppose all Mankind to be like the Harvest sprung from the Serpents Teeth; unnatural Sons of the Earth, born in Arms' (p. 6). In Ovid's tale of the 'Myrmidons', Zeus repopulates the island of Aegina with a new generation of men created out of a colony of ants; these men prove to be excellent mercenary soldiers.
[23] In 'Mary Astell and Possessive Individualism', Ruth Perry claims that, in this passage, Astell criticises those theorists who ignore women's reproductive role. In this sense, according to Perry, Astell's Tory pamphlet 'contains elements of an early feminist critique of liberal political theory' (447). But it is difficult to see this as a straightforward feminist claim, because when Astell points to the absurdity of being born 'without Father or Mother', she is clearly highlighting the significance of paternity as well as maternity.

responses to Locke's political views in the *Two Treatises of Government*. In the Second Treatise, the 'Essay Concerning the True Original, Extent, and End of Civil Government', Locke says that *'all Men by Nature are equal'* in the sense that they enjoy an equality in terms of their 'Jurisdiction or Dominion one over another'.[24] Every man has an equal right to his natural freedom, without being subject to the arbitrary will or discretionary power of another man. Locke says that

> The *State of Nature* has a Law of Nature to govern it, which obliges every one; And Reason, which is that Law, teaches all Mankind, who will but consult it, that being all equal and independent, no one ought to harm another in his Life, Health, Liberty, or Possessions. For Men being all the Workmanship of one Omnipotent, and infinitely wise Maker; All the Servants of one Sovereign Master, sent into the World by his order and about his business, they are his Property whose workmanship they are, made to last during his, not one anothers Pleasure.[25]

Locke maintains that in the state of nature, human beings are obliged to act in accordance with the 'Law of Nature, which is the Law of Reason'.[26] God has planted in all human beings a capacity for reason that directs them to pursue the will of their maker.[27] My reason tells me that I am God's property or workmanship and that therefore God (and no one else – including myself) has ultimate discretionary power over whether I live or die. For this reason, I am obliged to preserve not only myself but also the rest of humanity whenever the preservation of others does not compete with my own. In the natural condition, therefore, the 'Fundamental Law of Nature' is *self-preservation*, which is also defined as 'the first and strongest desire God Planted in Men', and a 'Fundamental, Sacred, and unalterable Law'.[28] This law gives me a 'Right to destroy that which threatens me with Destruction'.[29]

The problem, however, is that men inevitably have different ideas about how this law of self-preservation should be applied or executed. In the state of nature, everyone is their own judge and executioner, all are at liberty to judge for themselves about the best means to be pursued in order to preserve their lives, liberties, and estates. They do not have recourse to an 'umpire' – a common legislative, judiciary, or executive power – who has the authority to judge between them. While the state of nature is not identical with a state of war, as Hobbes had maintained, it is

---

[24] Locke, *Two Treatises*, II.54.   [25] Ibid., II.6.   [26] Ibid., I.101.   [27] Ibid., I.86.
[28] Ibid., I.88 and II.149.   [29] Ibid., II.16.

nevertheless 'full of fears and continual dangers'.[30] For this reason, human beings choose to quit the state of nature. They do so because they wish to avoid the inconveniences that result from the absence of a common judge, and in order to erect an authority who will ensure the preservation of their lives and that which tends to the preservation of life (such as liberty and health).

For Locke supreme power lies always with the community, not with the ruling political authority. The people retain the right to depose their rulers when those rulers fail to live up to the trust bestowed upon them, to preserve the lives, liberties, and estates of their subjects:

> For no Man, or Society of Men, having a Power to deliver up their *Preservation*, or consequently the means of it, to the Absolute Will and arbitrary Dominion of another; whenever any one shall go about to bring them into such a Slavish Condition, they will always have a right to preserve what they have not a Power to part with; and to rid themselves of those who invade this Fundamental, Sacred, and unalterable Law of *Self-preservation* for which they enter'd into Society.[31]

To be in a slavish condition, according to Locke, is 'to be subject to the inconstant, uncertain, unknown, Arbitrary Will of another Man'.[32] To protect his right of self-preservation, a man must enjoy freedom from absolute or arbitrary power.[33] If his rulers encroach on his right of self-preservation, he has the right to depose them.

Astell rightly perceives that Locke's concept of self-preservation plays an important role in his moral justification of the right to resist one's sovereign. She affirms that self-preservation is 'a fundamental right we cannot lose',[34] and, directly quoting Locke, she refers to it as 'that *Fundamental, Sacred and unalterable Law of Self-preservation*'.[35] But Astell's definition of the self differs significantly from that of Locke. In Astell's view, self-preservation is first and foremost preservation of the soul (or mind – she uses the terms interchangeably), and not preservation of the body or the soul–body composite. According to Astell, those writers who call self-preservation the 'Fundamental Law of Nature' are 'in the right if they are either Philosophers or Christian enough to take the *Soul* for *Self*'.[36] She advises readers to beware of 'the bare *meaning*' of

---

[30] Ibid., II.123.   [31] Ibid., II.149.   [32] Ibid., II.22.   [33] Ibid., II.22.

[34] Astell, prefatory discourse to *Moderation truly Stated*, p. xlviii.

[35] *The Christian Religion*, p. 133. Astell gives margin citations for the *Two Treatises*, II.149, II.23, and II.239.

[36] *Moderation truly Stated*, p. 24.

self-preservation, 'at least if you have any regard to real Self-Preservation, and think your Souls of greater moment than your Lives or Estates'.[37]

In the *Christian Religion*, Astell's concept of the self is supported by a careful argument for the Cartesian mind–body distinction. She begins with the proposition that we have two 'complete ideas' of thought and extension, in the sense that we do not gain either idea from abstraction or from a partial consideration of the ideas themselves. The ideas of a thinking being (a mind) and an extended being (a body) can be contemplated by us without 'any Relation to, or Dependance upon one another, so that we can be sure of the Existence of one, even at the same time we can suppose that the other does not Exist'. I can have two complete ideas of mind and body with 'different Properties and Affections': I can have a complete idea of the mind that does not include the idea of body; and I can also have a complete idea of body that does not depend upon my idea of the mind. From these premises, Astell concludes that the mind and body are 'truly Distinct and of Different Natures'.[38] Her argument proceeds in much the same way as Descartes's 'epistemological argument' for the real distinction in the Sixth Meditation of his *Meditations on First Philosophy* (1641).[39] From the proposition that he can clearly and distinctly conceive of the mind existing apart from the body, Descartes moves to the conclusion that I am really distinct from my body and can exist without it.[40] His argument relies on the premise that I am able clearly and distinctly to understand the mind apart from the body if there are properties or attributes such that I clearly and distinctly understand that one property (i.e. thought) belongs to the mind, and another property (i.e. extension) belongs to the nature of body; and I have a clear and distinct perception of mind which does not include extension, and a clear and distinct conception of the body which does not include thought. Astell seems to recognise the importance of this premise when she emphasises the 'completeness' of her ideas of mind and body, or the notion that I can consider each idea without any reference to, or dependence upon, the other. On these grounds, Astell asserts that 'because I and all other Reasonable Creatures Think, therefore we are

[37] *An Impartial Enquiry*, pp. 141–2.   [38] *The Christian Religion*, p. 250.
[39] There is no evidence that Astell read the *Meditations*, but we do know that she was familiar with Descartes's *Principles of Philosophy* and his *Passions of the Soul*. See Mary Astell, *A Serious Proposal to the Ladies, Parts I and II*, ed. Patricia Springborg (London: Pickering & Chatto, 1997), part II, pp. 123 and 165.
[40] For a discussion of Descartes's argument, see Margaret Dauler Wilson, *Descartes* (London and New York: Routledge, 1993), p. 189.

something that is not Body'.[41] The 'I' or the self is a non-bodily or immaterial substance, and 'for this reason, it is not liable to Separation of Parts or Corruption' – it is 'in its own Nature Immortal'.[42] Locke may not have subscribed to such a theory, but there is no doubt that Astell thought that, as a Christian, he ought to have.[43]

Astell thus agrees with Locke's central premise that an individual always has 'a right to Preserve what he has not a Power to part with', but, according to Astell, human beings have a right to preserve only their immaterial minds (or souls), not their bodies. In *The Christian Religion*, she explicitly addresses Locke's argument in the *Two Treatises*:

> What then is *Self-Preservation*, that Fundamental Law of Nature, as some call it, to which all other Laws, Divine as well as Human, are made to do Homage? and how shall it be provided for? Very well; for it does not consist in the Preservation of the Person or *Composite*, but in preserving the Mind from Evil, the Mind which is truly the Self, and which ought to be secured at all hazards. It is this *Self-Preservation* and no other, that is *a Fundamental Sacred and Unalterable Law*. . . . *No Man having a power to deliver up* this *Preservation, or consequently the means of it, to the absolute Will and arbitrary Dominion of another*, but *has always a right to Preserve what he has not a Power to part with (Two Treatises of Government, B. 2, S. 149)*, as a certain Author says in another Case where it will not hold.[44]

For Astell, self-preservation simply consists in the attainment of salvation for the soul, and the avoidance of damnation. The preservation of my soul is in my hands alone; I cannot transfer this power of self-preservation to another individual. On this definition, Locke's contractarian account of the origins of political society makes no sense: I simply cannot transfer or entrust that power to my rulers. According to Astell's interpretation of the 'fundamental law of nature', in other words, Locke can use the concept of self-preservation neither to support the foundations of political authority nor to mount an argument in favour of rebellion against political authority. It is a spiritual concept that pertains to spiritual matters alone, and any good Christian should acknowledge this fact.

For Astell, the doctrine of passive obedience is one that follows naturally from the law of reason and its concomitant law of self-preservation. In *The Christian Religion*, Astell begins with a consideration of the

---

[41] Astell, *The Christian Religion*, p. 251.   [42] Ibid.
[43] On Astell's critique of Locke's theory of 'thinking matter', see Broad, *Women Philosophers*, pp. 151–3.
[44] Astell, *The Christian Religion*, pp. 305–6.

obligations that a rational creature has to her maker.[45] She affirms that
'No body will be so absurd as to deny that it is the indispensable duty of
all reasonable Persons to conform themselves entirely to God's Will, so
soon as they can be inform'd of it.'[46] I can inform myself about the will of
God by following my reason, the 'Candle of the Lord' within me.[47]
Though Astell does not say it, these statements are entirely consistent
with the theological presuppositions in Locke's *Two Treatises*. Locke also
refers to reason as '*the Voice of God*' within us;[48] and he emphasises that
this reason tells us that our actions, and the rules for our actions, must be
conformable to the will of God.[49] Locke further adds that it is the will of
our maker that we preserve His workmanship, and that this law of preservation gives me a 'Right to destroy that which threatens me with
Destruction'.[50] According to Astell, this sentiment is correct – but I have
a right to resist only that which threatens the destruction of my soul. The
man who rebels against his sovereign is so far from preserving his soul, or
defending his right to self-preservation, that he actually places his soul
and its preservation in grave peril. This is the case because my reason tells
me that I must heed not only natural reason but also divine revelation, a
direct expression of God's will – and the Scriptures are perfectly clear
about my political obligations. According to St Peter's and St Paul's
commands, it is obligatory for '*Every Soul to be subject to the higher
Powers, not only to the good and gentle*, but even *to the froward*, to a
Persecuting *Nero*, who at that time Reign'd'.[51] Divine revelation does not
condone rebellion against one's rulers. God's revealed wisdom tells us
that rebellion against earthly authority actually constitutes rebellion
against God: 'He who takes upon him upon any pretence whatsoever, to
resist the Supreme Power, such an one *Resisteth the Ordinance of God*, is a
Rebel against the Divine Majesty, and must expect the terrible Punishment due to such Resistance.'[52]

Astell maintains that if we aim honestly to conform ourselves to the
will of our maker, we will see that passive obedience to our rulers is the
only acceptable course of action. It is not up to us to decide whether or
not the powers that be are truly deserving of their authority. All authority
is 'deriv'd from God's Absolute Dominion, which Dominion in its last
resort arises from the Excellency of His Nature, by which He is our
Creator, Preserver and constant Benefactor'. The 'reason and ground
of Superiority is the suppos'd Excellency of the Superior',[53] and our

---

[45] Ibid., p. 10.   [46] Ibid., p. 17.   [47] Ibid.   [48] Locke, *Two Treatises*, 1.86.   [49] Ibid., 11.135.
[50] Ibid., 11.16.   [51] Astell, *The Christian Religion*, p. 21.   [52] Ibid., p. 117.   [53] Ibid., p. 201.

superiors have dominion over us because they possess 'excellency' or virtue. In reality, we fallible human beings are not in a favourable position to judge whether or not our superiors truly possess this excellence. Our intellectual faculties are simply too weak and limited to penetrate that far. But

because Order and Government must be maintain'd, which cou'd not be, considering the Corruption and Partiality of Mankind, were every one left to be Judge in this matter, therefore we must Submit to him, who by the Laws and Usages of the Place, or by Prescription when there is not a better Title, has a claim to Superiority, even tho' he be not really better than his Neighbours.[54]

We must submit to those hierarchical structures providentially arranged by God, because

Order is a Sacred Thing, 'tis that Law which God prescribes himself, and inviolably observes. Subordination is a necessary consequence of Order, for in a State of Ignorance and Pravity such as ours is, there is not any thing that tends more to Confusion than Equality. It dos not therefore become the gross of Mankind to set up for that which is best in their own conceit; but humbly to observe where God has Delegated his Power, and submit to it, *as unto the Lord and not to Man.* Man, who because he is Man, will be liable to some mistakes in the Administration of the Divine Authority.[55]

We are not required to submit to just any old authority, but rather to the lawfully constituted government, 'for I hope no body will say, That Banditti and Pyrates, tho' they have a Constitution and Laws among themselves, Act by God's Authority'.[56]

In sum, like other Tories of her time, while Astell may be a constitutionalist, she is also an absolutist in one respect: she allows that the prince and the constitution together have an 'Absolute or Unaccountable Power'. The justification for this absolutism is that a 'last resort' or 'a last appeal must be lodg'd some where',

otherwise there is, there can be, no Government, whatever Men may talk, but all is in Confusion. Therefore the only way is for the Supreme Power wherever it is Lodg'd, to Govern it self, and to take all its Measures according to the Direction of the Laws; which, tho' they may not be Infallible, are yet the Supreme Wisdom

---

[54] Ibid.   [55] *Moderation truly Stated*, pp. 59–60.

[56] *The Christian Religion*, p. 117. Astell echoes Locke's observation that 'a Man can never be oblig'd in Conscience to submit to any Power, unless he can be satisfied who is the Person, who has a Right to Exercise that Power over him. If this were not so, there would be no distinction between Pirates and Lawful Princes' (*Two Treatises*, 1.81).

of the State. And whoever builds his Politicks on such a Scheme as this, will approve himself a Benefactor to Mankind; will equally provide for the Honour of the Prince and the just and wholsom Liberty of the Subject, and for the mutual Quiet, Interest and Prosperity of both.[57]

Astell thus advocates obedience to the prince and the constitution for reasons of practical necessity, as well as divine command. Human political power cannot be without fault: only power guided by Infinite Wisdom could be flawless. But if there were no single authority to decide on matters of justice in the state, then all would be anarchy and confusion. The consequences of rebellion are often worse than those of patient submission to one's rulers. The Interregnum, after all, had shown that the overthrow of a lawful prince with a 'just and necessary power' could lead us to become 'mere Slaves to the Arbitrary Rule' of some of the worst of our fellow citizens:[58]

Tyranny and Oppression are no doubt a great grievance; they are so to the Prince as well as to the Subject . . . But are Sedition and Rebellion no Grievances? they are not less, perhaps more Grievous than Tyranny, even to the People; for they expose us to the Oppression of a multitude of Tyrants.[59]

For this reason, it is 'better that I shou'd submit to an unjust Sentence, than that there shou'd be no end of Strife; and that some Private Persons tho' ever so Innocent shou'd suffer, than that the Majesty of Government, and herein the Divine Authority shou'd be violated, and the Public shou'd be disturb'd'.[60]

In short, Astell advocates a blanket policy of non-resistance to political authority: the people must comply with the commands of their rulers, and obey the powers that be, even if those rulers turn out to be irreligious tyrants. This amounts to a doctrine of active and passive obedience: 'Christians are under the strictest Obligation to render Active Obedience to Just Authority in all instances that are not contradictory to God's Commands, and to Submit quietly when they cannot actually Obey.'[61] Even in those cases where our rulers are irreligious, subjects must passively submit; they are never justified in attempting to bring down government.

Astell asserts that having 'a last appeal' or an 'unaccountable power' will ensure that 'the just and wholsom Liberty of the Subject' is respected. But it is difficult to reconcile this statement with her theory of passive

---

[57] Prefatory discourse to *Moderation truly Stated*, pp. xxxviii–xxxix.
[58] Ibid., pp. xxxvii–xxxviii.   [59] *An Impartial Enquiry*, pp. 196–7.
[60] *The Christian Religion*, pp. 200–1.   [61] Ibid., pp. 177–8; see also p. 371.

obedience to tyrannical and irreligious rulers. How can I be a free agent and yet subject to the capricious will of a tyrant? The difficulty disappears when we consider Astell's concept of liberty. In her view, 'the greatest Pretenders to Liberty, are the People that use their evil endeavours to put the vilest Chains upon their Fellow-Christians, whilst they clandestinely enslave their Minds, which are the true seat of Liberty'.[62] She says that

the difference between a Free and a Necessary Agent consists in this, That the Actions of the former, or more properly the Motions of his Mind, are in his own power. He has Ability, as every one of us is sensible, to determine them this way or that, according to his own pleasure, and as he is affected by the suppos'd agreeableness of the objects he pursues. Which power or faculty is what we call Liberty.[63]

Thus Astell defines liberty as an internal power of self-determination. In her view, God 'has not put the Liberty of his Creatures in any ones power but in their own'.[64] True liberty consists in the subject's choice to pursue or not to pursue that which is good for the soul. The power to preserve my soul lies entirely in my own hands – it is not a power that I can give up or transfer to another. This is liberty as a metaphysical state, as upheld by Suchon. Unlike Suchon, Astell does not think that our exercise of this liberty requires freedom from servitude or slavery. My destruction or salvation is entirely up to me, no matter what my social condition, because God has made me a free agent. In Astell's view, those men who advocate a right of resistance against lawful authority place the salvation of souls at risk. They attempt to prevent subjects from making their own free judgements about obedience, informed by their natural reason and a careful reading of the Scriptures. Modern dissenters thus 'effectually destroy the Liberties of the Subject under pretence of defending them'.[65] True liberty 'consists in making a right use of our Reason, in preserving our Judgments free, and our Integrity unspotted, (which sets us out of the reach of the most Absolute Tyrant) not in a bare power to do what we Will'.[66]

II

In *Some Reflections Upon Marriage* (1700), Astell extends these views about liberty and passive obedience to the situation of women in marriage.

---

[62] Ibid., p. 226.   [63] Ibid., p. 86.   [64] Ibid., p. 279.   [65] *An Impartial Enquiry*, p. 138.
[66] *The Christian Religion*, p. 278.

In this work, Astell offers a general assessment of marriage, and regrets the fact that this divine institution has been brought into disrepute by the irresponsible conduct of men and women. Despite her condemnation of divorce (her book was occasioned by the divorce case of Hortense Mancini, the Duchess of Mazarin), Astell is nevertheless sympathetic to the miseries of unhappily married women. She laments the fact that most women lack the fortitude to cope with abusive or tyrannical husbands. In the Preface to her 1706 third edition of *Reflections*, Astell points out that

if Arbitrary Power is an evil in itself, and an improper Method of Governing Rational and Free Agents it ought not to be Practis'd anywhere; Nor is it less, but rather more mischievous in Families than in Kingdoms, by how much 100000 Tyrants are worse than one. What tho a Husband can't deprive a Wife of Life with-out being responsible to the Law, he may however do what is much more grievous to a generous Mind, render Life miserable, for which she has no Redress, scarce Pity which is afforded to every other Complainant. It being thought a Wife's Duty to suffer everything without Complaint. If *all Men are born free*, how is it that all Women are born slaves? as they must be if the being subjected to the *inconstant, uncertain, unknown, arbitrary Will* of Men, be the *perfect Condition of Slavery*? and if the Essence of Freedom consists, as our Masters say it does, in having a *standing Rule to live by*? And why is Slavery so much condemn'd and strove against in one Case, and so highly applauded and held so necessary and so sacred in another?[67]

In this passage, Astell quotes without acknowledgement from two key sections of the *Two Treatises:* 11.22 and 11.24. To be in a 'perfect condition of *Slavery*' (11.24), Locke suggests, is 'to be subject to the inconstant, uncertain, unknown, Arbitrary Will of another Man' (11.22). The '*Freedom of Men under Government*', however, is 'to have a standing Rule to live by, common to every one of that Society, and made by the Legislative Power erected in it' (11.22). In the section immediately following (11.23), Locke once again spells out the view that I always have a right that may be exercised against those who would enslave me: the right of self-preservation.

   One common interpretation of Astell's passage is that it is an ironic statement directed at Whig thinkers of her time who do not extend their much-loved theory of passive obedience in the home into a theory of passive obedience in the state. In the *Reflections*, Astell does not advocate that wives 'Resist' or 'Abdicate' their spouses in order to retrieve their liberty.[68] Far be it from her, she says, 'to stir up Sedition of any sort, none

---

[67] *Reflections Upon Marriage*, in *Astell: Political Writings*, pp. 17–19.   [68] Ibid., p. 9.

can abhor it more'; and she heartily wishes that 'our Masters wou'd pay their Civil and Ecclesiastical Governors the same Submission, which they themselves exact from their Domestic Subjects'.[69] She points out that 'whatever may be said against Passive-Obedience in another case, I suppose there's no man but likes it very well in this; how much soever Arbitrary Power may be dislik'd on a Throne, not *Milton* himself wou'd cry up Liberty to poor Female Slaves, or Plead for the Lawfulness of Resisting a Private Tyranny'.[70] In turn, Astell aims to highlight the consistency of her own political position: in her view, passive obedience ought to be practised uniformly across the board, in both the political and familial spheres. Astell's justification of passive obedience to husbands is the same as her justification of passive obedience to rulers. She says:

Nor can there be any Society great or little, from Empires *down to private Families*, without a last Resort, to determine the Affairs of that Society by an irresistible sentence. Now unless this Supremacy be fixed somewhere, there will be a perpetual Contention about it, such is the love of Dominion, and let the Reason of things be what it may, those who have least force, or Cunning to supply it, will have the Disadvantage.[71]

Just as there must be a 'last appeal' in political society – a common umpire with the executive power to interpret and apply the laws – so too there must be a last appeal in the family. Astell implies that because women have the least force or the 'least Bodily strength' in the conjugal relationship, they inevitably find themselves in a position of subjection.[72] It is an unfortunate state of affairs, but it is not ours to question divine providence – and, in any case, lack of bodily strength does not imply a lack of understanding. Women have what it takes to serve God and attain salvation, and that is all that matters.

Astell's remarks about male freedom and female slavery are the subject of some scholarly debate. Springborg asserts that Astell's remark about women being born into slavery must be ironic:

Astell denied Locke's claim to one's property in one's person: a claim that applied in his day only to men. In Locke this right is crucially important in the

---

[69] Ibid., p. 8.   [70] Ibid., pp. 46–7.   [71] Ibid., p. 15; our italics.

[72] It is striking how similar Astell's views on the practical necessity of wifely submission are to those of Locke. In the *Two Treatises*, Locke says that 'the Husband and Wife, though they have but one common Concern, yet having different understandings, will unavoidably sometimes have different wills too; it therefore being necessary, that the last Determination, *i.e.* the Rule, should be placed somewhere, it naturally falls to the Man's share, as the abler and the stronger' (II.82). Astell does not, however, condone a wife's 'Liberty to *separate*' from her husband, as Locke does.

negative: as the incapacity of individuals (men) to incur hereditable impediments to their freedom or voluntarily to enter into slavery. To the extent that a positive right was entailed it was part of a package tailored by Locke to undermine hereditable monarchy. Since Astell denied property in one's person, vouched for in Locke by the right to real property (a right to which women were denied) she could not technically argue the slavery of women compared with the freedom of men. Nor does she seriously attempt to do so.[73]

There is good evidence, however, that Astell does intend her comments about women and slavery to be literal truths – at a certain level. On the one hand, we might interpret her as highlighting the hypocrisy of men such as Milton and Locke who do not uphold a uniform policy of passive obedience in both the state and the home. On the other, we might interpret her as highlighting the hypocrisy of men who do not have a consistent policy of resistance to absolute power – in this case, absolute power over women's minds. To see this, we have only to re-read the *Reflections* in light of Astell's alternative definitions of liberty and self-preservation. In the preface, she says that she aims to retrieve the 'Native Liberty, the Rights and Privileges of the Subject'.[74] The 'Subject' of the discourse is the wife, who is in subjection to her husband; her 'Liberty' is the liberty of all human beings – the freedom to pursue or not to pursue the good of her soul; and her 'Right' is the 'Natural Right of Judging for her self',[75] especially about religious matters. Married women are enslaved because they are taught to believe, without question, the views and opinions of their husbands. If men such as Locke truly abhorred absolute power – especially the power to direct someone else's judgement about right or wrong – then they would abhor the absolute power of husbands as much as they abhor the absolute power of sovereigns.

Similar sentiments are echoed in the *Reflections* when Astell addresses John Sprint's *The Bride-Womans Counseller* (1699). In this work, Sprint argues that a woman must practise absolute obedience to her husband, to the extent that she must yield to his every will and desire. As a matter of rule, Sprint recommends 'the very Desire of the Heart to be regulated by him so far that it should not be lawful to will or desire what she herself liked, but only what her Husband should approve and allow'.[76] In the *Reflections*, Astell paraphrases these remarks. Anticipating the arguments

---

[73] Astell, *Reflections*, p. 18, n. 20.   [74] Ibid., p. 8.   [75] Ibid., p. 10.
[76] John Sprint, *The Bride-Womans Counseller. Being a Sermon Preach'd at a Wedding* (London: H. Hills, 1699), p. 6.

of Eugenia and Mary Chudleigh, both of whom challenged the misogynist Sprint in print,[77] Astell says that

She who Elects a Monarch for Life, who gives him an Authority he cannot recall however he misapply it, who puts her Fortune and Person entirely in his Powers; *nay even the very desires of her Heart according to some learned Casuists, so as that it is not lawful to Will or Desire anything but what he approves and allows*; had need be very sure that she does not make a Fool her Head, nor a Vicious Man her Guide and Pattern, she had best stay till she can meet with one who has the Government of his own Passions, and has duly regulated his own desires, since he is to have such an absolute Power over hers.[78]

Astell's point is that, prior to marriage, women ought to improve their capacity for judgement in order to make the best decision possible. A woman cannot defy her husband's authority in the home, but she can refuse his offer of marriage in the first place. And if a woman does live to regret her decision to marry, then her intellectual improvements will offer consolation in the midst of her unhappiness.

In her *Serious Proposal to the Ladies*, Astell suggests a way in which women might improve their capacity for practical judgement before they consider marriage. Her proposal is for an academic retreat for single women, or a 'Seminary to stock the Kingdom with pious and prudent ladies'.[79] Astell did not read French,[80] and it is unlikely that she was familiar with Gabrielle Suchon's *On Morality and Politics* or *On Voluntary Single Life*. Astell encourages emulation of French women, but she recommends Anne Dacier and Madeleine de Scudéry, two authors who were translated into English.[81] Like Suchon, however, Astell thinks that women ought to have the option of remaining single until they can improve their capacity for judgement; and Astell's ideas on women and liberty also bear a resemblance to Suchon's. In the second part of her *Proposal*, Astell emphasises that it is prejudice, opinion, authority, and custom that 'erect a Tyranny over our free born souls'.[82] She urges women to embrace their essential humanity and to recognise the 'Natural

---

[77] Mary Chudleigh, *The Ladies Defence: or, The Bride-Woman's Counsellor Answered* (London: John Deeve, 1701); Eugenia, *The Female Advocate*.

[78] *Reflections*, pp. 48–9; our italics.   [79] *Proposal I*, p. 21.

[80] In a letter to Norris, dated 15 February 1693, Astell says of Nicolas Malebranche that 'I . . . wish I cou'd read that ingenious Author in his own Language, or that he spake mine' (Astell and Norris, *Letters*, p. 149).

[81] *Proposal I*, pp. 24, 58. Astell recommends Scudéry in the 1701 edition of the *Proposal*. In 1708, Astell's good friend Elizabeth Elstob published an English translation of Scudéry's *Essay upon Glory*; see Perry, *Celebrated Mary Astell*, pp. 110, 118.

[82] *Proposal II*, p. 89.

Liberty within' them.[83] Until 'we are capable of Chusing our own Actions and directing them by some Principle, tho we move and speak and so many such like things, we live not the life of a Rational Creature but only of an Animal'.[84] Liberty for women consists in freedom of the will, or the freedom to decide for themselves between good and evil.

Astell continues her project of feminist emancipation in *The Christian Religion*, a work that aims to convince women that they must study the content of the Scriptures for themselves and familiarise themselves with the foundations of their religious beliefs, rather than simply believe without knowing why. In this work, Astell emphasises that 'the mischiefs of a blind adherence to Authority are so many and so great'.[85] One of the worst consequences of such blind adherence is 'disobedience to Lawful Authority'.[86] Once again, Astell advocates a withdrawing from those who have 'usurp'd an empire over our Understandings' and the exercising instead of 'that most valuable Privilege, and indefeasible Right, of judging for our selves where God has left us free to do so':[87]

> How those who have *made themselves* our Governors, may like our withdrawing from their yoke I know not; but I am certain that this principle of judging for our selves in all cases wherein GOD has left us this liberty, will introduce no disorder into the World, or disobedience to our *Lawful* Governors. Rather, it will teach us to be as tractable and submissive to Just Authority, as we are careful to judge rightly for our selves, in such matters wherein God has not appointed any to govern for us.[88]

If we follow Astell's argument back to its beginnings, this right of judging for oneself ultimately derives from that 'fundamental law' of self-preservation – the right to preserve one's soul from eternal damnation. Astell applies this prime Lockean concept to the situation of women, but with an emphasis upon its religious or philosophical sense rather than its secular political meaning.

Mary Astell was not the only politically minded woman of her time to read Locke's *Two Treatises of Government*. In a 1705 letter to Sarah Churchill, Duchess of Marlborough (then the favourite of Queen Anne), Elizabeth Burnet says that she 'is extremly glad you have taken the trouble to read Mr Lock on Government, I think after those notions are digested one cant be much imposed on by the falacies of any party'.[89] Burnet says

[83] Ibid., p.148.   [84] Ibid., p.82.   [85] *The Christian Religion*, p.408.   [86] Ibid., p.36.
[87] Ibid., p.289.   [88] Ibid., p.36.
[89] Elizabeth Burnet to Sarah Churchill, 14 June 1705; in Add. MS 61458, f. 43v, British Library, London. On Burnet and politics, see Anne Kelley, '"Her Zeal for the Publick Good": The

of Locke that 'he was I am sure a true lover of truth, & sought it with as litle bias as is well possible'.[90] Astell may well have accepted Burnet's description of Locke as a lover of truth. In her *Moderation truly Stated*, Astell refers without irony to the '*Great* Mr. Locke', and more than once she praises his views about the association of ideas.[91] But Astell would not have accepted Burnet's remarks about the *Two Treatises*. According to Springborg, Astell regarded Locke's *Two Treatises* as the work of a devout Whig, and as representative of all that was wrong with the radical Whig political point of view. If we look beyond party political issues, however, to the philosophical aspects of her critique of Locke, we can see that Astell agreed with a number of Locke's fundamental principles – particularly the view that the law of nature is the law of reason, that reason tells us that we must conform ourselves to the will of our maker, and that we are therefore obliged to preserve ourselves and others from destruction. Astell's main criticism is that Locke does not take these principles to their logical conclusion with regard to our political obligations. For Astell, the fundamental right of self-preservation is the right to attain salvation for our souls. Any good Christian must recognise that this right takes precedence over the preservation of mere bodies or soul–body composites. This right of self-preservation cannot provide the foundation for a theory of government by consent of the governed. In her opinion, a necessary condition for our salvation is that we follow the biblical injunction to practise an active obedience toward just political authority, and to submit passively to tyrannical and despotic rulers. On this view, the people never have a right to resist their governors.

While Astell's critique of Locke may be brief, it is nevertheless perceptive to the extent that it points to a possible theological inconsistency at the heart of Locke's *Two Treatises*. In his *Second Reply* to Edward Stillingfleet, Locke complains that 'My Lord, the words you bring out of my book [the *Essay*] are so often different from those I read . . . I am sometimes ready to think you have got some strange copy of it, whereof I know nothing.'[92] Locke might be tempted to say the same thing to modern commentators about the *Two Treatises*. This work – now

---

Political Agenda in Elizabeth Burnet's *A Method of Devotion* (1708)', *Women's Writing* 13 (2006), 448–74.

[90] Elizabeth Burnet to Sarah Churchill, 14 June 1705; in Add. MS 61458, f. 43v, British Library, London.

[91] Astell, *Moderation truly Stated*, p. 11; *An Impartial Enquiry*, p. 177; and *Bart'lemy Fair: Or, An Enquiry after Wit; In which due Respect is had to a Letter Concerning Enthusiasm, To my LORD **** (London: Richard Wilkin, 1709), p. 77.

[92] *The Works of John Locke*, vol. 1, p. 716.

considered to be one of the most influential texts in the history of political thought – is sometimes regarded as a secular justification of political authority and political obligation, a defence of democracy, a justification of capitalism, and one of the first expressions of liberal individualism. It is probably fair to say that Locke consciously intended it to be none of these things. Astell's interpretation of Locke prompts us to read the *Two Treatises* through a historical lens, and to see that his arguments are ultimately based upon theological presuppositions rather than secular or modern liberal and democratic principles. As a contemporary, in other words, Astell sees this work as what many revisionist Locke scholars now believe it to be – a call to revolution[93] based upon religious arguments,[94] and an attack on Anglican royalist doctrine.[95] Astell's main criticism of Locke is that he does not take his theological presuppositions to their logical conclusion: acceptance rather than rejection of the theory of passive obedience. While today we might regard her argument as a *reductio* of Locke's position, she intended it to provide rational support for her own Anglican royalist views.

Like other English women political thinkers of the early modern period, Astell does not challenge revealed religion or a husband's dominion over his wife. While there are key differences between Astell's political views and those of Elizabeth I, Katherine Chidley, the women petitioners of the civil war era, the Quaker women, Margaret Cavendish, Elinor James, Anne Docwra, and Damaris Masham, on this issue little had changed. Astell was a constitutional monarchist rather than an absolutist; she was a strong critic of dissenters from the Church of England; she did not endorse the theory of popular sovereignty; she rejected the idea of a pre-political state of nature; and she upheld a religious argument for political authority, rather than one based solely upon practical necessity. Yet though she accepts women's political subordination to men, she incorporates the

---

[93] Once it was commonly thought that Locke's *Two Treatises* (revised and published in 1689) provided a post-Revolution argument in favour of allegiance to William III. But since the work of Peter Laslett, many scholars now believe that Locke's *Two Treatises* were written much earlier, during the Exclusion Crisis of 1679–83, and that the work was in fact intended to be a demand for revolution in the time of Charles II. Laslett's research shows that '*Two Treatises* in fact turns out to be a demand for a revolution to be brought about, not the rationalization of a revolution in need of defence' (Laslett, introduction to Locke, *Two Treatises*, p. 47).

[94] On theological presuppositions in Locke's political thought, see John Dunn, *The Political Thought of John Locke: An Historical Account of the Argument of the 'Two Treatises of Government'* (Cambridge University Press, 1969); James Tully, *A Discourse on Property: John Locke and his Adversaries* (Cambridge University Press, 1980); and Waldron, *God, Locke, and Equality*.

[95] Mark Goldie, 'John Locke and Royal Anglicanism', *Political Studies* 31 (1983), 61–85.

concerns of the female sex – *their* oppression under tyranny, *their* liberty, and *their* self-preservation – into her political vision. Her concepts of tyranny, liberty, and self-preservation differ markedly from those of modern liberal theorists, and as a result her gender concerns are somewhat remote from those of present-day feminists. But Astell cannot be criticised for failing to recognise the logical implications of her political thought for the female sex as a whole.

Conclusion

In 1991, Margaret King concluded her ground-breaking work on Renaissance women with the following bleak assessment:

When Renaissance women confronted the predicaments in which women found themselves, their solution was not to change society, irreparably dominated by male concerns, but to escape it. All three of the feminists considered in these last pages [Christine de Pizan, Moderata Fonte, Mary Astell] were social conservatives. They challenged the tyranny of men but not the tyranny of class or potentate. Within the structures their critique left undisturbed there was no place for women: no role for women in cities where only men could be citizens or kings. Until those ancient structures fell to male assault in the name of civil rights and natural law in the revolutions of the late eighteenth century, no truly modern feminist claims could be made.[1]

In this study, we have offered a more positive account of the place of women in the development of European political ideas. It is true, as King notes, that many women writers were socially conservative. A good number were prompted to write by their recent experiences of political turmoil, civil war, and social upheaval. They emphasise the need for submission to political authority, seeing it as necessary for the preservation of political stability and peace. And while some criticise the tyranny of marriage, others take the importance of political subjection so far as to argue for the legitimacy of a man's right to govern his wife. However, it is not true that there was no place for women in the political structures that these women proposed or imagined. We have shown that female royalists often represented the monarch as a parent, and their thought was ideologically accommodating to queens and female regents. Even those, such as Mary Astell, whose imagery was not explicitly parentalist accepted that women had all the attributes necessary to be successful monarchs. Christine de Pizan called women 'citoyennes', but thought all citizens

[1] King, *Women of the Renaissance*, p. 237.

288

should be loyal to their superiors. Laura Cereta imagined a female republic of letters. Marguerite de Navarre's women debate with men as equals, and she suggests that women may be men's spiritual superiors. Moderata Fonte and Lucrezia Marinella decried their lack of liberty within the Venetian republic; the civil war petitioners claim liberty of conscience as subjects with men; while Quaker women are socially egalitarian and claim equal spiritual authority with men. Madeleine de Scudéry and Mary Astell see women's acceptance of constraint as a positive characteristic in a subject, and Gabrielle Suchon makes tentative steps beyond freedom of conscience towards full political liberty.

Many of our conclusions emerge from taking a different methodological approach to the political thought of pre-Enlightenment women. We did not begin with the modern paradigm of political thought, with the aim of then looking back into the past and including only those works that fall within its purview. Rather, we began by considering the actual political traditions of late-medieval Europe – traditions derived from ancient Greek and Roman sources, and heavily modified by Christian doctrine – and then moved forward to the early modern era. By taking this approach, we found a greater number of women political thinkers than some historians have hitherto acknowledged. And, in terms of content, we found that interrogation of the nature of virtue and the relative virtues of the sexes, derived from Plato, Aristotle, and later Stoic writers, is ubiquitous in the works of women.

Early writers who promoted women's capacity to rule explicitly disputed the Aristotelian view that women lack the virtue of prudence. They thus implicitly undermined the Aristotelian argument for women's submission within marriage. Some, such as Laura Cereta, Marguerite de Navarre, and Madeleine de Scudéry, questioned classical models of virtue, variously putting in their place Christian faith, salvation, and humility. Reformation women used biblical sources to insist on women's spiritual equality with men and their right to liberty of conscience, following the Reformation trend of emphasising the place of conscience, salvation, and faith in the virtuous life. And although the appeal to the Bible often resulted in women's acceptance of submission to husbands in temporal matters, this was not invariably the case. Some, such as Madeleine de Scudéry, began to imagine marriage grounded in a tender love not too different from mutual friendship. Even when liberty does come to the fore in women's thought, it is typically as a means to virtue rather than as an end in itself.

Moreover, women did not accept that men were more virtuous than women, and they challenged the liberties that men assigned themselves. Women advocated submission to legitimate authority for men as well as for women, finding tyranny not in hierarchy *per se*, but in the illegitimate use of power for personal advancement in contravention of the public good. And many imagined that as subjects men and women could engage as equals in civic friendships whether within marriage or without.

Since women's ideas concerning the socio-political relations of men and women were often disseminated in popular forms, they were undoubtedly influential. But this influence has hardly been noted within the traditional academy, which has focused almost exclusively on male-authored political texts in which women are added as an afterthought, treated as an exception, or consigned to a 'private sphere' which is conceptualised as not fully political. Women, by contrast, approach the subject of politics as women, as rulers, and as ruled, attempting to articulate what they want of men as husbands, rulers, or subjects. For the women we have discussed, the political problem is not, in general, authority or hierarchy in itself, but the legitimate use of power, the danger of power corrupted by vice, the failure of the strong to protect individual conscience, and care for the weak and helpless, or the danger that liberty and dissent may lead to social upheaval. Thus, while rejecting Aristotle's claim that women are lacking in prudence, many remain Aristotelian and conservative in outlook, taking the central political problem to be the inculcation and practice of virtue in subjects and sovereigns alike. For many of our women, subjection to political authority is just, because political authority is necessary for peace, and in order to secure peace, authority ought to be subject to virtue.

One can even see a kind of sexual egalitarianism within some authors' acceptance of hierarchical authority. We might call it an equality of subjection. This does not mean that these women believe that all human beings suffer exactly the same subjection. There are definite hierarchies of subjection: men are subject to the crown; women, as wives, are the subjects of subjects (as are servants). But women's subjection to their husbands, and their free submission to the moral law, is often held up as a model to men, whose lack of submission and humility is characteristically painted by women as vice.

The history of men's political ideas is often represented as a progression towards liberalism, dominated by a series of great minds – Aristotle, Aquinas, Machiavelli, Hobbes, Locke, Rousseau, and Kant – perhaps supplemented by more minor figures such as John of Salisbury and Jean Bodin. Genuine feminism is then represented as an offshoot of this progress, as Margaret King suggests (see above). Men's ideas, more generally, have been represented as progressing by way of revolutions, initiated by key thinkers. Descartes is upheld as the originator of a modern faith that reason is the ground of knowledge, challenged only by the empiricist assertion that it is sensation, rather than reason, that is the source of our ideas. In writing this book, we have come to the conclusion that women's thought fits rather badly into these standard chronologies, and should not be represented as defective because it fails to fit the contours of the history of men's ideas. Long before Descartes, Christine grounded her defence of women on her own independent reason and experience, and her influence on women is significant up to the sixteenth century. Seventeenth-century women's political thought is more often opposed to Machiavelli and Hobbes, rather than built on them. Marie le Jars de Gournay defends women's equality with men, but is influenced by Montaigne, and not by Descartes. Quaker women are egalitarian but ground this on biblical injunctions, not modern political texts. Madeleine de Scudéry explores models of egalitarian love and friendship between the sexes, independently of ideas about the social contract, and while seventeenth-century English women do engage with Locke, this engagement is as often critical as it is complimentary.

It is only by expanding the definition of the political, and with it the range of texts that count as political, that we have been led to uncover an autonomous tradition of women's ideas. Women's political status is tightly bound up with marriage and their subordination to men. This in turn is justified within the Christian and Aristotelian tradition through the denial of women's capacity for virtue. Thus when women enter into political discourse they concentrate on themes such as virtue, sexual relations, love, and marriage. When women came to discuss these issues they often chose, not the Latin scholastic treatise, but more popular genres. In England, ordinary women voiced their opinions in broadsheets and pamphlets. Upper-class women were more likely to choose poetry, vernacular story, novel, or conversations. By the early eighteenth century, such popular genres came to be treated as appropriate for feminine entertainment, but not serious subjects for academic study.[2] And when some of these texts did enter the academy, with the rise of the study of literature during the twentieth century, they were studied for their literary qualities, not as political theory. But when we look more closely we see that works such as Marguerite de Navarre's *Heptameron*, Scudéry's novels,

[2] DeJean, *Ancients Against Moderns*.

and Cavendish's *The Blazing World* are clearly political. In works such as these, relations between women and men are often central to the discussion of social organisation and political obligation.

The women whose works we have discussed also attempted to locate themselves within a tradition of female political and intellectual authority. Mary Astell had read at least some of the works of Madeleine de Scudéry; Scudéry herself had earlier attempted to initiate a correspondence with Anna Maria van Schurman, as well as referring to Marguerite de Navarre and Madeleine and Catherine des Roches. Anna Maria van Schurman corresponded with Marie le Jars de Gournay and Elisabeth of Bohemia, and she was acquainted with Christina of Sweden. Schurman had also read Lucrezia Marinella, who acknowledged Moderata Fonte and earlier learned women such as Cassandra Fedele and Isotta Nogarola. Both Fonte and Marinella influenced Arcangela Tarabotti, whose ideas are sufficiently similar to those of Gabrielle Suchon to make one suspect some influence. One of Marguerite de Navarre's poems was translated by Queen Elizabeth, and both women in all probability read some of the works of Christine de Pizan. Marguerite de Navarre also corresponded with Vittoria Colonna, whose work built on that of earlier Italian women. Looking at these and other connections, we see how women appreciated the existence of other women who were their intellectual forebears and models, and saw themselves as part of an alternative intellectual tradition. While they certainly did not speak with a single 'other voice', we can see in their writings the outlines of a history of women's ideas that develops both alongside and in counterpoint to the history of men's ideas.

We have offered only a preliminary study of this history, based on scholarship currently available. No doubt there are gaps that some scholars will lament, and places where alternative interpretations might be proposed. We believe that, at the very least, we have drawn a partial map of this vast and rich terrain, which we hope will facilitate and provoke further research. We look forward to future collaborations, and to the work of other scholars who will extend the narrative of women's engagement with political ideas into the eighteenth century and beyond.

Bibliography

PRIMARY SOURCES

MANUSCRIPTS

Burnet, Elizabeth, letter to Sarah Churchill, British Library, London, Add. MS 61458, f. 43v.

Goggio, Bartolomeo, 'De laudibus mulierum', British Library, London, Add. MS 17415.

Masham, Damaris Cudworth, 'Letter to Jean Le Clerc, 12 January 1705', Amsterdam University Library (UVA), MS J.57.a.

Pizan, Christine de, *L'Epistre d'Othea*, British Library, London, MS Royal 14 E II; and MS Royal 17 E IV.

Livre de la Cité des Dames, British Library, London, MS Royal 19 A XIX.

Le Livre du corps de policie, BNF, Paris, MS fr. 1197.

Le Livre de Prudence, Bibliothèque Royale de Belgique, Brussels, MS 5698.

PRINTED TEXTS

'Anger, Jane', *Jane Anger her Protection for women*, London: Richard Jones and Thomas Orwin, 1589.

Anonymous, *A True Copie of the Petition of the Gentlewomen, and Tradesmens-wives, in and about the City of London. Delivered, To the Honourable, the KNIGHTS, Citizens, and Burgesses, of the house of Commons in Parliament, the 4th of February, 1641*, London: R. O. & G. D. for John Bull, 1641 [1642].

Anonymous, *To the Queens most Excellent Majestie. The Humble Petition of divers Gentle-women, Citizens Wives, Tradesmens Wives, and other Inhabitants in the Cities of London and Westminster, and the Suburbs thereof*, London: n.p., 1642.

Anonymous, *The Manner of the Deposition of Charles Stewart*, [London: n.p.], 1649.

Anonymous, *To the Supream authority of this Nation, the Commons assembled in Parliament: The humble Petition of divers wel-affected Women Inhabiting the Cities of London, Westminster, the Borough of Southwark, Hamblets, and Places adjacent*, London: 24 April 1649.

Anonymous, *To the Supream Authority of England The Commons Assembled in Parliament. The humble Petition of diverse wel-affected WEOMEN, of the Cities of London and Westminster, the Borrough of Southwark, Hamblets, and places adjacent*, London: 5 May 1649.

Anonymous, *To the Supreme Authority of this Common-wealth, The Parliament of England. The humble Petition of Severall of the Wives and Children of such Delinquents, whose Estates are propounded to be sold, as the Petitioners are informed* [London: n.p., August 1650].

Anonymous, *The Copie Of A Paper Presented to the Parliament: And read the 27th. of the fourth Moneth, 1659*, London: A.W. for Giles Calvert, 1659.

Aristotle, *The Nicomachean Ethics*, trans. H. Rackham, Loeb Classical Library, London: Heinemann, 1982.

Astell, Mary, *An Impartial Enquiry Into The Causes Of Rebellion and Civil War In This Kingdom: In an Examination of Dr. Kennett's Sermon, Jan. 31, 1703/4. And Vindication of the Royal Martyr*, London: E. P. for Richard Wilkin, 1704 republished in *Astell: Political Writings*.

Moderation truly Stated: Or, A Review of a Late Pamphlet, Entitul'd. Moderation a Vertue. With a Prefatory Discourse to Dr. D'Aveanant, concerning His late Essays on Peace and War, London: R. Wilkin, 1704.

The Christian Religion, As Profess'd by a Daughter Of The Church of England. In a Letter to the Right Honourable, T.L. C.I., London: R. Wilkin, 1705.

Bart'lemy Fair: Or, An Enquiry after Wit; In which due Respect is had to a Letter Concerning Enthusiasm, To my LORD ***, London: Richard Wilkin, 1709.

Astell: Political Writings, ed. Patricia Springborg, Cambridge Texts in the History of Political Thought, Cambridge University Press, 1996.

Some Reflections Upon Marriage, in *Astell: Political Writings.*

A Serious Proposal to the Ladies, Parts I and II, ed. Patricia Springborg, London: Pickering & Chatto, 1997.

Astell, Mary, and John Norris, *Letters Concerning the Love of God, Between the Author of the Proposal to the Ladies and Mr. John Norris*, London: J. Norris, 1695.

Aulnoy, Marie-Catherine, baronne d', *Relation du voyage d'Espagne*, Paris: Claude Barbin, 1691.

Nouvelles espagnolles, Paris: Claude Barbin, 1692.

Nouvelles ou Mémoires historiques, Paris: Claude Barbin, 1693.

Les Mémoires de la cour d'Angleterre, Paris: Claude Barbin, 1695.

Mémoires secrets de Mr L. D. D. O., ou Les avantures comiques de plusieurs grands princes de la cour de France, Paris: J. Bredou, 1696.

Les Illustres Fées, contes galans, Paris: M.-M. Brunet, 1698.

Le Comte de Warwick, Amsterdam: Desbordes, 1704.

L'Histoire d'Hypolite comte de Duglas, ed. Shirley Day Jones. Somerset: Castle Cary Press, 1994.

Contes I, ed. Philippe Hourcade, Paris: Société des Textes Français Modernes, 1997.

Contes II, ed. Philippe Hourcade, Paris: Société des Textes Français Modernes, 1998.

Barclay, Colonel D., *Reliquiae Barclaianae: Correspondence of Colonel D. Barclay and Robert Barclay of Urie and his son Robert, including Letters from Princess Elisabeth of the Rhine, the Earl of Perth, the Countess of Sutherland, William Penn, George Fox and others*, London: Winter & Bailey, 1870.

Barthélmy, Edouard and René Kerviler (eds.), *Un Tournoi de trois pucelles en l'honneur de Jeanne d'Arc. Lettres inédites de Conrart, de Mlle de Scudéry et de Mlle du Moulin*, Paris: Alphonse Picard, 1878.

Beaujeu, Anne de, *Les Enseignements d'Anne de France à sa fille Susanne de Bourboni*, ed. A.-M. Chazaud, Moulins: C. Desrosiers, 1878.

Beauvoir, Simone de, *The Second Sex*, trans. H. M. Parshley, Harmondsworth: Penguin, 1983.

Bellaguet, M. L. (ed.), *Chronique du Religieux de Saint-Denys*, 6 vols., Paris: Editions du Comité des travaux historiques et scientifiques, 1994.

Bergomensis, Jacobus Philippus, *De Claris Mulieribus*, Ferrara: Magistri Laurentii de rubeis Valentia, 1497.

Berquin, Le Chevalier de, *Déclamation des louanges de mariage*, ed. Emile Telle, Geneva: Droz, 1976.

Besse, Joseph, *A Collection of the Sufferings Of the People called Quakers, For The Testimony of a Good Conscience*, 2 vols., London: Luke Hinde, 1753.

Bodin, Jean, *Les Six Livres de la République*, Paris: Jacques du Puis, 1583; republished London: Scientia Aalen, 1961.

On Sovereignty, trans. Julian H. Franklin, Cambridge University Press, 1991.

Boethius, *The Consolation of Philosophy*, trans. Victor Watts, Harmondsworth: Penguin, 1999.

Bouchet, Jean, *Le Temple de Bonne Renommee*, Milan: Vita e Pensiero, 1992; first edition Paris: Galliot du Pré, 1516.

Triomphes de la noble et amoureuse dame et l'art de honnestement aymer, Poitiers: Jehan le Marnef, 1530.

Jugement poétique de l'honneur féminin, Poitiers: Jehan et Enguilbert de Marnef Frères, 1538.

Bourbon, Gabrielle, *Oeuvres spirituelles 1510–1516*, ed. Evelyne Berriot-Salvadore, Paris: Champion, 1999.

Brantôme, Pierre de Bourdeille, Seigneur de, *Oeuvres complètes*, 9 vols., Paris: Jules Renouard, 1866.

Briçonnet, Guillaume, and Marguerite d'Angoulême, *Correspondance*, ed. Christine Martineau and Michel Veissière, Geneva: Droz, 1975.

Carrier, Hubert, *La Fronde. Contestation démocratique et misère paysanne, 52 Mazarinades*, 2 vols., Paris: Editions d'Histoire Sociale, 1982.

Cary, Mary, *see* Rande, Mary.

Castiglione, Baldassare, *The Book of the Courtier*, trans. Thomas Hoby, London: Everyman, 1994.

Cavendish, Margaret, *The Philosophical and Physical Opinions, Written by her Excellency, the Lady Marchionesse of Newcastle*, London: J. Martin and J. Allestrye, 1655.

The Worlds Olio. Written By the Right Honorable, the Lady Margaret Newcastle, London: J. Martin and J. Allestrye, 1655.

CCXI. Sociable Letters, Written By The Thrice Noble, Illustrious, and Excellent Princess, the Lady Marchioness of Newcastle, London: William Wilson, 1664.

Philosophical Letters: Or, Modest Reflections Upon some Opinions in Natural Philosophy, Maintained By several Famous and Learned Authors of this Age, Expressed by way of Letters: By the Thrice Noble, Illustrious, and Excellent Princess, The Lady Marchioness of Newcastle, London: privately published, 1664.

The Life of the Thrice Noble, High and Puissant Prince William Cavendishe, London: A. Maxwell, 1667.

A Collection of Letters And Poems: Written by several Persons of Honour and Learning, Upon divers Important subjects, to the Late Duke and Dutchess of Newcastle, London: Langly Curtis, 1678.

Grounds of Natural Philosophy: Divided into Thirteen Parts: With an Appendix containing Five Parts, with an introduction by Colette V. Michael, facsimile reprint of 1668 edition, West Cornwall, CT: Locust Hill Press, 1996.

'A True Relation of My Birth, Breeding and Life', in *Paper Bodies: A Margaret Cavendish Reader*, ed. Sylvia Bowerbank and Sara Mendelson, Ontario: Broadview Press, 2000, pp. 41–63.

The Description of a New World, Called The Blazing World. Written by the Thrice Noble, Illustrious, and Excellent Princess, the Duchess of Newcastle, in Cavendish, *Political Writings*.

Political Writings, ed. Susan James, Cambridge Texts in the History of Political Thought, Cambridge University Press, 2003.

Orations of Divers Sorts, Accommodated to Divers Places. Written by the thrice Noble, Illustrious and excellent Princess, the Lady Marchioness of New Castle (1662), in Cavendish, *Political Writings*.

Cavendish, William, *Ideology and Politics on the Eve of the Restoration: Newcastle's Advice to Charles II*, transcribed with an introduction by Thomas P. Slaughter, Independence Square, Philadelphia: The American Philosophical Society, 1984.

Cereta, Laura, *Laurae Ceretae Brixiensis Feminae Clarissimae Epistolae Iam Primum e MS in Lucem Productae*, ed. Jacobo Philippo Tomasino, Padua: Sebastiano Sardi, 1640.

Laura Cereta: Quattrocento Humanist, ed. Albert Rabil, Binghamton: Medieval & Renaissance Texts Studies, 1981.

Collected Letters of a Renaissance Feminist, ed. and trans. Diana Robin, Chicago: University of Chicago Press, 1997.

Champier, Symphorien, *La Nef des dames vertueuses*, Lyon: Jacques Arnollet, 1503; Paris: Jehan de Lagarde, 1515.

Chapelain, Jean, *La Pucelle, ou la France délivrée*, 1656; reprint, Paris: Marpon & Flammarion, 1891.

Chartier, Alain, *The Quarrel of the Belle dame sans mercy*, ed. and trans. Joan E. McRae, New York and London, Routledge, 2004.

Chidley, Katherine, *The Justification of the Independant Churches of Christ*, London: William Larner, 1641.

A New-Yeares-Gift, or A Brief Exhortation to Mr. Thomas Edwards, [London: n. p.], 1645 [i.e. 1644].

Good Counsell, to the Petitioners for Presbyterian Government, [London: n.p., 1645].

Christina, Queen of Sweden, *Mémoires concernant Christine, reine de Suède*, ed. Johan Arckenholtz, 4 vols., Amsterdam: Pierre Mortier, 1751.

The Works of Christina Queen of Sweden. Containing Maxims and Sentences, In Twelve Centuries; and Reflections on the Life and Actions of Alexander the Great, London: Wilson and Durham, 1753.

Apologies, ed. Jean-François de Raymond. Paris: Editions du Cerf, 1994.

Christine de Pizan, *see* Pizan, Christine de.

Chudleigh, Mary, *The Ladies Defence: or, The Bride-Woman's Counsellor Answered: A Poem in a Dialogue between Sir John Brute, Sir William Loveall, Melissa, and a Parson. Written by a Lady*, London: John Deeve, 1701.

Collier, Thomas, *A Looking Glasse for the Quakers, Wherein They may behold themselves*, London: Thomas Brewster, 1657.

Coste, F. Hilarion de, *Les Eloges et les Vies des Reynes, des Princesses, et des Dames Illustres en Pieté, en Courage et en Doctrine, qui en fleury en nostre temps, et du temps de nos Peres*, Paris: Sebastien Cramoisy et Gabriel Cramoisy, 1647.

Cotton, Priscilla, *A Testimony of Truth to all Friends*, n.p.: Printed for M.W. [Mary Westwood], no date.

'Concerning the Passages of her Trial [at Exeter]' (1656?), in *Original Records of Sufferings*, 8 vols. Manuscript in Friends House Library, London, vol. III (items 251–375), item 310.

A Briefe Description by way of supposition holding forth to the Parliament and such as have but common reason, wherein a true Common-wealth consisteth, London: n.p., 1659.

A Visitation of Love Unto all People, London: Thomas Simmons, 1661.

Cotton, Priscilla and Mary Cole, *To the Priests and People of England, we discharge our consciences, and give them warning*, London: Giles Calvert, 1655.

Crenne, Helisenne de, *Les Angoysses douloureuses qui procedent d'amours (1538)*, ed. Paul Demats, Paris: Belles Lettres, 1968.

Oeuvres, Geneva: Slatkine Reprints, 1977.

A Renaissance Woman: Helisenne's Personal and Invective Letters, trans. Marianna M. Mustacchi and Paul J. Archambault, Syracuse, NY: Syracuse University Press, 1986.

Les Epistres familieres et invectives de ma dame Helisenne, Montreal: Les Presses de l'Université de Montréal, 1995.

The Torments of Love, trans. Lisa Neall and Steven Rendall, Minneapolis: University of Minnesota Press, 1996.

D'Albret, Jeanne, *Mémoires et Poésies*, ed. Le Baron de Ruble, Geneva: Slatkine Reprints, 1970.

Dante (Dante Alighieri), *Dante Alighieri: tutte le opere*, ed. F. Chiapelli, 3rd edition, Milan: Mursia, 1965.

The Divine Comedy of Dante Alighieri: Inferno, ed. Robert M. Durling and Ronald L. Martinez, New York: Oxford University Press, 1996.

Monarchy, ed. and trans. Prue Shaw, Cambridge University Press, 1996.

Davenant, Charles, *Essays upon Peace at Home, and War Abroad. In Two Parts*, 2nd edn, London: James Knapton, 1704.

Dentière, Marie, *Epistle to Marguerite de Navarre and Preface to a Sermon by John Calvin*, ed. and trans. Mary B. McKinley, Chicago: University of Chicago Press, 2004.

Descartes, René, *Descartes: His Moral Philosophy and Psychology*, translated with an introduction by John J. Blom, New York: New York University Press, 1978.

Oeuvres de Descartes, ed. Charles Adam and Paul Tannery, 11 vols., new edition, Paris: Librairie Philosophique J. Vrin, 1996.

Docwra, Anne, *A Looking-Glass for the Recorder and Justices of the Peace, and Grand Juries for the Town and County of Cambridge*, [London: n.p.,] 1682.

An Epistle of Love And Good Advice, To my Old Friends & Fellow-Sufferers in the Late Times, The Old Royalists And their Posterity, And to all others that have any sincere Desires towards God, London: Andrew Sowle, 1683.

Spiritual Community, vindicated amongst people of different perswasions in some things, London: [n.p.,] 1687.

An Apostate-Conscience Exposed, And The Miserable Consequences thereof Disclosed, For Information and Caution. By an Ancient Woman, and Lover of Truth, and the sincere Friends thereof, A.D., London: T. Sowle, 1699.

The Second Part of An Apostate-Conscience Exposed: Being an Answer to a Scurrilous Pamphlet, London: T. Sowle, 1700.

[Drake, Judith,] *An Essay In Defence of the Female Sex. In which are inserted the Characters Of A Pedant, A Squire, A Beau, A Vertuoso, A Poetaster, A City-Critick, & c. In a Letter to a Lady. Written by a Lady*, London: Printed for A. Roper, E. Wilkinson, and R. Clavel, 1696.

Edwards, Thomas, *Reasons against the Independant* [sic] *Government of Particular Congregations: As also against the Toleration of such Churches to be erected in this Kingdome*, London: Richard Cotes for Jo Bellamie and Ralph Smith, 1641.

Elizabeth I, *Collected Works*, ed. Leah S. Marcus, Janel Mueller, and Mary Beth Rose, Chicago and London: The University of Chicago Press, 2000.

'Eugenia', *The Female Advocate; Or, A Plea for the just Liberty of the Tender Sex, and particularly of Married Women*, London: Andrew Bell, 1700.

Fedele, Cassandra, *Oratio pro Bertucio Lamberto*, Modena, 1487; Venice, 1488; and Nuremberg, 1489.

Clarissimæ Feminæ Cassandrae Fidelis Venetæ Epistolæ & Orationes, ed. Jacobo Philippo Tomasino, Padua: Franciscus Bolzetta, 1636.

Letters and Orations, ed. and trans. Diana Robin, Chicago: University of Chicago Press, 2000.

Fell, Margaret, *Womens Speaking Justified, Proved and Allowed of by the Scriptures*, London: n.p., 1667 [i.e. 1666].

Undaunted Zeal: The Letters of Margaret Fell, ed. Elsa F. Glines, Richmond, IN: Friends United Press, 2003.

Fenster, Thelma and Mary Carpenter Erler (eds.), *Poems of Cupid, God of Love*, Leiden: Brill, 1990.

Filmer, Robert, *Patriarcha and Other Political Works of Sir Robert Filmer*, ed. Peter Laslett, Oxford: Basil Blackwell, 1949.

Fonte, Moderata, *La feste. Rappresentazione avanti il Serenissimo Prencipe di Venetia Nicolò Ponte il giorno di S. Stefano*, Venice: Guerra, 1581.

Tredici canti del Floridoro di Mad. Moderata Fonte, Venice: 1581.

La Passione di Christo descritta in ottava rima da Moderata Fonte, Venice: Guerra, 1582.

La Resurrezione de Gesù nostro Signore che segue alla Santissima Passione in ottava rima da Moderata Fonte, Venice: Imberti, 1592.

Il merito delle donne scritto da Moderata Fonte in due giornate ove chiaramente si scopre quanto siano elle degne e più perfette de gli huomini, Venice: Imberti, 1600.

Il merito delle donne, ed. Adriana Chemello, Venice: Eidos, 1988.

Tredici canti del Floridoro, ed. Valeria Finucci, Bologna: Mucchi, 1995.

The Worth of Women, ed. and trans. Virginia Cox, Chicago and London: The University of Chicago Press, 1997.

Forster, Mary, [and 7,000 others], *These several Papers Was sent to the Parliament, The twentieth day of the fifth Moneth, 1659*, London: Mary Westwood, 1659.

Gournay, Marie le Jars de, *Adieu de l'Ame du Roy de France et de Navarre Henry le Grand à la royne, avec, La Défence des Pères Iésuites*, Paris: Fleury Bourriquant, 1610.

Les Advis ou Les Présens de la Demoiselle de Gournay, reprint, Paris: Toussainct Du-Bray, 1634; reprinted with additions, 1641.

Adieu de l'ame du roy de France et de Navarre Henry le Grand à la royne. Avec, la défence des Peres Jesuistes, in Arnould *et al.* (eds.), *Oeuvres complètes*.

Apology for the Woman Writing and Other Works, ed. and trans. Richard Hillman and Colette Quesnel, Chicago: University of Chicago Press, 2002.

Oeuvres complètes, ed. Jean-Claude Arnould, Evelyne Berriot, Claude Blum, Anna Lia Franchetti, Marie-Claire Thomine, and Valerie Worth-Stylianou, 2 vols., Paris: Champion, 2002.

Hobbes, Thomas, *The Philosophicall Rudiments concerning Government and Society*, London: J. G. for R. Royston, 1651.

Leviathan, ed. Richard Tuck, Cambridge Texts in the History of Political Thought, rev. student edn, Cambridge University Press, 1996.

James, Elinor, *Elinor James*, in *The Early Modern Englishwoman: A Facsimile Library of Essential Works. Series II. Printed Writings, 1641–1700: Part 3, vol. 11*, selected and introduced by Paula McDowell, Aldershot: Ashgate, 2005.

Johnson, Elizabeth, 'Preface to the Reader', in [Elizabeth Singer Rowe], *Poems On Several Occasions. Written by Philomela*, London: John Dunton, 1696.

Knox, John, *The Political Writings of John Knox: The First Blast of the Trumpet Against the Monstrous Regiment of Women, and Other Selected Works*, edited with an introduction by Marvin A. Breslow, Washington: The Folger Shakespeare Library, 1985.

Labé, Louise, *Complete Poetry and Prose: A Bilingual Edition*, ed. Deborah Lesko Baker, trans. Deborah Lesko Baker and Annie Finch, Chicago: Chicago University Press, 2006.

La Boëtie, Etienne de, *The Politics of Obedience: The Discourse of Voluntary Servitude*, ed. Murray N. Rothbard, trans. Harry Kurz, New York: Free Life Editions, 1975.

De la servitude volontaire ou Contr'un, ed. Malcolm Smith, Geneva: Droz, 1987.

La Fayette, Marie Madeleine Pioche de la Vergne, Comtesse de, *Mémoires de la cour de France pendant les années 1688–1689*, Amsterdam: Chez Jean-Frédéric Bernard, 1731.

Histoire de Madame Henriette d'Angleterre, Paris: Chavaray Freres, 1882.

Oeuvres de Madame de Lafayette, Paris: Chardon, 1786.

La Princesse de Clèves. Geneva: Droz, 1950.

The Princess of Cleves, trans. Mary Mitford, Harmondsworth: Penguin, 1950.

Histoire de la princesse de Montpensier, ed. Micheline Cuénin, Geneva: Droz, 1979.

le Franc, Martin, *Le Champion des Dames*, ed. Robert Deschaux, 5 vols., Paris: Champion, 1999.

Lipsius, Justus, *Sixe Bookes of Politickes or Civil Doctrine. Done into English by William Iones [London 1594]*, Amsterdam: Da Capo Press, 1970.

Locke, John, *The Works of John Locke*, 4 vols., London: H. Woodfall *et al.*, 1768.

A Letter Concerning Toleration, ed. James Tully, Indianapolis: Hackett Publishing, 1983.

Two Treatises of Government, ed. Peter Laslett, Cambridge University Press, 1988.

Luttrell, Narcissus, *A Brief Historical Relation of State Affairs from September 1678 to April 1714*, 6 vols., Oxford University Press, 1857.

Maintenon, Françoise d'Aubigné, Marquise de, *Entretiens sur l'éducation des filles*, ed. Théophile Lavallée, Paris: Charpentier, 1854.

Lettres sur l'éducation des filles, ed. Théophile Lavallée, Paris: Charpentier, 1854.

Lettres historiques et édifiantes, ed. Théophile Lavallée, 2 vols., Paris, 1856.

Conseils aux demoiselles pour leur conduite dans le monde, ed. Théophile Lavallée, Paris: Charpentier, 1857.

Madame de Maintenon, extraits de ses lettres, avis, ed. Octave Gréard, Paris: Hachette, 1884.

Comment la sagesse vient aux filles, ed. Pierre-E. Leroy and Marcel Loyau, Paris: Bartillat, 1998.

Dialogues and Addresses, trans. John J. Conley, Chicago and London: Chicago University Press, 2004.

Marenbon, John, *Boethius*, ed. Brian Davies, Oxford University Press, 2003.

Marinella, Lucrezia, *La colomba sacra. Poema eroico di Lucrezia Marinella*, Venice: Ciotto, 1595.

Vita del serafico et glorioso San Francesco. Descritto in ottava rima da Lucrezia Marinella. Ove si spiegano le attioni, le astinenze e i miracoli di esso, Venice: Bertano, 1597.

Amore innamorato ed impazzato. Poema di Lucrezia Marinella, Venice: 1598.

La nobiltà et eccellenza delle donne co' diffetti et mancamenti de gli huomini, Venice: Ciotti Senese, 1601.

La vita di Maria Vergine imperatrice dell'universo, Venice: B. Barezzi, 1602.

Rime sacre, Venice: 1603.

Arcadia felice di Lucrezia Marinella, Venice: Ciotti, 1605.

Vita di Santa Giustina in ottava rima, Florence: 1606.

De' gesti heroici e della vita meravigliosa della serafica Santa Caterina da Siena, di Lucrezia Marinella. Libri sei, Venice: B. Barezzi, 1624.

L'Enrico overo Bisantio conquistato. Poema heroico, Venice: 1635.

Le vittorie di Francesco il serafico. Li passi gloriosi della diva Chiara, Padua: Crivellari, 1647.

Holocausto d'amore della vergine Santa Giustina, Venice: Leni, 1648.

The Nobility and Excellence of Women, and the Defects and Vices of Men, ed. and trans. Anne Dunhill, with an introduction by Letizia Panizza, Chicago University Press, 1999.

Masham, Damaris Cudworth, *A Discourse Concerning the Love of God*, London: Awnsham and John Churchil, 1696.

Occasional Thoughts in Reference to a Vertuous or Christian Life, London: A. and J. Churchil, 1705.

The Philosophical Works of Damaris, Lady Masham, with an introduction by James G. Buickerood, Bristol: Thoemmes Continuum, 2004.

Menut, A. D., (ed.), *Maistre Nicole Oresme, Le Livre de ethiques d'Aristote, Published from the Text of Ms 2902, Bibliothèque Royale de Belgique*, New York: G. E. Stechart, 1940.

Mézières, Philippe de, *Le Songe du vieil pelerin*, ed. G. W. Coopland, 2 vols., Cambridge University Press, 1969.

Mill, John Stuart, *On Liberty*, ed. C. L. Ten, New York: Oxford University Press, 1980.

Miller, Joshuah, *Antichrist in Man The Quakers Idol. Or a faithfull discovery of their ways and opinions by an eye and ear-witness thereof*, London: J. Macock for L. Lloyd, 1655.

Montaigne, Michel de, *Essays of Montaigne*, ed. William Carew Hazlitt, trans. Charles Cotton, 5 vols., London: The Navarre Society Limited, 1923.

Essais, ed. Maurice Rat, 3 vols., Paris: Garnier Frères, 1958.

The Essays of Michel de Montaigne, trans. and ed. M. A. Screech, London: Allen Lane, 1991.

Montpensier, Anne-Marie Louise d'Orléans, *Mémoires*, 2 vols., Paris: Fontaine, 1985.

'Munda, Constantia', *The Worming of a mad Dogge: Or, a Soppe for Cerberus the Jaylor of Hell*, London: Laurence Hayes, 1617.

Nalson, John, *The Common Interest of King and People*, London: Jonathan Edwin, 1677.

Navarre, Marguerite de, *L'Heptaméron*, ed. Michel François, Paris: Garnier, 1967.

    Suyte des Marguerites de la Marguerite des princesses, Lyon: Jean de Tournes, 1547; reprint, The Hague: Johnson Reprint and Mouton, 1970.

    Le Miroir de l'ame pecheresse, ed. Renja Salminen, Helsinki: Soulalainen Tiedeakatemia, 1979.

    The Heptameron, ed. and trans. P. Chilton, Harmondsworth: Penguin, 1984.

    Les Prisons, ed. and trans. Claire Lynch Wade, New York: Peter Lang, 1989.

    The Coach and the Triumph of the Lamb, trans. Hilda Dale, Exeter: Elm Bank Publications, 1999.

    Heptaméron, ed. Renja Salminen, Geneva: Droz, 1999.

Nemours, Marie d'Orléans, Duchesse de, *Mémoires de Marie d'Orléans, duchesse de Nemours. Suivis de Lettres inédites de Marguerite de Lorraine, duchesse d'Orléans*, ed. Micheline Cuénin, Paris: Mercure de France, 1990.

Nogarola, Isotta, *Isotæ Nogarolæ Veronensis Opera Quæ Supersunt omnia accedunt Angelæ et Zeneveræ Nogarolæ epistolæ et carmina*, ed. Eugenius Abel, Budapest: Gerold et Socios, 1886.

    Complete Writings: Letterbook, Dialogue on Adam and Eve, Orations, ed. and trans. Margaret L. King and Diana Robin, Chicago and London: University of Chicago Press, 2004.

Penn, William, *Good Advice to the Church of England, Roman Catholick, and Protestant Dissenter. In which it is endeavoured to be made appear that it is their Duty, Principles & Interest To abolish the Penal Laws and Test*, London: Andrew Sowle, 1687.

Pizan, Christine de, *The boke of the body of Polycye*, London: John Skot, 1521.

    Oeuvres poétiques de Christine de Pisan, ed. Maurice Roy, 3 vols., Paris: Librairie de Firmin Didot et Cie, 1886; reprint, New York: Johnson Reprints, 1965.

    Le livre des fais et bonnes meurs du sage roy Charles V, ed. Suzanne Solente, 2 vols., Paris: Champion, 1936–40; reprint, Geneva: Slatkine, 1975.

    Le Livre de la mutacion de fortune, ed. Suzanne Solente. 4 vols., Paris: Editions A & J Picard, 1959.

    The Epistle of Othea, trans. Stephen Scrope, London: Early English Text Society, 1970.

    Le Ditié de Jehanne d'Arc, ed. and trans. Angus J. Kennedy and Kenneth Varty, Oxford: Medium Aevum Monographs, 1977.

    The Book of the City of Ladies, trans. Earl Jeffrey Richards, London: Picador, 1983.

    The Treasure of the City of Ladies, trans. Sarah Lawson, Harmondsworth: Penguin, 1985.

    Le Livre des Trois Vertus, ed. Charity Cannon Willard and Eric Hicks, Paris: Champion, 1989.

Christine de Pizan's Letter of Othea to Hector, trans. Jane Chance, Newburyport, MA: Focus Information Group, 1990.

Christine's Vision, trans. Glenda K. McLeod, New York: Garland, 1993.

The Book of the Body Politic, ed. and trans. Kate Langdon Forhan, Cambridge University Press, 1994.

The Writings of Christine de Pizan, ed. Charity Cannon Willard, New York: Persea, 1994.

La Città dellè dame, trans. Patrizia Caraffi, ed. Earl Jeffrey Richards, Milan and Trento: Luni Editrice, 1997.

Letter of the God of Love, in *The Selected Writings of Christine de Pizan*.

Le Livre du corps de policie, ed. Angus J. Kennedy, Paris: Champion, 1998.

The Selected Writings of Christine de Pizan, ed. Renate Blumenfeld-Kosinski, New York: W. W. Norton & Co., 1998.

The Book of Deeds of Arms and of Chivalry, trans. Sumner Willard, University Park: Pennsylvania State University Press, 1999.

L'Epistre d'Othea, ed. Gabriella Parussa, Geneva: Droz, 1999.

Le Chemin de longue étude, ed. Andrea Tarnowski, Paris: Le Livre de Poche, 2000.

Le Livre de l'advision Cristine, ed. Christine M. Reno and Liliane Dulac, Paris: Champion, 2001.

The Book of Peace, ed. and trans. Karen Green, Constant J. Mews, and Janice Pinder, University Park, PA: Penn State University Press, 2008.

Poole, Elizabeth, *An Alarum of War, Given to the Army*, London: n.p., [17 May] 1649.

An [other] Alarum of War, Given to the Army, [London: n.p.], 1649.

A Vision: Wherein is manifested the disease and cure of the Kingdome, London: n.p., 1648 [i.e. 9 January 1649].

Pope, Mary, *A Treatise of Magistracy*, London: n.p., 1647.

Behold, Here Is A Word Or, An Answer To The Late Remonstrance of the Army, London: n.p., 1648.

Heare, heare, heare, heare, A Word or Message from Heaven, London: n.p., 1648.

Porete, Marguerite de, *Speculum Simplicium Animarum*, ed. Romana Guarnieri and Paul Verdeyen, Turnhout: Brepols, 1986.

The Mirror of Simple Souls, trans. Ellen Babinsky, New York: Paulist Press, 1993.

Poullain de la Barre, François, *De l'égalité des deux sexes*, Paris: Jean du Puis, 1676.

[Rande, Mary (Cary)], *Twelve Humble Proposals To the Supreme Governours of the three Nations now assembled at Westminster*, London: Henry Hills, for R. C. and Giles Calvert, 1653.

Richelieu, Cardinal, *Testament politique*, ed. Louis André, Paris: Laffont, 1947.

Testament politique de Richelieu, ed. Françoise Hildesheimer, Paris: Société de l'Histoire de France, 1995.

des Roches, Madeleine and Catherine, *Les Oeuvres*, Geneva: Droz, 1993.

From Mother and Daughter: Poems, Dialogues, and Letters of Les Dames des Roches, trans. Anne R. Larsen, Chicago: Chicago University Press, 2006.

Rousseau, Jean-Jacques, *Oeuvres complètes*, 5 vols., Paris: Gallimard, 1959.

Sabadino degli Arienti, Giovanni, *Gynevera de le clare donne*, ed. Corrado Ricci and Alberto Bacchi, Bologna: Gaetano Romagnoli, 1888; reprint, Bologna, 1968.

Sablé, Madame la Marquise de, *Maximes*, Paris: Sebastien Marbre-Cramoisy, 1678.

'Maximes de Madame de Sablé,' in Conley, *Suspicion of Virtue*, pp. 167–74.

Sablière, Madame de la, 'Maximes Chrétiennes de Madame de la Sablière', in Conley, *Suspicion of Virtue*, pp. 181–7.

Sarasin, Jean-François, *Oeuvres de J.-Fr. Sarasin*, ed. Paul Festugière, 2 vols., Paris: Champion, 1926.

Schiff, Mario, *La Fille d'alliance de Montaigne, Marie de Gournay*, Paris: Champion, 1910.

Scudéry, Georges de, *Alaric ou Rome vaincue*, ed. Cristina Bernazzoli, Fasano: Schena-Didier Erudition, 1998.

Scudéry, Madeleine de, *Conversations sur divers sujets*, Paris: Claude Barbin, 1680.

Nouvelles Conversations de morale dédiées au Roy, Paris: Chez la Veuve de Sebastien Marbre-Cramoisy, 1688.

Entretiens de morale dediez au Roy, Paris: Chez Jean Anisson, 1692.

Les Femmes Illustres: or Twenty Heroick Haranges of the most Illustrious Women of Antiquity, London: Dorman Newman, 1693.

Artamène, ou le grand Cyrus, 10 vols., Geneva: Slatkine Reprints, 1972.

'De l'air galant' et autres conversations. Pour une étude de l'archive galante, ed. Delphine Denis, Paris: Champion, 1998.

Clélie. Histoire romaine. Première partie (1654), ed. Chantal Morlet-Chantalat, Paris: Champion, 2001.

Clélie. Histoire romaine. Seconde partie (1655), ed. Chantal Morlet-Chantalat, Paris: Champion, 2002.

Clélie. Histoire romaine. Troisième partie (1657), ed. Chantal Morlet-Chantalat, Paris: Champion, 2003.

The Story of Sappho, trans. Karen Newman, Chicago and London: University of Chicago Press, 2003.

Segrais, Jean Renault de, *Les Nouvelles Françaises ou les divertissements de la princesse Aurélie*, ed. Roger Guichemerre, Paris: Société des Textes Français Modernes, 1990.

Sévigné, Madame de, *The Letters of Madame de Sévigné*, London: W. T. Morrell and Co., 1928.

Correspondance, ed. Roger Duchêne, Paris: Gallimard, 1972.

Shepherd, Simon (ed.), *The Women's Sharp Revenge: Five Women's Pamphlets from the Renaissance*, London: Fourth Estate, 1985.

'Sowernam, Ester', *Ester Hath Hang'd Haman: Or An Answere to a lewd Pamphlet, entituled, The Arraignement of Women*, London: Nicholas Bourne, 1617.

Speght, Rachel, *A Mouzell for Melastomus: The Cynicall Bayter of, and Foule Mouthed Barker against Evahs Sex*, London: Nicholas Okes, 1617.

Sprint, John, *The Bride-Womans Counseller. Being a Sermon Preach'd at a Wedding, May the 11ᵗʰ, 1699, at Sherbourn, in Doresetshire*, London: H. Hills, 1699.

Suchon, Gabrielle, *Traité de la Morale & de la Politique*, 3 vols., Lyon: B. Vignien, 1693.

Traité du Célibat volontaire, ou la Vie sans engagement, 2 vols., Paris: J. and Mich. Guinard, 1700.

Tarabotti, Arcangela, 'Antisatira', in *Contro il lusso donnesco, satira menippea con l'Antisatira di d.A..T. in risposta*, ed. F. Buoninsegni, Siena: Bonetti, 1646.

Le lagrime d'Arcangela Tarabotti per la morte dell'Illustriss. signora Regina Donati, Venice: Guerigli, 1650.

Lettere familiari e di complimento, Venice: Guerigli, 1650.

Che le donne siano della spetie degli huomini. Difesa delle donne di Galerana Barcitotti [pseud.] contro Horatio Plata, Nuremberg: J. Chercherberger, 1651.

'Women are of the Human Species', in *"Women are not Human"*, ed. and trans. Theresa M. Kenney, New York: Crossroad Publishing, 1998, pp. 89–159.

La semplicatà ingannata, Leiden: Gio. Sambix (Elzevier), 1654.

Il paradiso monacale, Venice: Gugliemo Oddoni, 1663.

'L'inferno monacale', in *L''inferno monacale' di Arcangela Tarabotti*, ed. Francesca Medioli, Turin: Rosenberg & Sellier, 1990.

Che le donne siano della spezie degli uomini: Women Are No Less Rational Than Men, ed. Letizia Panizza, London: Institute of Romance Studies, 1994.

Paternal Tyranny, trans. Letizia Panizza, Chicago and London: The University of Chicago Press, 2004.

Lettere familiari e di complimento, ed. Meredith Ray and Lynn Westwater, Turin: Rosenberg and Sellier, 2005.

Thenaud, Jean, *Le Triomphe des vertus. Premier Traité, le Triomphe de Prudence*, ed. Titia J. Schuurs-Janssen, Geneva: Droz, 1997.

Valois, Marguerite de, *Mémoires et autres écrits, 1574–1614*, ed. Elaine Viennot, 2 vols., Paris: Champion, 1999.

Vernon, Jean-Marie de, *L'Amazone chrestienne; ou, les avantures de Madame Saint-Balmon*, Paris: Gaspar Meturas, 1678.

Villedieu, Marie-Catherine-Hortense de (Mlle Desjardins), *Oeuvres complètes*, Geneva: Slatkine Reprints, 1971.

Selected Writings of Madame de Villedieu, ed. Nancy Deighton Klein. New York: Peter Lang, 1995.

Memoirs of the Life of Henriette-Sylvie de Molière, trans. Donna Kuizenga, Chicago and London: Chicago University Press, 2004.

Viollet, M. Paul, 'Comment les femmes ont été exclues en France, de la succession à la couronne', *Mémoires de l'Institut de France, Académie des Inscriptions et Belles-Lettres* 34 (1893), 125–78.

Whitrowe, Joan, *The Humble Address Of The Widow Whitrowe To King William: With a Faithful Warning To the Inhabitants of England, To Haste and Prepare by True Repentance, and Deep Humiliation, to meet the LORD, Before His Indignation burns like Fire, and breaks forth into a mighty Flame, so that none can quench it*, [London: n.p.,] 1689.

The Humble Salutation And Faithful Greeting of the Widow Whitrowe To King William, [London: n.p.,] 1690.

To Queen Mary: The Humble Salutation, And Faithful Greeting Of The Widow Whitrowe. With A Warning To The Rulers of the Earth Before The Day of the LORD breaks forth, that shall burn as an Oven, all the Wicked, and all the Ungodly shall be as Stubble: The Mouth of the LORD hath spoken it, [London: n.p.,] 1690.

To King William And Queen Mary, Grace and Peace. The Widow Whitrow's Humble Thanksgiving to the LORD of Hosts, the King of Eternal Glory, the GOD of all our Mercies, unto whom be Glory, Glory, and Praise for the King's safe Return to England, London: [n.p.,] 1692.

The Widow Whiterows Humble Thanksgiving For The Kings Safe return, London: D. Edwards, 1694.

Faithful Warnings, Expostulations and Exhortations, To The several Professors of Christianity in England, as well those of the Highest as the Lowest Quality, London: E. Whitlock, 1697.

Wollstonecraft, Mary, *A Vindication of the Rights of Man and a Vindication of the Rights of Woman*, ed. Sylvana Tomaselli, Cambridge Texts in the History of Political Thought, Cambridge University Press, 1995.

Woodhouse, A. S. P. (ed.), *Puritanism and Liberty: Being the Army Debates (1647–9) from the Clarke Manuscripts with Supplementary Documents*, introduction by A. S. P. Woodhouse, a foreword by A. D. Lindsay, London: J. M. Dent and Sons, 1951.

SECONDARY SOURCES

Achinstein, Sharon, 'Women on Top in the Pamphlet Literature of the English Revolution', *Women's Studies* 24 (1994), 131–63.

Adams, Tracy, '*Moyenneresse de Traictié de Paix:* Christine de Pizan's Mediators', in Green and Mews (eds.), *Healing the Body Politic*, pp. 177–200.

Åkerlund, Ingrid, *Sixteenth Century French Women Writers*, Lewiston: The Edwin Mellen Press, 2003.

Åkerman, Susanna, 'Kristina Wasa, Queen of Sweden', in *A History of Women Philosophers*, ed. Mary Ellen Waithe, Dordrecht: Kluwer Academic Publishers, 1991, pp. 21–40.

Queen Christina of Sweden and Her Circle: The Transformation of a Seventeenth-Century Philosophical Libertine, Leiden: E. J. Brill, 1991.

Akkerman, Tjiske, and Siep Stuurman (eds.), *Perspectives on Feminist Political Thought in European History from the Middle Ages to the Present*, London: Routledge, 1998.

Allen, Sister Prudence, *The Concept of Woman: The Early Humanist Reformation 1250–1500*, 2 vols., Grand Rapids, Michigan: Erdmans Publishing, 2002.

Altmann, Barbara K., and Deborah McGrady (eds.), *Christine de Pizan: A Casebook*, New York: Routledge, 2003.

Ankers, Neil, 'Paradigm and Politics: Hobbes and Cavendish Compared', in *A Princely Brave Woman: Essays on Margaret Cavendish, Duchess of Newcastle*, ed. Stephen Clucas, Aldershot: Ashgate, 2003, pp. 242–54.

Arbour, Roméo, *Les Femmes et les métiers du livre*, Chicago and Paris: Garamond Press & Didier Erudition, 1997.

Arnoult, Sharon L., 'The Sovereignties of Body and Soul: Women's Political and Religious Actions in the English Civil War', in Fradenburg (ed.), *Women and Sovereignty*, pp. 228–49.

Aronson, Nicole, *Mlle de Scudéry*, New York: Twayne, 1978.

'Amour et mariage dans les œuvres de Mlle de Scúdery', *L'Esprit créateur* 19 (1979), 26–39.

Axton, Marie, *The Queen's Two Bodies: Drama and the Elizabethan Succession*, London: Royal Historical Society, 1977.

Aylmer, G. E. (ed.), *The Levellers in the English Revolution*, London: Thames and Hudson, 1987.

Backhouse, Janet, 'Founders of the Royal Library: Edward IV and Henry VII as Collectors of Illuminated Manuscripts', in *England in the Fifteenth Century: Proceedings of the 1986 Harlaxton Symposium*, ed. Daniel Williams, Woodbridge: The Boydell Press, 1987, pp. 23–41.

Barash, Carol, '"The Native Liberty . . . of the Subject": Configurations of Gender and Authority in the Works of Mary Chudleigh, Sarah Fyge Egerton, and Mary Astell', in *Women, Writing, History 1640–1740*, ed. Isobel Grundy and Susan Wiseman, London: Batsford, 1992, pp. 55–69.

Barr, Alan P., 'Christine de Pizan's *Ditié de Jehanne d'Arc*: A Feminist Exemplum for the Querelle des femmes', *Fifteenth-Century Studies* 14 (1988), 1–12.

Battigelli, Anna, *Margaret Cavendish and the Exiles of the Mind*, Lexington: University Press of Kentucky, 1998.

'Political Thought/Political Action: Margaret Cavendish's Hobbesian Dilemma', in Smith (ed.), *Women Writers*, pp. 40–55.

Beasley, Faith E., *Revising Memory: Women's Fiction and Memoirs in Seventeenth-Century France*, New Brunswick: Rutgers University Press, 1990.

Salons, History and the Creation of Seventeenth-Century France: Mastering Memory, Aldershot: Ashgate, 2006.

Beaune, Colette and Elodie Lequain, 'Femme et histoire en France au xvme siècle: Gabrielle de la Tour et ses contemporaines', *Médiévales: Langue, Textes, Histoire* 38 (2000), special number on 'L'Invention de l'histoire', 111–36.

Bell, Ilona, 'Elizabeth I – Always Her Own Free Woman', in *Political Rhetoric, Power, and Renaissance Women*, ed. Carole Levin and Patricia A. Sullivan, Albany: State University of New York Press, 1995, pp. 57–82.

'Elizabeth and the Politics of Elizabethan Courtship', in *Elizabeth I: Always Her Own Free Woman*, ed. Carole Levin, Jo Eldridge Carney, and Debra Barrett-Graves, Aldershot: Ashgate, 2003, pp. 179–91.

Bell, Maureen, 'Mary Westwood – Quaker Publisher', *Publishing History* 23 (1988), 5–66.

Bell, Maureen, George Parfitt, and Simon Shepherd, 'Priscilla Cotton', in *A Biographical Dictionary of English Women Writers 1580–1720*, Hemel Hempstead: Harvester Wheatsheaf, 1990, p. 56.

Bell, Susan Groag, 'A Lost Tapestry: Margaret of Austria's *Cité des Dames*', in Dulac and Ribemont (eds.), *Une Femme de lettres*, pp. 449–67.

'A New Approach to the Influence of Christine de Pizan: The Lost Tapestries of *The City of Ladies*', in Ribemont (ed.), *Sur le Chemin de longue étude*, pp. 7–12.

The Lost Tapestries of the City of Ladies: Christine de Pizan's Renaissance Legacy, Berkeley: University of California Press, 2004.

Benson, David, *The History of Troy in Middle English Literature*, Woodbridge: D. S. Brewer, 1980.

Benson, Pamela Joseph, *The Invention of the Renaissance Woman: The Challenge of Female Independence in the Literature and Thought of Italy and England*, University Park, PA: The Pennsylvania State University Press, 1992.

Berriot-Salvadore, Evelyne, *Les Femmes dans la société française de la Renaissance*, Geneva: Librairie Droz, 1990.

'La problématique histoire des textes féminins', *Atlantis* 19 (1993), 8–15.

Bertolini, Sonia, 'Gabrielle Suchon: une vie sans engagement?', *Australian Journal of French Studies* 37 (2000), 289–308.

Bertoni, Giulio, *La biblioteca estense e la cultura ferrarese ai tempi del duca Ercole I, 1471–1505*, Turin: Loescher, 1903.

Biermann, Veronica, 'The Virtue of a King and the Desire of a Woman? Mythological Representations in the Collection of Queen Christina', *Art History* 24 (2001), 213–30.

Blamires, Alcuin, *The Case for Women in Medieval Culture*, Oxford: Clarendon Press, 1997.

Blumenfeld-Kosinski, Renate, 'Christine de Pizan and Classical Mythology. Some Examples from the *Mutation de Fortune*', in *The City of Scholars: New Approaches to Christine de Pizan*, ed. Margarete Zimmerman and Dina De Rentiis, Berlin: Walter de Gruyter, 1994, pp. 3–14.

Boislisle, M. A. de, 'Inventaire des bijoux, vêtements, manuscrits et objets précieux appartenant à la comtesse de Montpensier, 1474', *Annuaire-Bulletin de la Société de l'Histoire de France* 17 (1880), 269–309.

Booy, David, *Autobiographical Writings by Early Quaker Women*, Aldershot: Ashgate, 2004.

Bordo, Susan, *The Flight to Objectivity: Essays on Cartesianism and Culture*, Albany: State University of New York Press, 1987.

Bornstein, Diane (ed.), *Ideals for Women in the Works of Christine de Pizan*, Detroit: Michigan Consortium for Medieval and Early Modern Studies, 1981.

Bossy, Michel-André, 'Arms and the Bride: Christine de Pizan's Military Treatise as a Wedding Gift for Margaret of Anjou', in Desmond (ed.), *Christine de Pizan and the Categories of Difference*, pp. 236–56.

Bozard, Laurent, 'Le poète et la princesse. Jean Molinet, Jean Lemaire de Belge, Jean Marot et leurs "muses" Marguerite d'Autriche et Anne de Bretagne', *Le Moyen Français* 57–8 (2005–6), 27–40.

Brabant, Margaret (ed.), *Politics, Gender, and Genre: The Political Thought of Christine de Pizan*, Boulder: Westview, 1992.

Brailsford, H. N., *The Levellers and the English Revolution*, ed. Christopher Hill, London: Cresset Press, 1961.

Brailsford, Mabel Richmond, *Quaker Women 1650–1690*, London: Duckworth, 1915.

Briggs, Robin, *Witches & Neighbours: The Social and Cultural Context of European Witchcraft*, London: Harper Collins, 1996.

Broad, Jacqueline, *Women Philosophers of the Seventeenth Century*, Cambridge University Press, 2002.

'Astell, Cartesian Ethics, and the Critique of Custom', in Kolbrener and Michelson (eds.), *Mary Astell: Reason, Gender and Faith*, pp. 165–79.

'Liberty and the Right of Resistance: Women's Political Writings of the English Civil War Era', in Broad and Green (eds.), *Virtue, Liberty, and Toleration*, pp. 77–94.

'Damaris Cudworth Masham on Women and Liberty of Conscience', in *Feminist History of Philosophy*, ed. Eileen O'Neill and Marcy Lascano, Dordrecht: Springer, forthcoming.

Broad, Jacqueline, and Karen Green (eds.), *Virtue, Liberty, and Toleration: Political Ideas of European Women, 1400–1800*, Dordrecht: Springer, 2007.

Brown, Cynthia, 'The Reconstruction of an Author in Print', in Desmond (ed.), *Christine de Pizan and the Categories of Difference*, pp. 215–35.

Brown-Grant, Rosalind, '*L'Avision Christine*: Autobiographical Narrative or Mirror for the Prince?', in Brabant (ed.), *Politics, Gender, and Genre*, pp. 3–14.

'"Hee! Quel honneur au feminin sexe!" Female Heroism in Christine de Pizan's *Ditié de Jehanne d'Arc*', *Journal of the Institute of Romance Studies* 5 (1997), 123–33.

Brownlee, Kevin, 'Discourses of the Self: Christine de Pizan and the *Roman de la rose*', *Romanic Review* 79 (1988), 199–221.

'Structures of Authority in Christine de Pizan's *Ditié de Jehanne d'Arc*', in *Discourse of Authority in Medieval and Renaissance Literature*, ed. Kevin Brownlee and Walter Stephens, Dartmouth, NH: University Press of New England, 1989, pp. 131–50.

'Literary Genealogy and the Problem of the Father: Christine and Dante', *Journal of Medieval and Renaissance Studies* 23 (1993), 365–87.

'Le moi "lyrique" et généalogie littéraire: Christine de Pizan et Dante dans le *Chemin de long estude*', in '*Musique naturele*'. *Interpretationen zur französischen Lyrik des Spätmittelalters*, ed. Wolf-Dieter Stempel, Munich: Fink, 1995, pp. 105–39.

Bryson, David, *Queen Jeanne and the Promised Land*, Leiden: Brill, 1999.

Buckley, Veronica, *Christina, Queen of Sweden*, London: Harper Perennial, 2005.

Burke, Mary E., Jane Donawerth, Linda Dove, and Karen Nelson (eds.), *Women, Writing and the Reproduction of Culture in Tudor and Stuart Britain*, Syracuse, NY: Syracuse University Press, 2000.

Campbell, P. G. C., 'Christine de Pisan en Angleterre', *Revue de Littérature Comparée* 5 (1925), 659–70.

Cappello, Glori, 'Nicolò Cusano nella corrispondenza de Briçonnet con Margherita di Navarra', *Medioeva. Rivista di storia della filosofia medievale* 1 (1975), 96–128.

Cholakian, Patricia Frances, *Rape and Writing in the 'Heptaméron' of Marguerite de Navarre*, Carbondale: Southern Illinois University Press, 1991.

'The Economics of Friendship: Gournay's *Apologie pour celle qui escrit*', *Journal of Medieval and Renaissance Studies* 25, no. 3 (1995), 407–17.

Women and the Politics of Self-representation in Seventeenth Century France, Newark: University of Delaware Press, 2000.

Clarke, M. L., 'The Making of a Queen: The Education of Christina of Sweden', *History Today* 28 (1978), 228–35.

Clough, Cecil H., 'Daughters and Wives of the Montefeltro: Outstanding Bluestockings of the Quattrocento', *Renaissance Studies* 10 (1996), 31–55.

Collett, Barry, *A Long and Troubled Pilgrimage: The Correspondence of Marguerite d'Angoulême and Vittoria Colonna, 1540–1545*, Princeton, NJ: Princeton Theological Seminary, 2000.

Condren, Conal, 'Casuistry to Newcastle: "The Prince" in the World of the Book', in *Political Discourse in Early Modern Britain*, ed. Nicholas Phillipson and Quentin Skinner, Cambridge University Press, 1993.

Conley, John J., *The Suspicion of Virtue: Women Philosophers in Neoclassical France*, Ithaca: Cornell University Press, 2002.

Cottrell, Robert D., 'Inmost Cravings: The Logic of Desire in the *Heptameron*', in Lyons and McKinley (eds.), *Critical Tales*, pp. 3–24.

Cousin, Victor, *Madame de Sablé*, Paris: Didier, Libraire-Editeur, 1854.

La Société française au XVIIe siècle d'après Le Grand Cyrus de Mlle de Scudéry, 2 vols., Paris: Didier 1858.

Cox, Virginia, 'The Single Self: Feminist Thought and the Marriage Market in Early Modern Venice', *Renaissance Quarterly* 48 (1995), 513–81.

Crane, Mary Thomas, ' "Video et Taceo": Elizabeth I and the Rhetoric of Counsel', *Studies in English Literature 1500–1900* 28 (1988), 1–15.

Crawford, Patricia, 'Women's Published Writings 1600–1700', in *Women in English Society: 1500–1800*, ed. Mary Prior, London: Methuen, 1985, pp. 211–31.

'The Challenges to Patriarchalism: How Did the Revolution affect Women?', in *Revolution and Restoration: England in the 1650s*, ed. John Morrill, London: Collins and Brown, 1992, pp. 112–28.

Women and Religion in England 1500–1720, London and New York: Routledge, 1993.

' "The Poorest She": Women and Citizenship in Early Modern England', in *The Putney Debates of 1647: The Army, The Levellers, and the English State*, ed. Michael Mendle, Cambridge University Press, 2001, pp. 197–218.

Cropp, Glynnis, 'Boèce et Christine de Pizan', *Moyen Age* 87 (1981), 387–417.

'Philosophy, the Liberal Arts, and Theology in *Le Livre de la mutacion de Fortune* and *Le Livre de l'advision Cristine*', in Green and Mews (eds.), *Healing the Body Politic*, pp. 139–59.

Cuénin, Micheline, *Madame de Villedieu: Marie-Catherine Desjardins 1640–1683*, Paris: Champion, 1979.

Curnow, Maureen Cheney, '*The Boke of the Cyte of Ladyes*, an English Translation of Christine de Pisan's *Le Livre de la Cité des dames*', *Les Bonnes Feuilles* 3 (1974), 116–37.

'The *Livre de la Cité des Dames* of Christine de Pisan: A Critical Edition', PhD dissertation, Vanderbilt University, 1975.

DeJean, Joan, 'Amazones et femmes de lettres : pouvoirs politiques et littéraires à l'âge classique', in *Femmes et pouvoirs sous l'Ancien Régime*, ed. Danielle Hasse-Dubosc and Elaine Viennot, Paris: Rivages/Histoire, 1991, pp. 153–71.

Tender Geographies: The Politics of Female Authorship under the Late Ancien Régime, New York: Columbia University Press, 1991.

Ancients Against Moderns: Culture Wars and the Making of a Fin de Siècle, Chicago and London: Chicago University Press, 1997.

'Violent Women and Violence against Women: Representing the "Strong" Woman in Early Modern France', *Signs* 29 (2003), 117–47.

Delany, Sheila, ' "Mothers to Think Back Through": Who Are They? The Ambiguous Example of Christine de Pizan', in *Medieval Texts and Contemporary Readers*, ed. Laurie A. Finke and Martin B. Shichtman, Ithaca, NY: Cornell University Press, 1987, pp. 177–97.

'History, Politics and Christine Studies: A Polemical Reply', in Brabant (ed.), *Politics, Gender, and Genre*, pp. 193–206.

Delisle, Léopold, *Le Cabinet des manuscrits de la Bibliothèque impériale*, 3 vols., Paris: Imprimerie Impériale, 1868–81.

Desmond, Marilynn (ed.), *Christine de Pizan and the Categories of Difference*, Minneapolis: University of Minnesota Press, 1998.

Dotoli, Giovanni, 'Montaigne et les libertins via Mlle de Gournay', *Journal of Medieval and Renaissance Studies* 25 (1995), 381–405.

Downes, Stephanie, 'Fashioning Christine de Pizan in Tudor Defences of Women', *Parergon* 23 (2006), 71–92.

Dufour, Antoine, *Les Vies des dames célèbres (1505)*, Geneva: Librairie Droz, 1970.

Duggan, Anne E., *Salonnières, Furies and Fairies: The Politics of Gender and Cultural Change in Absolutist France*, Newark: University of Delaware Press, 2005.

Dulac, Liliane, 'Authority in the Prose Treatises of Christine de Pizan: The Writer's Discourse and the Prince's Word', in Brabant (ed.), *Politics, Gender, and Genre*, pp. 129–40.

'L'Autorité dans les traités en prose de Christine de Pizan: discours d'écrivain, parole de prince', in Dulac and Ribemont (eds.), *Une Femme de lettres*, pp. 15–24.

Dulac, Liliane, and Christine M. Reno, 'L'Humanisme vers 1400, essai d'exploration à partir d'un cas marginal: Christine de Pizan traductrice de

Thomas d'Aquin', paper presented at the conference 'Pratiques de la culture écrite en France au xvme siècle', Louvain-La-Neuve, 1994.

'The *Livre de l'advision Cristine*', in Altmann and McGrady (eds.), *Christine de Pizan: A Casebook*, pp. 199–214.

'Traduction et adaptation dans l'*Advision Christine* de Christine de Pizan', in *Traduction et adaptation en France à la fin du Moyen Age et à la Renaissance: Actes du Colloque organisé par l'Université de Nancy II (23–24 mars 1995)*, ed. Charles Brucker, Paris: Champion, 1997, pp. 121–31.

Dulac, Liliane, and Bernard Ribemont, *Une Femme de lettres au Moyen Age*, Orléans: Paradigme, 1995.

Dunn, John, *The Political Thought of John Locke: An Historical Account of the Argument of the 'Two Treatises of Government'*, Cambridge University Press, 1969.

Dupont-Ferrier, Gustave, 'Jean d'Orléans, comte d'Angoulême, d'après sa bibliothèque (1467)', *Mélanges d'Histoire du Moyen Age* 1 (1897), 39–72.

Elshtain, Jean Bethke, *Public Man, Private Woman*, Princeton University Press, 1981.

Famiglietti, R. C., *Royal Intrigue: Crisis at the Court of Charles VI*, New York: AMS Press, 1986.

Farinelli, Arturo, *Dante nelle opere di Christine de Pisan*, Halle: Niemeyer, 1905. *Dante e la Francia dall'età media al secolo di Voltaire*, 2 vols., Milan: Hoepli, 1908.

Fenster, Thelma, 'La Fama, la femme, et la Dame de la Tour', in Hicks (ed.), *Au champ des escriptures*, pp. 461–77.

'Who's a Heroine? The Example of Christine de Pizan', in Altmann and McGrady (eds.), *Christine de Pizan: A Casebook*, pp. 115–28.

Ferrante, Joan, 'Dante's Beatrice. Priest of an Androgynous God', in *Occasional Papers*, Center for Medieval and Early Renaissance Studies, No. 2, Binghamton: Medieval & Renaissance Texts & Studies, 1992, pp. 1–32.

ffolliott, Sheila, 'Exemplarity and Gender: Three Lives of Queen Catherine de' Medici', in Mayer and Woolf (eds.), *The Rhetorics of Life Writing*, pp. 321–40.

Fletcher, Jefferson B., 'The Allegory of the *Vita nuova*', *Modern Philology* 11 (1913), 19–37.

Fogel, Michèle, *Marie de Gournay*, Paris: Fayard, 2004.

Forhan, Kate Langdon, 'Reading Backward: Aristotelianism in the Political Thought of Christine de Pizan', in Hicks (ed.), *Au champ des escriptures*, pp. 359–481.

The Political Theory of Christine de Pizan, Aldershot: Ashgate, 2002.

Foxton, Rosemary, *Hear the Word of the Lord: A Critical and Bibliographical Study of Quaker Women's Writing, 1650–1700*, Melbourne: The Bibliographical Society of Australia and New Zealand, 1994.

Fradenburg, Louise Olga (ed.), *Women and Sovereignty*, Edinburgh University Press, 1992.

Frank, Felix, 'Marguerite d'Angoulême, sœur de François Ier, reine de Navarre, et l'esprit nouveau en France au xvie siècle', *Revue Moderne* 38 (1866), 220–42.

Freccero, Carla, 'Marguerite de Navarre and the Politics of Maternal Sovereignty', in Fradenburg (ed.), *Women and Sovereignty*, pp. 132–49.

Gallagher, Catherine, 'Embracing the Absolute: The Politics of the Female Subject in Seventeenth-Century England', *Genders* 1 (1988), 24–39.

Gardiner, Judith Kegan, 'Margaret Fell Fox and Feminist Literary History: "A Mother in Israel" Calls to the Jews', *Prose Studies* 17 (1994), 42–56.

Garman, Mary, Judith Applegate, Margaret Benefiel, and Dortha Meredith (eds.), *Hidden in Plain Sight: Quaker Women's Writing 1650–1700*, with a foreword by Rosemary Radford Ruether, Wallingford, PA: Pendle Hill Publications, 1996.

Genlis, Stéphanie Félicité de, *De l'influence des femmes sur la littérature française, comme protectrices des lettres et comme auteurs (ou Précis de l'histoire des femmes françaises les plus célèbres)*, Paris: Maradan, 1811.

Gentles, Ian, 'London Levellers and the English Revolution: The Chidleys and Their Circle', *Journal of Ecclesiastical History* 29 (1978), 281–309.

Gibaldi, Joseph, 'Child, Woman, Poet: Vittoria Colonna', in Wilson (ed.), *Women Writers of the Renaissance and Reformation*, pp. 22–46.

Gibbons, Rachel, 'Les conciliatrices au bas Moyen Age: Isabeau de Bavière et la guerre civile (1401–1415)', in *La guerre, la violence et les gens au Moyen Age*, ed. Pierre Contamine and Olivier Guyotjeannin, Paris: Comité des Travaux Historiques et Scientifiques, 1996, pp. 23–33.

'Isabeau of Bavaria, Queen of France (1385–1422): The Creation of an Historical Villainess', *Transactions of the Royal Historical Society*, series 6.6 (1996), 51–73.

'The Piety of Isabeau of Bavaria, Queen of France, 1385–1422', in *Courts, Counties and the Capital in the Later Middle Ages*, ed. Diana Dunn, Stroud: Sutton Publishing, 1996, pp. 205–224.

Gill, Catie, *Women in the Seventeenth-Century Quaker Community: A Literary Study of Political Identities, 1650–1700*, Aldershot: Ashgate, 2005.

'Pope, Mary (d. 1653?)', in *The Oxford Dictionary of National Biography*, Oxford University Press, 2004, http://www.oxforddnb.com/view/article/69153, accessed 6 August 2007.

Gillespie, Katharine, 'A Hammer in Her Hand: The Separation of Church from State and the Early Feminist Writings of Katherine Chidley', *Tulsa Studies in Women's Literature* 17 (1998), 213–33.

Domesticity and Dissent in the Seventeenth Century: English Women's Writing and the Public Sphere Cambridge University Press, 2004.

Goldie, Mark, 'John Locke and Royal Anglicanism', *Political Studies* 31 (1983), 61–85.

'The Theory of Religious Intolerance in Restoration England', in Grell, Israel, and Tyacke (eds.), *From Persecution to Toleration*, pp. 331–68.

'Mary Astell and John Locke', in Kolbrener and Michelson (eds.), *Mary Astell: Reason, Gender and Faith*, pp. 65–85.

Gough, Melinda J., 'Women's Popular Culture? Teaching the Swetnam Controversy', in Malcolmson and Suzuki (eds.), *Debating Gender*, pp. 79–100.

Grandeau, Yann, 'Les enfants de Charles VI: essai sur la vie privée des princes et des princesses de la maison de France à la fin du Moyen Age', *Bulletin Philologique et Historique du Comité des Travaux Historiques et Scientifiques* (1967), 809–50.

'Le Dauphin Jean duc de Touraine', *Bulletin Philologique et Historique du Comité des Travaux Historiques et Scientifiques* (1968), 665–728.

Jeanne insultée: procès en diffamation, Paris: Editions Albin Michel, 1973.

'De quelques dames qui ont servi la reine Isabeau de Bavière', *Bulletin Philologique et Historique du Comité des Travaux Historiques et Scientifiques* (1975), 129–239.

'Isabeau de Bavière ou l'amour conjugal', paper presented at the Congrès National des Sociétés Savantes, Limoges, 1977.

'L'exercice de la piété à la cour de France: les dévotions d'Isabeau de Bavière', paper presented at the conference 'Jeanne d'Arc: une époque, un rayonnement. Colloque d'histoire médiévale', Orléans, 1979.

Green, Karen, *The Woman of Reason*, Cambridge: Polity, 1995.

'Christine de Pisan and Thomas Hobbes', in *Hypatia's Daughters: Fifteen Hundred Years of Women Philosophers*, ed. Linda Lopez McAlister, Bloomington and Indianapolis: Indiana University Press, 1996, pp. 48–67.

'On Translating Christine de Pizan as a Philosopher', in Green and Mews (eds.), *Healing the Body Politic*, pp. 115–37.

'Philosophy and Metaphor: The Significance of Christine's Blunders', *Parergon* 22 (2005), 119–36.

'Isabeau de Bavière and the Political Philosophy of Christine de Pizan', *Historical Reflections/Reflexions Historiques* 32 (2006), 247–72.

'*Phronesis* Feminised: Prudence from Christine de Pizan to Elizabeth I', in Broad and Green (eds.), *Virtue, Liberty, and Toleration*, pp. 23–38.

Green, Karen, and Jacqueline Broad, 'Fictions of a Feminine Philosophical Persona: Christine de Pizan, Margaret Cavendish, and Philosophia Lost', in *The Philosopher in Early Modern Europe: The Nature of a Contested Identity*, ed. Conal Condren, Stephen Gaukroger, and Ian Hunter, Ideas in Context, Cambridge University Press, 2006, pp. 229–53.

Green, Karen, and Constant J. Mews (eds.), *Healing the Body Politic: The Political Thought of Christine de Pizan*, Turnhout: Brepols, 2005.

Grell, Ole Peter, Jonathan I. Israel, and Nicholas Tyacke (eds.), *From Persecution to Toleration: The Glorious Revolution and Religion in England*, Oxford: Clarendon Press, 1991.

Guibbery, Achsah, 'Conversation, Conversion, Messianic Redemption: Margaret Fell, Menessah ben Israel, and the Jews', in *Literary Circles and Cultural Communities in Renaissance England*, ed. Claude J. Summers and Ted-Larry Pebworth, Columbia and London: University of Missouri Press, 2000, pp. 210–34.

Gundersheimer, Werner L., 'Bartolomeo Goggio: A Feminist in Renaissance Ferrara', *Renaissance Studies* 33 (1980), 175–200.

'Women, Learning, and Power: Eleonora of Aragon and the Court of Ferrara', in Labalme (ed.), *Beyond their Sex*, pp. 43–65.

Hanley, Sarah, 'The Monarchic State: Marital Regime Government and Male Right', in *Politics, Ideology, and the Law in Early Modern Europe*, ed. Adrianna Bakos, Rochester, NY: Rochester University Press, 1994, pp. 107–26.

'The Politics of Identity and Monarchic Governance in France: The Debate over Female Exclusion', in Smith (ed.), *Women Writers*, pp. 289–304.

Harrison, Robert Pogue, *The Body of Beatrice*, London and Baltimore: Johns Hopkins University Press, 1988.

Hartle, Anne, 'Montaigne and Scepticism', in *The Cambridge Companion to Montaigne*, ed. Ullrich Langer, Cambridge University Press, 2005, pp. 183–206.

Hartmann, Van C., 'Tory Feminism in Mary Astell's *Bart'lemy Fair*', *The Journal of Narrative Technique* 28, no. 3 (1998), 243–65.

Heisch, Allison, 'Queen Elizabeth I and the Persistence of Patriarchy', *Feminist Review* 4 (1980), 45–54.

Heller, Henri, 'Marguerite of Navarre and the Reformers of Meaux', *Bibliothèque d'Humanisme et Renaissance* 33 (1971), 271–310.

Henderson, Katherine Usher, and Barbara F. McManus (eds.), *Half Humankind. Contexts and Texts of the Controversy about Women in England, 1540–1640*, Urbana and Chicago: University of Illinois Press, 1985.

Hepp, Noemi, 'La notion d'héroïne', in *Onze études sur l'image de la femme dans la littérature française du XVIIe siècle*, Paris: J.-M. Place, 1978, pp. 9–27.

Herrup, Cynthia, 'The King's Two Genders', *Journal of British Studies* 45 (2006), 493–510.

Hicks, Eric (ed.), *Le Débat sur le Roman de la Rose*, Paris: Champion, 1977.

Au champ des escriptures, Paris: Champion, 2000.

Higgins, Patricia, 'The Reactions of Women, with Special Reference to Women Petitioners', in *Politics, Religion, and the English Civil War*, ed. Brian Manning, London: Edward Arnold, 1973, pp. 177–222.

Hill, Christopher, *The World Turned Upside Down: Radical Ideas during the English Revolution*, London: Temple Smith, 1972.

Hinds, Hilary, *God's Englishwomen: Seventeenth-Century Radical Sectarian Writing and Feminist Criticism*, Manchester University Press, 1996.

Hodgkin, Lucy Violet, *A Quaker Saint of Cornwall: Loveday Hambly and Her Guests*, London: Longmans, Green and Co., 1927.

Hughes, Ann, 'Gender and Politics in Leveller Literature', in *Political Culture and Cultural Politics in Early Modern England: Essays Presented to David Underdown*, ed. Susan D. Amussen and Mark A. Kishlansky, Manchester and New York: Manchester University Press, 1995, pp. 162–88.

Hutton, Sarah, 'In Dialogue with Thomas Hobbes: Margaret Cavendish's Natural Philosophy', *Women's Writing* 4 (1997), 421–32.

'Philosophy and Toleration: A Discussion of Anne Conway's *Principia Philosophiae*', in *La formazione storica della alterità*, ed. Antonio Rotondo, Florence: Leo. S. Olschki Editore, 2001, pp. 541–58.

Anne Conway: A Woman Philosopher, Cambridge University Press, 2004.
Ilsley, Marjorie H., *A Daughter of the Renaissance: Marie le Jars de Gournay, Her Life and Works*, The Hague: Mouton, 1963.
Irwin, Joyce, 'Learned Woman of Utrecht: Anna-Maria van Schurman', in *Women Writers of the Seventeenth Century*, ed. Katharina M. Wilson and Frank Warnke, Athens and London: University of Georgia Press, 1989, pp. 164–85.
James, Alan, *The Origins of French Absolutism, 1598–1661*, Harlow: Pearson Education, 2006.
James, Carolyn, '"Machiavelli in Skirts": Isabella d'Este and Politics', in Broad and Green (eds.), *Virtue, Liberty, and Toleration*, pp. 57–75.
James, Margaret, 'The Political Importance of the Tithes Controversy in the English Revolution 1640–60', *History* 26 (1941), 1–18.
James, Susan, 'The Philosophical Innovations of Margaret Cavendish', *British Journal for the History of Philosophy* 7 (1999), 219–44.
Jardine, Lisa, 'Isotta Nogarola: Women Humanists – Education for What?', *History of Education* 12 (1983), 231–44.
Jordan, Constance, 'Women's Rule in Sixteenth-Century British Political Thought', *Renaissance Quarterly* 40 (1987), 421–51.
Jourda, Pierre, *Marguerite d'Angoulême, duchesse d'Alençon, reine de Navarre (1492–1549): Etude biographique et littéraire*, 2 vols., Paris: Champion, 1930; reprint, Geneva: Slatkine Reprints, 1978.
Jowitt, Claire, 'Imperial Dreams? Margaret Cavendish and the Cult of Elizabeth', *Women's Writing* 4 (1997), 383–99.
Kantorowicz, Ernst, *The King's Two Bodies: A Study in Mediaeval Political Theology*, Princeton University Press, 1957.
Keller, Abraham C., 'Montaigne on Women', in *Onze nouvelles études sur l'image de la femme dans la littérature française du dix-septième siècle*, ed. Wolfgang Leiner, Tübingen: Gunter Marr Verlag, 1984, pp. 33–7.
Kelley, Anne, '"Her Zeal for the Publick Good": The Political Agenda in Elizabeth Burnet's *A Method of Devotion* (1708)', *Women's Writing* 13 (2006), 448–74.
Kelley, Donald R., 'Elizabethan Political Thought', in *The Varieties of British Political Thought, 1500–1800*, ed. J. G. A. Pocock with the assistance of Gordon J. Schochet and Lois G. Schwoerer, Cambridge University Press, 1993, pp. 47–79.
Kelly, Joan, 'Did Women have a Renaissance?' in *Women, History and Theory: The Essays of Joan Kelly*, Chicago: University of Chicago Press, 1984, pp. 19–50.
King, Margaret L., 'Thwarted Ambitions: Six Learned Women of the Early Italian Renaissance', *Soundings* 59 (1976), 280–304.
  'Book-Lined Cells: Women and Humanism in the Early Italian Renaissance', in Labalme (ed.), *Beyond their Sex*, pp. 66–90.
  Women of the Renaissance, Chicago and London: University of Chicago Press, 1991.

King, Margaret L., and Albert Rabil (eds.), *Her Immaculate Hand: Selected Works by and about the Women Humanists of Quattrocento Italy*, Binghamton: Medieval & Renaissance Texts & Studies, 1992.

Kinnaird, Joan K., 'Mary Astell and the Conservative Contribution to English Feminism', *The Journal of British Studies* 19 (1979), 53–75.

Kirsop, Wallace, 'Gabrielle Suchon et ses librairies: une note complémentaire', *Australian Journal of French Studies* 37 (2000), 309–11.

Knecht, R. J., *The Fronde*, London: The Historical Association, 1986.

Kolbrener, William, ' "Forc'd into an Interest": High Church Politics and Feminine Agency in the Works of Mary Astell', *1650–1850: Ideas, Aesthetics, and Inquiries in the Early Modern Era* 10 (2004), 3–31.

Kolbrener, William, and Michal Michelson (eds.), *Mary Astell: Reason, Gender and Faith*, Aldershot: Ashgate, 2007.

Kolsky, Stephen, 'Moderata Fonte's *Tredici canti del Floridoro*: Women in a Man's Genre', *Rivista di Studi Italiani* 17 (1999), 165–84.

'Moderata Fonte, Lucrezia Marinella, Giuseppe Passi: An Early Seventeenth-Century Feminist Controversy', *The Modern Language Review* 96 (2001), 973–89.

The Ghost of Boccaccio: Writings on Famous Women in Renaissance Italy, Turnhout: Brepols, 2005.

Kunze, Bonnelyn Young, 'Religious Authority and Social Status in Seventeenth-Century England: The Friendship of Margaret Fell, George Fox, and William Penn', *Church History* 57 (1988), 170–86.

Margaret Fell and the Rise of Quakerism, New York: Macmillan, 1994.

Labalme, Patricia H. (ed.), *Beyond their Sex: Learned Women of the European Past*, New York: New York University Press, 1980.

'Venetian Women on Women: Three Early Modern Feminists', *Archivo Veneto* 5 (1981), 81–108.

Laidlaw, James, 'Christine de Pizan, le duc de Bourbon et le manuscrit de la reine (Londres, British Library, Harley MS 4431)', in *La Chevalerie du Moyen Age à nos jours: mélanges offerts à Michel Stanesco*, ed. Mihaela Voicu and Victor-Dinu Vladulesco, Bucharest: Editura Universitătii din Bucuresti, 2003, pp. 332–44.

'The Date of the Queen's MS (London, British Library, MS 4431)', 2005, www. pizan.lib.ed.ac.uk/harley4431date.pdf, accessed 6 August 2007.

Lecoq, Anne-Marie, *François Ier imaginaire*, Paris: Macula, 1987.

Le Dœuff, Michèle, 'Gabrielle Suchon', in *The Routledge Encyclopedia of Philosophy*, ed. Edward Craig, 10 vols., London and New York: Routledge, 1998, pp. 211–13.

Le Sexe du savoir, Paris: Aubier, 1998.

'Feminism is Back in France, or Is It?' *Hypatia* 15 (2000), 243–55.

The Sex of Knowing, trans. Lorraine Code and Kathryn Hamer, London: Routledge, 2003.

Lefèvre, Sylvie, 'Christine de Pizan et l'Aristote oresmien', in Hicks (ed.), *Au champ des escriptures*, pp. 231–43.

Legaré, Anne-Marie, 'Charlotte de Savoie's Library and Illuminators', *Journal of the Early Book Society* 4 (2001), 32–68.

Léger, Sophie, 'Gabrielle de Bourbon: une grande dame de la France de l'Ouest à la fin du Moyen Age. Etude de son cadre de vie à partir de l'inventaire après décès de ses biens demeurés au château de Thouars (1516)', in *Autour de Marguerite d'Ecosse. Reines, princesses et dames du XVᵉ siècle. Actes du Colloque de Thouars (23 et 24 mai 1997)*, ed. Geneviève and Philippe Contamine, Paris: Champion, 1999, pp. 181–99.

Lerner, Gerda, *The Creation of Feminist Consciousness: From the Middle Ages to Eighteen-Seventy*, Oxford University Press, 1993.

Leucke, Marilyn Serraino, '"God Hath Made No Difference Such as Men Would": Margaret Fell and the Politics of Women's Speech', *Bunyan Studies* 7 (1997), 73–95.

Levi, Anthony, *Renaissance and Reformation: The Intellectual Genesis*, New Haven: Yale University Press, 2002.

Lloyd, Genevieve, *The Man of Reason: 'Male' and 'Female' in Western Philosophy*, London: Methuen, 1984.

'Texts, Metaphors and the Pretensions of Philosophy', *Monist* 69 (1986), 87–102.

Ludlow, Dorothy P., 'Shaking Patriarchy's Foundations: Sectarian Women in England, 1641–1700', in *Triumph Over Silence: Women in Protestant History*, ed. Richard L. Greaves, London and Westport: Greenwood Press, 1985, pp. 93–124.

Lyons, John D., and Mary B. McKinley (eds.), *Critical Tales: New Studies of the 'Heptameron' and Early Modern Culture*, Philadelphia: University of Pennsylvania Press, 1993.

MacCaffrey, Wallace, *Elizabeth I*, London: Edward Arnold, 1993.

McCartney, Elizabeth, 'The King's Mother and Royal Prerogative in Early Sixteenth-Century France', in *Medieval Queenship*, ed. John Carmi Parsons, New York: St. Martin's Press, 1993, pp. 117–41.

McCrystal, John, 'Revolting Women: The Use of Revolutionary Discourse in Mary Astell and Mary Wollstonecraft Compared', *History of Political Thought* 14 (1993), 189–203.

McDonald, Lynn (ed.), *Women Theorists on Society and Politics*, Waterloo, Ontario: Wilfrid Laurier University Press, 1998.

McDowell, Paula, *The Women of Grub Street: Press, Politics, and Gender in the London Literary Marketplace, 1678–1730*, Oxford: Clarendon Press, 1998.

'James, Elinor (1644/5–1719)', in *The Oxford Dictionary of National Biography*, Oxford University Press, 2004, www.oxforddnb.com/view/article/14600, accessed 15 February 2007.

McEntee, Ann Marie, '"The [Un]Civill-Sisterhood of Oranges and Lemons": Female Petitioners and Demonstrators, 1642–53', *Prose Studies* 14 (1991), 92–111.

Maclean, Ian, *Woman Triumphant: Feminism in French Literature, 1610–1652*, Oxford: Clarendon Press, 1977.

Mack, Phyllis, *Visionary Women: Ecstatic Prophecy in Seventeenth-Century England*, Berkeley, CA: University of California Press, 1992.

'Whitrowe, Joan (*fl.* 1665–1697)', in *The Oxford Dictionary of National Biography*, www.oxforddnb.com/view/article/45833, accessed 15 February 2007.

Maître, Myriam, 'Sapho, *reine* de *Tendre*: entre monarchie absolue et royauté littéraire', in *Madeleine de Scudéry: Une femme de lettres au XVIIᵉ siècle*, ed. Delphine Denis and Anne-Elizabeth Spica, Arras: Artois Presses Université, 2002, pp. 179–93.

Malcolmson, Cristina, 'Christine de Pizan's *City of Ladies* in Early Modern England', in Malcolmson and Suzuki (eds.), *Debating Gender*, pp. 15–35.

Malcolmson, Cristina, and Mihoko Suzuki (eds.), *Debating Gender in Early Modern England, 1500–1700*, New York: Palgrave Macmillan, 2002.

Marot, Jehan, *Les Deux Recueils*, ed. Gérard Defaux and Thierry Mantovani, Geneva: Droz, 1999.

Matarasso, Pauline, *Queen's Mate: Three Women of Power in France on the Eve of the Renaissance*, Aldershot: Ashgate, 2001.

Mayer, Thomas F., and D. R. Woolf (eds.), *The Rhetorics of Life Writing in Early Modern Europe*, Ann Arbor: The University of Michigan Press, 1995.

Mendus, Susan, *Toleration and the Limits of Liberalism*, Basingstoke: Macmillan, 1989.

Mendus, Susan (ed.), *Justifying Toleration: Conceptual and Historical Perspectives*, Cambridge University Press, 1988.

Menut, A. D., 'Le *Livre des politiques d'Aristote* de Nicole Oresme', *Transactions of the American Philosophical Society* n.s, 60 (1970), 3–392.

Merkle, Gertrude H., 'Martin Le Franc's Commentary on Jean Gerson's Treatise on Joan of Arc', in *Fresh Verdicts on Joan of Arc*, ed. Bonnie Wheeler and Charles T. Wood, New York: Garland, 1996, pp. 177–204.

Mews, Constant J., 'Latin Learning in Christine de Pizan's *Livre de paix*', in Green and Mews (eds.), *Healing the Body Politic*, pp. 61–80.

Mintz, Samuel I., *The Hunting of Leviathan: Seventeenth Century Reactions to the Materialism and Moral Philosophy of Thomas Hobbes*, Cambridge University Press, 1970.

Mombello, Gianni, *La tradizione manoscritta dell' 'Epistre Othéa' di Christine de Pizan*, Turin: Accademia delle Scienze, 1967.

Moore, Will G., *La Réforme allemande et la littérature française. Recherches sur la notoriété de Luther en France*, Strasbourg: La Faculté des lettres à l'Université, 1930.

Motteville, Françoise Bertaut de, *Mémoires pour servir à l'histoire d'Anne d'Autriche*, Fontaine, 1982.

Müller, Catherine M., '"La lettre et la figure": lecture allégorique du *Mirouer* de Marguerite Porete dans *Les Prisons* de Marguerite de Navarre', *Versants* 38 (2000), 153–67.

'Marie de Clèves, poétesse et mécène du xvᵉ siècle', *Le Moyen Français* 48 (2001), 57–76.

'Autour de Marguerite d'Ecosse: quelques poétesses françaises méconnues du XVᵉ siècle', in *Contexts and Continuities: Proceedings of the IVth International Colloquium on Christine de Pizan (Glasgow 21–27 July 2000), published in honour of Liliane Dulac*, ed. Angus J. Kennedy, Rosalind Brown-Grant, James C. Laidlaw, and Catherine M. Müller, 3 vols., Glasgow University Medieval French Texts and Studies, Glasgow: University of Glasgow Press, 2002, vol. 11, pp. 603–19.

Mullett, Michael, 'Docwra, Anne (*c.* 1624–1710)', in *The Oxford Dictionary of National Biography*, www.oxforddnb.com/view/article/45813, accessed 15 February 2007.

Munro, James S., *Mademoiselle de Scudéry and the Carte de Tendre*, Durham: Durham Modern Language Series, 1986.

Murray, Margaret, *The Witch-Cult in Western Europe*, Oxford: Clarendon Press, 1921.

Nauert, Charles G., *Agrippa and the Crisis of Renaissance Thought*, Urbana: University of Illinois Press, 1965.

Nederman, Cary, 'The Living Body Politic: The Diversification of Organic Metaphors in Nicole Oresme and Christine de Pizan', in Green and Mews (eds.), *Healing the Body Politic*, pp. 19–33.

Nevitt, Marcus, *Women and the Pamphlet Culture of Revolutionary England, 1640–1660*, Aldershot: Ashgate, 2006.

Okin, Susan Moller, *Women in Western Political Thought*, Princeton University Press, 1979.

Pateman, Carole, *The Sexual Contract*, Stanford University Press, 1988.

'Women's Writing, Women's Standing: Theory and Politics in the Early Modern Period', in Smith (ed.), *Women Writers*, pp. 365–82.

Patton, Brian, 'Revolution, Regicide, and Divorce: Elizabeth Poole's Advice to the Army', in *Place and Displacement in the Renaissance*, ed. Alvin Vos, Binghamton, NY: Medieval & Renaissance Texts & Studies, 1995, pp. 133–45.

Penaluna, Regan, 'The Social and Political Thought of Damaris Cudworth Masham', in Broad and Green (eds.), *Virtue, Liberty, and Toleration*, pp. 111–22.

Perry, Ruth, *The Celebrated Mary Astell: An Early English Feminist*, Chicago and London: Chicago University Press, 1986.

'Mary Astell and the Feminist Critique of Possessive Individualism', *Eighteenth-Century Studies* 23 (1990), 444–57.

Petitfils, Jean-Christian, *Louis XIV*, Paris: Perrin, 1997.

Pettit, Philip, *Republicanism: A Theory of Freedom and Government*, Oxford: Clarendon Press, 1997.

Phillippy, Patricia, 'Establishing Authority: Boccaccio's *De Claris Mulieribus* and Christine de Pizan's *Le Livre de la cité des dames*', in Blumenfeld-Kosinski (ed.), *The Selected Writings of Christine de Pizan*, pp. 329–61.

Phillipson, Laurel, 'Quakerism in Cambridge before the Act of Toleration (1653–1689)', *Proceedings of the Cambridge Antiquarian Society* 76 (1987), 1–25.

'Quakerism in Cambridge from the Act of Toleration to the End of the Nineteenth Century', *Proceedings of the Cambridge Antiquarian Society* 77 (1988), 1–33.

Pincus, Steve, 'Neither Machiavellian Moment nor Possessive Individualism: Commercial Society and the Defenders of the English Commonwealth', *The American Historical Review* 103 (1998), 705–36.

Pinet, Marie-Josèphe, *Christine de Pisan*, Geneva: Slatkine Reprints, 1974.

Pintard, René, *Le Libertinage érudit dans la première moitié du XVIIe siècle*, Paris: Slatkine, 1983.

Purkiss, Diane, 'Material Girls: The Seventeenth-Century Woman Debate', in *Women, Texts and Histories 1575–1760*, ed. Clare Brant and Diane Purkiss, London and New York: Routledge, 1992, pp. 69–101.

Quilligan, Maureen, *The Allegory of Female Authority: Christine de Pizan's Cité des Dames*, Ithaca: Cornell University Press, 1991.

Rawls, John, *A Theory of Justice*, Oxford: Clarendon Press, 1972.

Reay, Barry, 'Quaker Opposition to Tithes 1652–1700', *Past and Present* 86 (1980), 98–120.

The Quakers and the English Revolution, with a foreword by Christopher Hill, London: Temple Smith, 1985.

Reeves, Marjorie, *The Influence of Prophecy in the Later Middle Ages: A Study in Joachimism*, Oxford: Clarendon Press, 1969.

Joachim of Fiore and the Prophetic Future, London: SPCK, 1976.

'Dante and the Prophetic View of History', in *The World of Dante: Essays on Dante and His Times*, ed. Cecil Grayson, Oxford: Clarendon Press, 1980, pp. 44–60.

Reno, Christine M., 'Feminist Aspects of Christine de Pizan's *Epistre d'Othea*', *Studi Francesi* 71 (1980), 271–6.

'Christine de Pizan: "At Best a Contradictory Figure?"', in Brabant (ed.), *Politics, Gender, and Genre*, pp. 171–91.

'The Preface to the *Avision-Christine*', in *Reinterpreting Christine de Pizan*, ed. Earl Jeffrey Richards with Joan Williamson, Nadia Margolis, and Christine M. Reno, Athens, GA: The University of Georgia Press, 1992, pp. 207–27.

'Autobiography and Authorship in Christine's Manuscripts', *Romance Languages Annual* 9 (1997), xxi–xxiv.

Ribemont, Bernard (ed.), *Sur le Chemin de longue étude ... Actes du colloque d'Orléans – juillet 1995*, Paris: Champion, 1998.

Richards, Earl Jeffrey, 'Christine de Pizan and Dante: A Reexamination', *Archiv für das Studium der neueren Sprachen und Litteraturen* 222 (1985), 100–11.

'Virile Woman and Womanchrist: The Meaning of Gender Metamorphosis in Christine', in *'Riens ne m'est seur que la chose incertaine': Etudes sur l'art d'écrire au Moyen Age offertes à Eric Hicks par ses élèves, collègues, amies et amis*, ed. Jean-Claude Mühlethaler, Geneva: Slatkine, 2001, pp. 239–52.

'Political Thought as Improvisation: Female Regency and Mariology in Late Medieval French Thought', in Broad and Green (eds.), *Virtue, Liberty, and Toleration*, pp. 1–22.

Robin, Diana, 'Cassandra Fedele's *Epistolae* (1488–1521): Biography as Effacement', in Mayer and Woolf (eds.), *The Rhetorics of Life Writing*, pp. 187–203.

    Publishing Women: Salons, the Presses, and the Counter-Reformation in Sixteenth-Century Italy, Chicago: University of Chicago Press, 2007.

Robin, Diana, Anne R. Larsen, and Carole Levin (eds.), *Encyclopedia of Women in the Renaissance: Italy, France and England*, Santa Barbara: ABC-CLIO, 2007.

Roelker, Nancy Lyman, *Queen of Navarre: Jeanne d'Albret (1528–1572)*, Cambridge, MA: Harvard University Press, 1968.

    'The Role of Noblewomen in the French Reformation', *Archive for Reformation History* 63 (1972), 168–95.

    'The Appeal of Calvinism to French Noblewomen in the Sixteenth Century', *Journal of Interdisciplinary History* 2 (1972), 391–418.

    One King, One Faith: The Parlement of Paris and the Religious Reformations of the Sixteenth Century, Berkeley, CA: University of California Press, 1996.

Rogers, John, *The Matter of Revolution: Science, Poetry and Politics in the Age of Milton*, Ithaca and London: Cornell University Press, 1996.

Ronzeaud, Pierre, 'La femme au pouvoir ou le monde à l'envers', *Dix-Septième Siècle* 108 (1975), 9–33.

Ross, Isabel, *Margaret Fell: Mother of Quakerism*, 3rd edn, York: The Ebor Press, 1996.

Sackville-West, Vita, *Daughter of France: The Life of Anne Marie Louise d'Orléans Duchesse de Montpensier*, London: Michael Joseph, 1959.

Saco, Diana, 'Gendering Sovereignty: Marriage and International Relations in Elizabethan Times', *European Journal of International Relations* 3 (1997), 291–318.

Sapiro, Virginia, *Vindication of Political Virtue: The Political Theory of Mary Wollstonecraft*, Chicago and London: The University of Chicago Press, 1992.

Sarasohn, Lisa T., '*Leviathan* and the Lady: Cavendish's Critique of Hobbes in the *Philosophical Letters*', in *Authorial Conquests: Essays on Genre in the Writings of Margaret Cavendish*, ed. Line Cottegnies and Nancy Weitz, London: Associated University Presses, 2003, pp. 40–58.

Schibanoff, Susan, 'Taking the Gold out of Egypt: The Art of Reading as a Woman', in *Gender and Reading*, ed. Elizabeth A. Flynn and Patrocinio P. Schweickart, Baltimore: Johns Hopkins University Press, 1986, pp. 83–106.

Schnell, Lisa J., 'Muzzling the Competition: Rachel Speght and the Economics of Print', in Malcolmson and Suzuki (eds.), *Debating Gender*, pp. 57–77.

Schochet, Gordon J., *The Authoritarian Family and Political Attitudes in 17th Century England: Patriarchalism in Political Thought*, New Brunswick and London: Transaction Books, 1988.

Schwoerer, Lois G., 'Women and the Glorious Revolution', *Albion: A Quarterly Journal Concerned with British Studies* 18 (1986), 195–218.

'Women's Public Political Voice in England: 1640–1740', in Smith (ed.), *Women Writers*, pp. 56–74.

Scott, Joan W., *Only Paradoxes to Offer: French Feminists and the Rights of Man*, Cambridge, MA: Harvard University Press, 1996.

Segarizzi, A., 'Niccolò Barbo, patrizio veneziano del sec. xv e le accuse contro Isotta Nogarola', *Giornale storico della letteratura italiana* 43 (1904), 39–54.

Sénemaud, Edmond, 'La bibliothèque de Charles d'Orléans, comte d'Angoulême, au château de Cognac (1496)', *Bulletin de la Société Archéologique et Historique de la Charente*, 3rd ser., 2 (1862), 130–87.

Setterwall, Monica, 'Queen Christina and Role Playing in Maxim Form', *Scandinavian Studies* 57 (1985), 162–73.

Skinner, Quentin, 'Thomas Hobbes and his Disciples in France and England', *Comparative Studies in Society and History* 8 (1965), 153–67.

The Foundations of Modern Political Thought, 2 vols., Cambridge University Press, 1978.

Liberty Before Liberalism, Cambridge University Press, 1998.

'Hobbes on the Proper Signification of Liberty', in *Visions of Politics, Volume 3: Hobbes and Civil Science*, Cambridge University Press, 2002, pp. 209–37.

'Conquest and Consent: Hobbes and the Engagement Controversy', in *Visions of Politics*, Volume 3: *Hobbes and Civil Science*, Cambridge University Press, 2002, pp. 287–307.

Slerca, Anna, 'Le *Livre du chemin de longue estude* (1402–1403): Christine au pays des merveilles', in Ribemont (ed.), *Sur le chemin de longue étude*, pp. 135–74.

Slomp, Gabriella, 'Hobbes and the Equality of Women', *Political Studies* 42 (1994), 441–52.

Smith, Hilda L., '"A General War Amongst the Men ... But None Amongst the Women": Political Differences Between Margaret and William Cavendish', in *Politics and the Political Imagination in Later Stuart Britain: Essays Presented to Lois Green Schwoerer*, ed. Howard Nenner, Rochester, NY: University of Rochester Press, 1997, pp. 143–60.

All Men and Both Sexes: Gender, Politics, and the False Universal in England, 1640–1832, University Park, PA: Pennsylvania State University Press, 2002.

'"Cry up Liberty": The Political Context of Mary Astell's Feminism', in Kolbrener and Michelson (eds.), *Mary Astell: Reason, Gender and Faith*, pp. 193–204.

Smith, Hilda L. (ed.), *Women Writers and the Early Modern British Political Tradition*, Cambridge University Press, 1998.

Smith, Hilda L., and Susan Cardinale, *Women and the Literature of the Seventeenth Century: An Annotated Bibliography based on Wing's 'Short-title Catalogue'*, Westport: Greenwood Press, 1985.

Smith, Hilda L., and Berenice A. Carroll (eds.), *Women's Political and Social Thought: An Anthology*, Bloomington, IL: Indiana University Press, 2000.

Smith, Hilda L., Mihoko Suzuki, and Susan Wiseman (eds.), *Women's Political Writings, 1610–1725*, 4 vols., London: Pickering and Chatto, 2007.

Sommers, Paula, 'Marguerite de Navarre as Reader of Christine de Pizan', in *The Reception of Christine de Pizan from the Fifteenth through the Nineteenth Centuries*, ed. Glenda K. McLeod, Lewiston, NY: Edwin Mellen Press, 1992, pp. 71–82.

Speizman, Milton D., and Jane C. Kronick, 'A Seventeenth-Century Quaker Women's Declaration', *Signs* 1 (1975), 231–45.

Springborg, Patricia, 'Mary Astell (1666–1731), Critic of Locke', *American Political Science Review* 89 (1995), 621–33.

'Astell, Masham, and Locke: Religion and Politics', in Smith (ed.), *Women Writers*, pp. 105–25.

'Mary Astell and John Locke', in *The Cambridge Companion to English Literature, 1650 to 1750*, ed. Steven Zwicker, Cambridge University Press, 1998, pp. 276–306.

'Republicanism, Freedom from Domination, and the Cambridge Contextual Historians', *Political Studies* 49 (2001), 851–76.

'Mary Astell, Critic of the Marriage Contract/Social Contract Analogue', in *A Companion to Early Modern Women's Writing*, ed. Anita Pacheco, London: Blackwell, 2002, pp. 216–28.

Mary Astell, Cambridge University Press, 2005.

Stephenson, Barbara, *The Power and Patronage of Marguerite de Navarre*, Aldershot: Ashgate, 2004.

Stevenson, Jane, *Women Latin Poets: Language, Gender and Authority from Antiquity to the Eighteenth Century*, Oxford University Press, 2005.

Stone, Donald, '"La malice des hommes": "L'Histoire des satyres" and the *Heptameron*', in Lyons and McKinley (eds.), *Critical Tales*, pp. 53–64.

Strong, Roy, *Gloriana: Portraits of Elizabeth I*, Oxford: Clarendon Press, 1963.

The Portraits of Queen Elizabeth I, New York: Thames and Hudson, 1987.

Sutherland, Nicola M., 'Catherine de' Medici: The Legend of the Wicked Italian Queen', *Sixteenth Century Journal* 9 (1978), 45–56.

Suzuki, Mihoko, *Subordinate Subjects: Gender, the Political Nation, and Literary Form in England, 1588–1688*, Aldershot: Ashgate, 2003.

Taylor, C. C. W., 'Politics', in *The Cambridge Companion to Aristotle*, ed. Jonathon Barnes, Cambridge University Press, 1995, pp. 233–58.

Taylor, Craig, 'The Salic Law and the Valois Succession to the French Crown', *French History* 15 (2001), 358–77.

Telle, E. V., *L'Œuvre de Marguerite d'Angoulême reine de Navarre et la Querelle des femmes*, Toulouse: Lion, 1937; reprint, Geneva: Slatkine Reprints, 1969.

Tetel, Marcel, 'Marguerite of Navarre: The *Heptameron*, a Simulacrum of Love', in Wilson (ed.), *Women Writers of the Renaissance and Reformation*, pp. 99–131.

Thomas, Keith, 'Women and the Civil War Sects', in *Crisis in Europe 1560–1660*, ed. Trevor Aston, London: Routledge and Kegan Paul, 1965, pp. 317–40; reprinted from *Past and Present* 13 (1958), 42–62.

Thomas, Owen C., 'Beatrice or Iseult? The Debate about Romantic Love', *Anglican Theological Review* 79 (1997), 571–87.

Thysell, Carol, *The Pleasure of Discernment: Marguerite de Navarre as Theologian*, Oxford University Press, 2000.

Timmermans, Linda, *L'Accès des femmes à la culture (1598–1715)*, Paris: Champion, 1993.

Trevett, Christine, *Women and Quakerism in the Seventeenth Century*, York: Sessions Book Trust, The Ebor Press, 1991.

Tuck, Richard, 'Scepticism and Toleration in the Seventeenth Century', in Mendus (ed.), *Justifying Toleration*, pp. 21–36.

Tuetey, Alexandre, 'Inventaire des biens de Charlotte de Savoie', *Bibliothèque de l'Ecole des Chartes* 26 (1865), 338–66.

Tully, James, *A Discourse on Property: John Locke and his Adversaries*, Cambridge University Press, 1980.

Vosevich, Kathi, 'The Education of a Prince(ss)', in Burke *et al.* (eds.), *Women, Writing and the Reproduction of Culture*, pp. 61–76.

Waldron, Jeremy, 'Locke: Toleration and the Rationality of Persecution', in Mendus (ed.), *Justifying Toleration*, pp. 61–86.

   God, Locke, and Equality: Christian Foundations of Locke's Political Thought, Cambridge University Press, 2002.

Walker, Julia M., 'Re-politicizing the *Book of the Three Virtues*', in Hicks (ed.), *Au champ des escriptures*, pp. 533–48.

Wallace, Terry S. (ed.), *A Sincere and Constant Love: An Introduction to the Work of Margaret Fell*, Richmond, IN: Friends United Press, 1992.

Walters, Lori, 'The Royal Vernacular: Poet and Patron in Christine de Pizan's *Charles V* and the *Sept Psaulmes Allégorisés*', in *The Vernacular Spirit. Essays on Medieval Religious Literature*, ed. Renate Blumenfeld-Kosinski, Duncan Robertson and Nancy Bradley Warren, New York: Palgrave, 2002, pp. 145–82.

   'Christine de Pizan as Translator and Voice of the Body Politic', in Altmann and McGrady (eds.), *Christine de Pizan: A Casebook*, pp. 25–42.

Warner, George F., and Julius P. Gilson (eds.), *British Museum, Catalogue of Western Manuscripts in the Old Royal and King's Collection*, 4 vols., London: British Museum, 1921.

Waters, Kirstin, 'Sources of Political Authority: John Locke and Mary Astell', in Waters (ed.), *Women and Men Political Theorists*, pp. 5–19.

Waters, Kirstin (ed.), *Women and Men Political Theorists: Enlightened Conversations*, Malden, MA, and Oxford: Blackwell Publishers, 2000.

Weil, Rachel, *Political Passions: Gender, the Family, and Political Argument in England, 1680–1714*, Manchester: Manchester University Press, 1999.

Weiss, Penny A., 'Mary Astell: Including Women's Voices in Political Theory', *Hypatia* 19 (2004), 63–84.

Wetherbee, Winthrop, 'The Body of Beatrice,' *Modern Philology* 88 (1991), 299–301.

Whitaker, Katie, *Mad Madge: The Extraordinary Life of Margaret Cavendish, Duchess of Newcastle, the First Woman to Live by Her Pen*, New York: Basic Books, 2002.

Willard, Charity Cannon, 'A Portuguese Translation of Christine de Pizan's *Livre des trois vertus*', *PMLA* 78 (1963), 459–64.

'The Manuscript Tradition of the *Livre des Trois Vertus* and Christine de Pisan's Audience', *Journal of the History of Ideas* 27 (1966), 433–44.

Christine de Pisan: Her Life and Works, New York: Persea, 1984.

'The Patronage of Isabel of Portugal', in *The Cultural Patronage of Medieval Women*, ed. June Hall McCash, Athens, GA: University of Georgia Press, 1996, pp. 306–20.

Williams, Charles, *The Figure of Beatrice: A Study in Dante*, Woodbridge and Rochester, NY: D. S. Brewer, 1994; originally published, London: Faber and Faber, 1943.

Wilson, Katharina M. (ed.), *Women Writers of the Renaissance and Reformation*, Athens, GA: University of Georgia Press, 1987.

Wilson, Margaret Dauler, *Descartes*, London and New York: Routledge, 1993.

Winn, Mary Beth, 'Books for a Princess and her Son: Louise de Savoie, François d'Angoulême and the Parisian libraire Anthoine Véraud', *Bibliothèque d'Humanisme et Renaissance* 46 (1984), 604–17.

Wootton, David, 'Leveller Democracy and the Puritan Revolution', in *The Cambridge History of Political Thought 1450–1700*, ed. J. H. Burns, with Mark Goldie, Cambridge University Press, 1991, pp. 412–42.

Wright, Joanne H., 'Going Against the Grain: Hobbes's Case for Original Maternal Dominion', *Journal of Women's History* 14 (2002), 123–55.

Yates, Frances A., *Astraea: The Imperial Theme in the Sixteenth Century*, London: Routledge and Kegan Paul, 1975.

Zimmerman, Margarete, 'Christine de Pizan: Memory's Architect', in Altmann and McGrady (eds.), *Christine de Pizan: A Casebook*, pp. 57–77.

Zook, Melinda, 'Contextualizing Aphra Behn: Plays, Politics, and Party, 1679–1689', in Smith (ed.), *Women Writers*, pp. 75–93.

'Religious Nonconformity and the Problem of Dissent in the Works of Aphra Behn and Mary Astell', in Kolbrener and Michelson (eds.), *Mary Astell: Reason, Gender and Faith*, pp. 99–113.

Index

works:
Discourse Concerning the Love of God,
242
Occasional Thoughts, 242
Medici, Catherine de, 113, 132, 181
Medici, Marie de, 126, 131, 132, 181, 184, 186
Mendus, Susan, 227, 239, 240
Mill, John Stuart, 150, 260
Milton, John, 266, 281
monarchists and monarchism *see* royalists and
royalism
monarchs and monarchy:
absolutist conception of, 110, 124–5, 186, 187,
199, 225, 269, 277
conjugal (marital) conception of, 102, 103,
124–5, 132, 157 8
constitutional, 269–70, 277
hereditary, 128
parental conception of, 31, 36, 37, 91, 102–3,
124–5, 126–7, 128, 132, 157–8, 186, 198,
240, 241
pastoral conception of, 6, 94, 114, 227, 230,
240
Montaigne, Michel de, 125–37
Montefeltro, Battista da, 40, 58
Montpensier, Anne-Marie Louise d'Orléans *see*
La Grande Mademoiselle
mothers and maternity, 36, 102–3
Motteville, Françoise Bertaut de, 184–5

Nalson, John, 271
Navarre, Marguerite de:
biographical details, 65–7, 74–5, 112
and Christine de Pizan, 67–8, 70–1
and Elizabeth I, 76
influence of, 119, 181
on love, 71, 78, 81–5
on marriage, 61, 83–5
political epistemology of, 68, 77, 87
on political organisation, best form of, 72
and prudence, 66, 74
religious thought of, 68–70, 72–3, 76, 81
on women's virtue, 70, 71, 78, 79, 80, 82
on women and men, relations between, 77,
79–80
works:
'The coach' ('La coche'), 71
Heptameron, 71, 77–87
Mirror of the Sinful Soul, 75, 76
Les Prisons, 69–70, 71, 81
Suyte des Marguerites, 72
Newcastle, Margaret *see* Cavendish, Margaret,
Duchess of Newcastle
Nicholas of Cusa, 87
Nogarola, Isotta, 41, 43–5, 46, 58, 119

obedience:
passive, 199, 229, 230, 231, 233, 246, 268,
275–8, 280, 285
of subjects to sovereigns, 6, 35, 92, 93, 94, 199,
212–18, 229, 230, 231, 232, 233, 237, 246,
268, 275–8, 280, 285
of women to men, 44, 95
obligation, political, 201, 204, 212–18, 219, 222
occasional conformity, 242, 268
original position, 170

parental conception *see under* monarchs and
monarchy
Pateman, Carole, 3, 224
patriarchalism, 155, 157–8, 159–60, 261
peace:
as political ideal, 15, 19, 20, 23, 24, 35, 114, 203,
227, 262
and women, 55, 102, 105–6, 122
Penn, William, 232–3
Perry, Ruth, 228, 271
petitioners, women *see* civil war women
petitioners
Petrarch, 16, 17, 40, 47, 119, 181
Pettit, Philip, 151
phronesis see prudence
Piscopia, Elena Lucrezia, 43
Pizan, Christine de:
and Aristotle, 5, 17, 18, 30, 60
and Boethius, 14, 16, 18, 26
biographical details, 10–12
on body politic, 13, 25, 35, 107
and Dante, 12, 14–26
influence of, 9, 37, 57, 63–4, 65, 67–8, 70–1,
107, 224
and Isabeau de Bavière, 28–9, 224
and John of Salisbury, 13, 25, 107
on peace, 15, 19, 20, 23, 24, 35
political epistemology of, 12, 24
on political organisation, best form of, 18, 19,
20, 22, 25, 30, 30–6
and prophecy, 13, 20, 21, 22, 23, 24
on prudence, 24, 27, 29, 31–3, 74
religio-political thought of, 14, 15, 24, 25, 26,
28, 30
on women and political authority, 12, 14, 15,
17, 26–30, 33–4, 36, 60
on virtue, 17, 24, 26, 31–3
works:
Book of the Body Politic, 12, 24, 25
Book of the City of Ladies, 12, 27, 28, 29, 30,
33, 57, 60, 63, 224
Book of the Mutation of Fortune, 23
Book of Peace, 12, 24, 29, 31, 35, 45
Book of Prudence, 31